TURNING LATHES.

Turning Lathes

A GUIDE TO TURNING, SCREW-CUTTING, METAL-SPINNING, ORNAMENTAL TURNING, &c.

And including the 1896
BRITANNIA COMPANY CATALOGUE

OVER 400 ILLUSTRATIONS

EDITED BY JAMES LUKIN, B.A.

FOURTH EDITION
1894

THE ASTRAGAL PRESS
Lakeville, Minnesota

Library of Congress Catalog Card Number: 94-70622
International Standard Book Number: 1-879335-49-2

Published by
The Astragal Press
An Imprint of Finney Company
8075 215th Street West
Lakeville, Minnesota 55044

www.finneyco.com
www.astragalpress.com

Manufactured in the United States of America

PREFACE TO FOURTH EDITION.

THREE Editions of "Turning Lathes" having quickly been sold, we have no apology to make for introducing this the Fourth Edition. The Press, both English and American, with one exception, are unanimous in praise of the book, and we give short Extracts from some of the reviews of the mechanical journals.

The book has been appreciated by numerous learners and users of Lathes, and many letters of approval have been received. It will be found in the principal libraries in England, Canada, and Australia.

This Edition contains sixty-eight pages of new matter, on the Eccentric, the Oval, and the Dome Chuck, the Goniostat, the Eccentric, and the Horizontal Cutting Frame, and a Chapter on Handy Receipts and Wrinkles. Sixty - seven new Engravings illustrate these new Chapters.

OPINIONS OF THE AMERICAN PRESS

ON BRITANNIA COMPANY'S BOOK ON
"TURNING LATHES."

"Amateurs and technical students will find this book of great advantage to them, as the aim of the author, whoever he may be, has been to explain very thoroughly the processes of the art of turning."— *American Machinist.*

"This is a work of 158 pages, very fully illustrated, and with clear, descriptive matter on branches of lathe-work which are usually followed by amateurs. For these last it is valuable, as it contains succinct directions how to do certain work, how to avoid the many difficulties and the causes of failure in using certain kinds of tools; both wood and metal working are covered."—*American Engineer.*

"This book is an illustrated treatise on lathe-work, designed for use in technical schools. The minuteness and practical nature of the directions given, however, make it of value to amateur turners. To those wishing to learn the art from the beginning, it would be hard to recommend a more useful book. Wood and metal turning are both considered, and the description of hand turning is especially full."—*Scientific American.*

"We heartily commend the book to those interested in the subject. It will be found of special value to apprentices and others whose knowledge of lathe-work is limited."—*The National Car Builder* (American).

"This work assumes that the reader has had no previous knowledge of the lathe whatever, and starting with an elementary description, the author advances in a very clear and intelligible manner, explaining the various operations of hand and slide-rest work in a thoroughly satisfactory manner."—*Mechanics.*

"The author does not presuppose any technical knowledge whatever in the reader, but begins by describing and naming the various parts and attachments of a lathe, so that a schoolboy can pick up the book and work his way through it without any difficulty. The illustrations are very numerous and well-executed."—*Practical Engineer.*

"The several types of lathes, both for wood and metal turning, and their parts in detail, are fully described and illustrated, as also are the various operations of the latheman's art. Amateur turners will find in it many useful hints."—*Popular Science News.*

"The small price and general excellence of this book will commend it to the large class of ambitious apprentices for whose benefit it has been written."—*Boston Journal of Commerce.*

NOTICE.—*The Reviews of the English Press were equally favourable.*

CONTENTS.

TURNING LATHES.

—∘◦⦂◦⦂◦∘—

CHAPTER I.

DESCRIPTION OF THE LATHE.

THE novice who has never examined a Lathe, but, having seen others using it, thinks he should also like to try his hand at the work, naturally wants to know its construction. He hears of chucks, and mandrels, and poppets, but the terms convey to his mind nothing but mystery. We shall, therefore, at once enlighten him. Beginning at the stand, he will see two cast-iron uprights, supporting between them parallel bars, nicely planed. These are called the standards, and are sometimes, but not very generally, made of wood. The parallel bars are called the bed, sometimes gantry, which appears to be an American coinage, not very expressive, and decidedly ugly. Half-way between the bed and the floor, the crank axle is suspended, generally upon centres or pointed steel screws; but sometimes this axle runs in brasses, called bearings or bushes, and sometimes it rests upon small turned wheels, called friction wheels, which are supposed to give it an easier motion. At the lowest part is hung a treadle for the foot, and this is connected to the crank by an iron hook, or by crank chain passing over a roller in the treadle bar. This gives a smooth rolling motion. Sometimes the crank hook is called the pitman.

B

The bed of a Lathe is usually made of two bars in a single casting, planed quite flat on the top and edges. It may be of beech, mahogany, or hard wood, but it is now so easy to obtain complete Lathes of iron, and they are so cheap and convenient, that it is not worth while to build them up at home. In some of the small Lathes, there is no crank axle, but the flywheel is hung upon a short bolt or stud, which screws into the left standard. The crank is then merely a pin fixed into one of the spokes of the wheel. Standing on the bed are two poppets, or, as they are also called, headstocks. The one on the left hand is permanently fixed in place by a strong bolt and nut. This headstock carries a small wheel or pulley, the axle of which is the mandrel. The pulley is turned with grooves for the Lathe cord; that of smallest size giving the greatest speed. This is used for wood, and the slower motion is for metal. Soft wood, like deal, needs the quickest speed of all to make it cut clean. The harder woods, and also bone and ivory, are usually turned at a slower rate.

The mandrel is the most important part of the Lathe. It is made generally with the conical neck passing through a hard steel or gun-metal collar in the headstock, while its other end rests on a hard, pointed screw of steel, which is called the tail pin. By means of the latter, any wear of the neck or collar can be taken up by screwing the tail pin so as to push the mandrel neck forward into its collar. This must always be attended to, as the mandrel must turn very easily, but without the least shake. There are oil-holes drilled in the top of the headstock, and lubrication must never be omitted. The best sewing-machine oil should be used, and a few drops of paraffin will make it still more suitable. Never use vegetable oil, like linseed or olive, Lucca or colza, if it can be avoided. Sperm oil is good, either alone or with paraffin, and if only olive or salad oil is obtainable, always add paraffin to it, as it materially improves it. A good lubricant makes a surprising difference in the running of a Lathe. The crank axle screws, and also the crank hook or chain, must also receive due attention in this respect; likewise, now and then, the bearings of the treadle.

PLATE I.—PLAIN FOOT LATHE.

The second Lathe head, or back poppet as it is usually called, is movable along the bed, and can be fixed at any point by the bolt and nut attached to it. The upper part is bored out accurately to carry the cylinder, or smooth, round bar into which the pointed steel centres fit, which are used to support work while it is being turned. This cylinder is advanced and withdrawn by a hand wheel at the back, which carries a screw working into a nut in the cylinder. All this is out of sight in the upper part of the poppet. Between the poppets stands the hand rest, on which the tool is supported. This can be placed where needed, and the upper part, or tee, can be raised or lowered at pleasure, according to the size of the work that it is proposed to turn. This hand rest is often replaced by the slide rest, if metal is to be turned; but a good deal can be done without this addition to the Lathe, which can be added at any time, after wood turning has been thoroughly mastered.

In the illustration (Plate I.), all the parts above described are lettered as follows:—

A, A, Standards.

B, Bed or gantry.

C, Treadle.

D, Crank hook, pitman, or chain gearing.

E, Crank axle.

F, Flywheel.

G, Lathe cord.

H, Fast headstock.

I, Movable headstock or back poppet.

J, Hand rest; and K, its T or tee.

L, Hand wheel to move M, the cylinder.

N, Mandrel, with its pulley, O.

P, Screw for chucks.

Q, Tail pin.

R, R, Treadle centres or bearings.

S, Movable back centre.

T, Bearings or centres of crank axle.

We now come to what are known as chucks. These are contrivances by which the work to be turned is secured to the Lathe mandrel, and they vary according to the size and nature of the work, such as whether it is long or short, whether to be bored or hollowed out, or solid; and also whether it is of wood, ivory, or metal. Chucks are, there-fore, rather numerous, but for general use we may readily make an inexpensive selection. Plate II. gives illustrations of several chucks. Nos. 5 and 6 are main or adapter chucks, into which fit many of the smaller ones, such as No. 1, the fork or prong chuck, for soft wood, used with the back centre to support the work at its other end. No. 2, the cross or blade chuck—a capital one for hard or soft wood. A saw cut is made at the end of the piece, crossed by another at right angles. Into these the blades fall, and the work cannot shift or slip. The back centre is needed as in the last case. No. 3 is the square hole chuck, made to take carpenters' boring bits, or rods of metal squared to fit, and for many similar purposes. This is a very useful chuck. No. 4 is a solid chuck of gun-metal, that can be drilled out to any desired size. No. 7, taper screw, an indispensable chuck, for holding short bits of stuff for boxes and other hollow work. These are also sometimes held by means of No. 8, a plain face plate with holes countersunk at the back. The work is attached by ordinary wood screws. No. 9 is a mandrel for circular saws, emery wheels, buffs, &c. When required for saws, a saw table is needed, which is fitted into the socket of the hand rest, or fastened upon the bed. No. 10, a bell chuck, with clamping screws, for holding short bars of metal. It is less used since the scroll chuck was invented; but is a good contrivance, its only fault being that it is a knuckle-duster. Made with very thick metal, however, the screw heads can be countersunk. Nos. 11 and 12, the amateur's self-centreing scroll chuck, often called American, as it has been chiefly developed and perfected there. It has one or two sets of jaws, which draw together concentrically, by means of the key, and hold drills or work truly and securely. Of late years these chucks have come into very general use. They are of all sizes and prices : the 2in., 24s.; 4in., 34s. They are fitted to a face plate screwing on the mandrel; the smaller ones on a cone.

No. 13 is a four-jawed chuck, of which each jaw is inde-

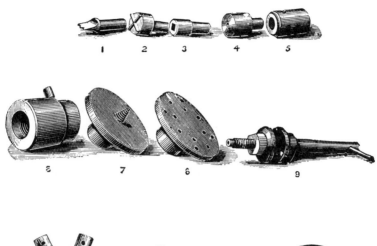

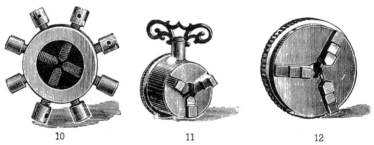

PLATE II.—LATHE CHUCKS.

pendent of the others, so that work can be held eccentrically when desired. It is an excellent chuck, holding very firmly; it is, in fact, an engineer's chuck, and is seldom of less diameter than 6in. Fig. 1, cup chuck, made in iron or gun-metal, from 1in. inside diameter upwards. Before self-centreing chucks were invented, every amateur's Lathe was fitted with a dozen or two of these. They are useful as ever, and a few

FIG. 1.—CUP CHUCK.

may well be added; the wood is simply driven into the chuck, and so secured.

The amateur will soon learn to make boxwood cup chucks, which will prevent any necessity for a large supply of metal ones. These are always very largely used, and are hollowed out to suit any work in hand; they soon accumulate, and when used up are easily replaced. A day at chuck-making

FIG. 2.—PLAIN DRILL CHUCK.

affords capital practice; the method is given on a later page. The advantage of a metal chuck is that it always screws up to run truly; it is usually plugged with wood, and this is turned out to the size necessary. Fig. 2, a plain drill chuck, with ⅜ hole; a smaller one fits inside for drills of less diameter in the shank. Fig. 3, face plate, used for large work, secured to it by variously shaped clamps and bolts; it is of extensive use for metal-turning. Fig. 4 is a neat little jeweller's chuck for very small saws, circular brushes, and buffs; it also holds drills of small size. Another drill chuck is here shown, called the Essex (Fig. 5). The parts are numbered separately. 1 is the complete chuck with drill. The shank is turned to a

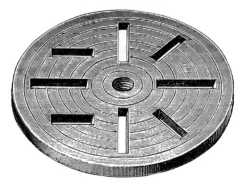

FIG. 3.—FACE PLATE.

gentle taper, or long cone, and fits into a taper hole in a receptacle chuck, truly bored out to a similar angle. 2 is the outer case; 3, the cap, which is conical within, and when screwed on it compresses the jaws (4), of which two sets are supplied, one for very small, and the other for larger drills. 5 is the wrench fitting the hexagonal top of the cap. This is

FIG. 4.—THE JEWELLER'S CHUCK.

the cheapest of all the adjustable drill chucks, the price being 10s. 6d. It will hold drills up to ¼in. A larger size is made with four jaws, to take drills of ½in. diameter in the shank. These are the chucks chiefly used for general work, but there are one or two more needing description. That used for turning bars of metal is called a driver chuck, and is

composed of two essential parts—viz., the carrier plate, **or**
driver chuck, and the carrier, which is of various forms,

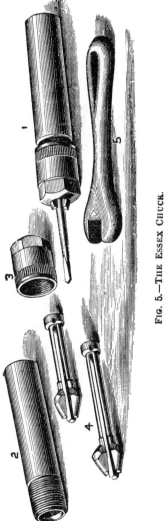

FIG. 5.—THE ESSEX CHUCK.

but usually like that of Fig. 6. The chuck is like the main
or receptacle chuck, a centre point fitting into it; but, made

crosswise through it, is a squared hole, receiving a cranked arm, which is secured by a side screw, and is, consequently, adjustable. The bar to be turned is mounted " between centres " — *i.e.*, supported at one end by the point of this chuck, and at the other by the point of the back poppet, shallow holes called hollow centres being drilled at each end, exactly at the respective centres of the ends of the article to be turned. One of the carriers is now selected,

FIG. 6.—DRIVER CHUCK.

which is of suitable size, and this is clamped on the end nearest the mandrel. The tail of this catches the cranked arm of the driver, or pin of the carrier plate, if that form is used, and causes the whole to revolve together. The bar is then turned as far as the tool can reach, and afterwards it is reversed, and the carrier is attached at the finished end, after which that part previously covered by the carrier is turned. When the chuck is made like a face plate with a

FIG. 7.—SELF-CENTREING CHUCK (WOOD).

projecting pin, it is often termed a " catch plate." This is the chuck almost always used for iron bars, and it has this advantage, that, if the hollow centres are left in the ends of the work, it can at any time be re-mounted, and will run as true as before. With other chucks it is always difficult to readjust work centrally.

One other deserves mention in this place, on account of its

convenience, but it must be always used with the back centre. It is of metal, but easily made of boxwood. It is a cup chuck with thicker walls, and is hollowed out conically, and the inside is then grooved to form ridges. A piece of wood placed in it centres itself and is held by the ridges catching any rough parts sufficiently to resist the action of the turning tool. It is shown by Fig. 7. A block of boxwood thus hollowed, with grooves cut by a gouge, will answer just as well. This is a capital chuck for holding bars of wood for tool handles; a finished piece of work can also be centred in it for polishing or altering. Two or three wooden ones, with conical holes of from 1in. to 3in. at their largest diameter, will be serviceable. Sometimes, a chuck is made with a square taper hole an inch or more across the face, and then the bars of wood are squared; but the other will take them without preparation.

CHAPTER II.

THE TURNING TOOLS.

FOR wood-turning, which is probably what a novice will, and certainly ought to, commence with, the gouge and chisel are the special tools, and are almost the only ones to be met with in the workshop of an ordinary turner. With these alone may be turned solid work of all kinds, besides a good deal of hollow ware, as it is called. It is true that, for turning hard wood, many others are used, but, for the present, at any rate, we may with advantage pass them by. The gouge is the roughing-down tool, and the chisel is used to level all ridges and give a finish to the surface. After this, a bundle of shavings held against it while it rapidly revolves, is all that should be necessary to polish it; but, for a time, at any rate, fine glass-paper will very likely be found necessary. The finish produced, however, by a sharp chisel, efficiently used, beats all that can be obtained by any amount of papering. The tool, in fact, leaves a high polish.

We will begin by turning a tool handle, which will suffice very well to teach the way of setting to work. Put the prong or fork chuck on the mandrel—or, if preferred, the cross chuck or that last described may be substituted; after a little practice, one or the other will have preference. The fork or prong is not a very sure one to hold, and sometimes the work will slip round, which it cannot do upon the cross or blade chuck.

Now cut a piece of beech or ash, or other suitable wood

—elm will do, but the first-named are better—or a bit of acacia will serve, which is of a yellowish-brown tint, and is a capital turning wood. Saw off a bar about 6in. or 7in. long, and 1½in. in diameter or thereabouts, cutting it off as squarely at the ends as you can; chop off the corners if it is square, so as, in a rough way, to round it slightly. Make a little hole in each end as centrally as possible, just to give a slight entrance to the Lathe centre and the central point of the prong chuck, or make saw cuts if the cross chuck is used. Then loosen the back poppet, and slide it forward until there is just room enough for the wood to be mounted. Screw up the nut so as to hold the poppet securely, and then, turning the hand wheel, secure the work in its place, taking care that the cutting edges of the fork chuck, if it is used, get a good hold by sinking into the wood. If this is very hard, it may be better to make a cut with a saw across the end, to receive the chuck edges; but it will not be necessary to do so with beech, ash, or elm, nor, of course, with deal, lime, sycamore, willow, and other such soft woods. These, however, are not very useful for tool handles. Indeed, of all woods for general turning, beech is most desirable.

Now start the Lathe, causing the work to revolve towards you, and see if the wood runs fairly true, which it is sure to do if the holes in the ends were central. Put just one drop of oil on the point of the back centre. The next thing to do is to place the rest as near as it will go without touching the wood, securing it by the hand nut below the bed, and also setting the tee so high as to stand a little lower than the centre of the work. This is also to be secured by its side screw. The gouge is now to be used thus: grasp the handle firmly with the right hand, palm upwards, and lay it on the rest with its hollow side up, and the whole tool not horizontal but inclined somewhat by lowering its handle. The blade is to be grasped by the left hand with knuckles upwards, and very near the rest, upon which it can thus be held down tightly, while at the same time it is shifted along the rest as the work proceeds. And here will the tyro's first difficulty be met with.

The wood as it revolves will strike the gouge, and cause

it to jump about on the rest, and, when trying to prevent this, he will forget the treadle, and the Lathe will stop or run backwards. But it is a case of "Never say die!" Keep cool. Do not push the gouge too forward, and presently you will get the knack requisite, and the cutting will proceed, not very well at first, but fairly. The best way is not by any means to run the gouge along the rest, as will be done after a little practice, but to hold it so as to cut a little bit at a time, beginning at the end next to the back centre, and so cutting by successive steps till the whole piece is fairly rounded. Then, using the side more than the point of the tool, it will not be difficult still further to level the surface, and, indeed, so nearly to finish it that the chisel, which is far more difficult to use, may be dispensed with, and the work finished by glass-paper.

This is, however, not to be dreamed of after mastering the use of the chisel, but only permitted for one or two introductory essays. And for the first lesson, though I have suggested a tool handle, I would not recommend one requiring a curved shape. It would be better at first to make it like A on Plate IV.—*i.e.*, only a long, straight taper down to the ferrule. This, indeed, is a good form to adopt for files and many hand tools, though seldom used for such as belong specially to the wood-turner. There is, however, great difference of opinion as to the best form, and also as to the length of the handle. Chisels and gouges usually have much longer ones than those used for metal and hard wood or ivory. The ferrule is generally sawn off a piece of brass tube of the requisite size, or from an old gun-barrel, or any bit of thin tube. At some shops they can be bought cut ready for use, but in most towns and villages suitable stuff may be found; and here let me observe that the young turner should be constantly on the look-out for odds and ends of wood, metal, ivory, or bone, of which a well-selected assortment will often supply an unexpected demand. A hack saw, consisting of a steel frame with a thin saw stretched across it by a tightening screw, is used to saw metal. Often an old scythe-blade, roughly notched into teeth, is used, and even preferred; but the real metal saw is the neatest and best. The ferrule being

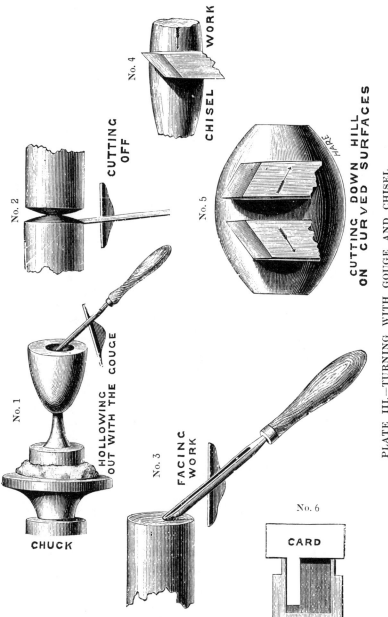

No. 2

CUTTING
OFF

No. 4

CHISEL WORK

No. 5

HARE

CUTTING DOWN HILL
ON CURVED SURFACES

No. 1

HOLLOWING
OUT WITH THE GOUGE

CHUCK

No. 3

FACING
WORK

No. 6

CARD

PLATE III.—TURNING WITH GOUGE AND CHISEL.

ready, the end of the tool-handle is reduced to fit it. If the back centre is withdrawn a little, the ferrule can be tried on as the work proceeds, for the wood will run true again when the centre is screwed up as it was before. Ferrules should go on tightly, or they drop off when the wood becomes more thoroughly dry. A little glue or cement of any kind assists to hold them, but it is not absolutely needed. In rounding off the opposite end, the gouge is to be laid on its left side, with the hollow part away from the surface which is being cut. This is the rule: Work down hill when making a moulding or rounding off a surface, and keep the hollow of the tool away from the surface that is being cut (see the Numbers on Plate III.). In turning a ball, for instance, the gouge will lie on its back, when in the diametrical line, and as the cut is carried towards the right hand, it will lie more and more on its right side, the hollow part towards the right hand. Then, starting again down hill the other way, the tool will lie gradually over on its left side; used thus, the tool will leave a clean cut, but otherwise the edge will soon catch in and bite out a chip, or break itself. It is easy enough to cut the piece off with a gouge or chisel (see No. 2, Plate III.) by working a notch, cutting down hill each way till the piece is so far severed as to break off with a touch; after which a penknife and glass-paper will finish it off.

THE CHISEL is the plane of the wood-turner, and, rightly managed, will leave a surface so smooth that a touch of glasspaper would spoil it; but it needs to be gripped with a firm hand, and used with decision. Suppose a cylindrical piece of wood to have been turned by a gouge, and that it is desired to finish it to a truer surface than it is possible to produce with a gouge, the chisel is the tool to use. It is not ground straight across, and with the bevel on one side only, as is the case with a carpenter's chisel, but there is a bevel on both sides, and the edge is ground slanting, so that there is formed one sharp point and one blunt one (No. 4, Plate III.). As a rule, the blunt point leads, whether the tool is being worked to right or left (No. 5, Plate III.), and, also, in cutting down hill on a curve or incline. But this tool is not laid flat on the rest, but slightly on edge, for this reason: if laid flat, as a tyro would probably place it, it could only scrape, and would tear up the fibres of any soft wood. It is, therefore, slightly raised upon edge, care being taken that the upper sharp corner never comes in contact with the wood, or it will hitch in and spoil the work. Only the middle part of the edge, therefore, actually cuts, and this, engaging the fibres at an angle, no longer tears them apart. When there is a rounded surface to be worked, this tool is made to travel, like the gouge, both ways down hill; and so, also, in a hollow, it never sweeps the curve from end to end, but the cuts are carried down each way, meeting at the bottom. It may be conjectured that, just at the point of juncture, the two cuts will not exactly meet, but practice will make them do so. The cut is made so as to reduce the shaving at this point to almost nothing; a slight rub of glass-paper will obliterate any little defect that still remains. After a while, even this will be unnecessary. Of course, a beginner must not expect to succeed all at once with this tool, but I strongly advise him for a long time to work entirely with gouge and chisel, and not to attempt hollow work till he has become an adept at what is solid. Let him turn a set of handles, ninepins, towel-rollers, rolling-pins, ring-stands, chair-rails, and anything else he can think of : drawer-knobs, door-handles, and other articles of curved surface will give him excellent practice, and pave the way for those which require greater skill—a skill only to be gained by steady, consistent, and painstaking practice. I have given drawings here (Plate IV.) of some such articles, including variously shaped tool-handles. The little pilasters will do for rails of book-trays, overmantels, brackets, shelves, and a score of similar articles. A round ruler, well and truly finished by the gouge and chisel alone, may be considered a proof that the young turner has passed his novitiate. Indeed, he may attempt simple hollow work long before his hand and eye are equal to so severe a test of skill.

HOLLOW WARE is chuck work—i.e., the work is held by the chuck alone, the back poppit being pushed entirely out of the way. Very deep or long articles, however, need extra support, by means of a boring collar, of which we need not

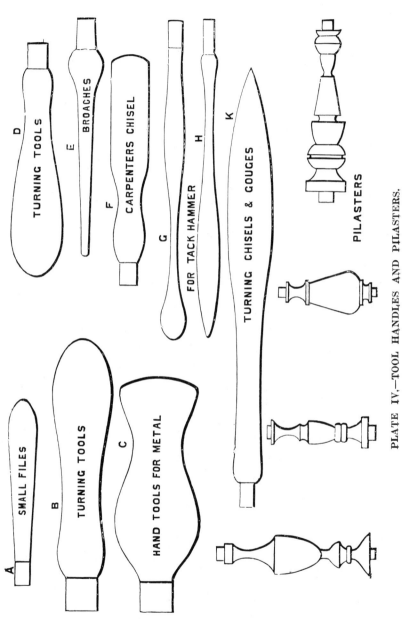

A SMALL FILES

B TURNING TOOLS

C HAND TOOLS FOR METAL

D TURNING TOOLS

E BROACHES

F CARPENTERS CHISEL

G

H FOR TACK HAMMER

K TURNING CHISELS & GOUGES

PILASTERS

PLATE IV.—TOOL HANDLES AND PILASTERS.

speak further at present. An egg-cup will be a capital thing to begin with. Saw off a bit of beech, birch, or other wood, long enough to serve the purpose, the length and size being easily determined by reference to a pattern. Allow a little more than absolutely necessary, and screw it upon the taper screw chuck, after securing the latter in its place on the mandrel. If care is taken to bore a hole centrally, and not too large, the piece will abut fairly against the face of the chuck, and will run evenly; but to insure this it must be cut off squarely at the end. The back poppet may be brought up to help sustain it while the rougher excrescences are being cut away, and the whole brought into approximate form, after which it must be removed. The outside will present no special difficulty if sufficient practice has been obtained upon solid work, but the hollowing out needs some care, and especially needs a knowledge of how to do it in the best way. The end must be first of all faced nicely, using the gouge, as explained, with its bevelled back against the work, and its hollow outwards towards the right hand (No. 3, Plate III.). The rest is still to remain parallel to the Lathe bed, as in turning the outer surface. Now, keeping the back or bevel as before, bring the point or middle of the edge to the centre of the work, and cause it to penetrate slightly, by moving the right hand, which holds its handle, a little outwards. This will cut a little conical recess. Repeat this, pushing the gouge onwards each time beyond the centre, and also gradually raising the point and rolling the tool over, till, at what may be called the top of the cut, it lies almost face downwards. It is difficult to describe the action, but the shaving should curl out rapidly in little coils, leaving a smooth surface. For deep cuts, it may be necessary to turn the rest round somewhat, so as to bring its tee more across the face of the work (as shown in No. 1, Plate III.), but not entirely so. This is a curious way of using a gouge, causing it to cut *beyond the centre* instead of on the near side; but nothing can exceed the ease with which it will cut when so used, and the hollow can be extended and deepened, within certain limits, with great rapidity: a few minutes will suffice for an egg-cup. It is worth while to risk spoiling one such

article, by turning round the rest to stand across the work—
(it is so placed for hard-wood turning)—and then to lay the
gouge on its back, and try to hollow out the egg-cup by
turning the near side instead of the further one. Probably,
any novice would try thus if left to himself. The tool held
still will bore a hole of its own size, just as a quill bit would
do, if used in a carpenter's brace. But as soon as the
attempt is made to enlarge it, the gouge will catch in. Even
here, however, something may be done by remembering the
rule to keep the back, or bevel, against the surface to be cut.
By this, however, it is evident that the tool must be on its
side, and not on its back; the hollow being towards the
centre, and the cut proceeding from without inwards. There
will be no "catch in" in this case, and the hollowing may
often be carried forward thus. But as long as the tool can
be got to work in the other manner, cutting from the bottom
of the recess outwards, this will be found to produce the
better work. The egg-cup is so comparatively shallow, and of
such small size, that it may be begun and finished thus; but
for larger work both methods may be combined—now working
from the centre outwards, and now the other way. In fact,
a turner can use his tools in all sorts of ways with equal
facility, but a learner should not take such liberties.

It may readily be seen that it will be impossible to get a
flat bottom with a sharply-defined angle in this way with
the gouge; and, therefore, when such is necessary, the last
touch must be given by a chisel, held quite flat on the rest.
A common carpenter's chisel will answer very well for this.
A dozen egg-cups will enable a learner to manage the gouge
only, as they do not require to be finished inside to a flat
surface; nor, indeed, is it necessary with a match-vase or spill-
pot. But it will soon be discovered that a gouge cannot be
used as described for deeper work, as the limit of its cutting
power is soon reached. For deep work in soft wood, tools
called hook tools are used in the trade, but are so difficult to
manage as to be seldom found in amateurs' workshops.
Round-end tools, chisels, and gouges are therefore used,
and the surface finished with inside tools similar to those for
hard wood, the finish being given by glass-paper. These

tools will be fully described in treating of hard-wood turning.

BOXES. — These will come next in order as needing a little more skill than egg-cup turning, as the cover has to be fitted nicely. The first thing is to cut off a bit of wood long enough for box and cover, with something extra to allow for the length of the taper screw and for waste—say, 4in. for a 3in. box or 2½in. one. The wood can be held in a cup chuck instead of the taper screw, if preferred; and in that case it is merely trimmed roughly to a cylindrical form, and driven into the chuck about ½in. To save the mandrel from violence, it may be thus driven in while the chuck stands on the bench, or on a block of wood, although it will most frequently be done after screwing the chuck on the mandrel. In this case, there is no need for heavy blows, which tend to damage the tail pin or mandrel; but a few steady taps from a light mallet will suffice if the wood fits fairly well. The learner will, however, find it necessary to drive the wood in more deeply than an adept, as he is more likely to have a hitch in of the tool, and in that way to throw the wood out of the chuck altogether. Supposing it to be secure, the first thing is to reduce it to a cylinder by gouge and chisel, and for this the back centre may be brought up to steady it. When, however, it is once shaped, the loose poppet is to be slid back, as before, out of the way. The usual way is to hollow out the extreme end for the cover, then to cut this off, and, from what remains in the chuck, to hollow out the box; and this is the best plan, as it enables the turner to try on the cover again and again, until a satisfactory fit results. Following this plan, the cover is to be faced off true with the chisel held quite flat on the rest; or, if it is very rough, the gouge is first used, laid on its back and held horizontally, the rest being, of course, turned round so as to bring the tee across the face of the work. Then, as soon as the surface is made flat, begin as for the egg-cup, only keep the hollow very shallow; and then, with the chisel held flat, square the recess thus made, and especially take care to make the side quite perpendicular to the bottom, and not in the least conical, for on this will the exact fit of the cover chiefly depend—and a

well-fitted cover is a credit to the learner. Light cuts will
have to be taken at last, using the more pointed corner of
the turning chisel to get into the angle and to finish smoothly
the inside. When the cover is done, a tool called a parting
tool is generally used to cut it off. It is like a very narrow
chisel, with (when meant for soft wood) a groove or notch
in it. But this tool is not absolutely necessary. A tenon
saw, held against the wood as it revolves, will soon cut it off;
or the chisel set on edge and made gradually to cut a
deeper and deeper notch till the piece is severed, or used
to cut a deep notch, to be followed by the saw. After this,
the end of the work is again faced off truly, and the rebate
is cut, with the chisel, upon which the cover of a box always
rests; but, in this case, it is left a little too large at the
present stage, as it will be cut down again, and accurately
finished after the box itself has been hollowed out. This is
the work to be now taken in hand.

In either case the top of the box will be neither smooth
nor level, but that will be rectified presently. The box itself
must now be hollowed out as described, using the gouge as
far as possible, but finishing with the chisel. Care must
be taken not to go too deep, or in cutting it off when done
there will not be found enough stuff left for the bottom,
and it will come off in the form of a ring. After it is sufficiently hollowed out, and the inside is levelled and smoothed,
the rebate or flange is finished till the cover will just go on
tightly. This part must be left exactly cylindrical. It will be
generally conical in the hands of a beginner, either small at
top or at bottom of the rebate. The cover must slide on
and fit all the way, and not go on easy at first and then fit
tightly when pressed quite down. This accuracy will be
found difficult, but patience must be exercised, and a very
light cut taken each time after trying on the cover. The
latter should fit so well that its junction with the box
is only visible as a thin line. When the fit is perfect, the
cover is left on, the rest put across the bed, and with the
chisel laid flat upon it, the outside of the cover is turned to
a dead level. With the sharp angle of the tool a few circles
are often cut, by way of ornamentation, both on the top of

the cover and also on the side of the box itself. The work now has to be cut off, just as the cover was severed. If a parting tool is used, it is placed exactly upright on its edge and steadily advanced, keeping it horizontal, or with the point only very slightly raised. This point must not be allowed to get, at any time, below the level of the centres, or the tool will be drawn in. Also, although its edge is so broad as to clear itself as it enters, it is safer to make it cut now a little on this side and now on that, so as slightly to widen its own groove as the cut is made. All danger of a catch in is thus avoided, and the tool can be advanced quite to the centre, when the box will fall off. With care and a little practice the bottom of the box should be quite level, but it will probably be found necessary to re-mount it on a wooden chuck, turned to fit inside it, so as to get at the bottom of the box for a final cut, to finish it. A very common fault to be guarded against is getting the bottom of the box rounded, so as not to stand well when placed on the table. It may be made very slightly hollow, which will not matter, but every care must be taken that the centre shall not project in the least. Of course, the outside of a box need not be of pill-box uniformity, but can be moulded to any shape, and, if so intended to be formed, the sides should be left rather thick when it is hollowed out.

In order to insure the perpendicularity of the rebate of the box, an instrument is used called a turner's square, but it is easy to cut a rectangular notch in a bit of card or tin, and to test with this as shown in No. 6, Plate III. The long edge of the card is to be placed in contact with the top, and the short edge of the notch will test the accuracy of the inside, which it should exactly coincide with. The inside of the cover may be tested with a similar card. These little home-made contrivances are very useful, cost nothing, and can be made in a few minutes. A similar gauge is useful where a number of articles are to be of exactly the same size, either in length or thickness. Cut gauges cannot shift like calipers, which, again, are not practically very easy to use for accurate testing; but such a gauge as that shown, even of card, is of great use, and well worth making.

Suppose, for instance, you wish to make several tool-handles, all of one length and size, with mouldings like No. 1, Plate V. We may make a gauge of its length by two nail-points in a bit of wood (C), and two others a little shorter, which are to mark the highest points of the moulding when the gauge is held against the wood as it revolves after it has been turned to a cylindrical form. Then it can be roughly shaped, and from time to time tested for size by gauge B. This is a far speedier plan than to measure the length by rule or compass and then to use calipers for size, which would have to be set separately to test the hollows and the convex curves.

Carrying on a little further our description of hollow work, we will take that simple article a needle-case or bodkin-case, in which the length very much exceeds the diameter. In this the gouge cannot be used as in larger work, and may advantageously be replaced by an ordinary shell bit or nose bit, such as carpenters use with a brace; or by the twisted or spiral drill used for metal. The latter, held in a tool-handle, answers splendidly, doing its work in a few seconds without undue strain. Drive the bit of wood, as before, into a cup chuck, not of metal but of wood, or wood driven in to plug the metal one and then hollowed out to the necessary size. Turn it with gouge and chisel as before; run the drill in deeply enough to bore the cover, following it up with a narrow chisel or slightly larger drill, and keeping the bore nicely parallel; then cut it off and set it aside for subsequent finish, and go on with the case itself, using the drill, and, if necessary, following it with chisel or with a narrow round-end tool, if in stock, or with a larger bit or drill; only it must be bored out smaller than the cover, to allow of the rabbet on which the latter fits, and which is made long to prevent the cover from dropping off so readily when the case is carried in the pocket. For work of this kind, sycamore will be found very useful if obtainable. Birch, poplar, beech, alder, and many other soft but not splintery woods can also be used; and of those ordinarily found in the country hornbeam is exceedingly useful. Acacia, again, is a nice and also handsome wood, but almost any stuff will do for simple work of this kind.

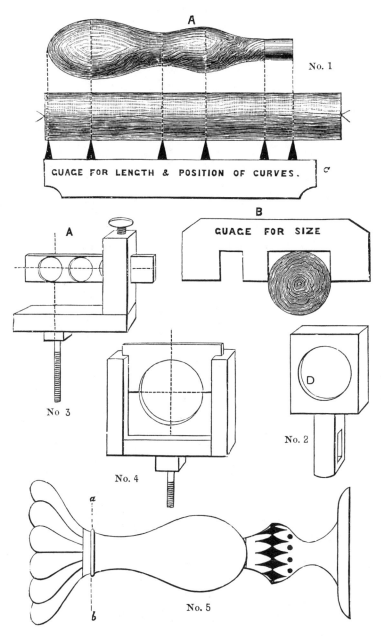

A

No. 1

GUAGE FOR LENGTH & POSITION OF CURVES.

B

GUAGE FOR SIZE

A

No 3

D

No. 2

No. 4

a

b

No. 5

PLATE V.—BORING-COLLARS : USE OF GAUGES.

If the article to be bored is over three or four inches long it will be found difficult to turn and bore it without further support. In such cases, what is known as a cone plate or boring-collar is used, or very frequently a temporary substitute made of wood. The cone plate properly so called consists of a short poppet from which projects a stout pin secured by a nut at the back. Upon this is fitted a circular metal plate, having near its circumference a ring of conical holes of gradually increasing size, the centre of any one of which is exactly level with the Lathe centres when such hole is at its highest point. The largest part of the cone stands towards the mandrel, and that hole is selected which will allow the end of the work to rest in the cone without passing through it. Thus supported, the extreme end of such work as a needle-case or deep spill-pot can be got at by a boring tool, and, being thus supported, there is no danger that the work will be thrown out of centre or forced out of its chuck. In such a cone plate the largest hole cannot be over 2in. diameter or thereabout, and is, in fact, seldom even so large. It is, therefore, hardly suitable for the general work of a wood-turner, and may be advantageously replaced by one of the home-made contrivances on Plate V. The first is merely a piece of plankwood cut with a tenon to fit between the bearers or bed of the Lathe, and fastened with a wedge or bolt—generally the former. The hole is preferably cut in the Lathe, which alone enables a nice cone to be formed, but it is often sawn out and bevelled by the chisel, followed by a cabinet rasp and file. Of course, it is only suited for one size of work; but a wood-turner will arrange his work accordingly, as he generally makes a large number of articles alike, turning them in sets —a dozen or two of one size, and then a dozen of another; so that with two or three such boring-collars he can get along very well. No. 2 D will sufficiently explain this simple arrangement. No. 3 represents another plan in which a mortice in an upright part of a specially made base carries horizontal plates of wood, with one, two, or more conical holes in it. A wooden thumbscrew or plain wedge secures the plate in position. The bottom part stands on the bed, and a plain bolt and nut will secure it. It is better made with a tenon piece screwed on underneath to fit between the bearers as before. A still more complete and stiffer arrangement is made by having a frame put together firmly with dovetails, in a groove in which the boards containing the conical holes slide. These are also for convenience sawn across, which renders it easier to adjust them to the work. This, shown at No. 4, is far better worth making, because it can often be fitted over a neck or smaller part of the work if not large enough in the bore to fit the larger diameter. It might, for instance, grasp the vase (No. 5, as shown at the narrow part, a, b), and it will hold it quite steadily for hollowing out.

It would probably not be supposed that a simple cylinder without any mouldings is far more difficult to turn than such a piece as a baluster or pillaret, but so it is. Nevertheless, a wood-turner, skilled in the use of gouge and chisel, will accomplish it readily enough by hand, where an amateur would fall back on the slide rest to give the rectilinear motion to the tool. In short, a slide rest, or other mechanical appliance, is not to be found in a wood-turner's shop, and is, indeed, quite unnecessary, except for ornamental work in hard wood and ivory, and for turning metal.

To turn a cylinder, the top of the rest should be level, and if notched it should be corrected with a file, so that a gouge or chisel may slide along it with regularity. After the wood has been roughened down almost to size, the gouge should be carried along quietly and steadily, using its side more than its point, and the chisel must follow; great care being taken to keep it at the same angle throughout, that it may not cut more deeply in one place than in another. A series of light cuts with a good quick speed will best insure success. Quick speed is absolutely essential in turning soft wood—it can hardly be too high—but for hard wood it may be more moderate. But in all these mechanical arts we can only say how the tool is to be held and used: we cannot give skill, which nothing but long and careful practice can afford. It is no use for a learner to think he will turn out good work; he will turn one handle or egg-cup while a good workman will turn a couple of dozen, and his work will also be inferior. But that workman also was once a learner, and his acquired skill is likewise attainable by perseverance. In nothing is this so true as in turning soft wood, because in this you are not able to use those mechanical contrivances which insure correct results. With ivory and hard wood, you may turn and hollow out and decorate a true sphere almost with hands in pockets, leaving the Lathe and tool to do their own work. Hence it is that an amateur spends so much and finds turning so costly. He does very little, and that little is expensive. He then goes, perhaps, into such a shop as Oetzmann's or Maple's, and sees overmantels, and cabinets, and tables, and all kinds of serviceable articles of great beauty, to which the Lathe has contributed very largely; and he may rest assured that neither slide rest nor any costly apparatus has been used in the manufacture: only plain Lathes, two or three tools, and a good deal of labour and skill. Turning should cost very little—such turning as the generality of amateurs ought to take up—and Lathes are getting cheaper than ever, so that even a labourer, with spare time upon his hands, might profitably employ himself in turning, and add a few pounds to the family purse. Where most amateurs fail is in the matter of patience. In some of the articles, for instance, just alluded to, there are, perhaps, fifty to a hundred little turned pillarets, all exactly alike, and about 2in. in length. To an amateur, this would be a tedious job; but a professional will go on, day after day, and all day long, till the Lathe bed is piled with pillarets; and although the gouge and chisel alone are used, and, probably no measurements are taken, yet all are alike in size and pattern.

CHAPTER III.

TURNING BOXWOOD AND FOREIGN HARD WOOD.

THE tools used for the above work differ considerably from those used for soft wood, which they will not, in fact, cut so as to produce a good surface. The gouge and chisel are, however, still used, and, generally speaking, the former is the roughing-down tool. But hard wood admits of much finer beads and mouldings, and will take a higher polish, and it can be covered with a network of fine tracery and delicate carving, which is quite impossible in the case of soft wood. Screws, moreover, can be cut upon this material, either coarse or fine, which can only be managed with difficulty on soft wood, on which also, if cut, the pitch must be coarse. All hard-wood tools lie flat on the rest, and are, in consequence, easy to use, and whatever the profile of the edge may be, it is, of necessity repeated on the work, if the tool is held still, such profile being, of course, reversed. The tools are of various shapes for cutting to right and left, turning hollows, and beads and mouldings. The more general ones are illustrated here, so far as their cutting edges are concerned.

A, Plate VI., the flat tool, is sharpened on both sides as well as on the edge; B, C, bevel tools, are sharpened in the same way (the bevels of all the tools shown being supposed to be underneath); D, similarly sharpened, is the round tool, used for turning hollows, and sometimes for roughing-down hard wood and ivory, instead of the gouge; E, the bead tool, is made of all widths for turning beads and small spheres, like those on the head of a chess pawn; F is sharpened only on the

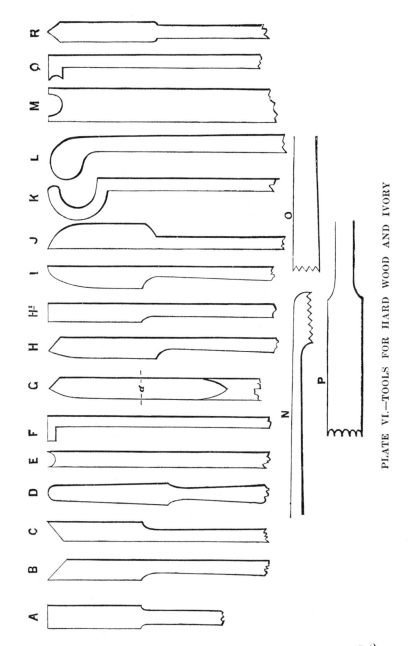

PLATE VI.—TOOLS FOR HARD WOOD AND IVORY

end of the bent part—it is an inside parting tool, and is made
in sets with longer or shorter bent part; G is a side view
of an ordinary parting tool—it cuts at the extreme end, and
is ground thinner downwards to about A on each side, so as
to cut itself clear; H, I, J, are inside, or right and left,
tools, cutting on the ends and sides for hollowing out work—
they vary in shape as shown; K, is ground all round the
outside of the curve, and is used to hollow out bulging or
spherical work, like a humming-top—so also is L; M is a
bead and astragal, turning a bead with flats on each side;
Q is a ring tool—for instance, in turning a curtain ring on
wood, E would round it on the outside, and Q on the inner
face: all such tools are made of various sizes, and can be had
in complete sets; R is a point tool, for turning angular
grooves, and, like D, it is often used for roughing-down work;
P is a reeding tool, and is practically a row of small beading
tools; N, O, are a pair of chasing tools, for cutting outside
and inside screws—they are made of various pitches, coarse
and fine. The average price of these tools is 1s. 6d.
Screw tools vary in price, according to pitch. It is not easy
to determine how many to buy, but perhaps three different
sizes of D, E, F, and Q, will do for a start, as these can be
added to as may prove necessary, and the parcel post now
brings all such tools within easy reach of country customers.
A slight sketch of the tool required, with size needed, will
enable a tool-dealer to supply it. Handles are from one
penny each and upwards, and for these beech is preferable
to hard wood.

The hard-wood cylinder can be turned wholly with the
gouge and chisel, if the latter lies flat on the rest, with
the leading angle kept clear, so as not to mark it. But a
chisel thus held is so quickly blunted, that the flat tool,
which is thicker, and ground with a shorter bevel, is for this
purpose superior to it. The leading angle in this case, also,
is kept clear. The cylinder must, of course, be first reduced
to nearly the required size by the gouge or round tool, or
both, leaving the flat tool as little work as possible. With
some woods, a very thin tool for the final touches proves the
best, and this is held as a mere scraping tool slightly under-

hand—that is, the edge depressed below the level of centres, instead of being applied horizontally. The ends may be trimmed by the parting tool if anything has to be cut off, and finished by a side tool or point tool held at the required angle. All is easier than the manipulation of the soft-wood tools. Hollow work is commenced by drilling a hole with either a twist drill or nose bit, held in a tool handle, or with a round tool, and enlarging it with the latter, or with one of the bevel or inside tools; and if the recess is to be flat at bottom, like that of a box, the flat tool will level it accurately, and with ease.

Bowls and tazzas, egg-cups, vases, &c., are worked also with any of the round end or other suitable tools, held flat on the rest and swept round the curve. The last cuts have to be made slowly and lightly, taking the whole surface, if possible, without stopping, so as to prevent any lines or tool-marks remaining visible.

In turning beads and mouldings, it is almost necessary economy to spare the beautifully made tools by which this kind of work is done. The tools are easily damaged, as the points are fine, and in the smaller sizes the tools are necessarily slender. Hence, it is usual to reduce the parts just as much as possible with point tool, chisel, or bevel tools, and with these to bring the bead or moulding to its approximate size and shape. Then the beading tool has but to clear away the irregularities and finish the bead to a perfect curve. In the use of the above-named tools, the rest is placed just below the level of centres, so as to allow for the thickness of the tool itself. Although, however, the latter is, as a rule, held level and horizontal, it is sometimes tilted up a little in finishing off a surface. All such variations of position must be decided at the time, and their expediency or otherwise will only appear after some amount of practice. Much depends upon the wood, of which some specimens are far more troublesome than others to bring to a good surface. The maximum of such trouble I have found to accrue in the case of a bit of canary wood turned plankway and cut into a bowl.

With the harder and more costly woods, the highest

perfection of workmanship should always be aimed at, and this mainly consists of sharply defined curves and cleanly cut surfaces, bold and neatly cut mouldings, of which the contour or profile can be plainly seen. Glass-paper tends to obliterate angles, and, if necessary, it must be very carefully kept from attacking acute edges; but if these are damaged by its use, they must be renovated by a fresh touch of the tool. In this sharp, clear definition of outline lies all the difference between good and bad work. It may also be remarked here that although glass-paper is sometimes absolutely necessary to cut down fibres which cannot be cleanly cut by the tool, it will not hide bad cutting. If, for instance, the inside of a bowl, instead of presenting to the eye one uniform, curved surface, shows a series of flat rings when closely examined, the paper will not obliterate these, and they should be honestly looked for in a good light, and not shirked under the impression that polish or varnish will ultimately conceal them. Instead of doing so, it will render them painfully conspicuous; and with those who know what good work is, these common defects will at once condemn the workman. Moreover, he himself, being cognisant of such defects, will feel no pleasure in his own work. Therefore, although we are of course addressing learners who cannot be expected to become suddenly proficient in an art requiring the skill obtained by long practice, it has seemed better to point out such defects and errors as they are most likely to fall into in their early essays, that they may know what to strive after, and what to avoid, and, so far as possible, *how* to avoid. In this very matter of bowls and cup-shaped hollows, it will be found easier to work with a curved tool of a size proportioned to that which it is proposed to form; as a broad tool such as K or L, is more likely to produce a hollow free from flat bands and irregularities than a smaller tool with round end like that illustrated at D.

TURNING THE PLANKWAY OF THE GRAIN.—This has to be frequently done both with soft and hard wood, as it often happens that it is not possible in any other way to get stuff wide enough for the intended purpose. There is no great difficulty in working this: even with soft wood the gouge and chisel are used flat upon the rest, light cuts being taken generally from the centre outwards; but for final cuts the tool must be keen. The part which it is most difficult to cut smoothly, is just where the fibres begin to crop out endwise. There will be two spots in a circular disc, where this will be the case, and sometimes they give a great deal of trouble, and need alternate cutting and papering to lay them down smoothly. The harder woods seldom present this difficulty. It would, of course, be a wasteful mode of work to turn such an article as a large bowl or tazza, with stem and stand, out of a piece large enough for the bowl itself, and the latter would be turned separately, perhaps out of a piece sawn plankway, and the stem out of a smaller piece; the stand also probably out of a third. This building-up of work is of constant occurrence, the several pieces being tenoned together, or cut with screws, which is the better plan where the workman is skilful enough to manage it.

The pins or tenons are turned at the ends of pedestals or stems, and the other pieces are drilled in the Lathe, to insure centrality and squareness to the surfaces. Glue or other cement is then used to unite them.

CUTTING SCREWS IN WOOD BY THE HAND CHASER.—This somewhat difficult art is well worth all the trouble that it needs to acquire it. As soon as it is gained, it renders the work more independent of all costly apparatus used to render the process easy to such as cannot succeed with hand tools alone, and the screw can be made in a shorter time than it takes to set up even the simplest of such apparatus; but it would be a mistake to suppose the art in question easy of acquirement, and it needs constant practice to keep up the knack of using the chaser.

The directions given by most of our leading authorities are as follows: "Having turned smooth and true the cylinder upon which the screw is to be traced, round off the edge or arris so that it shall not catch into the teeth at starting, and check the traverse of the tool. The rest is placed very near the work, and must have its edge filed smooth and level if it is at all notched from other work. The tool is to be held by its handle in the right hand, and its blade between the first finger and thumb, so as to cushion it somewhat, and allow it barely to lie on the rest. Then the Lathe is to be set in easy motion, and after a trial or two, without actually touching the work, just to get the swing of it, a steady, decisive cut is to be attempted, traversing the tool without nervousness or hesitation." Exactly so; but, unless the workman is already an adept, the chances are sadly against his hitting off the thread; and, knowing this, he will be as nervous as a skater making his first essay on the ice. Yet there is no royal road to screw-cutting, and the above directions are as good as any. The best way is to cut threads outside chucks, and any odd bits of boxwood, on all occasions: go at it and keep at it, and the skill will not long be wanting.

The inside thread has also to be struck haphazard, only the movement of the tool is now straight forward into the hole. Many use for this purpose an arm rest, which is a long-handled, flat bar of iron, about ½in. wide, tapering down to about ¼in. at the extremity. The end is turned up ¼in., and the chaser rests on the end just behind this hook. The T of the rest is now retained in its usual position parallel to the Lathe bed, and the arm rest is held under the left armpit, with the blade of it across the rest. This places the shank and hook at right angles, or nearly so, across the face of the hollowed work, and the tool is laid on it, instead of having to turn round the T of the rest itself. The hands grasp the end of the arm rest as well as the tool, so that the two move as one. A great deal of inside work, besides screw-cutting, is done with this contrivance, as it prevents having to shift round the T of the rest. Inside screws are easier to cut with its aid, as it moves on the T as on a fulcrum, and gives to the tool an easy swing, as if it moved on a ball-and-socket joint. Each cut of the chaser, especially at the commencement, must be very light, and it must carry itself along by the thread first traced, and not be driven in the least until the thread is well and deeply cut.

The great difficulty will be found with the coarse pitches: the finer, from 16 to 24, are easier than from 8 to 16— the traverse of the latter is necessarily so much faster

and more difficult to hit off, as regards speed. Except
for chucks and large boxwood cases, it is not often that
the coarse pitches will be needed, and 12 to 24 will
amply suffice for general purposes. Holtzapffel, in his
valuable work, directs that the first stroke of the chaser
is to be across the centre of the curve where the sharp angle
has been turned off, like Nos. 1 and 2, Plate VII., *a b* showing
the first stroke, and *c d* the second. Thus the screw is gradually
worked round to the cylindrical part. The traverse is, of
course, from right to left, and from the edge to the interior
of hollow work. Personally, I have found it quite as easy
to begin at once upon the end of the cylindrical part; but
it is, I suppose, a question of habit. I have also generally
found it better at the commencement to keep the points
clear, and to let the tool touch just below them. This will
carry it along sufficiently to let the required speed of traverse
be seen, after which the tool may be lowered, so as to bring
into action its full cutting powers. But there is no sort of
doubt about the difficulty of screw-chasing by hand — a
difficulty that is only to be overcome by such constant work
as falls to the lot of brass-turners and others who are at
work with the chaser every day, and, for the most part,
confine the chasing to one or two pitches only, of which they
thus soon get the exact pace. By way of encouragement,
I may add that a fortnight's apprenticeship often makes a
lad at an optician's workshop a fair proficient, provided he is
kept to one pitch of thread only, as he soon gets used to
traverse the tool at one rate of speed.

Considering, however, that screw-chasing is an acknowledged
difficulty, we are not surprised to meet with various suggested
contrivances for effecting the work in an automatic manner,
especially as this can be done without difficulty in more than
one way. Naturally, the first idea is to continue the use of
the hand chaser, but to arrange some additional apparatus to
insure its accurate traverse. No. 3, Plate VII., will serve to illustrate the principle which, variously modified, has been used for
the purpose. There is cut outside the chuck B a screw of
the required pitch, or a ferrule with such guide-screw cut
on it is slipped on the chuck, and prevented by a feather

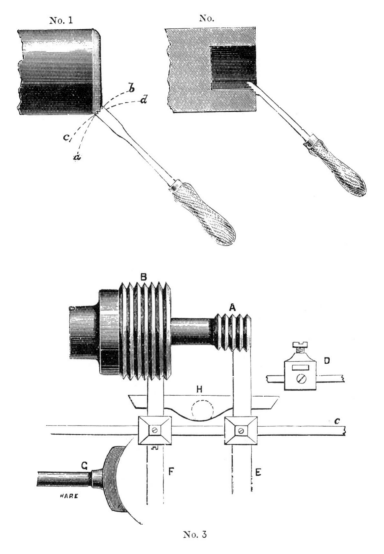

No. 1

No.

No. 3

PLATE VII.—SCREW-CHASING APPARATUS

from revolving upon it. In the latter case, the same chuck will admit of various ferrules, each of different pitch. A is the work upon which a similar screw is required. By means of a bar, C, and a pair of clamps, shown again at D, the chaser, E, is connected with F, a similar chaser, which, however, is not intended to cut, and may be of brass, or even of wood. The tools thus connected at a suitable distance apart, now act as one, and as F is carried along by contact with the screw guide, E, the actual cutting tool will follow at exactly the same rate, tracing a screw on A. Both tools lie upon the rest, H. Theoretically, this is an excellent arrangement, and valuable from its extreme simplicity. In practice, however, it is less satisfactory. The resistance of the cut is apt to throw the guide-chaser out of gear with its ferrule; and, indeed, this chaser needs to embrace a segment of the ferrule, like G, instead of ending merely in one or more points.

Then, again, it is not easy to keep the eye upon both work and guide, especially if they are at all far apart. Hence, without materially altering the original plan, the bar, C, has been made to slide in two suitable sockets, in arms attached to the Lathe—thus steadying the whole arrangement. The sockets, D, are then attached to the bar, C, by screws, but the cutting tool may pass freely through its slot to allow of independent advance. This arrangement has proved to be a perfectly practical one, and is, probably, the best for the purpose, with the sole exception of the traversing mandrel, to be presently described. The supporting arms and sockets need not be in the way, and the bar can be readily unshipped and removed entirely. For inside threads a slightly different arrangement is needed. Suppose E, on the right, to be a plain bar to act as a rest, and the tool to be laid across it, just as it is with the arm rest. If the tool is firmly held, and the bar also gripped, the thread will be cut as before. In practice, this rest arm has a clamp to secure the chaser.

There are several other ways of guiding a tool, but these do not belong here, as they all need a slide rest and gearing by wheels or by cords, and are not to be classed with hand tools and their manipulation. Of all contrivances which admit the use of hand chasing tools, none equals in simplicity, combined with efficiency, the traversing mandrel of which the old pattern, but without the headstock, is shown in plan in Plate VIII., No. 1. B, B represent in section the collars, which used to be of brass, or even of a softer metal—pewter or type-metal—which were made in two parts, so as to be tightened up when worn. The two ends of the mandrel are cylindrical, that they may be able to slide lengthwise, as well as to revolve in their collars. When used for ordinary turning, a pin—seen on the left-hand collar—or a falling stop entered a groove in the mandrel, preventing longitudinal motion. Upon the mandrel were cut short lengths of screw of various pitches. Only three are shown here, but six or eight were often cut, of which one was usually of the pitch of the mandrel nose, to assist in cutting screws in the wooden chucks.

To cause the traverse a very simple expedient was used. A block of soft but close-grained wood, seen at F, was pressed by a wedge against the selected thread, and the pin or catch in the back collar was removed. As soon as the mandrel was made to revolve, a thread was impressed in the wood block, which thus at once became a stationary nut, or section of a nut; and, as this remained immovable, the mandrel itself was compelled to run forward at the exact rate of the particular screw thread that had been selected. A single point tool, or a chaser of similar pitch, needed only to be held quite still upon the rest, and a screw was cut perfectly identical with that on the mandrel. With this apparatus even a tyro can cut a screw in boxwood or ivory, or other material, and even in soft wood. But, in the latter case, a V tool, as it is called, is used, which is in shape like a narrow strip of writing-paper, folded lengthwise, and sharpened at the end. That for inside work is similar, but cuts at right angles to its length: with these only a single cut is taken, which finishes the screw to its full depth; but with hard wood the chaser is generally allowed to retrace its course two or three times. The old pattern of screw mandrel illustrated is mounted on wooden headstocks, the front and back collars being attached with bolts. They are greatly used at Tunbridge, and abroad,

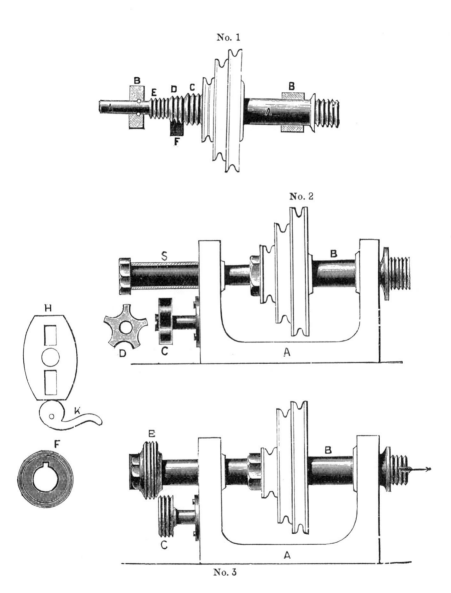

PLATE VIII.—THE TRAVERSING MANDREL.

both in Germany and France, but are not now made to any extent in England, having been, in a great measure, displaced by the neater and more expensive form, in which the screws, instead of being cut directly upon the mandrel, are cut upon rings or ferrules of brass or steel, and attached to the back part of the mandrel which projects beyond the collar, and is outside the headstock.

Before explaining in detail this modern arrangement, it may be as well to go a little into the mode of using the traversing mandrel, as this will apply equally well to both forms of it. The work, it will at once be understood, will travel forward towards the right hand; and, therefore, the back poppet cannot be used: it is only for work chucked on the mandrel, that cannot be done without such other support, that this contrivance is available. A screw cannot be cut with it on the end of a long rod. Thus, also, as this traverse will carry the work forward, the rest must be far enough away, when cutting the inside thread, to allow of this forward movement taking place to the full extent required. This must be tested, both for inside and outside work, before the cutting is commenced. Again, when there is, as always is the case with a box, a short tenon with a shoulder, care must be taken to see that the tool will not, at the end of the traverse, come up against this shoulder, which, by causing a sudden shock, would damage the thread; and the same would happen if, in cutting a screw inside the cover of a box, the end of the tool should strike the inside of the top. It is easy to test this before finally setting the tool to its work. The Lathe is also not allowed to get into full motion, the flywheel only taking a half-turn to and fro, which will give, however, several full rotations to the mandrel. The crank must, therefore, not be allowed to go over, or, in all probability, serious damage will occur, as the threads on the guide ferrules will get jambed. The treadle motion is, therefore, kept carefully under control of the foot, and only a gentle to-and-fro swing is given to the crank axle and flywheel.

A beginner generally finds a little difficulty in holding the chasing tool quite still, and is apt to let it be carried along the rest by the advance of the work. An easy way to prevent this is to drill a hole in the flat-topped rest, and insert a pin on the right of the tool, which will then be kept steadily in its place; or a block of boxwood may be made, with a stem to fit into the socket of the rest, having a groove or channel cut in it for the reception of the chaser, which will be free to move forward into cut, but not to traverse sideways. After a little practice, the difficulty will disappear; but these little aids need never be despised, and may save work, otherwise well turned, from being spoiled. The chief thing is to allow the tool only to take light cuts, so as to present as little resistance as possible to the forward motion of the mandrel.

It is not necessary to finish the thread with the guide-screw in gear, as there is no difficulty after the first cut has been made sufficiently deep to catch fairly the points of the chasing tool. As soon as this is done, it is better to remove the guide, or, at any rate, to throw it out of action, and to finish the thread to its full depth by hand alone. Then, if it is not a good fit, but too tight for its nut or box-cover or other part that is to be attached to it (let it always err on the side of tightness), the chisel can be used, or the flat tool, to take off the tops of the thread, and the chaser can be applied again by hand alone to re-touch and finish the threads again; and this process can be repeated again and again, if necessary, until an accurate fit has been obtained.

In metal-work done with stocks and dies, there is a standard of size for the bore of a nut, to enable it, when tapped, to exactly fit the screw. But in ordinary turned work, in which the traversing mandrel is to be used, a little trying-on of a box-cover is both lawful and very expedient indeed. Suppose the cover to have been just made, and its inside screw cut and finished, the outside of the box tenon must be turned to a diameter equal to that of the inside of the cover, measured to the bottom of the thread cut in it. To measure this is not very easy, because, if done with inside calipers, with points sufficiently fine, you cannot pull them straight out: you may do it with in-and-out calipers if very accurate; but, without pulling them out of the thread, you must, with a second pair of outside calipers, take the width of the points of the first pair—*i.e.*, of course, the points outside, which are just as wide apart as those buried in the threads; you can then close and remove the latter, and the second pair will gauge the tenon. But it is far more usual to work by guess, trying the screwed cover upon the tenon till it appears to be the required size, but leaving it, if anything, too large. It is then cut with a screw thread, and tried as already explained, and, if necessary, cut down, and the thread renewed as often as may prove necessary until it goes on well. But for boxes and scent-bottle cases, and all work that will be constantly taken apart, do not make too tight a fit. It ends in splitting the cover, or being compelled to use the vice to hold the work while it is being unscrewed; and, although a rub of soap will help the matter as an effective lubricant, it is seldom that the work escapes damage, if not entire destruction. A *tight* fit is not to be called a *good* fit.

The modern screw mandrel (No. 2) is a neater arrangement than the last, but in principle it is exactly the same. A is the poppet, not of wood, but of cast iron; and this is usually japanned black, except in the front face, where it is made bright. Hard steel collars are let into it to receive the cylindrical hardened mandrel (B), which is free to revolve and to slide lengthwise, but is so well fitted as not to have the least atom of side play. Such a mandrel of best quality will wear very many years without running loose in its bearings. The front end has a short conical neck, and the mandrel is put in in that direction. To draw back the conical part into its bearing in the front collar, a sleeve (shown in section at S) is slipped over the projecting part of the mandrel, and secured by a nut and washer at the back. This, which is also hardened at the end, bears against the back collar, and retains the mandrel in its place. This sleeve fits over a short feather or pin, that prevents it from itself rotating upon the mandrel. For ordinary turning, all parts remain in the position indicated. There being no tail pin to take up the end thrust in such operations as drilling and boring, this comes entirely upon the front cone. These Lathes are not, therefore, well suited for such work, and are mostly purchased by those who practise ornamental turning, in which there is no heavy or detrimental work to be done. The conical neck is, of course, so proportioned that it shall not jamb by the ordinary thrust of the back poppet, when this is in use for turning cylindrical work of such length as to need its support. When it is desired to cut a screw, the box or other article is carefully turned to a form truly cylindrical, the rebate being also accurately rectangular.

The rest is then placed about ¼in. from the work, and (as explained) well towards the right, in which direction the traverse will take place. If the stem of the rest is placed about where the traverse will begin, the hand grasping it and the tool together will be better able to prevent the latter from being carried sideways when the cutting action begins. The sleeve (S) is now removed by unscrewing the nut which holds it, and a ferrule, having been selected, is slipped on in its place. The nut is again attached to secure it (see No. 3). The disc (D C) is turned round by the fingers, to bring uppermost the half-nut matching the ferrule, and then it is raised until it just gears with one or two threads; a drop or two of oil is added, and the mandrel run forward without applying the tool to the work, in order to see that everything works easily and smoothly, as it should.

If all appears satisfactory, the treadle is now used to give half-revolutions to the crank, and the tool is gently but firmly advanced to the work, upon which it will trace an accurate thread, which can be deepened with or without the traversing apparatus, as already stated. In the drawing, the stud, upon which the segment-plate or scalloped disc is mounted, is represented as attached to the headstock by two screws. The plate (seen at H, Plate VIII.), with two slots in it, permits of being slid up and down upon these screws, by which it may also be held when in position. It may be raised by hand, but it is more convenient to do this by an eccentric, like K.

CHAPTER IV.

METAL-TURNING WITH HAND TOOLS.

THE principle of the cutting action of all tools is the
same. They are thin wedges, which force apart the
substance of the material upon which they are engaged; they must, consequently, be harder than such substance, and their edges must be as thin as is consistent with
the necessary strength. They must also be held in the
position most favourable for the operation.

The resistance which has to be overcome by a cutting
tool is twofold: first, the hardness of the material which
it has to penetrate; and secondly, the rigidity of the shaving
which has to be separated, and which must be capable of
curling away as it is cut, and escaping from the upper
surface of the tool. If too deep a cut is attempted, so that
the shaving is too thick to curl away and escape, it holds
the tool fast by compression, and breaks its edge; or, if
strong enough to resist breakage, the machine driving such
tool is brought to a standstill. Metal, offering considerably
greater resistance than wood, needs tools with stronger edges;
and as their strength is, on the other hand, limited by the
necessity of keenness, they require careful adjustment in
order to enable comparatively keen edges to do their work
without breaking. The shaving must be thin enough not
to endanger such fracture, and its thinness or the contrary
depends upon the angle at which the tool meets the work.

Again, it is essential that metal-turning tools be well
supported, owing to the strain which comes upon them in

the act of cutting. They cannot be held like the chisel at
A B (Plate IX.), because the direction of the strain is as
nearly as possible in a line with the tool, which, in the case of
metal-turning, would slip down towards the hand. Hence, a
rest with flat top, like C, No. 2, has to be substituted, which
supports entirely the heel of the bent tool, such as is used
for iron, and of which the edge, thin and sharp, is also
supported by the metal below it, the strain tending to fracture it being reduced to a minimum. An exception in the
need of a flat-top rest, occurs, however, in the case of the
graver, which is seen at E, No. 3. This tool would be placed
as shown, ready to cut a shaving from the bar of metal,
commencing at the end. It is evident that as the strain is
downwards, this tool is perfectly supported by the T of
the ordinary rest. The tools for iron always have sharp edges,
which are not suitable for those intended for brass and gun-
metal. The tool H, No. 5, called a triangular tool, and which,
having cutting angles of 60deg., can be made of old saw files
ground till the teeth are removed, is the usual tool for inside
work; and for turning the ends of cylinders and sides of collars
and flanges it is a splendid tool, cutting with great freedom.
There is not much light work that cannot be done with this
tool and the graver alone, but for heavier cuts the one shown
at D of No. 1 is more serviceable. This is made in two
forms, O, P, one for smoothing, the other for roughing.
The heel is often drawn out a little, to grip the rest more
firmly. G is, as a brass-turning tool, what H is for iron and
steel. The edges are rectangular, as a sharp edge proves too
eager for yellow metal and is apt to catch in and spoil the
work. L, No. 6, is a side view, for instance, of such tools as
J and K, having an angle of 80deg. or thereabout, which
is sharp enough for most purposes. The tools J, K, are
almost counterparts of those for hard wood, which, indeed,
are not unfrequently pressed into service in default of others.
The round-end is the best of all for roughing-down brass.
At P is shown a rest which has been greatly used by turners
of brass, but is not so often seen now that slide rests have
become so general: a few years ago, owing to the cost, they
were the exception. The pins are inserted in a flat-top rest,

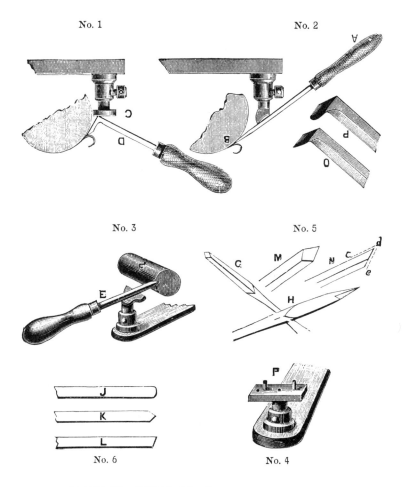

No. 1   No. 2

No. 3   No. 5

No. 6   No. 4

PLATE IX.—METAL-TURNING BY HAND TOOLS.

as fulcrums to assist in steadying the tools and prevent them
from slipping sideways out of cut. They are easily fitted,
and will prove of great convenience, saving the muscles of
the hand and wrist a good deal of hard work. It will be
seen at a glance that metal-turning tools, used by hand,
cannot be run along the surface of work as wood-cutting
tools are, but must, for the most part, be swept round in
short curves, then shifted, and a similar cut made. The
ridges between these curves are then attacked and the surface levelled by degrees in stages. But very good work can,
nevertheless, be so done, and metal-turning by hand will be
found far more interesting and easy than might be supposed;
even with a slide rest at hand, it is impossible wholly to lay
aside hand tools.

It may, indeed, seem strange to the ambitious tyro, whose
heart is bent on a slide rest, to be told that hand tools are
easier to use, and that he must not think for a moment that
all he has to do is to put a tool in the rest, turn a handle,
and produce excellent work. If it were so, a Lathe man
would hardly need the apprenticeship which he is called on
to serve. But it is equally true that the use of hand tools
may be very quickly acquired, and that good work may be done
with them. The principle guiding their use is, nevertheless,
exactly the same as that which governs the others; and it is,
perhaps, accuracy of position which is of more real importance
than accuracy of the cutting angle of edge. For instance,
if a cutting edge of 60deg. is the best for wrought iron, one
of 62deg. or of 59deg. would cut it almost as well; but one
of 60deg., though perfectly ground, not placed exactly right,
will do far worse work than one of 70deg. placed correctly.
The rule, which is so generally applicable that it may be
taken as absolute, is to keep the lower face of the tool, or the
face which is nearest to the surface of the work, as accurately
tangential as is possible while allowing it to cut—in a word,
keep it almost in contact, but not quite. The graver will
illustrate this better than any other. The back of the tool is
seen at E, No. 5, and the front of it is like M, the side
view or profile N. Now, in order to set this tool into cut,
let it first lie quite flat against the end of the bar—*i.e.*, lay

the bevel, or sloping face, of it in that position. This is technically called "without any clearance." Draw back the tool upon the rest, so as only to let ½in. of its point overlap, but still keep the face as before. Now tilt up the tool very slightly indeed, giving it a very small clearance angle. It will at once cut the metal beautifully. Increase the clearance more and more, noting the result. It will be found to cut worse and worse. Take up the triangular tool, and try the same. It will shave off quite a broad, thin shaving if the clearance is very small, a thicker one by tilting it a little more; but presently it will be found too much tilted over for good work. Either tool may be held in one hand, easily, with a small clearance, so slight is the resistance. Nothing can teach better than this the fundamental principle of a small amount of clearance. This lesson is preparatory to the right understanding of slide-rest tools, the difficulty with these being the impossibility of thus gently altering the angle of clearance, or of slightly varying the position of their edge, or edges engaged with the work : yet it is this very slight variation that makes all the difference between good cutting and bad. It is the same with the heel tool (D of Plate IX.) The lower face, next the work, must make a very small angle with the bar upon which it is engaged, in order to cut the material easily and smoothly. It is just the same, but is not, perhaps, so plainly perceptible in turning hollow work with the triangular tool. Experiment may here, however, be made with great advantage, because, if the tool fails to cut as it should, it must necessarily be because it is not correctly placed, as its angles are 60deg., and are quite the best for use on wrought iron. We may now go a step further. Suppose D (the heel tool) to be placed correctly in the drawing—which it is—it will be seen that, if the handle is lowered, cutting will cease, and the tool will rub against the work. This, therefore, is our limit in that direction. But what will result if we raise the handle? Not only shall we increase the clearance angle, but we shall also alter the position of the top face of the tool, and shall bring it more nearly into a horizontal position. From this another evil will result. The shaving will be bent up sharply, pressing upon the top face of the tool, and greatly adding to the resistance; and, at the same time, the edge of the tool will become more of a scraper than a cutting tool. It is just the same as with a knife. If you want to cut a pencil, you lay the blade pretty flat. If you wish to scrape the lead to a point, you set the blade up on edge. In the first case, the clearance angle is very small; in the second case, it is actually 90deg., or a right angle. This will show how we are limited in the position we can give a turning tool.

As regards speed for metal-turning, it may be briefly stated here that cast iron needs a very slow speed, and this is best obtained by back gear, which is very useful also for boring metal. But wrought iron of small size may be turned by means of the slowest speed on the flywheel, and brass can be cut upon the next speed, or the first on the rim of the wheel. Small brasswork, indeed, may be turned at the same speed as hard wood. The finishing touch is given to brass by a planisher, as it is called, which is, in fact, a flat tool, thin at the edge, and ground off square; and if this tool is rubbed with a burnisher after being ground and set, it will in turn, not only cut the metal, but leave upon it a burnished surface, which looks exceedingly well on any fillets or beads which form rings above the general surface. These may also be finished with the milling tool, which acts by pressure, and impresses its own pattern on the work while revolving in close contact with it. Heads of screws to be turned by the finger and thumb are nearly always thus finished, as the minute teeth so formed produce a rough surface, not liable to slip when laid hold of. There is one vexatious tendency in brass which often causes trouble—namely, its tendency to chatter or vibrate under the action of the tool. This causes a series of striæ, or minute undulations, to be cut on its surface, which, once begun, are difficult to check. The only way to prevent the mischief appears to be to move the tool ceaselessly, so as to alter the direction of the vibrations constantly, thereby counteracting them. A similar result may be attained by a pad of sole leather on the rest, or by allowing the tool to bed itself partially against the thumb and finger. But short cuts, with the tool slightly tilted, and frequently altered in position, are the most general antidotes. It is, however, often necessary to go over the whole surface with a router, or round-end tool, to get rid of striæ formed in a few seconds. Some kinds of brass are more subject to this tendency than others.

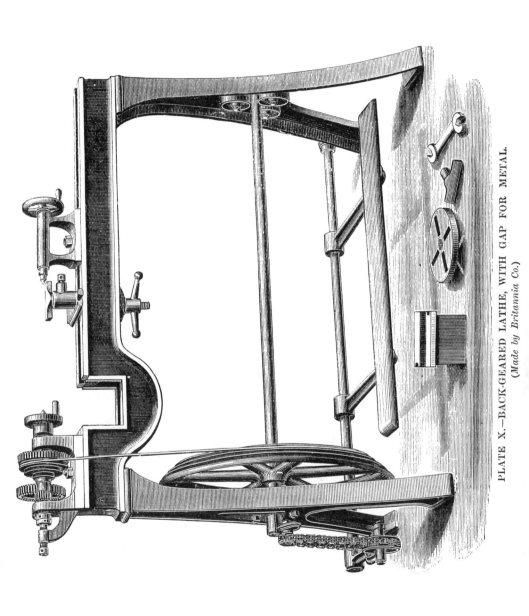

PLATE X.—BACK-GEARED LATHE, WITH GAP FOR METAL.

(Made by Britannia Co.)

CHAPTER V.

SLIDE-REST WORK IN METAL.

IT will be as well to commence this chapter with a description of one or two Lathes more specially suited for metal-work than those already illustrated, which are chiefly for beginners, and for work of small size. The Lathe of which an engraving is given here. is a very strong one, and is made from 4in. to 6in. centre. It has back gear for slow motion, and can be had with extra hard mandrel and steel collars, but is generally made with gun-metal collars. Price, £13 to £18; weight, 4½cwt. The crank shaft runs on friction rollers, and everything is done to prevent the Lathe from working heavily. Such a Lathe as this is powerful enough for metal-work of a tolerably heavy character, and should be fitted with a good strong slide rest. This latter Lathe appliance has gone through many changes of form, but consists mainly of two slides, working at right angles to each other—the lower one moving to and fro across the Lathe bed, the upper moving parallel to it. There is, however, in addition, a quadrant plate, allowing the upper part to swivel round horizontally, so as to adjust the tool for turning cones. Sometimes the upper slide is made to advance or withdraw the tool, and the lower is the one parallel to the Lathe bed; in which case, the whole rest is fitted with a sole plate, or foot, similar to that of a hand rest, and this—which generally slides on a separate cradle, fitted on the Lathe bed, to keep it accurately square to such bed—constitutes a third slide (see Fig. 8). The rest is good for special purposes, but not so

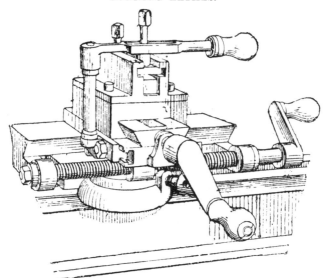

FIG. 8.—W. S. BROWN'S SLIDE-REST
(*Made by Britannia Co.*)

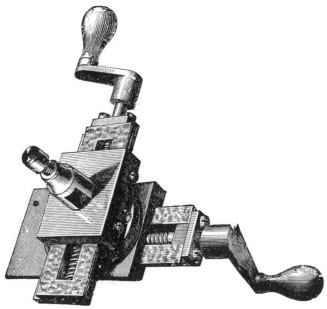

FIG. 9.—SMALL SLIDE-REST.

well suited for general metal-work, where the greatest
rigidity is needed. A small slide-rest of the ordinary make is

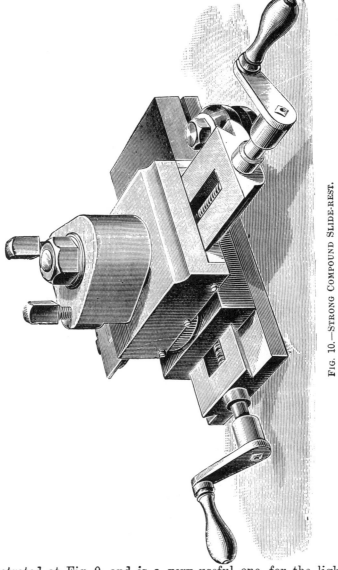

FIG. 10.—STRONG COMPOUND SLIDE-REST.

illustrated at Fig. 9, and is a very useful one for the lighter

D

Lathes to 4in. centre already described.   Below, and parallel
to the top frame, is a tenon, to fit accurately in the bed of
the Lathe, to which it is attached by a bolt and hand nut.
The tool-holder swivels round to any horizontal position.
The quadrant plate and its clamping nut are seen on the
right hand, just above the square plate of the lower slide.
The next Figure (10) shows a much stronger rest, suitable for
turning any work admissible in a Lathe of 5in. or 6in. centres.
The tool-holder is also better for heavy work.

With a slide rest it is no longer necessary to cut the
metal by short strokes, which produce inequalities demanding
to be levelled down by subsequent cuts.   The tools traverse
steadily along the surface of the work, removing a continuous
shaving which is often of a yard or more in length in the
case of a self-acting Lathe driven by steam.   There is, moreover, not the least strain upon the muscles of the hand, as
the tool is rigidly clamped on the upper plate of the slide
rest, and all that has to be done by the workman is to turn
the handle which causes the traverse.   The horizontal angle of
the tool is under perfect control by means of the swivelled
tool-holder, but all others are evidently fixed and unalterable;
front, top, and side rake being determined once for all in
grinding the tool.   If the chapter on hand turning tools has
been carefully studied, it will not be difficult to understand
what is required to make a slide-rest tool act perfectly.   We
have to consider, first, the cutting edges, which must be of
such an angle, and such sharpness, as to suit the metal on
which they are to be used; secondly, the low clearance angle,
as before, which brings the front face or faces at nearly a
tangent to the work; and, thirdly, the height of cutting edge,
which is always, as a normal rule, to be at the height of the
Lathe centres—a rule which it is rarely necessary to alter.
The solid tools forged from steel bar are represented here,
Fig. 11, from A to G.   Some are straight, some bent to right or
left, some cranked, and others for inside work.   They stand
flat on the sole plate of the rest, always lying horizontally.
They can be packed up to exact height of centre by parallel
slips of iron placed underneath them.

One of the most common tools for roughing-down work is

the round end or router, Fig. 11, A; bent to the right or left
if the work requires it, B. If well ground and correctly
placed, it takes a good bite, and gets over its work rapidly,
but does not leave a finished surface. It is, in fact, the gouge
of the metal-turner. Another tool for the same purpose is
the point or diamond point tool, C. This is a more delicate
affair, and it leaves on the work a fine spiral line, which is,
in fact, a screw of very fine pitch. These tools are, for iron,
bent up somewhat, so as to give an inclined upper face,
because the tool cannot be held at a tangent like a wood
chisel, and the top face must therefore be ground permanently
to a suitable top angle. Then, again, if we look down upon the
top of the tool and work, as in the plan view, Fig. 12,'S, we shall

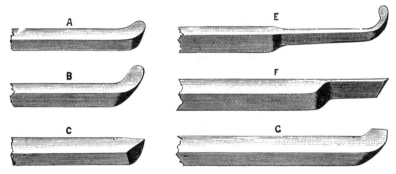

FIG. 11.—SOLID FORGED TOOLS.

see that the cut is made by the left side of the curved end as
far as the dotted line, supposing, for the sake of distinctness,
that a deep cut is taken. The tool is travelling to the left
in the direction of the arrow. The part a, therefore, which
leads, must have its clearance, or it will rub against the
side of the cut; and the point or front must have clearance,
or it will rub against the cylinder. To get a good cut out
of this tool, the top face or top clearance should be ground
in the direction of a b, and not straight down towards the
shank. This will give what is called "side rake," rendering
the tool sharpest where the line a b touches the work. This
is easier to manage if the end is not only bent up, but bent
over towards the left, like B of the set just described.

D 2

To make still more clear the principles which guide the action of slide-rest tools, we must recollect that a shaving has to be detached in two directions—viz., from the shoulder *a* of K, Fig. 12, and from the surface of the cylinder at *b*. A shaving has to be thus separated at two points, and, to effect this in the best way, it must be cut, and not torn, in either direction. Hence, a perfect tool must evidently have two edges — a front and a side edge; and, as it is the ultimate object of turning to leave a smooth surface upon the work, it is evident that the tool edge which cuts this cylindrical surface must be formed and

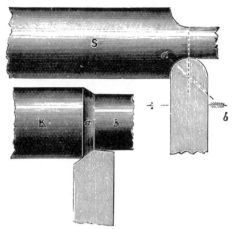

Fig. 12.—SLIDE-REST WORK.

sharpened as carefully at least as the other, although the latter, as the leading edge, has most of the work to do, and, if there is any difference, needs to be sharpest. This is the double-edge principle, which is often regarded as a sort of scientific theory suited only for amateurs, and of no real use to a workman; but it is not so: it is the fundamental principle of slide-rest tools—easy to understand, and equally easy to apply practically; and no chapter on tools would be complete without an explanation of it. In a round-end tool we may take half the edge as the leader and the other half as the follower; as we may suppose it to be, what it practically is, a double-edged tool of very wide angle, with its extreme point rounded off. It is a very common practice to apply a tool *end on*, whether pointed or rounded (A and B, Fig. 13); but evidently the tools, after having started, cut no further than to the dotted line dividing them centrally, and the part *x, x* might be cut away altogether. Where, then, is the second edge of the point tool? Nowhere; and hence the shaving is torn, and not cut, in that direction, and a rough line remains on the surface of the work. Power is also

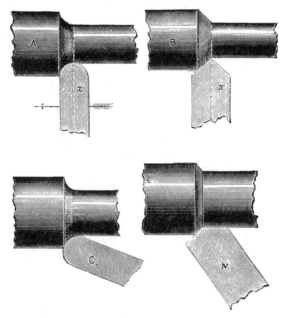

FIG. 13.—PRINCIPLE OF DOUBLE EDGES.

wasted, because it takes more power to tear apart the particles of iron than to cut them cleanly. An "end-on" tool is not, therefore, a scientific one, its proper position being that of M, so as to bring both edges into cut. The same is true of a round-end tool. It is evident that here the extremity is the sharpest part of it, and that the edge gets gradually blunter, as it is situated further and further round the curve; then it is plain, from what has been said, that it should not stand "end on," like *x* of Fig. 13, because the

blunter part at the side is leading. Placed as at C, or bent
to the left, it will cut much better. It is never *quite* satisfactory, owing to the sharpness of edge varying all round the

FIG. 14.—SET OF TOOLS FOR SLIDE-REST.

curve, but it is a useful tool which is sure to find a place
in every workshop.

The variously formed slide-rest tools ordinarily supplied in

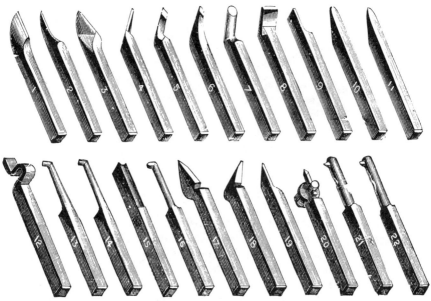

FIG. 15.—VARIOUS SLIDE-REST TOOLS.

complete sets are illustrated together in Fig. 14, set up in a
block, and in Fig. 15 they are shown separately; and it would

be difficult to devise other shapes, as there can hardly be any work, hollow or otherwise, which one or more such tools will fail to cut. The three on the right hand of the second row are, however, not solid tools, but bars with loose cutters—the first for outside, and the two others for inside work. Of the first, in all its details, we shall speak very fully under the head of the Haydon Bar. The others have square shanks to lie upon the rest, and are then turned for the remainder of their length. At the end is a small mortice, which is cut slightly conical, and is intended to receive small bits of steel, filed to fit the mortice, and then sharpened and hardened. The mortice is cut either square to the bar or at an acute angle, by which plan the cutting end of the tool is made to project a trifle beyond the end of the bar, for the purpose of

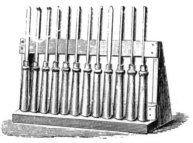

FIG. 16.—STAND FOR TOOLS.

getting into corners. These replace the holing or boring tools, of which E, Fig. 11, is a larger drawing. Third from the right, in the first row, is a drawing of the knife tool. Of these, there are always a pair. The edge is on one side, and the tool is meant to true up the ends of cylinders and sides of collars. It is ground to a very slight clearance angle in the face next the work, and will take off a broad, thin shaving. The left-hand tool of the second row is a spring tool for finishing off a shaft; it acts as a chisel, and cannot possibly hitch in. The edge is placed almost parallel to the work, but so as to keep the angle clear.

Illustrated here (Fig. 16) is a very simple stand for tools which is most useful, as each tool can be seen at a glance. This one is for handled tools for wood.

The further consideration of this important subject will be better carried on in connection with cutter bars, especially as these are fast displacing the solid forged tools of which we have been speaking. Those that are cranked are made on the same principle, but are more convenient to grind, and naturally lead up to the cutter bar, as they may be considered

FIG. 17.—PRINCIPLE OF LOOSE CUTTERS.

as a shank acting as a handle to support a straight bar, ground off at an angle at its upper end (see dotted lines in Fig. 17, representing a cranked tool).

Passing by, for the present, other bars which are made to hold round, square, or oblong section steel, we may go at once to one called, from the name of its inventor, the Haydon

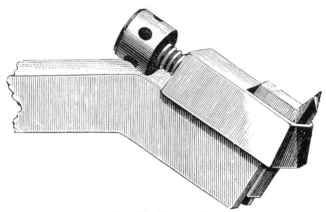

FIG. 18.—HAYDON BAR.

Bar. It was designed to carry out to the utmost the principles of double-edged tools. Intended chiefly for square section bars, it will also·hold round ones and gouges—the latter being, of course, broken off into short bits about 1in. long. Fig. 18 represents this bar, and its construction is evident at a glance. It is sold, accompanied by a full printed description, and with directions for grinding the little cutters. The price varies from 9s. 6d. to 17s. 6d., according to size. The top part, or sling, is a separate piece, and the clamping screw, by drawing it up towards the front end of the bent part of the bar, grips the steel cutter firmly. The latter requires to be ground on three faces—two in front, and one on top. This gives full scope to the workman, in shaping the tool, to meet all requirements. The bar can also, for special purposes, be bent to either side, but it is seldom necessary, as the cutters can be shaped to cut in front or sideways. It is not, however, possible to use such bar for boring and inside work. For this a straight one is used, or an ordinary solid boring tool. In the engraving of the bar we see the top face of the cutter, and one of the two lower ones, the other being precisely similar. In these we have to get, not exactly *front* clearance (nor does the front line signify), but the clearance of the one face of the tool, which will lie against the shoulder, and of the other, which will be opposite to the cylinder. The meeting of these two with the top face produces, evidently, the two edges which are to remove the shaving. Naturally, we should first grind the front faces, and for this the tool is pushed up, after slackening the screw of the sling, so that the latter may not come into contact with the grindstone. If the shank of the bar is laid on a wooden block resting on the bearers of the grindstone, and the bar is slewed round so as to bring parallel to the stone the face which is to be first ground, a few turns will grind it. The slope, or clearance angle, will be greater or less, according to the height of the block, and the distance the tool has been pushed up in its sling. The thicker the block, or the higher the tool, the greater will be the clearance produced, because the stone will grind more the heel or lower part of the face on which it is engaged. Take Fig. 19, A, to represent the cutter, held up with its two lower faces towards you, and B, the side view which will, of course, show but one face; this will be ground with not much clearance. Then C and D will be similar views, in which the grinding, carried lower down the tool, has produced longer faces—*i.e.*, more clearance. But observe, it is the *face*, and not the middle line, of which we are speaking : this front clearance we have nothing to do with so far. The slope of it depends on the grinding of the faces, and may be called accidental.

But now it will come into use in quite another way. As yet we have no edges, the shape being like E, if it is a square tool not ground before. Its side view will, in this case, be represented by F. It has, therefore, to be ground off on about the line *x*, *y*, until the square end is obliterated. It is now that the front line comes into service, for, in grinding the top face, it will make a given angle with this line, and according to that angle will the sharpness of the two cutting

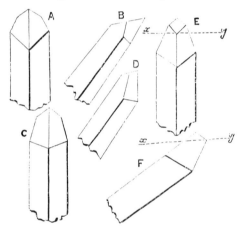

FIG. 19.—GRINDING CUTTERS.

edges be. All this, when it has to be put into words, appears very complicated ; but now it has been once explained, it can be summarised in a few words. To grind a cutter : Set the bit of steel up in the sling, to prevent the latter from receiving damage; lay the shank on a block, resting on the bearers of the stone; grind the two lower faces in succession at a tolerably wide angle—90deg. to 120deg., as a rule, will do. Take out the cutter and turn it round in the sling, so as to bring the face which is left to be ground outwards; lay it on the stone, and grind it to the desired angle with the front line. This is not at all complicated, after all; and when the thing is being actually done, all will be seen clearly enough. Grinding this third or top face will obliterate the square, as it will bring the face to the line $x\,y$ of this Figure.

Now here is at once seen the handiness of the cutter bar. There is no forging to be done. The little steel rods, ⅛in. to ⅜in., or in large bars ⅝in., square, are readily procured, and can be cut in lengths of an inch or two; and as they are gradually shortened by grinding, they are merely pushed up higher in the sling, so as always to bring the point of the tool to the height of the Lathe centres. After grinding, the steel cutter is not left standing up high, but is pushed down again, so that the point shall never stand above the level of the shank of the tool: if too high, it will have a tendency to chatter; and if it should catch in, it will probably also break.

We may now consider another point connected with the formation of the cutters. It is necessary to know how to obtain the two cutting edges of exactly the angle preferred—say, for instance, 60deg. for wrought iron. Now, this angle depends upon two things conjointly—first, the angle at which the two lower faces meet, called the plan angle of the tool; and then, secondly, upon the angle at which the top face is ground to the front line, formed by the meeting of the aforesaid faces. A graver is a square bar: it has, therefore, a plan angle of 90deg. Grinding off the face at 45deg., with the line formed by the meeting of any two given faces, the edges produced will be 60deg. each, and these are the angles usual with that tool. If we grind the faces of the little cutter, therefore, similarly to make an angle of 90deg., and then grind off the top face at 45deg., we get 60deg. of cutting edge. But an angle of 90deg. gives rather a weak point to the graver or to our cutter, and the latter is preferably ground to a larger angle, the faces meeting at 120deg. The top must be then ground to make 55deg. with the front line, and the result will be two cutting edges of 60deg., as before, but the point of the tool will be strong. The extreme point, even then, is preferably rounded on the oilstone.

One precaution has always to be taken, in order to produce two edges equally sharp, and that is, to keep the front line

formed by the two faces, and which will be upwards when
grinding the last face, in the "run" of the grindstone. It
does not follow that the line in question will be in the
centre of the tool, because it is to be clearly understood
that there is no restriction as to the direction of the edges.
Fig. 20, A, B, C, may represent the grindstone forming the
third, or top, face—the back of the tool, being, of course,
seen. Then it may chance that, to get the middle line between the front faces right in the run of the stone, the bar
may have to lie like B or C; for it may seem convenient to
grind the first edge like the left hand of D, all on one side,
so that the second edge, making 120deg. with the first, may
lie square across the end of the bar. When the tool is

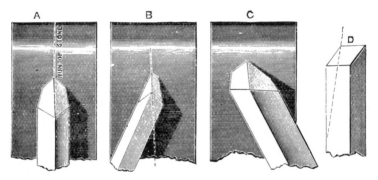

FIG. 20.—GRINDING THE TOP FACE.

reversed, it will have to lie as seen at C, or the edges will
not be equally sharp. Such a tool, having its leading edge
very much to one side, may be useful on the side of a flange
or shoulder. The position of this leading edge is the first
consideration. It will depend on the work: is the tool to
cut more towards the right or left, or straight ahead? Grind
that face to suit the case, and then grind number two at
120deg., 90deg., or, for a small corner, 60deg., or 55deg. for
screw-cutting, and then the top face at such a slope or rake
as to give the cutting edges desired. Consider, also, if you
are likely to find in the way any part of the tool edge that
will not be actually engaged. Generally speaking, only a
small part of the edge is in cut. Then, if you like, file

away all that is of no use. Never mind the shape thus
produced: all you want are the *edges*.

It is very advisable that every turner who wishes to take
up this Haydon bar, and to work it thoroughly, should begin
by what may be called the normal tool for outside work on
cylinders. This is the simplest of the many possible forms;
the angles are of a size easily remembered, and the work
which it will do is of the very best. The front angle, formed
by the meeting of the lower faces, is to be 120deg., and the
angle made by the front line with the top face is to be
55deg., giving 60deg. as the angles of the edges. A notch in
a sheet of tin, made by two three-square saw files held together,
will make a gauge for 120deg.; a second notch made by one
such file will be 60deg.; and a third notch, *marked* for 60deg.
by a bit of tin filed to fit the 60deg. notch, and then cut a
little within the marks, will serve nearly enough to measure
the profile of 55deg. Of course, it may be done with mathematical accuracy, by means of a proper protractor, but the
plan suggested serves fairly well as a workshop expedient.
In grinding the two faces, the clearance may be stated at
3deg., as it has been shown that the smaller this angle is
the better. After grinding to gauge, give a rub, face down,
on an oilstone, and also take off with it the extreme point,
rounding it just visibly and no more. This tool will, if
rightly placed, do the finest and most beautiful outside work,
needing no further finish of any kind. To place it, gauge
height by the Lathe centre, after the bar is fixed in the rest,
pushing up the cutter in the sling until it is exact to height;
then clamp it by the screw. To adjust it now to the work,
remember the principle is to be carried out of two edges—a
leader to cut down the shoulder, and a follower to cut the
shaving from the cylinder in such a manner as to leave it
perfectly smooth, and, if desired, as bright as a looking-glass.

For this the follower is to lie almost parallel to the work, but
not quite so. About two-thirds of that edge may, in fact, be
allowed to cut. If the result is not a continuous shaving
clean cut, examine for the cause, specially for the following—
viz., too great clearance angle, and the tool point too high
or too low; the latter, having, perhaps, resulted from screwing

down the bar in the tool-holder, after adjusting height of centres, with the bar merely lying upon the rest. Also, see to possible softness of the tool, a defect often over-looked. Nothing has, indeed, been said about hardening and tempering the cutters; but this is a matter of necessity, and a very easy one to accomplish. Just heat each, after forming it, to a full red, and drop it in a basin of water. This gives perfect hardness; and, though brittle, the tools will, with ordinary work, seldom break. But they are easily let down a little by heating a bar of iron, or shovel, red hot, and placing them on it until they take a light straw colour, or deeper straw, beginning to verge into blue. Then drop again into cold water, and they will stand well upon most bars of rolled iron. The latter may itself cause broken and short shavings, owing to cracks and defects; but, after a little practice, it will soon be seen whether this or the tool is at fault.

Never rest satisfied with bad work or hitching, chopping, scraping, or anything but an evidently clean cut. If not obtained, the grinding is faulty, or the tool badly placed. When both these conditions are correctly carried out, the tool cannot possibly fail to work well.

After thoroughly getting hold of both the principle and practice, by the use of the normal tool, another simple form should be tried—e.g., one ground to 90deg. front angle and 45deg. top rake, which is exactly the graver used as a double-edged tool, instead of as a single-edged one, as it is when used by hand in the way already described. Then, taking the normal tool as a foundation, file away one edge almost to nothing, taking a great sweep out with a round file, and you have a tool for the side of a shoulder or an odd corner. File out both sides till you get a parting tool—and, in fact, see how many useful shapes you can obtain out of that one plain tool. You thus learn, step by step, the real value of the cutter-bar system. Even workmen who have never heard of double edges, or who scorn to depart from their ancestral inheritance of rule of thumb, do unconsciously adopt the principle when they give more top rake to that side of a round-end tool that is leading. They set the tool "end on," at right angles to the Lathe bed, and then find it cuts badly, unless the leading edge is higher than the other.

It is a rule in double-edged tools that, if any difference of acuteness exist, this extra sharpness of the leading edge shall be secured by leaning the tool slightly over in grinding the top face. But not only is this the case, but, whether recognised by the workman or ignored, it is a fact that nearly all his tools are double edged, and, in fact, must be so, unless he is content to tear off the shaving instead of cutting it. If a shaving has breadth and thickness (and some are of considerable thickness), it must be cut in two directions, and, therefore, two edges are a necessity, although they may be, and are, often disguised by being rounded off into each other. It is much better to admit this fact, and then to think out the result of it.

A workman thus using his intelligence will soon prove a better practical workman than he was before. There has been a vast amount of prejudice in this matter, which still exists to some extent, because a latheman who has learnt practically how to grind a tool, and how to use it, will not listen to any theory of why the tool in question was to be so ground or placed. But the result is that a great deal of Lathe work is very badly done, and that if any unusual job of turning is called for, demanding a special tool, the workman is at his wits' end to produce it; and if any tool works inefficiently, it very often happens that the latheman has no knowledge of where the fault is.

Technical schools are doing something to rectify matters; and probably before long the rule of thumb will find itself deposed, and that workman will get the highest wages who understands the theory of cutting tools, and can reduce it to practice.

CHAPTER VI.

THE SELF-ACTING LATHE.

IT will always be found difficult to turn the handle of the
slide-rest so evenly that the work shall be left uniformly
smooth and true. If the tool rests too long on one spot
a deeper cut is the result, which, although very shallow,
shows as a line upon the work; and this always occurs,
again and again, when the slide-rest handle receives an
intermittent motion, which, more or less, it nearly always
does. Hence, for one reason, a self-acting motion is superior
to that produced by hand, and this is easily managed by
the aid of gearing or cog-wheels, and, with slightly less
certainty, by means of cords and pulleys, generally connected
to the mandrel through the medium of an overhead shaft.

But another reason for the adoption of self-acting Lathes
is that in a factory one man can attend to two or three
instead of one—a matter of economy that cannot be dis-
regarded. And, thirdly, this mechanism enables a workman
to cut screws of any desired pitch, say from one to sixty
threads in an inch, with certainty; and also coarser screws
called spirals, having perhaps but one complete turn in
six inches. Apart, therefore, from such other uses as the
self-acting Lathe may be occasionally put to, the above
are ample reasons for its general use where much and varied
work is carried on. The general form of these Lathes may
be gathered from the accompanying engravings of Lathes,
numbered 15 and 16 in the catalogue of the Britannia
Company, of Colchester (Plates XI. and XII.). A screw

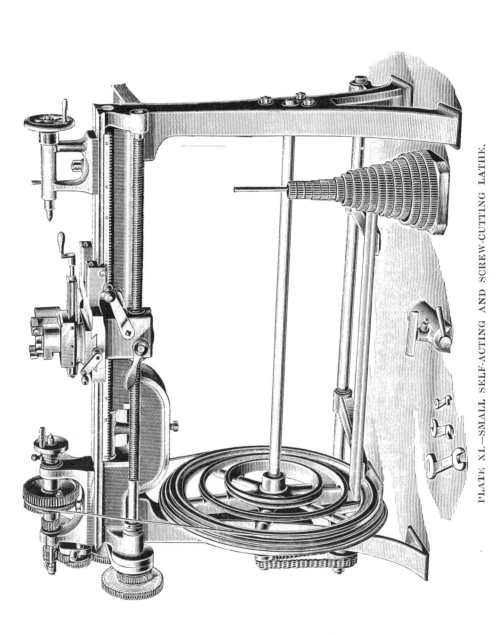

PLATE XL.—SMALL SELF-ACTING AND SCREW-CUTTING LATHE.

runs the whole length of the bed in front, of a quarter pitch—*i.e.*, of four threads to the inch. This passes through a nut in the apron of the slide-rest, just behind the straight handle. The rest is free to move along the bed from end to end, the edges of the bed being planed to a ∨ shape, and being embraced by guide-bars similarly planed, and adjustable to take up wear. Turning the main or "leading" screw, as it is called, in one direction, causes the rest to travel from right to left, and reversing the motion causes it to return. This is the main principle of all self-acting Lathes.

But it is also evident that means will be needed to stop the traverse at any given point, without having at the same time to stop the Lathe. This is accomplished by sawing in half the nut through which the screw passes, and attaching each half to a short, vertical slide working in guides. The handle seen in front carries a plate with two spiral grooves in it, in which pins standing out from the halves of the nut engage, so that by turning the handle on one side the two halves are separated in an instant, leaving the screw free; while turning it back closes the nut upon the screw, and causes the slide-rest to resume its motion. The slide-rest is placed upon a saddle which fits to and slides upon the bed; and it is very often so made that the whole upper part can be removed, leaving the saddle free, so that work can be clamped upon it for boring or planing (if the Lathe has a planing head fitted to it). To the left is seen a large cog-wheel, attached to the screw, and by which, through other changeable wheels and pinions, the rate of motion of the screw can be varied, so as to give to the slide-rest either a quick or slow motion at pleasure. Two small wheels (seen on the left of the headstock below the mandrel) are fitted on the same plate, which is centred on a pin; so that either can be made to gear with the small pinion on the mandrel. This serves to reverse the motion of the screw, while the flywheel still continues to revolve in the same direction as before. Bolted to the back of the saddle, but removable at pleasure, is a die stay, or support for long work liable to bend under the tool. Being carried along the bar as the turning proceeds, and being all the time close to the tool, it supports the work perfectly, and quite removes all tendency in it to deviate from its proper position. A drip-can, with soap and water, is also similarly mounted, to lubricate the work.

The action of the screw causes a very slow movement of the saddle and its rest, and, therefore, when the cut is finished, and it becomes necessary to run back the rest, to commence a new cut, means are required for doing this with rapidity. For this purpose there is a rack attached to the front of the Lathe bed, into which a pinion gears, which has its bearings near the half-nut slides, in the apron of the saddle. The handle to this is the long one seen in front. The half-nuts being opened, to free the rest and its screw, a few turns of the handle carry the tool back again to its starting-point, ready to commence a fresh cut. The Lathes illustrated have friction wheels to the crank axle, which is straight, a slotted crank being attached outside the left standard, and this is worked by an anti-friction chain motion passing to the treadle. The pile of cog-wheels seen in front, twenty-two in all, are for attaching to a stud, on a radial arm, which is mounted concentrically with the screw, and can be clamped in position after the gear wheels are arranged on screw, mandrel, and stud. These are necessary for automatic screw-cutting. It is evident that, with a given set of wheels and pinions—geared, on the one hand, with the mandrel, and, on the other hand, with the screw—any desired rate of speed can be obtained between the two; thus, while the screw makes one turn, and draws the slide-rest and tool $\frac{1}{4}$in., the mandrel may be made to revolve either once or twice, or a dozen times, according to the sizes of the wheels and pinions used, as will be fully explained in the chapter on screw-cutting. The slide rest can, therefore, be arranged for merely turning a smooth surface—which is, in reality, an infinitely fine screw—or it can be made to travel so fast in proportion to the speed of the mandrel as to cut a coarse spiral.

The tools required are the same as those already described, and either the solid ones can be used, or the cutter bar; but when once set into cut, nothing is needed but to work the treadle, when the tool will be carried along with a perfectly

PLATE XII.—LARGE SELF-ACTING AND SCREW-CUTTING LATHE.

(*No. 16 Lathe, by Britannia Co.*)

even motion, such as no hand feed can rival. Among Lathe novelties introduced by the Britannia Company, of Colchester, two are well worthy of notice, and they may be taken as extremes of power—viz., their Nos. 13 and 18: the first a small screw-cutting Lathe of 3in. centre only, with 2ft. 6in. or 3ft. bed; and the other a treble-geared Lathe, specially made for the Admiralty for use on shipboard—a Lathe with gap bed, to swing 24in., and with power enough, under treadle

FIG. 21.—TREBLE-GEARED LATHE.

action alone, to take a ½in. cut off a 2in. or 3in. bar. It would be hard to find a tool of such power more compact, better designed, or better made; and the price—£36 for one of 5in. centre—is marvellously low. That it is possible to turn a pump-cover, or similar article, 24in. diameter, by foot power is, at first sight, incredible; but the treble gear multiplies enormously the power applied. This Lathe is illustrated here in Fig. 21, which gives a good idea of its general appearance. In a country fitting-shop or agricultural implement maker's where steam is not available, this Lathe would be invaluable.

The No. 13 (*see* Plate XIII.) is the amateur's Lathe *par excellence* for all light work in engineering, such as model-making and the construction of electrical and scientific instruments. Fitted also, however, with overhead, as shown here, it becomes suitable for ornamental and plain turning in wood or ivory. As a screw-cutting Lathe, it is an exact miniature of those already described, except that there is no crank axle, the flywheel being mounted on a fixed stud on the standard. With a handle fitted to the slide-rest screw, and a revolving cutter or drill, driven by the overhead, the most beautiful spiral work can be done. When the gap piece is out of the bed, it will admit a disc of 10½in. diameter, instead of 6in. The drawer in the table on which it is mounted is intended for spanners, tommies, mandrel taps, and such like. Price £15 15s.; or £21 with overhead, including the ornamental drill spindle. This Lathe is such as an ingenious amateur can hardly fail to turn to good account, removing, as it does, both the difficulty of screw-cutting, and also of highly-finished plain turning in metal. It can be made with a crank shaft at a small extra charge. With castings, now so easily obtained, engine-making should become, by the help of this unique Lathe, comparatively easy work. The overhead is, moreover, an advantage that need only be tried to be appreciated, especially in cutting screws in wood. These can be beautifully cut with small, revolving cutters, which make a clean thread far better than is attainable with a fixed tool, owing to the very slow motion of the mandrel, which is not well suited for wood. In fact, wood cannot revolve too quickly against the tool, especially if it is of the kind known as soft wood. A V tool, however, will cut the latter quite cleanly, and make a nice thread, and this can be held in a cutter bar, and fixed on the slide-rest of this Lathe.

It is not to be supposed that the amateur, or anyone not a thorough adept, will succeed in either plain turning or screw-cutting — most decidedly not the latter — merely by

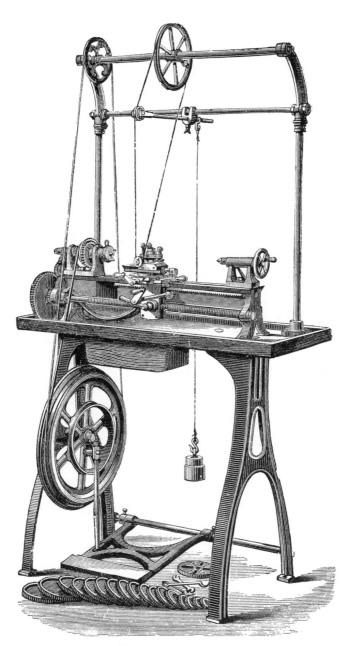

PLATE XIII.—MINIATURE SCREW-CUTTING LATHE.

obtaining one of these handy little machines. A screw-cutting Lathe is a very ingenious bit of mechanism, and its capabilities are not to be learnt in a day. When, therefore, it first comes to hand, it should be thoroughly examined, and its various parts studied until well understood. Let the various wheels be mounted—first, a mere idle wheel, or the stud brought into gear with that or the screw, and with the small one below the two that are on a pivoted plate at the back of the headstock, which two, I have explained, are meant to reverse the motion of the screw for cutting left-handed threads. Then, when the single row of wheels has been thoroughly understood, let the wheel and pinion on the sleeve be mounted on the stud, and the effect of this arrange-ment tested as regards change of speed. Put a cylinder of wood in the Lathe, to experiment upon; and, with a sharp point tool, try the result of different wheels geared singly and also doubly. This will teach, better than any written description, the nature of screw-cutting, to be hereafter carried out, in metal. It will be found that wheels geared singly—i.e., in one plane—only produce the effect of the first and last; the result, as regards speed, being the same as if these were geared together. But the intermediate one alters the *direction* of motion, and is necessary to fill up the space between the mandrel wheel and that on the leading screw. Any intermediate wheel that is of suitable size may, there-fore, be used indifferently, without altering the ratio of speed between the screw and mandrel. In illustration of this, suppose a wheel of sixty teeth on the screw, and one of ten on the mandrel, which is the driver or originator of the motion: it is evident that the rate will be six to one—that is to say, the small wheel will turn six times while the large wheel turns once—and they will turn in opposite directions. Insert between them one of twenty teeth, which will, at the same time, reverse the direction of the driven wheel. The ten wheel (driver) makes one turn, while the twenty on the stud makes *half* a turn—i.e., uses ten of its teeth—and, as six times ten are sixty—the number of teeth on the screw wheel—the latter still makes, as before, six turns, to one of the driver. Instead of an intermediate wheel of twenty cogs, any other

will answer equally well that may be of convenient size. The
small wheel under the pair on the plate is of the same size
as that on the mandrel, and consequently may be considered
the mandrel wheel. Consequently, the wheel placed on its
projecting axle may be reckoned as being placed upon the
mandrel itself, and is to be considered the first driver of the
train. Screw-cutting depends upon the rate at which the
slide-rest carrying the tool travels compared with that at
which the work revolves. The leading screw is of half or
quarter pitch—two or four threads to the inch—the latter
in all small Lathes; so that one turn of the screw moves the
rest ¼in. along the bed. If the wheels are so arranged, therefore, as to carry the mandrel once round in the same time
as the tool takes to travel ¼in., or four times while the tool
travels 1in., the screw cut will be quarter pitch also—the same
as the original leading screw. Here the mandrel and screw
make turn for turn, and, therefore, each will need a wheel
of equal number of teeth, and to fill up the space, any idle
wheel may be placed on the stud.

Plainly, it is not difficult, so long as we can get the proper
proportion out of wheels in the same plane, to get any even
number of threads to the inch from a leading screw of a quarter
pitch. Starting with a pair of the same number of cogs, we
have seen that the pitch of the leading screw will be exactly
copied. Halve that on the mandrel, and the pitch will be
twice as fine, because now the work will turn twice while
the screw turns once; and so on—the smaller the mandrel
wheel, the greater the number of threads that will be cut in
1in. of length. The wheels generally rise by five cogs, from
20, the smallest, to 120, with two of 60 for use to get the
equal pitch with that of the screw. It is convenient to keep
the one on the screw unchanged, and this is commonly of
60 teeth in small Lathes, which is a convenient size; or, if
preferred, that on the mandrel may remain the same, and
the screw wheel be the one to change—it is merely a
matter of convenience: but, for a time at least, while getting
into the way of reckoning, one or the other should be
constant. A short Table is annexed, suitable for a 60 wheel
on mandrel, unchanged:—

Threads to inch required.	Mandrel Wheel.	Stud Wheel.	Screw Wheel.	
1	60		15	And so on for all even
2	60		30	numbers, as long as the
3	60		45	requisite wheel is in ·the
4	60	Any of suitable size.	60	set, *e.g.*, 24 threads would
5	60		75	require four times 90 =
6	60		90	360, which will not be
7	60		105	supplied.
8	60		120	

But, again, suppose with a 60 wheel we try to find a screw wheel to produce $3\frac{1}{2}$ threads to the inch, we find it would be one with $52\frac{1}{2}$ cogs. We must, therefore, change our 60 mandrel wheel for another—say, of 80 cogs—and with 70 on the screw, the required pitch will be obtained; for 70 bears the same proportion to 80 as $52\frac{1}{2}$ does to 60.

Perhaps the simplest way to get at it is this. Set down the number of threads required, and under it the number of threads to the inch on the leading screw, making it a fraction thus: Required 6 threads to the inch, with a leading screw of 4 to the inch, $\frac{6}{4}$. As we have no wheels of so few cogs, multiply both by the same number—say, 10—we get $\frac{60}{40}$. The bottom figure will be the mandrel wheel, the top one the screw. Both these wheels are in the set. But if we want, instead, to use our 60 wheel on the mandrel, we can manage it, for we have but to multiply the $\frac{6}{4}$ by 15 instead of 10— thus, $\frac{90}{60}$. We now get the 60 on the mandrel, and 90 on the screw, as already set down in the Table. We will now take the fractional pitch, $3\frac{1}{2}$ to the inch. Set it down as before, and multiply by 10, thus $\frac{3\frac{1}{2}}{4} \times 10 = \frac{35}{40}$; or, if more con- venient to use larger wheels, multiply again by 2, and we obtain $\frac{35}{40} \times 2 = \frac{70}{80}$, which is also the same as shown in the table, 80 on the mandrel and 70 on the screw.

When the wheels set in one plane are incompetent to pro- duce the speed required, we have to break up the single fraction into two, and thus get the sizes of the stud wheel and pinions. I may observe here, that it is of no consequence whether we place the pitch required above or below in the so-called fraction, and for one reason we may perhaps conveniently reverse it in treating of stud wheels. Thus, to cut 6 with a screw of 4 to the inch, $\frac{4}{6} \times 10 = \frac{40}{60}$, or $\frac{6}{4} = \frac{60}{40}$; only we have to remember that the mandrel wheel will be that which we get from the pitch of guide-screw—*i.e.*, in this case, the 40 wheel—a fact easy to remember. To work with the extra wheels, suppose we have to cut 9 to the inch with a screw, as before, of 4, $\frac{4}{9} \times 10 = \frac{40}{90} = \frac{4}{9} \times \frac{10}{10}$. We can multiply $\frac{4}{9} \times 5 = \frac{20}{45}$, which wheels we have at hand, and, as we have a pair of 60, we can multiply $\frac{10}{10} \times 6 = \frac{60}{60}$. We thus get $\frac{20}{45}$, $\frac{60}{60}$. The top are the drivers, the bottom the driven. So we put 20 on mandrel, driving 45 on stud, on which we also place 60 as driver, and gear it to 60 on the screw. We have worked as before, only we have cut up the one fraction into two. Now, it might have happened that we had but one 60 wheel, in which case, for the sake of practice, we will work differently.

We begin with $\frac{4}{9} \times 10 = \frac{40}{90} = \frac{8}{45} \times \frac{5}{2}$. We may leave the 45 and 5, and multiply the 8 and 2 by 5. We now get $\frac{40}{45}$, $\frac{5}{10}$, and can again multiply the latter pair by 10, and get $\frac{50}{100}$, or by 6, and get $\frac{30}{60}$. Let us suppose the latter to be found preferable. The whole will stand $\frac{40}{45}$, $\frac{30}{60}$, and we put 40 on mandrel, to gear with 45 on stud, which also carries 30, to gear with 60 on the screw. To prove it, multiply the drivers together, and also the driven, and the original fraction will recur $\frac{40}{45} \times \frac{30}{60} = \frac{1200}{2700} = \frac{12}{27} = \frac{4}{9}$. Screw-cutting Lathes have attached, generally speaking, a plate, with the numbers engraved, for ordinary Whitworth pitches, to suit the particular guide-screw and set of wheels, rendering calculation unnecessary. But the above has been given to explain the principle, and to enable the workman to calculate for himself in respect of any unusual pitch of screw he may have to cut. It may happen that, with the usual set of twenty-two wheels, it may not be possible to get certain pitches exactly, and then the nearest that is practicable within a very small fraction must take its place, and will often answer very well for a short length; for the difference in that case will not be perceptible. A nut, *e.g.*, cut with nine threads, may apparently fit a screw of eight or ten, if it has only to go on a few turns. Of course, it is only for such a common, rough job that such fit would pass muster.

The principles here laid down are carried out, in a later chapter, by a practical workman, accustomed to all operations of the kind. A Table is there added, to save, to a certain extent, the trouble of calculation. At the same time, it is of great importance to a latheman to become independent of such Tables, which are rather conducive to laziness. They are, however, useful as a means of checking and verifying calculations previously made by the workman.

CHAPTER VII.

CHUCK-MAKING.

IT will now be as well to fulfil a promise made in one of the earlier pages of this work, by describing the proper method of making a chuck in wood and in metal, because this is a task almost necessary for the amateur, and involves a little screw-cutting, in which he is now supposed to be fairly proficient. To commence with a plain cup chuck of boxwood. Let a piece be sawn from the log, of adequate size, say 2½in. or 3in. in diameter by 3in. in length; care must be taken to saw it off squarely, or there will be unnecessary waste, and boxwood is precious. If a self-centreing scroll chuck is at hand that will grasp it, nothing can be more suitable. If not, let a hole be bored centrally, and mount the block on the taper screw chuck. It must bed down fair and true against the plate of the chuck, and be very firmly secured, because it has to stand both turning and boring. Bring up the back centre to help hold it, while the outside is being reduced to a cylindrical surface, and the end cut exactly square to the axis. Of course you can, in this last operation, only carry the cut as far as to the back centre. The poppet head must, therefore, now be removed, and the face of the work finished by means of a chisel, held flat on the rest as before explained; try it with a straight-edge, and see that it is neither hollow nor convex, but truly flat. Now, with a nose bit or gouge, or round-end tool, bore a hole to a depth rather greater than the length of the screw on the mandrel nose; and if the latter is 1in. diameter,

let this hole be $\frac{7}{8}$in., as the thread will be, probably, $\frac{1}{8}$in.
deep; anyhow, don't let it be too large, as it is easy to en-
large it if too small. Here, again, care is needed to prevent
the bore from being conical in either direction—it must be
quite parallel. An inside tool, or right-hand tool, as it is
often called, is the proper one to finish it with. Now bevel
slightly, or round off the sharp edge, or "arris," as directed
in the chapter on screw-cutting by hand, which is the next
process to carry out; but, unless the turner is an adept at
screw-cutting, he had better avail himself of some kind of
guide—a traversing mandrel, if he has one; but if not, the best
way is to use a special tap, made to cut sharply, so as to
make a screw line deep enough to give a lead to the
chasing tool. The sort of tap to have is one similar to what
is sold with a screw-box. The taps for metal are of no use for
this work. The ordinary taper tap will not get a hold, unless
you can make the hole a deep one; the plug will not enter,
and the intermediate will not have sharp cutting threads near
its end. What is needed, and should be sold always with a
lathe, is a very short tap, with four sharp edges, and a long
stem with a hollow centre made in the end; the cutting part
must, of course, taper a little. It is certainly possible to use
an ordinary intermediate tap for a cup chuck, because you
may bore it as deep as you please; but it is not really suitable. The way to enter it is to bring up the poppet head so
that its point may fall into the hollow centre in the end of
the stem or shank, a small spanner or hand vice being secured to the square head of the tap, or a proper tap wrench,
which is better. The tap is then slowly revolved, a little at a
time, while the back centre is screwed up so as to follow it;
and this is carried on until the requisite depth is reached.
There will now be, on gently withdrawing the tap, by turning
it backwards, a clear, sharply-cut screw line, quite sufficient to
give a lead to the chaser—and it will be parallel, and true to
the lathe centres. The hand rest is now to be set across the
end of the chuck, and the inside screw tool is to be gently
applied, when its points will be caught at once in the spiral
groove, which will carry it forward at the required rate. In
this way the thread is to be deepened gradually, until it is

E

found to be of full depth, and equally cut from end to end of the hole.

To allow of this, it is usual to bore a little deeper than the length of the mandrel nose, and then to take a side parting tool, and with it to cut a groove at the bottom the full depth of the thread. The chaser will then fall partly into this, giving time to withdraw its teeth out of cut, and thus enabling it to cut to the end of the thread without striking the bottom of the hole. Now unscrew the chuck (not the one you are engaged upon), and, turning the latter round, try how it will go on. If it is too tight, do not force it, but put all back, and ease it. The sharp edge of the thread will be better removed, and a chuck should run on quite easily, and bed up well and truly against the face of the mandrel. Try and try again, therefore, until such is the case. All that remains is to screw the wooden chuck in its place on the mandrel, turn up the outside, and bore it out to the size needed; which latter job should be left, of course, until the chuck is actually required for use. It is usual to round off and shape to a nice curve the back end of the chuck, next to the mandrel; but this is a matter of taste. If all has been well done in boring and screwing, the chuck ought, theoretically, to run true at once, when in its place; but this is seldom the case, although the error is often very slight. In any case, a few strokes of gouge and chisel are all that will be needed, and, once true, it will generally so remain for a long time.

To make a similar chuck in metal, the process, roughly speaking, is the same; but here we have to deal with a casting of iron, brass, or gunmetal. This must, of course, be chucked differently, though if of brass, a strong American scroll chuck may possibly suffice; yet it is hardly a safe plan. Preferably I would chuck it *upon*—*i.e.*, outside—a wood chuck, or outside a block of wood driven into a metal cup chuck, and turned to fit it tightly. If it is a good casting, and is mounted to run fairly true, there will be no shocks caused by the tool, even at the first cut—only a steady strain, that should not loosen it, or throw it out of centre The skin should be ground or worked off with a coarse old file before mounting it on the lathe, as it will make it much easier for the tool to face it up. Such skin is often exceedingly hard, and will instantly take off the edge of a tool; the latter, however, should always have a clean place to start upon, by filing off the edge of the work to form a slight bevel—it then gets at once underneath the skin. There are face-plate clamps which will also serve our purpose, but on the whole the plan suggested will be the simplest, and therefore the best. The chuck to be turned need not occupy more than an inch of the block on which it is mounted, if it is well fitted. Being rough inside, it will take a secure hold of the wood. The great thing is to drive it on carefully and truly at once, so as not to have to keep on tapping it this way and that, to set it correctly, or it will be loose on the block, and yield to the tool. Supposing the work fairly mounted, a cut should be taken, all over it, either by hand, or, better, by a tool in the slide-rest; a round-end will be the usual one. Then, the end that has to be bored is to be very truly faced; and, if the hole is not cored out in the casting, it will have to be drilled—and in a cup chuck it is generally drilled quite through into the hollow of the chuck. It is not easy to make a 3in. chuck solely by hand, but as regards boring out the hole for the screw no turning is necessary. If not cored out, a little centre hole is first made, by the point of a graver, and then a drill is run in, and the bore enlarged by another; or a little recess is turned, and then a half-round engineer's bit of the exact size needed, bores and completes the hole at one operation. This tool has a centre drilled at its opposite end, and is always advanced into cut by the screw of the back centre. It is a splendid tool if well made, and will cut a clean hole in solid iron; but it will save it to run a drill in first. You must turn a slight recess, however, just to in-sure a true start. The tap now comes into operation as before, and here again it needs one made sharp to cut a clean line, but a tap a good deal less in size than the mandrel nose, as it will be followed by the chaser, as in the case of the wood chuck. The chief thing is to keep the tap in line with the mandrel, and this is secured always by advancing it by means of the back poppet centre.

All taps of the size of a lathe mandrel have centres left, and are so used in lathe-work. Generally speaking, the screw on the mandrel is not cut clean up to the shoulder against which the chucks abut, and therefore, after finishing the screw to a nice fit as far as it will go, two or three threads must be turned off. It will then bed correctly home, and also run fairly true. As soon as it does this, finish the outside while it is in its place, and, if you like, turn the inside out quite smooth, and *very* slightly taper—so slightly as to leave it almost cylindrical. Such is the proper, orthodox, and best way; but a great many chucks are mounted in the lathe and bored, and then, if a through or thoroughfare hole is allowable, as in the present case, the entire thread is done with ordinary taps, and the chaser wholly dispensed with. It is then screwed on the mandrel; and, as it is rarely that it can run true, the outside is freely cut away to make it run correctly. If the end does not touch the shoulder of the mandrel all round, it is filed till it does, and the result is a badly-fitted chuck, that will again and again work out of truth.

CHAPTER VIII.

TURNING ARTICLES OF SQUARE SECTION.

IT would at first sight be deemed impossible to turn articles in an ordinary lathe of any other form than cylindrical, although, by means of rocking headstocks, actuated by rosettes, or cams, or special appliances, such work is done every day, and wheel spokes, axe handles, and other irregular forms, are shaped by thousands. Nearly a century ago, nevertheless, Bergeron published a method of effecting such work by the aid of a sort of chuck, round the periphery of which several bars of material were mounted, so that they might come in succession under the operation of the gouge and chisel. The method was precisely similar to that now to be explained, the chuck and its fittings being, however, improved and simplified. The apparatus is very cheap, and the work produced sufficiently satisfactory to be worth doing. There is also the advantage of being able to make from four to six articles at once, and precisely similar. The apparatus consists: first, of a square bar of iron, with centres drilled at the ends, to be mounted as if for turning. Upon it are fitted a pair of round discs of wood, which can be adjusted at any desired width apart, according to the length of the work. These are backed by smaller flanges of metal, which secure them to the bar by a wedge or screw. In the edges of the wooden discs are cut rectangular notches, to fit the bars of wood which are to be turned. The latter are secured, either by such iron clamps as are shown, or by any other efficient means, such as an iron hoop slightly larger than the discs, and thin wedges of hard wood.

Whatever may be the mode adopted, it must be capable of easy removal and readjustment. The drawings given, of the

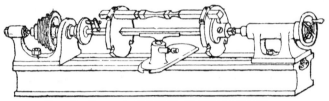

FIG. 22.—TURNING ARTICLES OF SQUARE SECTION.

complete apparatus and its essential details (Figs. 22 and 23), will suffice to explain clearly the arrangement. The square bars thus mounted can now be moulded by turning tools held upon the rest as usual; but as they do not themselves revolve,

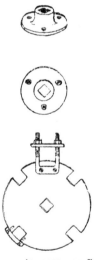

FIG. 23.—CHUCK FOR ARTICLES OF SQUARE SECTION.

except upon an axis common to all, the tools will only reach a small part of their respective surfaces, three-fourths remaining untouched. The bars are now loosened and remounted, with another side outwards, which will enable another fourth of the surface to be cut, the mouldings running into those previously made. Again the bars are loosened, and the process repeated, and after three readjustments the several bars will be found to have obtained a form of which the cross-section is apparently a square. The faces are, in point of fact, not quite flat, but curved, approaching nearest to a flat if the discs of the chuck are of large size.

This method is also capable of producing work of triangular section, the only alteration requisite being triangular instead of square notches in the discs of the chuck. The work also, or, at any rate, its extreme ends, must be carefully planed with three flat faces, to fit these notches. Other sections, such as octagon, hexagon, or quasi-elliptic, are possible, by different forms of notches to receive the ends of the rods; and, instead of four only, several pieces may be secured and turned at the same time. This kind of work looks very well associated with that of circular form. The top of a candlestick, for instance, may be made cylindrical, and the stem and base, or stem alone, square or triangular. The whole will also stand conspicuous as a turner's puzzle. A half-crown will purchase the whole apparatus, so that it is within the reach of all. This work requires care and sharp tools, taking very light cuts; and in making the discs, it is essential that the notches stand opposite each other. The two should, in fact, be clamped together, so as to enable the pair to be notched as one. Even the square bar may be of wood—so that the whole apparatus might be home made; or it may be purchased, either in the rough parts or finished, of the Britannia Company.

CHAPTER IX.

SCREW-CUTTING BY SELF-ACTING LATHE.

WITH many amateurs it is a source of much perplexity how to manipulate the change wheels and leading screw of a screw-cutting lathe, in order to produce a screw of any desired thread, or " pitch."

It is therefore proposed in this short chapter to present the matter in a very plain and simple manner, which will elucidate the whole mystery.

What we have to do is to traverse the tool along the work revolving between the lathe centres, at such a ratio to the speed of the revolution as shall produce a screw of the desired fineness or coarseness, which is called the " pitch," and usually expressed as of so many threads to the inch in length of screw.

Now it will be obvious that if equal-sized wheels be used to connect the spindle of headstock and the leading screw which traverses the saddle, and with it the cutting tool, along the lathe bed, the speed of the revolution of the spindle (and with it the work driven by it) will be the same as that of the leading screw, and the screw produced will be precisely a counterpart in pitch to the leading screw; and as this may be often required, every set of change wheels is supplied with one pair of equal wheels, usually forty or sixty teeth, and to vary this ratio of speed the other twenty wheels are required.

Our object now is to see how to adjust these various wheels, so as to traverse the tool in such a relative speed to the speed of the revolution of the headstock spindle as shall cut our desired pitch.

A modern screw-cutting lathe is usually provided with a fixed pinion on the tail end of the spindle, and a second precisely similar pinion on a fixed stud screwed into the head-stock below it; and these are geared together by a third and intermediate wheel of the same or any convenient size; while a fourth wheel, precisely a counterpart of the third, is fixed to gear into it, and is running idly so long as the third is being used, but may be brought into gear with the head pinion by disengaging the third, and will thus reverse the motion of the second pinion. These three wheels, which we have called the second, third, and fourth, are fixed on a plate, swivelling on the stud of the second for a centre, and are called the reversing gear, and are used for the purpose of causing the leading screw to revolve in one direction or the other, to traverse the saddle from right to left, or *vice versâ*, and thus to cut screws either right or left handed.

Now, as the pinion on the end of the spindle, and that (the second) on the fixed stud below it, are precisely the same, it follows that they will revolve at the same speed, and we may treat them as the same, and the sleeve connected to pinion on stud of reversing gear is now a correct substitute for the spindle of headstock, and in all our subsequent arrangements we shall treat it as the latter, and speak of it as the "spindle."

This sleeve, fixed to and revolving with the second pinion, is prepared with a key to receive the change wheels; and when we say we put such a change wheel on the spindle, we intend putting it on this sleeve.

Now, we have at our disposal for change wheels the "spindle," and the end of the leading screw, similarly prepared with a key for the wheels, and which we will more briefly speak of as the "screw."

But as these two revolve on fixed centres, we must have some adjustable means of connecting them by gearing, and this gearing, we have seen, must vary greatly to produce the results we desire; hence the use of the swing frame, or quadrant plate, which swivels at the end of the screw, and is provided with one or two slots, having a stud and sleeve long enough to admit of two wheels side by side, and adjustable along this slot. By this means, and the swivelling motion of the swing frame, it will be found that any gearing may be arranged to connect the spindle and the screw.

The sleeve revolving on the sliding stud of swing frame is called the "stud," and the driven wheel on it is called the stud wheel; and should there be occasion to use a second wheel on this sleeve, it would be called the "pinion." So we now have—

Spindle   Stud   Pinion   Screw

or, as they are frequently called—

Driver   Driven   Driver   Driven

We have now to consider the changing of the wheels on these three centres, to give the requisite ratio of speed between spindle and screw.

For simple pitches below twelve threads per inch, a single train of wheels—that is, three—only is needed, viz., one driver, on the spindle; one driven, on the screw; and one intermediate wheel, on the stud. Let it always be borne in mind that a mere idle or intermediate wheel, simply conveying motion, does not affect the ratio. Now the size of the change wheels, that is, the number of teeth, must always bear the same ratio as does the screw to be cut to the leading screw of the lathe; hence we will adopt the following:

Rule 1.—Place the pitch of the leading screw as numerator, and the pitch of the screw to be cut as denominator, in the form of a simple vulgar fraction; multiply both by 5 or 10, and the products will be the wheels required, the numerator being the spindle wheel, or driver, and the denominator the screw wheel, or driven.

Example.—To cut a screw of seven threads per inch with a leading screw of four threads per inch.

$$\frac{\text{Leading screw}}{\text{Screw to be cut}} \ \frac{4}{7} \times 5 = \frac{20}{35} \ \frac{\text{Spindle or driver}}{\text{Screw or driven}} \ \} \ \text{wheels required.}$$

To cut a screw of twelve threads per inch, with a leading screw of two threads per inch:

$$\tfrac{2}{12} \times 10 = \tfrac{20}{120} \text{ wheels required.}$$

Or, if the pitch required be fractional, all we have to do is to reduce the fraction or mixed number to a whole number for a simple denominator, and proceed as before.

Example.—To cut a screw of four and three-quarter threads per inch, with a leading screw of four threads per inch:

$$\tfrac{4}{4\frac{3}{4}} \times 4 \text{ (denominator of fraction)} = \tfrac{16}{19} \times 5 = \tfrac{80}{95} \text{ wheels required.}$$

Pitches above twelve per inch may require, for convenience of gearing or bringing the sizes within the compass of the wheels usually supplied, that a double train (four wheels) be used—usually termed compounding; to effect which we will adopt

Rule 2.—Proceed according to Rule 1, setting forth the ratio of screw to be cut to leading screw in simple fractional form; then assume any two other equal wheels, for second driver and driven, also set forth in fractional form, and divide one driver and one driven by any convenient divisor to bring the figures within the compass of your wheels.

Example.—To cut a screw of twenty-five threads per inch, with a leading screw having four threads per inch:

$$\tfrac{4}{25} \times 10 = \tfrac{40}{250}; \text{ assume } \tfrac{100}{100};$$

divide one driver and one driven by five, and we have

$$\tfrac{40}{50} \; \tfrac{20}{100}, \text{ the four wheels required.}$$

Again.—To cut twenty-two threads per inch, with a leading screw of two threads per inch:

$$\tfrac{2}{22} \times 10 = \tfrac{20}{220}; \text{ assume } \tfrac{100}{100} \div 4 = \tfrac{20}{55} \; \tfrac{25}{100} \text{ wheels required.}$$

Again.—To cut nineteen threads per inch, with a leading screw of four threads per inch:

$$\tfrac{4}{19} \times 10 = \tfrac{40}{190}; \text{ assume } \tfrac{100}{100} \div 2 = \tfrac{40}{95} \; \tfrac{50}{100} \text{ wheels required.}$$

It need only be added, that if any mechanical difficulty arise in gearing any wheels, when once the correct ratio is established, any drivers or driven may be subjected to addition, subtraction, multiplication, or division, without affecting the result, so long as the ratio is maintained.

Thus: $\frac{40}{60}$ + a quarter = $\frac{50}{75}$, will be the same.

or $\quad \frac{60}{75}$ — a third = $\frac{40}{50}$ „ „

or $\quad \frac{20}{50} \times 2 = \frac{40}{100}$

or $\quad \frac{15}{25} \times 3 = \frac{45}{75}$

or $\quad \frac{90}{120} \div 3 = \frac{30}{40}$, &c., &c.

In order to insure the tool dropping into the same track at each cut, the simplest way is to mark a stop on the bed, or, better, put a stop of wood, or anything convenient, abutting against the front of the poppet, to bring the saddle back to at each cut.

When commencing, have the saddle up to this stop, the nut closed on screw, and all ready to start the first cut. Carefully mark the position of both spindle and screw by chalking the wheels; then proceed.

When the cut is taken, withdraw the tool and disengage the nut; run the saddle back to the stop; turn the lathe till both spindle and screw come to their marked position; close the nut; advance the tool, and it will drop into its correct track for the next cut.

This precaution is not necessary in simple pitches either the same as or multiples of the pitch of leading screw, in which cases our tool will drop into its place correctly without trouble.

In setting up the tool to start each fresh cut, be careful not to be too eager to get the work done, and spoil all; but take just so deep a cut as will best and quickest do the work.

In this adjustment of the tool, the rough-and-ready method prevailing among workmen is to chalk the collar of the slide screw and its bearing, and after withdrawing the tool at the end of each cut by means of the slide screw, to set it up for the next to the chalk mark of the last cut, and so much more of a revolution of the slide screw as practice shows will give the requisite depth of cut; then wipe out the last chalk mark, and mark afresh. But this method lacks science and system, and is, after all, but a rough method, constantly liable to variation of depth of cut.

To better insure accuracy in this matter, the Britannia Company have patented a little appliance which they call a micrometer. It is made to apply to any ordinary lathe, and consists of a small frame, or bed, attached in a minute to the saddle, and carrying a carefully-cut screw of ten threads per inch, with a collar again divided into ten parts, and a milled head for turning it by thumb and finger. On this is a nut, which can thus be advanced or withdrawn to any desired fixed distance, correctly indicated by the index point of the frame, and read off the graduated collar of the screw. A stop pin is fixed into the transverse slide of the saddle,

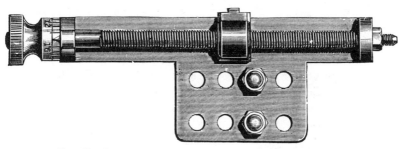

FIG. 24.—BRITANNIA COMPANY'S PATENT MICROMETER GUIDE.

and the nut brought up to this pin; and thus the exact position of the slide, and the tool it carries, is correctly indicated, and any required advance of the tool for a new cut is measured by turning the screw such portion of its revolution as may give the required depth to the one-hundredth part of an inch. It is adapted for inside or outside screw-cutting; and, while one cut is in progress, the tool can be accurately adjusted for the following cut. It can also be applied to any lathe with a slide-rest—for accurately measuring the cut, and so insuring uniformity; and for ornamental drilling and fluting.

For the guidance of the novice, a few useful hints in preparing his work for screw-cutting are added.

He will, by this time, have carefully read and put into practice the operations set forth in Chapter VI., and will be able to turn—or, in workshop parlance, " slide "—a parallel shaft. We will assume this has been done, and it is now desired to cut a thread on the same. When it is practicable, turn the shaft down to the depth of the thread, at the part where the screw will end (as the shank of a tap is), that the tool may run off. But this cannot always be done; the thread may have to end abruptly at a given point, in the full diameter; in this case it is usual to drill a small hole for the tool to run into, and it is safer to stop the lathe about a turn or half a turn before reaching the end, and pull round the rest by hand. In starting a thread to end thus, the work will be set between the centres, with carrier on, and driver of lathe touching, hole for end of thread to front; bring the saddle up, and set the tool point into the hole, close the nut into the leading screw, and mark the position of both spindle and screw, by chalking the wheels, as before described. Release the nut, and run the saddle back to position to commence the cut, and proceed as already explained. Let it be remembered that the handle of the screw of slide-rest, *parallel* with the lathe bed, must not be touched when the tool is set, or the relative position of the tool and nut, which has just been obtained, will be varied Where a screw has to be cut close up a collar or shoulder a hole may be drilled, or a groove to depth of thread may be permissible for the tool to run into; but the latter is generally objectionable, as it weakens the screw. When both ways are objected to, the lathe must be stopped about a thread from the end, and pulled round the remainder by the left hand, the right hand meantime gradually withdrawing the tool. Practice will soon give the necessary skill for these operations.

The greatest care is necessary to set the tool exactly at right angles to the axis of the work, in order that the thread shall be upright, not sloping like saw teeth, or when the screw and nut are cut, though both of one diameter and pitch, they will not fit each other. And in grinding the tool, in the case of Whitworth V-shaped threads, see that the correct angle of 55° is maintained. In V threads it is not usual to give the tool any rake or slope; but clearance is necessary, or the under part of the cutting point of the tool may scrape and spoil the thread. But in cutting square threads, especially if coarse or double threads, it is necessary to form the tool with a rake or slope, to follow in the space cut by the edge, either inclining to right or left, as the case may be. To get the correct angle of this rake, draw a right-angled triangle, having the pitch for a base, the circumference of screw for perpendicular, and the hypothenuse will then be the required angle. For all the above purposes, a very useful little gauge is sold, invaluable to screw-cutters, costing only about 3s. It may be observed, that in square threads the depth is usually half the pitch of thread.

Appended are some calculated tables of change wheels which may save time and trouble. To these we have already referred on page 95, pointing out the use or abuse of them. They are certainly an assistance to a young workman, enabling him to set the proper wheels for the job in hand, and to go confidently to work. But if, on trial, some error is found to exist, he will probably be unable to rectify it, and his work may prove to be spoilt, just as it was almost finished. It is a better plan, even where such tables are hung up in a workshop for reference, to make an apprentice work the sum first of all, and then compare the result with the figures given—he will soon find himself independent of such aid, and will leave the tables for those too lazy or too indifferent to make the calculations for themselves.

TABLES OF CHANGE WHEELS.

I.—*Leading Screw having Two Threads per Inch.*

No. of Threads per in.	Drivers.		Driven.	
1	40	—	—	20
	50	—	—	25
	60	—	—	30
1¼	40	—	—	25
	30	40	15	50
1½	40	—	—	30
	40	60	20	90
	40	50	25	60
1¾	40	—	—	35
	20	40	20	35
2	40	—	—	40
	60	—	—	60
2¼	40	—	—	45
	20	80	30	60
2½	40	—	—	50
	20	90	30	75
2¾	40	—	—	55
	60	40	30	110
3	20	—	—	30
	40	—	—	60
	25	40	20	75
	50	40	30	100
3½	20	—	—	35
	40	—	—	70
	20	80	40	70
4	20	—	—	40
	40	—	—	80
	20	60	30	80
5	20	—	—	50
	30	—	—	75
	40	—	—	100
	25	60	75	50
6	20	—	—	60
	20	50	40	75
	50	40	75	80

No. of Threads per in.	Drivers.		Driven.	
7	20	—	—	70
	30	—	—	105
	30	40	60	70
8	20	—	—	80
	25	—	—	100
	50	20	40	100
9	20	—	—	90
	20	50	75	60
	20	100	75	120
10	20	—	—	100
	20	40	50	80
	30	40	75	80
11	20	—	—	110
	20	50	100	55
	20	40	55	80
12	20	—	—	120
	20	25	50	60
	20	50	100	60
13	20	25	65	50
	20	30	65	60
	20	50	65	100
14	20	30	60	70
	20	50	100	70
	20	60	120	70
15	20	40	50	120
	20	30	50	90
	20	60	90	100
16	20	50	80	100
	20	25	40	100
	30	25	60	100
17	20	50	85	100
	20	25	50	85
	20	60	85	120
18	20	40	80	90
	20	50	120	75
	20	60	120	90

No. of Threads per in.	Drivers.			Driven.	
19	20	40	...	80	95
	20	50	...	95	100
20	20	40	...	80	100
	20	60	...	120	100
21	20	25	...	75	70
	20	30	...	90	70
22	20	40	...	80	110
	20	30	...	120	55
23	20	50	...	115	100
	20	60	...	115	120
	20	45	...	90	115
24	20	40	...	80	120
	20	30	...	80	90
	20	45	...	120	90
25	20	30	...	75	100
26	20	30	...	120	65
27	20	40	...	120	90
	20	25	...	75	90

No. of Threads per in.	Drivers.			Driven	
28	20	30	...	105	80
	20	45	...	105	120
	20	25	...	70	100
30	20	30	...	90	100
	20	25	...	75	100
	20	40	...	100	120
32	20	25	...	80	100
	20	30	...	80	120
	25	30	...	100	120
34	20	30	...	85	120
	20	25	...	85	100
36	20	25	...	90	100
	20	30	...	90	120
38	20	25	...	95	100
	20	30	...	95	120
40	20	30	...	100	120
48	20	25	...	100	120
60	20	30	...	120	150

II.—Leading Screw having Four Threads per Inch.

	Drivers			Driven	
1	80	—	...	—	20
	60	100	...	30	50
	50	120	...	20	75
1¼	80	—	...	—	25
	40	80	...	20	50
1½	80	—	...	—	30
	40	120	...	30	60
	40	90	...	30	45
1¾	80	—	...	—	35
	40	80	...	20	70
	60	80	...	20	105
2	40	—	...	—	20
	50	—	...	—	25
2¼	80	—	...	—	45
	40	80	...	60	30
2½	80	—	...	—	50
	40	90	...	30	75
	60	90	...	45	75

	Drivers			Driven	
2¾	80	—	...	—	55
	40	50	...	25	55
	50	80	...	110	25
3	60	—	...	—	45
	40	—	...	—	30
	50	40	...	20	75
3½	40	—	...	—	35
	60	50	...	35	75
	80	50	...	35	100
4	40	—	...	—	40
	60	—	...	—	60
5	40	—	...	—	50
	60	—	...	—	75
	60	30	...	25	90
6	60	—	...	—	90
	30	—	...	—	45

No. of Threads per in.	Drivers.			Driven.	
	40	—	...	—	70
7	20	—	...	—	35
	45	80	...	90	70
	20	—	...	—	40
8	30	75	...	45	100
	20	—	...	—	45
9	30	80	...	60	90
	30	40	...	60	45
	30	—	...	—	75
10	40	—	...	—	100
	30	40	...	60	50
	20	—	...	—	55
11	30	40	...	60	55
	20	—	...	—	60
12	30	50	...	45	100
	20	—	...	—	65
13	25	40	...	50	65
	20	—	...	—	70
14	20	50	...	35	100
	20	60	...	35	120
	20	—	...	—	75
15	30	40	...	90	50
	25	—	...	—	100
16	30	50	...	60	100
	20	—	...	—	85
17	35	40	...	70	85
	20	—	...	—	90
18	30	40	...	60	90
	25	40	...	45	100
	20	—	...	—	95
19	25	80	...	100	95
	25	40	...	50	95
	20	—	...	—	100
20	25	40	...	50	100
	25	60	...	75	100
	20	—	...	—	105
21	20	40	...	70	60

No. of Threads per in.	Drivers.			Driven.	
	20	—	...	—	110
22	20	40	...	55	80
	20	50	...	55	100
	20	—	...	—	115
23	30	60	...	115	90
	30	80	...	115	120
	20	—	...	—	120
24	25	40	...	75	90
25	20	40	...	50	100
	20	60	...	75	100
26	20	40	...	65	80
	20	35	...	65	70
	20	40	...	60	90
27	20	80	...	90	120
	20	70	...	90	105
	20	60	...	70	120
28	20	40	...	70	80
	30	40	...	80	105
	20	40	...	60	100
30	30	40	...	100	90
	20	50	...	75	100
	20	30	...	80	60
32	20	60	...	80	120
	25	40	...	80	100
	20	50	...	85	100
34	25	40	...	85	100
	30	40	...	85	120
36	25	40	...	90	100
	30	40	...	90	120
38	25	40	...	95	100
	30	40	...	95	120
40	20	40	...	80	100
	20	30	...	75	80
48	20	25	...	75	80
	25	30	...	75	120
60	20	25	...	75	100

CHAPTER X.

USES OF THE OVERHEAD.

A BOOK on the Lathe would hardly be complete without an explanation of that attachment briefly called "The Overhead." There are many forms of this, but that shown on the miniature screw-cutting lathe (Fig. 13, page 89) is as good as any other, and is the plan most commonly adopted. The main object of it is to enable a turner to connect the movement of the fly-wheel with the slide-rest, or with various pieces of apparatus held therein, such as drills and revolving cutters. The screw of the slide-rest may also be itself so connected, which will render it self-acting, thus imitating, in a small way, the large screw-cutting lathes. For this purpose the winch handle is removed, and replaced by a pulley of any desired size. The overhead consists of a revolving shaft, supported on a pair of light but firm standards, attached to the backboard of the lathe. Upon this shaft is a pulley like that on the mandrel, and a roller, or second adjustable pulley. A cord from the fly-wheel, or sometimes from the mandrel, passes over the first of these, and a second cord descends from the roller to the pulley of the slide-rest screw, or to that of the drill, or of any revolving cutter which may be in use. It will evidently be necessary to keep this cord tightly strained under all circumstances, whether the driving pulley of the apparatus be large or small, and whether it is advanced nearer to the work or withdrawn by the action of the cross slide of the rest. To attain this end, there is a bar just under the shaft of the overhead, acting partly as a tie-bar between the standards, but, secondly, as a support to a sliding block, capable of being placed at any part of the bar, about which, also, it can turn as a hinge. Through this block passes a round rod, of stout iron, which carries at one end a pair of pulleys, whose peripheries bear against the cord, the pressure depending upon a weight slung to the opposite end of the bar, as well as upon the leverage. For this reason, the entire affair is called the "tension apparatus." Sometimes a spring arrangement takes the place of the weight; but the latter, being constant in its action, is decidedly preferable, and if it is suspended near the floor there is nothing objectionable about it.

The principle of the overhead having been explained, it will be as well to enter briefly upon some of its uses, although we do not intend to set forth *in extenso* the details of ornamental turning, which, indeed, require an extra volume.

Let us suppose a drilling spindle securely held in the rest, having a round-ended drill in its socket, such drill pointing to a smooth cylinder of boxwood held between centres or in a chuck. Let the height of drill be level with the lathe centres. Now suppose the ordinary lathe cord removed, and that from the fly-wheel to the overhead to be arranged, and a second cord to lead down from the overhead to the driving pulley of the drill. If, by means of the cross slide, the drill is advanced, it will simply bore a hole through the cylinder. But now let us suppose that the cross slide advances the drill only about $\frac{1}{10}$in., while the other handle of the rest is steadily turned, so as to carry the entire drilling apparatus horizontally along the work, lengthwise. In this case, the result will be a rounded groove, or recess, or *flute*. The mandrel, it will be observed, is not revolving at all, because its cord was removed. In practice it is held fast by an index point, resting in one of the holes of a division plate fixed to the face of the mandrel pulley; the circles of holes for this purpose are, however, very frequently drilled in the face of the pulley itself. By these means we can advance the pulley as many divisions as we please between each traverse of the drill, and make the flutes as near to each other or as far apart as we please.

Now let us substitute for the round-ended drill one with a semicircular hollow at the end, such as would be made with a rat-tail file. This, if gently advanced by the rest, while kept in rapid rotation by the overhead, will not drill a hole, but will form a bead. It must not, however, be traversed along the work, because it would not form a flute. But if now we use the division-plate and index as before, it will be easy to drill a ring of beads round the work, close together, or at any desired distance apart. This is the principle of fluting and beading work, and also of cutting watch and clock wheels, a revolving saw or cutter taking the place of the drill. If this were the sole use of the overhead, it is evident that it would be a very valuable adjunct to the lathe; but there are other uses, to which our attention must be directed. It has been remarked that one great advantage of a self-acting lathe is that it enables a perfectly regular feed to be obtained in making a cut. The tool is advanced evenly and steadily, making a very beautiful finish to the work, if the tool cuts well, and is correctly placed. All that is here needed is a pulley, instead of a winch handle, on the feed-screw of the rest, and that this shall be driven at a suitable rate, by means of a cord from the overhead. The balance-weight of the tension apparatus must be so adjusted as to keep the cord tightly strained, and then there will be no slip, but the action will be as sure as if it was attained by cog wheels or gearing. Now let us go a step further : it was explained in the Chapter on Screw-cutting in the self-acting lathe, that we can obtain any desired pitch of screw by gearing the slide-rest with the mandrel, by means of cog wheels of varying sizes. We can do exactly the same by means of cords and pulleys of proportional size. If we have a pulley on the overhead of exactly the size of any one of those on the mandrel, and connect them by a cord, they will revolve at exactly the same speed ; and if we have on the slide-rest screw a pulley equal to the roller in size, the mandrel, and overhead shaft, and slide-rest screw, will revolve exactly together, each turn of the mandrel giving one revolution to the other two, which are thus geared with it. Suppose the screw to have ten threads to one inch of its length; then, at each turn of the mandrel (and any work attached to it), the tool held in the rest, and actuated by the screw, will advance one-tenth of an inch. If, then, a pointed screw-tool is in the rest, and a cylinder in the chuck, a screw-thread of $\frac{1}{10}$ pitch will be traced upon it, ten turns completing one inch. This will be a screw of ten pitch. Double the size of pulley on the slide-rest, leaving the others as before, and the tool will traverse at half the speed, cutting a twenty-pitch screw. The practical difficulty of this arrangement arises from the nicety required to size the pulleys with accuracy; but it is more theoretical than practical after all, as a little care will overcome it. A greater difficulty arises from the speed with which the mandrel is driven by the fly-wheel. The traverse is proportionally affected, and is correct; but it is too quick for most purposes. The remedy is to have one speed-pulley of the fly-wheel so small that the mandrel shall make but one turn to one of the crank axle, and then to have a large pulley on the overhead, to gear with the smallest on the mandrel. The same thing is done better by having a worm wheel and tangent screw fitted to the rest-screw or mandrel; but this will be more costly, and, unless for exceptional purposes, is not necessary.

We do not, indeed, advocate this plan for screw-cutting in a general way, unless a second shaft can be added, to facilitate the variations of speed. To take down the main shaft, in order to affix a pulley which again needs to be tested several times, and then, after each trial, to replace it, entails a deal of awkward and unsatisfactory work. Hence, in one form of overhead, a short, intermediate shaft has been added, which can be replaced between the lathe centres, in· order to turn its pulleys, and again placed in its bearings without having to remove the main shaft at all. The latter is, in fact, too long to be thus mounted between the centres of its own lathe. Sometimes a shaft is added upon two short standards at the back of the lathe, instead of, or in addition to, the high ones which carry the long shaft and its pulleys. In that case, the lower shaft may be quite short, to receive the change wheels, or sized pulleys, which take their place.

From what was said about change wheels in the screw-cutting lathe, it will be seen that a large variety of threads can be cut with two pulleys only; and here we can do without the intermediate idle wheel, as we can at once change the direction of traverse by merely crossing the driving cord. We can even reckon the sizes of pulleys by the same tables which give us the sizes or number of teeth in the wheels. A wheel of sixty teeth we may match with a pulley of 60in. circumference, or sixty half or quarter inches, and then one of twenty or ten teeth will match a pulley of 20in. or 10in., or half or quarter inches. Thus there will be no guesswork, and the pulley may even be turned accurately to size at once, without repeated testing.

Another use of the overhead is to drive emery wheels or grinders, held in a proper shank, similar to that used for drilling. By this a bar of iron or steel, between centres, can be ground to absolute truth after it has been turned, and even hardened. The lathe centres too, can at any time be ground true, and the points renewed when worn.

From the remarks we have now made, it will be seen that an overhead is such a useful addition to a lathe as to be well worth its original cost. It can, if desired, be also easily rigged up by the amateur with standards of wood. and an axle made of gas pipe, plugged at each end, and with centres drilled and hardened. At the same time, a properly-fitted one, entirely of metal, not only looks neater, but is unquestionably better. The roller should preferably be made hollow, so as to lighten it, and the standards should be substantial enough to check vibration as much as possible.

Before quitting this subject, it may be as well to point out that the drilling spindle, which is supplied with the overhead in the lathes of the Britannia Co., may be fitted to do eccentric work of interlacing circles, by the simple expedient of cranking the drills, so that they shall trace circles as they revolve. According to the length of the cranked part, so will be, of course, the size of circle, each requiring a different drill; but these are so easily made, that the defect in question is unimportant. The proper tool for such work is the eccentric cutter, in which the little tool can be placed at any distance from the centre of rotation; so that it may be called a cranked drill, with self-contained power of adjustment. With this, or the simpler substitute, the index plate must, of course, be used to determine the distance between the several circles. Their position on the work is regulated by the slide-rest.

CHAPTER XI.

ON CHOOSING A LATHE.

THE selection of a lathe is not a difficult task, if certain things are granted. Let the necessary outlay be of no importance, and let the purchaser know what he wants, and he may obtain his desire without much trouble. But these two requirements are not always, nor generally, forthcoming; and if the first is there, it by no means follows that the second is. A wealthy amateur may, it is true, enter the shop of a first-class lathe maker, and give a general order for an outfit, and on the receipt of the same, together with a bill, in which the sum total is as likely to contain four figures as three, he will not know the use of one-half the things that meet his view. Admire them he certainly will, if his tastes are mechanical; but we do not usually buy lathes as we buy pictures—merely to look at—so that little satisfaction is produced by the purchase. Letting our millionaire alone to order what he pleases, let us address the amateur who can only muster a few pounds, and who, therefore, wishes to get the best he can for his money. If he has never turned at all, but is really a beginner, a very plain and simple lathe will be all that he will need—no slide-rest and no overhead; a 3in. plain lathe, for instance, sold by the Britannia Co. at about £5. This is really a beautiful little tool, running easily, and is capable of a great deal of light work. Draughts, chessmen, egg-cups, ring stands, salt-cellars, bottle cases, boxes of various designs, needle and bodkin cases, tool handles, drawer knobs, rulers—all

kinds of things up to 4in. diameter, and a foot or so in
length, can be as well done as upon a larger lathe, costing
a score of pounds; or if he is inclined to take up model
engineering, he may turn up all parts of small engines in
this lathe, as well as any job of light work in brass, iron,
or gunmetal. But even in this case we would recommend
a lot of practice in turning wood with hand tools before
embarking in metal. All metal-workers should be able,
for instance, to make their own chucks and wooden patterns,
and to turn the handles of their own tools. It is sometimes
recommended to learners to buy at once a larger and more
expensive kind of lathe, because it will always be capable
of additions, and worthy of them. A lathe, e.g., of 5in.
centre, with first-class mandrel, and all parts of best make
and quality, may, by additions, be gradually converted into
an ornamental lathe capable of first-class work in ivory
and hard wood. The advice, good as it is under certain
circumstances, may be modified somewhat with advantage.
Suppose such a lathe to have been purchased at, perhaps,
£30 or £35, it has to stand the rough treatment which almost
of necessity a beginner will bring to bear upon it. By the
time the learner has so far advanced as to begin to aim at
higher class work, the bed and other parts will exhibit
marks of injury; or it may be—and it is a frequent contingency
—the tyro becomes tired of turning, finding it less satisfactory
or less pleasurable than he expected, and the occupation
gives place to some other hobby. The lathe is then
delegated to the lumber-room, or returned to the maker,
or sold, at a ridiculous sacrifice, to some knowing purchaser. Hence, it is certainly a more sensible plan to
begin with one of the small, cheap lathes, and eventually to
replace it entirely by a larger and better, if the art of turning
has been found satisfactory. The little lathe will then come
in for grinding, sawing, or drilling, if no customer takes a
fancy to it; but a £5 lathe is more easily resold at £3, than
a £50 one at £30; in point of fact, it will probably not
fetch £20.

Let us now suppose that the art has been fairly learnt
upon a cheap lathe, and a tolerable amount of skill gained

in the use of hand tools alone. It is now desired to purchase
a better lathe, as a permanent machine for the workshop.
By this time the turner will have discovered for himself in
what direction his tastes lie—whether he is inclined to stick
to plain hand turning in wood, or to advance to eccentric and
ornamental work in ivory; or whether, on the other hand, he
prefers working in metal. He may, of course, intend to
work at each of these as occasion offers; but one or the
other is pretty sure to have the preference. Ornamental
turning, especially in its higher grades, is by far the most
costly of all. A little may be done with an inexpensive lathe
and tools—but *very* little; and few who get thus far are
contented to remain there, but are ambitious to rival the
greater works of the masters in this captivating branch of
the turner's art. The exact opposite in the matter of expense,
is plain hand turning, by which chair and table legs,
pillarets for various purposes, Elizabethan twisted work—*et
id genus omne*—may be made, and indefinitely multiplied.
For this a 5in. centre lathe is very suitable. It should have
a bed 5ft. or 6ft. long, either of wood or metal, and should
run very easily, and be arranged for high speeds—*i.e.*, the
fly-wheel should be large, and the mandrel pulley proportionately
small. Mandrel and collars should be of hard steel, kept
well oiled.

A wood-turner should be able to stand at his lathe many
successive hours without undue fatigue, and he cannot possibly
do this if his lathe runs sluggishly. In that case, a few
hours at the treadmill would be preferable. Now, this
kind of lathe may be purchased complete, and ready for
immediate use, and, if properly constructed, will wear for
years without deterioration. No slide-rest is necessary, the
chucks will be few and inexpensive, and mostly of wood,
to be made by the workman himself. Suppose, however,
that our friend prefers to take up metal turning, and to
make, for sale or for his own amusement, models of engines
and machinery which will involve drilling, boring, and occasional screw-cutting. With a plain lathe, without back gear,
he can do all this; but he should add a slide-rest. Accurate
boring of an engine cylinder can hardly be accomplished

by a hand tool, and, where metal-work is to be freely practised, a slide-rest must be considered indispensable. If nothing else but such small model making is to be done, or the making of scientific instruments, no lathe will beat the little Miniature Screw-cutter, a 3in. centre lathe, fitted complete with self-acting slide-rest and twenty-two change wheels—the cheapest and best lathe ever made of its kind. The price asked (£15 15s.) can hardly pay the makers a fair profit.

If work of a somewhat heavier class is to be attempted, such as a small 1 horse power engine for real use, it will be better to get the next size, viz., a 4in. or 5in. screw-cutting lathe, costing £20 to £25. This is no mere amateur's lathe, but a strong and serviceable workshop tool. The Britannia Co., of Colchester, may be fairly said to have popularised the screw-cutting lathe. Only a few years ago, £50 to £80 was about the lowest price at which it could be obtained; whereas now, the treble-geared lathe, which has been described and illustrated on a previous page, can be purchased at that price, inclusive of various chucks and fittings not hitherto included in the estimate. These are, moreover, not shoddy, but sound, substantial tools, which stand the severe tests required by the British Government, for whom they were originally designed.

For short screws, and for all kinds of work in hard wood and ivory, no lathe can equal that with a traversing mandrel and screw guides—generally six in number. Such lathes are not intended for careless use, nor are they fit for metal work of any size, although any light work may be done on them. They are chiefly intended for high-class ornamental work, and have hitherto been sold at prohibitive prices. A newly-designed lathe has now been introduced, which is strong, durable, and cheap, and as a lathe for general amateur work it is exactly what was needed. Fitted with an overhead and a drilling spindle, and eccentric cutter, it will enable a turner to do a great deal of really handsome work; and if an eccentric chuck is added, the outfit will be complete for anyone who cannot afford to give fabulous prices for complicated apparatus.

CHAPTER XII.

GRINDING AND SETTING TOOLS.

IN no mechanical trade can good work be done by badly sharpened tools. Keenness of edge is necessary, and also something more, namely, a *correct form* of edge. To the turner this is essential; yet it is the very detail of practical work which an amateur often neglects. Tool-grinding, being anything but a pleasant job, is put off as long as possible, and then it is done hurriedly and inefficiently. A grindstone worked by a treadle should find a place in every workshop. Such a machine is now readily obtainable, with an iron water-trough below, hinged so that it can be lowered when done with, thus preventing the stone from resting in the water, and becoming soft in one place—a defect that will rapidly throw it out of truth. Even when grinding, the water need not flood the stone. Let it be wet enough to prevent particles of steel from becoming bedded in it, as well as to prevent heating in the tool; but a stone running over with water is a nuisance, and makes such a mess as ought not to be tolerated, even if the water does not run down the arm, and sodden the shirt sleeves, which is a very good lesson of "How *not* to do it."

The faces applied to the stone in the case of a turner's chisel, which is ground on both sides to equal bevels, are to be made as flat as it is possible to make them; and the bevels must be also long, so as to produce a very small angle at the cutting edge. A short bevel is of no use for soft-wood turning. The general fault is a rounded or convex face, made still more so by the final touches on the oilstone, by

which a finish is given. If the bevel is not flat or slightly
hollow, no satisfactory work can be done. A turner's chisel
is not ground off square to its length, but slanting, so as to
form one obtuse and one acute point; therefore, during the
process of grinding, the tool must not lie quite in the run of
the stone, but a little on one side, causing the blade to lie
at a small angle across it. In grinding and setting a plane
iron, the face is ground to an acute angle, and then this angle
is reduced some two or three degrees by the oilstone, which
makes a second narrow facet. But with a turning chisel, the
oilstone should merely remove the slight burr or wire edge
caused by the stone, without enlarging the angle perceptibly.
This will give the utmost possible keenness to the tool. There
are one or two appliances for assisting an amateur in this
operation, by supplying a guide to insure the flatness of face;
but it is better to do it by hand alone, and not to become
dependent on artificial aids.

The gouge requires similar treatment to a chisel, but is
more difficult to sharpen nicely. Of course, the part to be
ground is semi-cylindrical, and, to prevent cutting a groove
in the stone, the tool should lie across it, and be rolled to
and fro upon it; but in the other direction there must be
no rounding. The bevel, as such, must be flat, so that a
straight-edge, applied to it lengthwise, will touch it equally
from the end to the point. In this case the inside, or hollow
part, is not bevelled, but is kept quite flat, and, to take off
any wire edge, an oilstone slip is used, called a gouge slip.
It is wedge-shaped, with one thick and one thin edge, and
both are rounded, so as to be suited to gouges of different
sizes. Two such slips will suffice. We may sum up the
previous remarks by saying that the rule for grinding chisels
and gouges for soft-wood turning is to form flat, long bevels,
merely using the oilstone to remove wire edge, and bring the
process to a perfect finish, without increasing the angle to
which the tool has been ground to any perceptible degree.
This, like other mechanical operations, always presents a
certain amount of difficulty, which practice will overcome.
The secret of success is patience; to hurry the job is to
spoil it.

This perfect flatness of the face of a tool holds good on such as are to be used upon hard wood and metal; but in these the actual edge is not so keen, but contains a larger angle. Most of these tools are ground on one side only, those which are hollow, like beading tools, being laid quite flat on the stone, and the hollow part only receiving a rub from a gouge slip. When they absolutely require grinding, owing to breakage, they are ground upon cones of brass fed with emery. This, however, is only likely to be required in the case of tools for ornamental turning. Hand beading tools are merely rubbed quite flat upon the oilstone. It will be almost self-evident that accurate grinding needs an accurately level stone, the face of which must be neither hollow nor rounding, nor convex. A convex face will, of course, produce a concave edge, and *vice versâ*. Hence, a careful workman takes as much care of his grindstone as of any other tool, and, as soon as ever he finds it the least out of truth, he sets to work to true it up again. This is best done by turning its face with a tool formed of a bit of nail rod, which is rolled over as one part gets blunt. It is rested on the frame, or on a block of wood laid across the bearers. The stone is kept damp, and the turning continued, until a perfectly true face is obtained. It is then finished with a bit of hoop iron. The job is a tiresome one, and dirty, but more so the longer it is delayed.

Among other tools which will need occasional grinding are screw or chasing tools. Now these are formed upon hobs, or revolving screw-taps, which cut the teeth. They are, consequently, never ground except upon the upper side, or flat face, which will perfectly renew their cutting edges. Sometimes this face is slightly bevelled off at the end where the teeth are; but this is a lazy plan, not to be recommended. They seldom need either grindstone or oilstone, but when necessary let the upper face be kept quite flat. The tools will, of course, get thinner, but are equally serviceable; and if they become too weak for metal, they will do perfectly well for hard wood, and even better for bone and ivory.

The graver, the tool *par excellence* for iron and steel, is a square bar of steel ground off at an angle of 45° from

corner to corner.   In this case, again, a perfectly flat face is
alone capable of producing accurate cutting edges of 60°.
If the face is rounded, all is uncertainty, for the cutting edges
are then of no determinate angle, nor are they capable of being
placed accurately in the best position for cutting.   There are
small grindstones and emery wheels, fitting on a spindle, to run
between the lathe centres.   These are of necessarily small
diameter, so that, if a tool is held still as they revolve, a flat
cannot be ground, but a concave surface.   Now, of the two evils
—a rounded or a hollowed face—the latter is unquestionably
the least, as it does not prohibit the production of a sharp
edge.   But it is an evil nevertheless.   By drawing the tool
to and fro lengthwise upon the stone, the error may be partially
annulled; but, on the whole, these small grinders are more suited
for drills and punches, and small tools, than for chisels and
such like.   Moreover, no one who values a good lathe will
use such apparatus, especially emery wheels.   The grit gets
into the collar, and grinds the bearings, especially if the collars,
or bushes, are of brass or gunmetal.   The particles become
embedded in the softer metal, and will cut a nick in the
mandrel in a very short time.   It is far better, and but little
more expensive, to have all grinding apparatus on a separate
stand.   Of oilstones there are several kinds.   The Arkansas
is good, and for rough work, the Tam o'Shanter.   But a real
good Turkey beats all the rest.   A bit of even grit, without
hard spots, is a treasure worthy of all care.   Perhaps, next to
this, carpenters appreciate a "Charley Forrester," the real
name being, not Charley, but Chorley, in Cheshire, whence the
supply is obtained.   This stone will produce a very fine edge.

CHAPTER XIII.

ON METAL-SPINNING.

THE art of metal-spinning is the most interesting subject that an amateur or novice can practise, and on which very little has, up to the present, been written to guide, or, at least, to be of any practical value; therefore I will describe the process, &c., in as few words as possible, and without going into technical details.

Assuming that the amateur possesses a lathe on which a high speed can be obtained (as the success of the operation depends a great deal upon this); also taking it for granted that he understands the working of his lathe, and is able to use his tools, at least for wood turning—all the addition he will require is a tool-rest with at least six $\frac{1}{4}$in. round holes drilled in about $\frac{3}{4}$in. apart, in which small iron or steel pegs are placed to serve as a side rest for obtaining a powerful side leverage to his tool (see Figs. 2 and 3, Plate XV.). These have to be shifted as the work advances or is spun over the wooden pattern.

The tools required are a roughening and a finishing tool, sometimes called burnishers; also a beading tool (see *aa*, *bb*, and *c*, Plate XIV.). Having all these, I will now proceed to describe the process :

After having chucked, or screwed a piece of hard wood on your lathe mandrel, turn it to the shape or pattern desired, care being taken at first not to attempt an elaborate pattern, but a plain one, that is not too deep; after this, cut out a circular disc of sheet copper, or brass, which,

F

of course, requires to be previously well annealed by placing it into a bright fire, and making it just red, and then cooling—which latter is best done by plunging it into cold water, and wiping dry with a bit of waste, which gets rid of a large portion of the oxide—and it is ready for use. Place this next your pattern, backed by a piece of turned wood to keep the metal in place and from shifting; then bring up your tail-stock (see Figs. 2 and 3, Plate XV.: B, turned wooden pattern; C, circular metal disc; D, piece of turned wood or backing; and E, tail-stock). Next lubricate the front face of the metal disc on which you are going to operate with a little machine oil, applied with a brush or piece of oily waste, to prevent the tool scratching, and save unnecessary friction, adjust your rest (A, Figs. 2 and 3, Plate XV.) at a suitable distance, place in your pins or pegs, and you are now ready to commence operations.

Place your tool (aa, Plate XIV.) in the position as shown in Fig. 3, Plate XV., and bring a side pressure to bear on your metal disc, and, with a sweeping motion from the centre to the outer edge of disc, try to force the metal over your pattern, taking care that the outer edge and sides of disc always run perfectly true, as the success of forcing the metal over greatly depends on this. Should you by accident slip over the outer edge with your tool, which would cause your metal to buckle, remove it, and straighten; and do not have your disc larger than is actually required—if too large, turn down with a graver. Having got the metal satisfactorily forced or spun over the wooden pattern, finish with tool bb, Plate XIV., by using the flat edge against your metal, which, if properly done, ought to give it the appearance of a highly burnished surface, without showing any of the ridges previously made by tool aa (Plate XIV.).

Figs. 5 and 6 (Plate XVI.) are examples of two different patterns which will best show the gradual shapes the metal ought to assume, commencing at 1, and finishing at 5. The novice, in his first attempts, will have to give the metal as it progresses several annealings before he will get it spun over, but after practice will do so without any difficulty.

The gauge or thickness of metal to be used at first should

FIG. 1

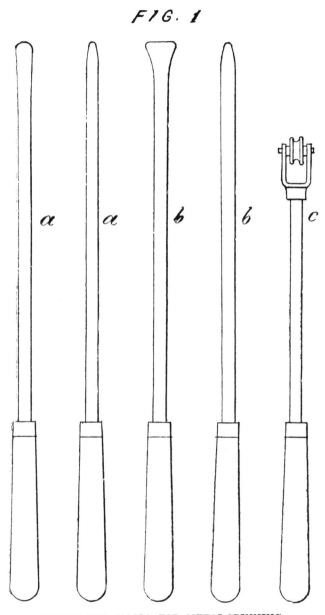

a   *a*   *b*   *b*   *c*

PLATE XIV.—TOOLS FOR METAL-SPINNING.

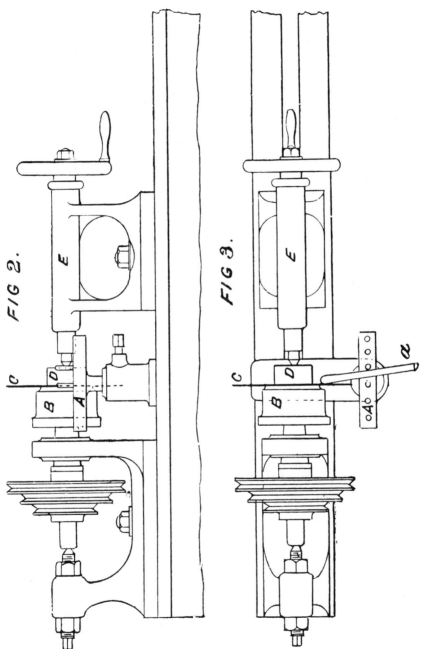

FIG 2.

FIG 3.

PLATE XV.—LATHES FOR METAL-SPINNING

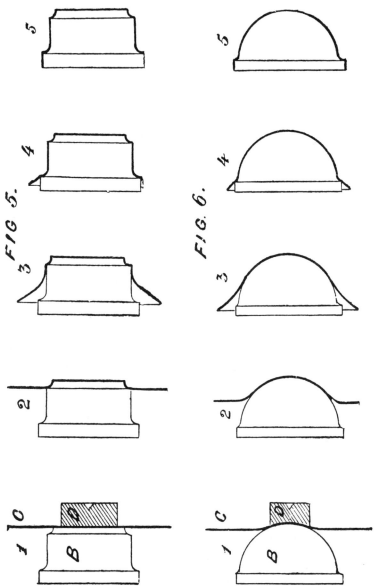

PLATE XVI.—SIMPLE SHAPES FOR METAL-SPINNING.

be 26 B.W.G.; but after the novice has become proficient, thicker metal may be used, and other metals may be substituted, such as zinc, tinplate, nickel silver, &c.

The variety of work that may be done is very great; elaborate patterns may be spun and joined together by beading or soldering, &c., to suit the taste and requirements of the amateur. The examples given here are only to illustrate the process.

After practice, the worker will see numerous objects which he can spin; and as he can make his own patterns, the cost of experiments are trifling—the metals being thin, cost but little, and if spoiled can be sold for old metal.

CHAPTER XIV.

BEDDOW'S (COMBINED), EPiCYCLOIDAL, ROSE-CUTTING, ECCENTRIC-CUTTING, DRILLING, FLUTING, AND VERTICAL-CUTTING APPLIANCE.

(Also easily adapted for cutting spirals on the cylinder.)

Patent Application, No. 23,743, of 1893.   Price £10.

THIS apparatus meets a long-felt want, viz., that of a cheap and efficient appliance for performing in the handiest manner, and by an entirely new method, a singular variety of ornamental work in the lathe, some of it entirely new, and the rest hitherto out of the reach of most amateurs owing to the prohibitive prices of the various instruments, each doing one special kind of work only.   The surface designs which may be produced, are absolutely unlimited in number and variety, and their character again is entirely altered when deep cut to show facets with, say, a broad round-nosed cutter. Any epicycloidal pattern, having a decided loop, may be cut in this manner.

All manner of the most beautiful work may also be executed with this appliance on the cylinder.

It can be used in any lathe that is provided with a slide-rest and an ordinary jaw chuck.   The only fitting or alteration required being a wheel fitted to the chuck (or mandrel), and a movable bracket bolted to the mandrel-head.   (For vertical cutting a plain spindle with no graduated arm but a hole and set-screw to take the cutters is preferable, and for spiral work on the cylinder a fixed collar and a wheel added to the slide-rest is also required.)

PLATE XVII.—BEDDOW'S EPICYCLOIDAL, ROSE-CUTTING, &c., APPLIANCE.

For the epicycloidal and compound geometric work (see Plates XVIII. to XXIII. inclusive) no over-head motion, or division-plate and index, is required, and if the slide-rest is not an ornamental one any graduation required on it is easily done by the aid of the instrument itself.

Its strength and simplicity are notable points, and there is little doubt when its capabilities become known and are realized that it will form an indispensable adjunct to the lathe, as it is not a toy but a really useful tool for a great variety of purposes.

The engraving, Plate XVII., shows the apparatus as fixed in an ordinary lathe ready for surface-cutting. T is an ordinary slide-rest, in which is clamped the frame L, L¹, carrying a revolving spindle (called the tool spindle), on which is fixed by a set-screw the wheel D, the boss being to the left and close to the frame, which prevents the spindle from moving to the right or left. This wheel is connected with the wheel C, on shaft G, by means of the carrier wheels X, X, fixed in the frame E, which is in turn fixed in any desired position by means of a screw and nut to the adjustable arm Q. This arm is centred upon one of the steel collars in which the tool spindle works, so that in whatever position it is fixed the carrier wheels always remain in gear with wheel D. Similarly, by means of the jointed arm R, they may be kept in gear with wheel C, so that by slackening the set screw, which retains the arm Q in any desired position, the slide-rest may be advanced to or from the centre of the work V to be ornamented, all the wheels remaining in gear and with exactly the same play between the teeth.

The shaft G is supported on the right by the pillar H fixed in the socket of the hand-rest S to the desired height and position, and having a hole near the top to receive the pointed end of the shaft. On the left it is similarly supported by the small bracket or metal-plate I attached to the mandrel-head W by a set-screw, and so fixed in any position, according to the size of wheel B (fixed on shaft by set-screw), so that it may properly gear with the wheel A fixed on ordinary jaw chuck U. The wheel A is fixed at the back of the chuck in any convenient manner, as it is not required to be removed.

Or it may be fixed to the mandrel pulley, in which case the
shaft G must be longer and the bracket I bolted further
back accordingly.

The shaft is readily fixed in a horizontal position and also
parallel with the lathe-bed, and its position is not afterwards
altered except wheel B is changed.

The wheels all being in gear, it will now be seen that if
the mandrel is slowly revolved by means of the fly-wheel or
treadle of the lathe (the band passing round the smallest pulley
of fly-wheel and largest one of mandrel) the tool-spindle will
also be revolved at any desired ratio of speed with the mandrel according to the various change wheels employed, and
the cutter P being advanced by the slide-rest to meet the
revolving work, patterns of varying numbers of loops, cusps,
straight-sides, &c., including all manner of epicycloidal work,
will be the result.

The tool-spindle has at one end, at right angles to it, a
graduated arm M, in which slides the steel bar O which
carries the cutter P, and also a small index. By this means
eccentricity is given to the cutter, and the bar is fixed in the
desired position by a set-screw underneath. The cutter is
tapered at one end and fits into a tapered hole in the bar;
a slight tap secures it. It is also ground off a little on
opposite sides, so that it may readily be fixed to slide freely,
but without shake, in the arm M. The set-screw also secures
the drills inserted in the central hole of spindle for ornamental
and other drilling, and the small cutter used for facing-up
the work previous to ornamentation (the bar O and properly-
shaped cutters may be used for all such work if preferred).
When required the spindle is prevented from rotating by a
set-screw in the frame, and it is obvious that the motions
of the slide-rest may be thus used to shape the work in any
desired manner without removing the instrument from the
rest, the arm Q being simply moved backwards to throw it
out of gear.

For eccentric - cutting, ornamental - drilling, rose - cutting,
radial-fluting, &c., it is necessary that the work should be at
rest, and the division-plate is then employed for placing the
circles, &c., in the desired positions round the work. Wheel B,

therefore, is slipped out of gear, and a band passing round the overhead (which is driven by the fly-wheel at a slow speed) and the grooved pulley F revolves the shaft and spindle only. This answers well for rose-cutting, the spring with which the frame is provided acting as a drag on wheel D, but for other work, if preferred, the pulley F may be placed upon the tool-spindle in place of the wheel D and driven direct from the overhead in the usual manner. A stop of some kind should be used when a series of cuts are to be made, so that each may be of the same depth.

On the left-hand side of the frame, as fixed in the rest, the steel bushing projects a little, and on this is centred the rosette or pattern disc K, having a curved slot in it, so that it may be bolted to the frame in the desired position, as to whether the crossing lines in the compound geometric patterns shall bisect one another or not. The sliding-bar O is graduated at one end, so that the metal-plate, carrying the roller N, may be easily shifted equal distances upon it and fixed by the set-screw. The roller is kept in contact with the edge of the rosette (which may be of any pattern) by means of a spring or an elastic band. If now the apparatus is driven, as above directed, the pattern produced will be the shape of the rosette, of any desired size, and superposed or interpolated on the work in any desired manner. But if instead of the overhead the gearing is employed, as for the epicycloidal work, the compound geometric patterns are produced, which are really the result of three motions, viz., the revolution of the work and of the revolving cutter, and also the reciprocating motion of the latter governed by the pattern disc.

When the rosette is used, each separate cut should be very light lest the spring fail to keep the roller to the edge.

Epicycloidal patterns are placed equidistant from one another by throwing the tool spindle out of gear by means of the top traverse of the slide-rest—a few turns of the handle to the right effects this—and before putting back again turning the fly-wheel slightly so that one, two, or more teeth, as desired, are omitted or passed over. Omitting only one tooth places them close together, as, for instance, in Fig. 22, which is eleven cuts of a five-looped figure placed side by side in this manner.

The spring attached to frame and pressing against wheel D prevents the spindle from accidentally moving while this is being done. They are placed spirally in a similar manner. In Fig. 23, for instance, besides the reduction of eccentricity of cutter one tooth was omitted between each cut.

Compensation for obliquity sometimes required when cuts are repeated nearer to or further from the centre (see Fig. 15) is *automatically* obtained in the following manner : The arm R (which is not often required except for this purpose) being connected with the frame E it is advisable (to prevent accidental movement) to lock the train of wheels by means of the division-plate index, or by any other convenient method. The spindle is now locked by the set-screw, the set-screws of wheel D and arm Q are both slackened, and the bottom traverse of the slide-rest is advanced or drawn back as desired ready for the next cut, which may be made after again tightening the set-screws to wheel D and arm Q, slackening the set-screw in frame, and removing the index from division-plate. If when moving the rest wheel D moves in the same direction in which it has been revolving all loss of time is taken up; but if in the contrary direction, the loss of time must be taken up by hand before fixing the wheel. When one carrier-wheel only is employed, the spring, if used, is placed so as to press on the *top* of wheel D.

When the slide-rest has no adjustments for levelling and centreing, this is effected by means of the set-screws with which the frame is provided, but the latter is made $\frac{9}{16}$in. square to suit the receptacle of ornamental rests when required. A little time and patience must not be grudged to get it dead true, both as to height of centre and parallelism of the revolving cutter with the work; but once true, block after block, or piece of work after piece, may be faced up, or turned, as desired, with the same instrument, and ornamented.

The following is, perhaps, the best manner of quickly levelling and centreing : Adjust the frame as near as can be judged by the eye to height of centre (*i.e.* the centre of spindle corresponding with centre of lathe) and square with the block which has been roughly shaped and fixed in the chuck. Secure a round-nosed cutter in the spindle, by means of the set screw, and

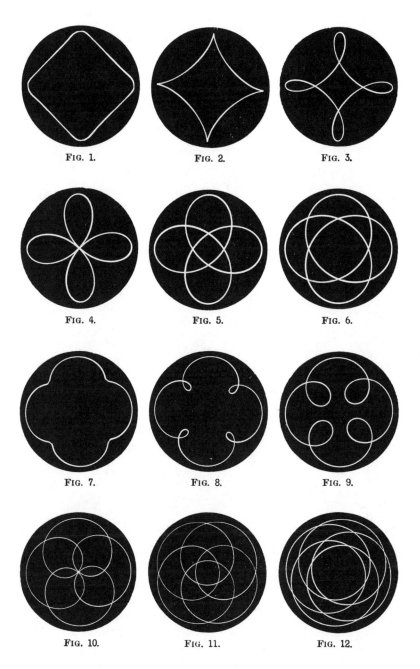

FIG. 1. FIG. 2. FIG. 3.

FIG. 4. FIG. 5. FIG. 6.

FIG. 7. FIG. 8. FIG. 9.

FIG. 10. FIG. 11. FIG. 12.

PLATE XVIII.—PHASES OF FOUR LOOP COMBINATION, EXTERNAL
AND INTERNAL.

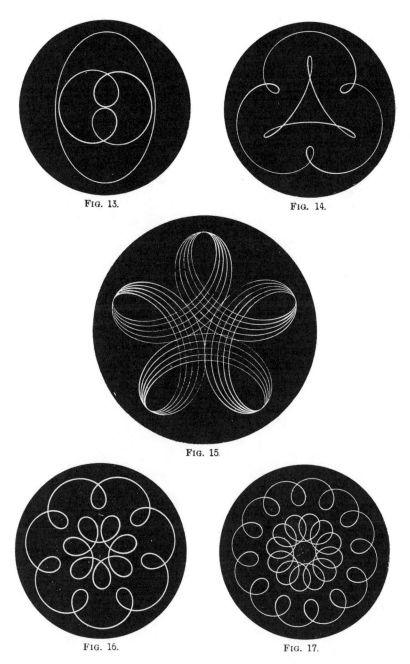

FIG. 13.

FIG. 14.

FIG. 15.

FIG. 16.

FIG. 17.

PLATE XIX.—EXAMPLES OF TWO, THREE, FIVE, SEVEN, AND TWELVE
LOOP COMBINATIONS, DIRECT, EXTERNAL AND INTERNAL.

FIG. 18.

FIG. 19.

FIG. 20.

FIG. 21.

FIG. 22.

PLATE XX.—FIG. 18.—FIVE CUTS NINE LOOP COMBINATION, CIRCULATING, EXTERNAL. FIG. 19.—FOUR CUTS NINE LOOP COMBINATION, CIRCULATING, INTERNAL. FIG. 20.—SEVEN CUTS FOURTEEN LOOP COMBINATION, CIRCULATING, EXTERNAL. FIG. 21.—SEVEN CUTS FIVE LOOP COMBINATION, CIRCULATING, EXTERNAL. FIG. 22.—TWELVE CUTS FIVE LOOP COMBINATION DIRECT, EXTERNAL.

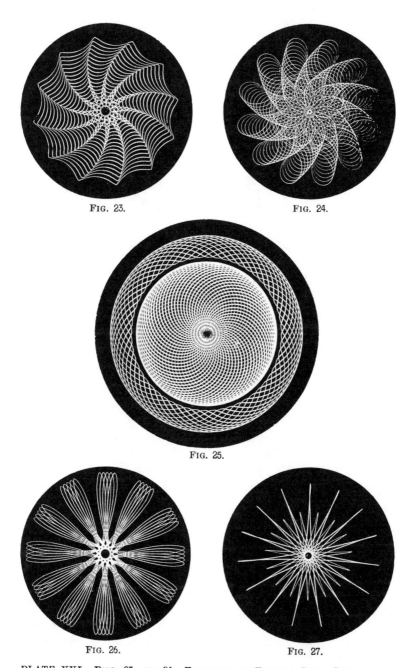

FIG. 23.

FIG. 24.

FIG. 25.

FIG. 26.

FIG. 27.

PLATE XXI.—FIGS. 23 AND 24.—EXAMPLES OF TWELVE LOOP COMBINATION
DIRECT. FIG. 25.—TWO CUTS OF FIFTY-SIX LOOP COMBINATION, INTERNAL.
FIG. 26.—FIVE CUTS OF TWELVE LOOP COMBINATION, CIRCULATING.
FIG. 27.—TWO CUTS OF FIFTEEN LOOP COMBINATION, CIRCULATING.

FIG. 28.

FIG. 29.

FIG. 30.

FIG. 31.

FIG. 32.

PLATE XXII.—EXAMPLES OF NEW COMPOUND GEOMETRIC DESIGNS
IN ONE SINGLE CONTINUOUS LINE.

Fig. 33.

Fig. 34.

Fig. 35.

Fig. 36.

Fig. 37.

PLATE XXIII.—Figs. 33 and 34.—Examples of Eccentric Circle Cutting. Fig. 35.—Groups of Elipses. Figs. 36 and 37.—Examples of Rose Cutting.

lock the spindle. Now face up the block, leaving a tiny portion projecting in the centre. Remove the cutter, replacing it by the sliding bar containing the pointed cutter, which should be fixed so that the latter is in the exact centre (readily ascertained by revolving the spindle by hand when a dot only, not a circle, would be cut by the point). Now raise or lower the set screw at the end of the frame until the point of the cutter corresponds with the projecting point on the block. Give some eccentricity to both cutter and slide-rest, and cut a trial circle (revolving spindle by hand). If it touches evenly all the way round nothing more is required, but if not, the other set-screws (which must of course rest on the table of the slide-rest) must be raised or lowered as required, and the frame perhaps shifted as well, the trial cuts showing exactly what is required to be done. When the circle is cut evenly all the way round, again put the cutter at the centre, and see that it corresponds with the centre of the work, and if not, raise or lower the set-screw as before, the clamping screws being sufficiently slackened to allow of this, but not so much that the frame easily shifts, or the truth may again be interfered with.

In the event of the clamping top Y of the rest extending to the edge of the table T, it must be filed away sufficiently to allow of the set screws at L¹ to rest well on the table.

The annexed Table gives the numbers of loops mostly required in practice. The wheels are changed in the readiest manner. When both carrier wheels are employed the loops turn outwards, and when one only they turn inwards. The direct loops are those which follow one another consecutively (see Figs. 17, 24, &c.), and they are circulating when one or more loops are missed before the next is described (see Figs. 18, 26, &c.).

The two-loop combination, *external*, forms an ellipse (see Fig. 1), grouped in Fig. 35.

The two following examples will be sufficient to show how the numbers of loops are arrived at that any given combination or train of wheels will produce (the carrier wheels not affecting the train), and will enable anyone to work out other variations for himself:

1. $\dfrac{\text{Wheel C } 30}{\text{Wheel D } 30} \div \dfrac{24. \text{ Wheel B}}{72. \text{ Wheel on chuck}} = \dfrac{30}{30} \times \dfrac{72}{24} = 3$

producing, therefore, three *direct* loops, a whole number being left.

2. $\dfrac{\text{Wheel C } 48}{\text{Wheel D } 24} \div \dfrac{30. \text{ Wheel B}}{72. \text{ Wheel on chuck}} = \dfrac{48}{24} \times \dfrac{72}{30} = \dfrac{24}{5}$

producing, therefore, twenty-four *circulating* loops, a fraction being left.

It may be mentioned that in the case of circulating loops roughly speaking, the higher the denominator (up to half the value of the numerator) the narrower will be the loops, the eccentricity of cutter and slide-rest being unaltered; thus the fraction $1\frac{6}{3}$ would give sixteen broad loops, and $1\frac{6}{7}$ would give sixteen narrow ones.

By fastening a spring at one end of bar, and attaching to it a glass pen or a pencil, designs may be traced on paper instead of being cut, with, however, some slight and unavoidable loss of accuracy as compared with the fixed cutter.

THE SPIRAL-CUTTING APPLIANCE.—For spiral and twist cutting on the cylinder the cutters are fixed in the spindle used for vertical cutting, and revolved in a similar manner, *i.e.*, direct by the overhead motion. The bracket I is bolted on the front part of the mandrel-head (or if sufficiently long, and curved, in the same position as described), and the hand-rest containing the pillar H is brought forward so that the shaft G is in front of the work to be ornamented instead of behind it as before. This new position obviates the necessity of using very large wheels, and also allows of the poppet-head being advanced to support the work if desired. A collar is fastened to the slide-rest and centred on the handle, and on this collar the arm Q works, just as on the projecting collar of the frame, the carrier wheels being bolted on the right-hand side of it instead of on the left. These wheels gear with a small wheel fixed on the handle of the rest (the latter traversing the tool during the cutting of the twist), and with the wheel C on shaft G as before, wheel B gearing with wheel A on this side of it instead of at the back as previously directed. By using wheels of various sizes the twist, or spirals, will be varied accordingly.

TABLE SHOWING SOME OF THE COMBINATIONS OBTAINABLE WITH WHEELS

72, 54, 48, 42, 36, 30, 30, 24, 18, 18,

AND THE NUMBERS OF LOOPS, OR CUSPS, INTERNAL OR EXTERNAL, PRODUCED BY EACH.

30 ON TOOL SPINDLE IN GEAR WITH

WHEEL (B) ON BACK, SHAFT IN GEAR WITH WHEEL ON CHUCK.	18 Circ.	18 Direct	24 Circ.	24 Direct	30 Circ.	30 Direct	36 Circ.	36 Direct	42 Circ.	42 Direct	48 Circ.	48 Direct	54 Circ.	54 Direct
18	12		16			4	24		28		32		36	
24						3	18		21		24		27	
30							72		84		96		108	
36						2			14		16		18	

24 ON TOOL SPINDLE IN GEAR WITH

WHEEL (B) ON BACK, SHAFT IN GEAR WITH WHEEL ON CHUCK.	18 Circ.	18 Direct	24 Circ.	24 Direct	30 Circ.	30 Direct	36 Circ.	36 Direct	42 Circ.	42 Direct	48 Circ.	48 Direct	54 Circ.	54 Direct
18		3				5		6		7		8		9
24														
30						3	18		21		24		27	
36					5				7			4	9	

18 ON TOOL SPINDLE IN GEAR WITH

WHEEL (B) ON BACK, SHAFT IN GEAR WITH WHEEL ON CHUCK.	18 Circ.	18 Direct	24 Circ.	24 Direct	30 Circ.	30 Direct	36 Circ.	36 Direct	42 Circ.	42 Direct	48 Circ.	48 Direct	54 Circ.	54 Direct
18			16		20			8	28		32			12
24						5		6		7		8		9
30			16		20		24		28		32		36	
36			8		10				14		16			6

SUMMARY.—DIRECT:—2, 3, 4, 5, 6, 7, 8, 9, and 12.

CIRCULATING:—5, 7, 8, 9, 10, 12, 14, 16, 18, 20, 21, 24, 27, 28, 32, 36, 72, 84, 96, and 108.

CHAPTER XV.

THE ORNAMENTAL DRILL AND ECCENTRIC CUTTER.

ALTHOUGH we have already disclaimed all intention of treating fully on ornamental turning, which would need many costly illustrations, and a vast extension of the size of this book, the two instruments heading the present chapter seem to call for attention. The first is, indeed, supplied very frequently with the overhead, and the latter enables certain work to be done which is not strictly of the ornamental class.

THE DRILLING INSTRUMENT,

Of which an illustration is appended (Fig. 25), consists of a square stem of steel, usually finished to the size of $\frac{9}{16}$in., which enables it to enter and fit accurately the receptacle of an ornamental turning slide-rest. It lies in the channel of this

FIG. 25.—THE DRILLING INSTRUMENT.

receptacle, and can be faced about in either direction, so as to stand parallel with the mandrel, at right angles to it, or at any other intermediate angle. The top or side of a box, or other article, may therefore be operated on with equal facility. At each end of the square bar or stem a steel collar is inserted, which is hardened to reduce friction and prevent wear. The front collar, next the drill, is coned out accurately. The spindle, with a socket at one end for the drills, and a steel pulley at the other, is also of steel, and is hardened where it passes through the collars. The utmost care is needed in fitting it; and when it begins to run loose, it is tightened in its bearings by giving a turn to the nut behind the pulley.

So great is the accuracy required in this instrument, that the drills have to be turned in the spindle itself after fitting

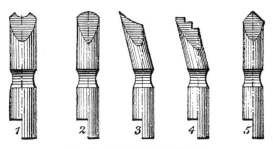

FIG. 26.—ORNAMENTAL DRILLS.

their shanks into it. In no other way can the cutting ends of the drills be made sufficiently true. Take, for instance, the drill used for beading, on which a few words have been written in a previous chapter. It is seen, by the annexed drawing (No. 1, Fig. 26), to consist of two cutting points, united by a semicircular hollow. If it runs accurately true, the result will be a hemispherical knob, or bead, perfect in form, and free from any fash or roughness on either side at its base. If, however, the points are not equally distant from the axial line, one will cut into the work of the other; and if the curved part, which is also keenly sharpened, is irregular in shape, the same result will occur, and no good work can be done. Or if, again, a pointed drill is used, and the point is a hair's breadth out of centre, it will describe a minute circle, and mar the work. Hence, also, the curved edges of these little tools cannot be finished with a file alone, but are ground upon little conical grinders of brass, fed with fine emery, which gives them

G

the necessary accuracy, as well as a keen and polished edge. The drills with flat or stepped edges are finished with little square slips of oilstone.

Evidently, tools needing all this care in construction cannot be very cheaply made, and, being costly, many amateurs learn to make their own. It is not a very difficult task, but it is decidedly a tedious one, and the better way is to be contented with a small set, and to take care of them. A good deal of very pretty work may be done with a dozen, carefully selected, and kept in good working order.

The way to make them is to take a small bar of steel, as near the size of the socket as possible, and to fit it very carefully with a file, so that it shall enter truly, and fit without shake. Even this requires care, and turning is better than filing; but, at any rate, the bar should be centred in the lathe, and filed while in rotation. The socket is usually made with a taper hole, or with a cylindrical one having a cross-mortice, in which case the drill shank has a flat on one side. This secures its position, and affords a ready means of pushing it out by the insertion of a small lever. That illustrated (Fig. 25) has a side screw, to secure the drills, and the screw will mark the tool, so that it can always be put into its socket in the same position. In fitting such a socket, the bit of steel must be secured by the screw before turning it of the required form, otherwise, the next time it is inserted the screw will force it out of truth. Supposing the bit of steel fitted and cut off, so as to stand out about half an inch, the shank is secured in the slide-rest, and a cord arranged to drive it from the overhead. A hand-rest is now brought up, and the drill is turned up by means of a graver and small files. If it is for beading, the end is turned cylindrical for a distance of about ⅛in., or rather less, which, when the sides are subsequently flattened, and the end forked by a rat-tail file, will insure the points being equidistant from the axial line of the spindle. The curve filed out, will, as stated, have to be finished to accuracy on a conical grinder. If, instead of a beading, a fluting drill is needed, the end will be turned to a hemi-spherical form, and the sides will be afterwards filed flat. There is an apparatus often sold to assist in grinding the curve of a fluting drill; but it is sometimes done by the eye. It will, nevertheless, make a great difference in the appearance of the work to have a perfectly-formed curve at the cutting end of the drill.

These precautions may be considered, by some of our readers, unnecessary; but if they could compare good ornamental work with that which is, at least, of indifferent quality, they would at once recognise the great difference between the two. In the one, the tool leaves not only a clean, decided cut, of well-defined outline, but a polished surface, which is due to the sharp, accurate, and burnished edge of the tool; in the other will be irregularity and indecision of outline, and a rough surface, which cannot afterwards be smoothed and polished. This polish produced by the tool is an essential of ornamental turning. No sand-papering or varnishing is permissible, as it rounds off edges, and gives a poor look to the work; all that is ever done is to give a rub with a hard, dry brush; and even this is often impossible with delicate tracery, for drilling can be so finely executed as to produce something comparable to lacework.

The actual work of drilling is carried out as follows: We will suppose it desired to arrange a row of beads round a box cover, and on the face of the same: the manipulation will, however, be the same if the beads are to be on its convex surface. Having selected a drill of suitable diameter, and inserted it firmly in the socket of the drilling spindle, the rest is turned, so as to place the instrument parallel with the lathe bed, and with the centre line of the drill spindle exactly true with the lathe centres. This position is essential. We will suppose that the division-plate has 180 holes, and that the index point is in Zero. As the work is, presumably, smaller considerably than the face of the mandrel pulley, there will not be room for 180 beads, but the index will have to be shifted a certain number of holes after each advance of the drill. A large pulley has 360 holes in the outer circle; but, very possibly, there may only be 180 for the outside circle, with, perhaps, other smaller circles of 100, 112, 96, or other generally useful numbers, those divisible into as many equal parts as possible being selected. Now, 180

will divide by 2, 3, 4, 5, 6, and is a very good number to have
on the pulley; we can therefore drill 90, 60, 45, 36, or 30
beads, and have only to decide whether they shall touch each
other, or nearly so, or whether there shall remain a decided
space between. Suppose we start on a trial of 60 : there
will be three holes to move the index each time. Bringing
up the drill very gently, a slight circle is traced—just barely
visible. The index is then shifted three divisions, after
withdrawing the tool, and a second very light cut is made.
If these actually touch, they are too close for a beading
drill of that size ; but a smaller one can be used, or the
index must be shifted one hole—*i.e.*, there will now be four
holes to move it each time, and instead of 60 beads we shall
get but 45. These trials must always be made with care,
or, when the cut is deepened, one bead will be found to be
cut into and spoilt in cutting the adjacent one. If it is found
correct, all that remains is to advance the tool each time to
precisely the same distance, and to shift the index correctly
after each cut. This entails careful counting, and, in practice,
becomes very tedious; but there is no help for it, except by means
of a very expensive automatic counter. We may now suppose
the circle of beads correctly drilled, and that, as an additional
ornamentation, radial flutes are required. Fluting the outside of
a cylinder has already been described, and, of course, for the
present operation on the face of the work, similar round-ended
drills are needed, which must, therefore, be substituted for the
beading drill. In all work intended for face ornamentation, a
minute centre point should be left when it is turned, to form
a guide for exact centrality of the drill, or for the tools used
in the eccentric cutter. If such is not the case, let the index
be removed, so as to free the pulley, and let such a mark be
now made. Then bring up the fluting drill, and set it spinning, and note if it is exact to height of centre; if not, let
it be accurately adjusted. It is assumed that, for such work
as this, an ornamental slide-rest is at hand; but it is a
costly affair, and it is just possible to use that intended for
metal, only the screws are less accurate, and there are no
adjusting stops to check the advance of the tool, so as to
insure all cuts being of equal depth, and all flutes of equal

length. Some mark must therefore be made, or some stop apparatus contrived instead. In any case, such work can only be done *tolerably* with a rest of this kind; but care and patience will accomplish wonders, and, with even worse appliances, marvellously good results have been attained.

But to resume. The drill being carefully set to height of centres, and its pulley, of course, banded to the overhead, the tool is traversed bodily by the slide-rest to form the flutes, while the index point determines, as before, the distances between them. Trial is also made of such distances—as was done in the case of the beads—so as to determine how close together they shall be, and whether or not each shall touch its neighbour. The length of each must be determined; and, unless a proper rest is used, which has divisions marked, and also a pair of proper fluting stops, a little mark is to be made, with a fine centre punch, at which, at each traverse, the slide of the rest is to stop. Now, with radial flutes on a flat surface, such as the top of a box-cover, it will not look well to have them equally broad and deep at both ends; yet the same drill must cut them. How is it to be managed? Simply by placing the rest at a slight angle, by means of the quadrant-plate, instead of having it truly parallel to the face of the work. Thus, the drill must be quite out of cut when it arrives at the centre, and at its fullest depth at the other end of its course. There is an advantage, moreover, in this plan, because it is not necessary to have any mark or stop at the shallow end of the flute. The tool will cut itself clear with accuracy, each time, just before it reaches the centre, or, if preferred, at a point more or less distant from the centre, according to the setting of the rest. Radial fluting always has a nice effect, and is a simple and easy process. A very effective kind of fluting is the stepped fluting, cut with different-sized drills. A broad flute is first cut, as already described, of equal depth from end to end. A narrower drill is then substituted, and carried along so as to cut away the bottom of that first made, and this is carried to a given depth. With a still smaller drill, the second flute has its centre cut away and deepened. Beads of this kind are also done at one cut by a stepped drill, which leaves its counterpart upon the

work. It is also cut with drills having a square end, like a
chisel, which gives a different effect to that produced by a
round-end tool; but the mode of work is the same in all
cases.

THE ECCENTRIC CUTTER.

This instrument—of which an illustration is annexed (Fig. 27)
—enables a turner to do much of the preceding work; but, in
addition, he has the means of carving out many forms otherwise
incapable of being made in the lathe—such, for instance, as
cubes and polygons. The eccentric cutter will also produce
most beautiful and intricate patterns on face work, when such

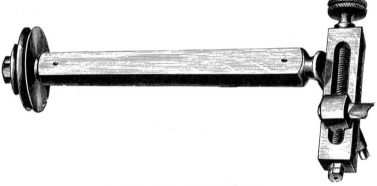

FIG. 27.—THE ECCENTRIC CUTTER.

can be composed of interlacing circles, as is the case with
the majority of such patterns. For stepped fluting it is
also a superior instrument to the drilling spindle, because
its range is greater. By its means, broad recesses can be cut
out; and, the more it is used, the more will its many uses be
discovered.   The simpler operations carried out by its aid
we shall proceed to describe; the rest will soon be discovered
by the turner.

The eccentric cutter is made, up to a certain point, exactly
like a drilling instrument, but, instead of a socket, a small
steel frame is attached, of which, when the apparatus is lying
in the tool receptacle of the rest, the upper face is exactly
level with the lathe centres. It will be seen by the drawing

that it is filed down for that purpose. The frame constitutes a little slide-rest, to hold the small cutters, which are carried along by a leading screw of ten threads to the inch, and are secured, by a screw clamp, at any distance from the centre. The screw head is graduated to ten divisions, so that each shall represent upon the slide $\frac{1}{10}$in. Generally there are also engraved half-divisions. To set the instrument for face work, a point tool is inserted, and made to tally with the minute mark left in the centre of the work, as described in reference to the drill. If all is "at centre," and the instrument made properly, the tool will drill a hole, and not cut a circle. Unless it will do this, it will be useless for ornamental turning; and when the tool is thus set, the index at the milled head of the slide ought to read Zero. If it does not, however, it is not fatal to the tool, but is inconvenient, especially in copying any published patterns. It must be always remembered that, as the *face* of the slide is diametrical, the face of the tool, and not the bevelled side, must lie upon it; and in testing it, that side must be really dead flat, and not in the least bevelled off at the point, otherwise the instrument may be condemned unjustly. Evidently, to a certain extent—*i.e.*, if the frame is not in the way—the eccentric cutter can be used, with suitable tools, for the work more generally effected by the drilling instrument, only the shanks of the tools must be flat.

But the range of work that this instrument is capable of is far wider than that of the drill. With a quarter-hollow flat tool, very large beads can be cut, and with a pointed tool an immense variety of patterns can be traced and deeply cut. All such patterns are produced by interlacing circles of various sizes. These can be placed diametrically, like A, Fig. 28, or carried round the circle like B. In the former case, the work would be held still by the index peg; in the latter, the mandrel would be moved round so many divisions after each cut. With a metal turning rest it would be very difficult to space the radial circles, especially if they are to be cut at very small distances apart. The spacing must necessarily be done by the cross slide, moved a certain distance after each cut by the screw; and unless it is

an unusually accurate one, and its head divided, the result
would show great unevenness and inequality. Here, again, as
in all such work, the very slightest irregularity in a pattern is fatal. Hence, with such a rest, it will be easier to
make circular work, because the circles will be spaced by the
division plate and index. Even then, however, each advance
of the tool must be to an equal degree, or some circles will
be cut more deeply than others, which will in effect alter the
distances between them. Fig. 28, of course, merely shows
the nature of this work. In practice, there would be five

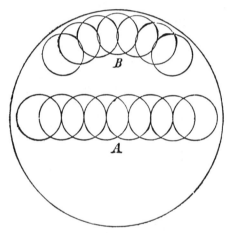

FIG. 28.—INTERLACING CIRCLES.

or six circles where one is drawn here. Coarse work, however, *deeply cut,* looks well in ivory.

Passing from traced, or mechanically engraved patterns—a
variety of which will suggest themselves in practice—we must
go on to show how this instrument is used as a carving
tool, and especially to cut out rectangular work. Figure 29
represents a cylinder which has been turned, and is held
in the chuck (A), and by the back centre, if necessary.
The part B is flat, and to cut it so the eccentric cutter is
used, with a small, flat, or round-ended cutter in it. The
slide-rest is adjusted so as to place the stem of the instrument exactly at right angles to the lathe bed and mandrel.
The ornamental rest has a cradle, to ensure this position, but

it is quite possible to do without it. If the cylinder is itself true, it can be secured, as usual, by the index peg, and then, when the rest is set true—as nearly as can be done by hand— the tool may be set just to touch one end, and can be carried along the work horizontally, at height of centres. If it just touches throughout its traverse, the setting is true; if not, the rest must be re-adjusted. If now the tool is set just to cut the cylinder, and rapidly rotated by the overhead while carried along by the slide-rest, a series of circular cuts

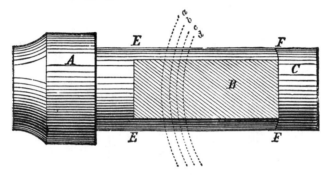

FIG. 29.—SQUARING CYLINDER BY ECCENTRIC CUTTER.

(a, b, c, d) will result, running into each other, and a flat will be produced upon the cylinder. It is represented as bounded at E F by straight lines; but these will, in reality, be curved if the flat is not cut clean out at each end of the cylinder. If it is so cut, the curve will be obliterated. If the index peg is, to begin with, in hole 180, it is plain that, by moving it to hole 45 ($\frac{180}{4} = 45$), we shall turn the cylinder exactly one quarter round. If, therefore, we cut one face by guess, until nearly the right size, and then, shifting to 45, we do the same, the cuts will at last meet, and produce an angle of 90°, or a square. It will be exactly right if the tool at 45 A has been advanced exactly as far as it was at 180. When the two cuts thus meet, therefore, the distance the tool has advanced is noted, and marked upon the rest-slide. In cutting the other two flats, it will only be necessary to work exactly to the mark thus made. Here, again, an ornamental rest has a stop-screw, as well as marked divisions. At present, an ornamental rest cannot be got under £10, and may reach £75 with all recent additions. But the Britannia Company, Colchester, are scarcely likely to allow this state of things to continue. Undoubtedly, a very useful rest may be produced for less money, although the finish may not equal that of the

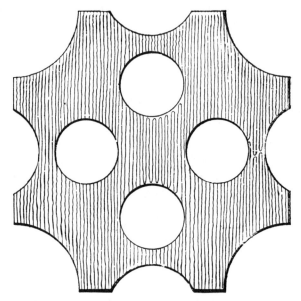

FIG. 30.—SHAPING WORK WITH ECCENTRIC CUTTER

more costly article. Ornamental turning would, probably, in that case be more extensively practised; and it has a fascination which few can resist who have once given it a trial, or seen it done by a skilled hand. From the very slight sketch given here, it will be readily conjectured that the eccentric cutter is of very extensive service as a carving, beading, fluting, and engraving tool. It can be used to cut out rings and washers from flat pieces of ivory, and small or large discs, such as are used for counters. Such a plate as represented in Fig. 30, which might be the base of a vase, or anything or nothing, can be cut out by this instrument with great facility, even if $\frac{1}{4}$in. thick. The tool has to be set in very rapid revolution, and advanced very gently;

but the work proceeds with fair celerity, and the cut is clean, without leaving tool marks, if the cutter is itself well made and strong, and its spindle works, without the slightest shake, in its bearings. With proper adjustments, cubes, and geometrical solids of various kinds can be accurately carved, and the several surfaces left from the tool highly finished, and even polished.

CHAPTER XVI.

THE ECCENTRIC CHUCK.

THERE is no more useful lathe appliance than the eccentric chuck, shown in Plate XXIV., of which a drawing is given here. It consists of a base plate A, with a screwed boss at the back for attaching it to the mandrel—a sliding plate B working between guide-bars of steel, and actuated by a screw of which the end is seen at D, with also a micrometer or divided head E reading against a line upon the face of the chuck. A divided circular plate, carrying a nose which is in size and pitch a counterpart of that on the mandrel, takes the cup chuck holding the piece to be ornamented. This plate is turned by a tangent-screw by means of a winch-handle or key fitting its squared head. The leading screw which moves the slide has generally ten threads to the inch, so that ten complete revolutions will move the slide exactly that distance. The divided head, which may be turned by its milled head, or by a key, has ten divisions marked upon it, of which every second is usually numbered. The circular plate is commonly marked with 96 divisions, as being a number divisible by 2, 3, 4, 6, 8, and therefore very convenient; but my own chuck has 100 divisions, which, on the whole, prove quite as satisfactory, although not divisible by 3 or 6, but is, of course, divisible by 5, which 96 is not.

The eccentric chuck enables the turner to bring almost any point on the surface of a flat disc into the axial line of the mandrel. It enables intersecting circles therefore to be cut upon any diameter of the work, as illustrated in Fig. 1, Plate XXV.,

PLATE XXIV.—THE ECCENTRIC CHUCK.

of this Chapter, which gives such circles of different sizes. Fig. 2 shows similar circles of larger size placed less closely together. Fig. 3, a ring of similar circles; and, although it would hardly be supposed to be so, Fig. 4 is precisely the same—only the circles are much larger; and Fig. 5 repeats the pattern, but the circles are now so large as to pass beyond the block, which is here cut away to show this effect more clearly.

The following experimental cuts will show exactly what an eccentric chuck will and will not do. Let all be at centre— i.e., let the slide remain without eccentricity, the pin at K being in place to aid in taking any undue strain off the slide and its screw. This little steel pin passes through both the plates when the slide is in its normal position, and the chuck-nose therefore central. If a point tool is now placed in the slide-rest and brought into the axial line of the mandrel, it will only cut a small dot when advanced to touch the work. By now moving down the slide of the chuck, a second and any number of such dots can be made, and these will be seen to lie in one line, upon a diameter. By means of the circular division-plate a circle of dots can be made, either near to the centre of the work, or nearer to its circumference. These dots may be made centres of circles, and they can evidently be placed upon any radius—practically therefore upon any part of the work, because any one such point is evidently on some one radius or diameter. To convert these dots, which are centres, into circles, all that is required is to move the tool a little distance towards the workman, such distance determining the size of circle. Hence, again, we can place circles in straight lines, on radii, or, using the division-wheel, convert them into rings of circles, which can be put near to one another, or at a distance, or so as to intersect. The *size* of a circle therefore evidently depends on the slide-rest, and its *position* depends on the chuck, and both are regulated by the number of turns given to their respective leading screws. There is, it will be seen, no difficulty in placing intersecting circles on radii, or on the circumference of circles—i.e., we can make straight lines of circles or rings of circles. Can we now make a line of rings

on each side of a square, forming a square pattern? As I
have shown that we can put dots or circles on any part of
the surface of the work, we might evidently draw a square
in pencil and put dots along the lines or circles as before.
True it is quite possible to do this, but it is far from
easy. It has to be done by trial at every cut, as both
the chuck-slide and the division-plate have to be used
together, with different degrees of movement at each cut.
Hence a square or similar pattern is not considered suitable for this chuck alone, and it is generally accomplished
by the eccentric cutter in the slide-rest in combination with
the eccentric chuck upon the mandrel. The variety of patterns
that can be worked by the chuck alone is very great; but
there are some one or two, which have become standard
designs. Fig. 4, Pláte XXV., goes by the name of the Turk's
Cap; Fig. 1, Plate XXVI., is a shell; and Fig. 2 a double-shell.
A little consideration will make the nature of this pattern
evident. It is plain that both the size of the circles diminishes,
and that the circles themselves shift their position so that
their centres form a row of points upon the diameter of the
largest circle. In the present case, however, the cuts have
been carried beyond the circumference of this largest circle
to produce more correctly the form of the outline of a scallop
shell. The double shell was begun in the middle; the single
one was begun with the largest circle; and after each cut the
main screw of the chuck was moved three divisions and the
screw of the slide-rest three or four—the latter diminishing
the size of the circles after each cut, and the former shifting
its position. The double shell was cut the reverse way : first,
all at centre, resulting in a mere dot at the centre of the
block; then the slide-rest screw was turned three or four
divisions and a circle cut, and then the slide-rest screw and
eccentric were both thrown out at each cut till one shell
was completed; then all was returned to its first position—
all at centre—but the division-plate of the chuck was
moved fifty divisions—that is half round, and the second shell
was cut in the same manner. Of course, if twenty-five
divisions had been taken instead of fifty, and the work
similarly done, four shells instead of two would have resulted.

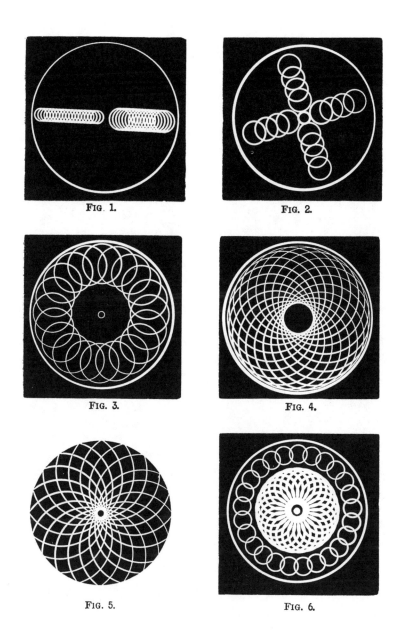

FIG. 1.

FIG. 2.

FIG. 3.

FIG. 4.

FIG. 5.

FIG. 6.

PLATE XXV.—ECCENTRIC CUTTING.

FIG. 1.

FIG. 2.

FIG. 3.

FIG. 4.

PLATE XXVI.—ECCENTRIC CUTTING.

The centre of the double shell is imperfect, and it is so left as an instance of the defect already alluded to as backlash, or loss of time, due to a nut and screw action; but especially so when, as in this case, both have had considerable wear. If this double shell had been differently worked this central defect would have been avoided. It results from coming back to "all at centre" for a fresh start, the defective chuck not returning to that point with absolute exactness. If the central circle were first made, then the chuck and rest shifted to cut the first circle of the shell, and then the division-wheel moved 50deg. and a second shell cut, and so on, building up the pattern on both sides alternately, there would have been no need to come back to centre at all. In the same way, to cut four, six, or eight of such shells this is generally the best plan, cutting one circle and then moving the division-plate through the necessary number of divisions. The majority of patterns in which a particular design has to be repeated are cut in this way, working round the block step by step, instead of completing each design separately.

In the larger block, Fig. 3, of Plate XXVI., four shells are cut, which were worked in the above way, the division-plate being shifted twenty divisions after each cut. It is evidently only a matter of easy calculation to devise eccentric patterns, it being always remembered that when this apparatus is used it is the rest which determines the sizes of the circles, and the chuck which decides their position, the opposite result to that being obtained by the use of the eccentric cutter. One more block is given here with a diversity of eccentric designs upon it (Fig. 4, of this Plate). The eccentric-cutting frame used in combination with this chuck enables a workman to enlarge the series of face patterns, and, in short, to cut almost any designs that consist of interlacing circles. That which is cut on Fig 2, Plate XXVII., for instance, is a compound pattern of this description, which could not be cut without the aid of the eccentric-cutting frame. Each of the four rings of interlacing circles are placed by the eccentric chuck, while the cutter determines their size, and the rest their distance from their common centre. Supposing all at centre, and the block accurately faced, the slide of the chuck is thrown down until what I have called the "common centre" of one ring of circles is brought into the axial line of the mandrel. If now a fixed tool were put on the slide-rest, and the chuck with the mandrel made to revolve, a circle would be cut, the size depending upon the distance the tool is placed from the new centre obtained by the chuck. Instead, however, of a fixed tool, a double-pointed drill (of which, usually, I prefer to break off one point), or the eccentric cutter, is mounted in the slide-rest, either of which being put in revolution by means of the overhead will cut a small circle, and by using the division-plate of the mandrel, and passing over five divisions of the 100 circle at each cut, one complete ring like those on the block will be formed. The dividing plate of the chuck is then moved 25 divisions of its 100 circle, and a second chain of circles is made, and this is repeated at divisions 50 and 75. The pattern is a simple and easy one, but serves as well or better than a more complex one to teach the use of the eccentric chuck and drill, or cutter, in combination. All these blocks are cut shallow, but for specimens they would be cut deeply with a burnished tool, and the effect of the work is much enhanced if the surface of the block is "grailed," as it is technically called— that is, covered first of all with very fine and shallow concentric circles, as closely together as they can be placed; this gives a sort of uniform grey tint, which, by rendering the surface dull, causes the clean bright cuts of the ornamenting cutters to show up with great brilliance. Grailing is, however, an exceeding slow, tedious operation.

SQUARE PATTERNS.—I have shown one square pattern as an illustration of this class of work. It is a very telling design when cut on a circular piece, such as a box-cover, and although at first sight it may appear to present some difficulty, it is really very simple and can be cut with rapidity. The tool used was a double-pointed drill intended for cutting beads, but one of the points was broken off and the broken end filed down to be out of the way. Such a tool often cuts cleaner than if both points are left, for unless the tool is perfectly ground it may happen that the two points do not fall exactly into the same track, in which case the cut made by one point is burred by the

Fig. 1.

Fig. 2

PLATE XXVII.—SQUARE AND COMPOUND ECCENTRIC CUTTING.

other. The block was set square to the sides of the chuck when the index was at Zero of the division-plate, and when the chuck was on the mandrel it was set square to the lathe-bed and the mandrel pulley fixed by its index, without specially troubling about the hole it chanced to fall into. The chuck-slide was then lowered until the upper line of the square came opposite the tool. Nothing then remained but to set the overhead at work, and placing the circles side by side by the divisions on the slide-rest main screw, work straight across the face, turn the chuck-wheel by its tangent-screw until a second side, tested by a square set up on the lathe-bed, is also truly vertical, and cut a second row of circles by working the slide of the rest back again—only be careful to attend to what was said about backlash — for it will be seen that on reversing the motion of the rest-screw the slide will not be moved until the divided head of the screw has passed by one or two divisions. It should be noted and remembered what amount of backlash the screw has. My own is now equal to two divisions, and in some rests which have been much used it may amount to three or four. When the exact amount is known, this does not give rise to much difficulty in working a pattern, but it must never be ignored or accurate work will be impossible. The third and fourth sides are cut exactly in the same way, the important thing being to set the chuck always exactly true by the square, even though the division-plate figures may appear correct. Most lathes for ornamental work have an adjusting index—i.e., one which, after its point has been set in some one of the holes, can be moved a little by means of a slot in the spring and set screw, thus pulling the mandrel round a little way. This enables a chuck to be set square to the lathe-bed with the most perfect accuracy, which is often a difficult matter unless there are several circles of holes.

SOLID WORK WITH THE ECCENTRIC CHUCK. — Sur-face-patterns are, after all, only a question of interlacing circles that may be almost indefinitely varied. Time, patience, keen tools, and a calculating brain are needed to produce them, but when finished they are of no practical use except to decorate covers of boxes. There is another mode, however, of using this chuck, by which some very curious and far more

satisfactory work can be done, and in which it becomes more
of a carving machine. The drawings show the nature of this
work, which is more specially applicable to the stems of
tazzas or shallow bowls, ring-stands, pillarets, and many
similar articles upon which the turner is wont to exercise his
skill. The simpler form of ornamentation is easy to work
out, and is managed thus : The bit of wood or ivory is fixed
firmly in a cup chuck, without the eccentric chuck, and is
turned truly cylindrical. The size is, of course, dependent on
the ultimate use intended to be made of it. About 1in.
diameter, and 3in., 4in., or 6in. long, will probably be found
most convenient for a first experiment, and for such a bit of
boxwood will suffice. It is to be turned in the first place truly
cylindrical by means of the slide-rest, being fixed in a cup chuck,
in which it is to be inserted till firmly held, and the back
poppet, with a sharply-pointed cone centre, is to be brought
up to support the end. The piece with its chuck is now to
be removed, and the eccentric chuck mounted on the mandrel
to which the cup chuck is then to be attached. It is always
as well to start work with the index of the division plate at
0°, and that of the slide-rest also at Zero. If the eccentric
chuck was specially made for the lathe, its index should point
to Zero when it has no eccentricity. Thus it will be easy to
begin counting on either of the screws or division-plate, with
also less chance of forgetting the selected number or mis-
calculating when at work. In the present case the position
of the index of the chuck-screw is of less importance, as when
once its eccentricity is determined it remains throughout at
the same position, but the count-wheel is moved after each
cut is taken. To work this geometrical staircase, as it is
called, and which is represented in Plate XXVIII., throw down
the slide of the chuck one complete turn of the screw, which
should move it $\frac{1}{10}$in., first moving back and then replacing the point of the back centre, which will, of course, make
for itself a new depression in the end of the wood. This must
be repeated without fail before each cut is made. The point
must be released before the chuck-wheel is moved, and replaced
before taking a fresh cut. The tool to be used is a flat
end, $\frac{1}{10}$in. or so in width, but its actual width is not

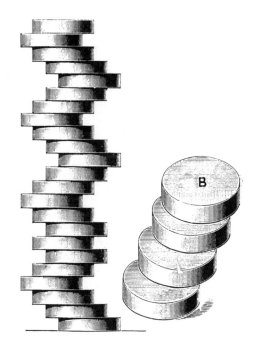

PLATE XXI.—SOLID ECCENTRIC CUTTING.
(Geometrical Staircase).

important, only it is to be keen and sharpened quite squarely so as to leave a surface that is truly parallel to the axis of the mandrel. A cut is to be taken very gently and carefully until the eccentricity is entirely removed, and a new cylindrical bit $\frac{1}{10}$in. wide is made. The stop-screw is to be set to that depth and to remain there; then the tool is to be withdrawn, the back centre drawn back, the count wheel turned 10 or (if it has 96 divisions instead of 100) 8, and the slide-rest screw made to move the tool *exactly* its own width, and the back centre replaced. A second cut is now made until the work is again cylindrical at that point, and so on, till the one, two, or three coils, as desired, are completed. Let it be noted that the back centre goes into a fresh spot each time according to the number of times the division-plate is moved, after which it will always fall into one of these. The number of discs, or steps, in each complete turn of the spiral will also be the same as the number of such centres; and, of course, by continuing the operations described, as many coils can be given as desired. This is evidently an ordinary spiral twist, made up of a number of flat discs piled on one another (XXVIII. B.). The edges of these discs can be gone over subsequently by a vertical or fly cutter, or by an ornamental drill, altering and beautifying the effect considerably. A hollow drill will stud them at equal intervals, and if it has a hollow and two flats, or astragals, the studs can be made to stand up, leaving the surface generally quite flat.

Instead of turning the original piece cylindrical, it can be made of a different shape. Mouldings are no use, but the general form may be wavy in outline, or merely smaller in the centre than at the extremities. The discs, again, may be cut thick or thin, according as the tool used is wider or narrower, and other possible modifications will occur to the ingenious turner; as, for instance, hollowing out the piece and mounting it on a central spindle of black wood, if the work is done in ivory. The latter, though a far more delicate piece to work, will give very beautiful results, worth all the care and patience expended upon it. In decorating a piece of curved outline, it is evident that the stop-screw of the rest cannot be used, because the cuts do not penetrate to the same depth. An ingenious and simple plan in such a case is to blacken the surface with a lead pencil, and let each cut just penetrate till this black is removed. A little care will make it fairly easy to do this.

The discs shown in Plate XXVIII., of full size, may be reduced alternately to mere pins, giving a different effect altogether. It is, however, difficult to express in a drawing the twisted appearance of such designs. I have sketched a few discs in perspective to make the matter clear. All this work is very well worth doing, and when it is once thoroughly understood there is little difficulty in varying the designs.

A vast difference in appearance results between thick and thin discs, and between those cut with a flat-ended tool and one of a hollow, round, or other shape. But, in point of fact, all this, though it is perfectly legitimate lathe-work, reduces the lathe to the condition of a carving machine, its dignity being compromised somewhat by compelling it merely to hold the material in certain positions while a revolving cutter chisels it into form. All the finest work, however, is done in this way; and on a considerably larger scale this system is carried out in various wood-working factories—gun-stocks, shoemakers'-lasts, axe-handles, and a multitude of such common articles are thus formed—an iron pattern, on a second mandrel, being so connected to the tool slide of the rest that it shifts it to-and-fro according to the design.

CHAPTER XVII.

THE DOME OR SPHERICAL CHUCK.

THE chuck, shown in Plate XXIX., differs from others, inasmuch as it holds the work vertically instead of horizontally. Moreover, it is not made to revolve when in use by the rapid rotation of the mandrel on which it is fixed. Motion is given to it by the hand or, when the lathe is so fitted, by the worm-wheel and tangent-screw affixed to the mandrel pulley. Although it is often called a spherical chuck, a perfect sphere cannot be turned upon it, and its usual purpose is the formation and subsequent decoration of domes. These will if thus formed be true segments of spheres, and may be either hemispheres or smaller segments, or, if desired, they may exceed the hemisphere. The work of forming a dome by means of this chuck is somewhat tedious, but it is always partially done by hand, while the work held in a cup chuck is on the mandrel. The chuck is transferred to the vertical nose of this apparatus and finished to a truly spherical outline.

It is, I think, a little difficult, unless this chuck is in actual use, to realise its capabilities, or, in the workman's lingo, " to get the hang of it "; but I will do the best I can to make it clear by the help of a drawing or two.

Two views are given of the chuck itself—one as seen directly in front, and one in profile; and where the same parts are seen in both the same letters of reference are used. A is the usual boss on the back, which is bored and tapped with a screw-thread for attachment to the mandrel. E is

the main plate, which is seen in the second drawing to have
a long slot or mortice running down the centre. Into this
mortice fits the tenon of another plate, which is lettered B,
and which stands out horizontally. The tenon which fits the
slot or mortice is drilled with a hole tapped to receive the
leading screw F G, which is fitted so as to turn freely in the
plate, but is prevented from moving endwise by a collar
or nut A. When turned, therefore, by the milled head
F it causes the horizontal plate to move up or down, and the
plate can then be clamped by a nut seen at H. Upon the
horizontal plate is fitted a worm-wheel, acted on by a tangent-
screw marked K in both drawings. On the upper surface of
the wheel, and cast in the same piece, is the screw nose to
take the chucks, this being a counterpart of the mandrel
nose. The chuck is therefore not at all of a complex
character, and it is evident that it will hold the piece to be
turned in an upright position, and by turning the main-
screw it can be raised or lowered; the tangent-screw and wheel
will also enable us to turn the work round to any required
position.

Suppose now that a bit of box or other wood, held in a
cup chuck, has been turned to the shape of a dome or
hemisphere—not with absolute correctness of form, but as
nearly as can be effected by help, let us say, of a card or
tin template, cut out after drawing an arc of a circle upon
it with a pair of compasses. The piece with its chuck is
removed and the dome chuck mounted upon the mandrel
instead, and the cup chuck is now placed vertically on the
nose D of this dome chuck. A point, or round-nosed tool,
which is perhaps better, is now fixed in the slide-rest, which
is placed parallel to the lathe bed, and the tool is accurately
adjusted to height of centres. The horizontal plate is now
raised by the screw until the centre of the intended dome
is in a line with the axis of the mandrel. The tool is, of
course, drawn back so as not to be in the way during such
adjustment. Now advance the tool so as just to touch the
side of the work, and by means of the stop-screw mark its
forward position; then draw it back, and, turning the
mandrel pulley *by hand,* after removing the lathe-cord, move

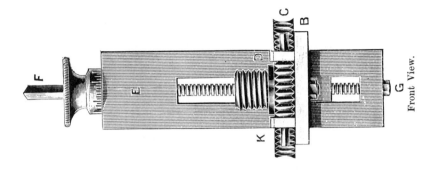

Front View.

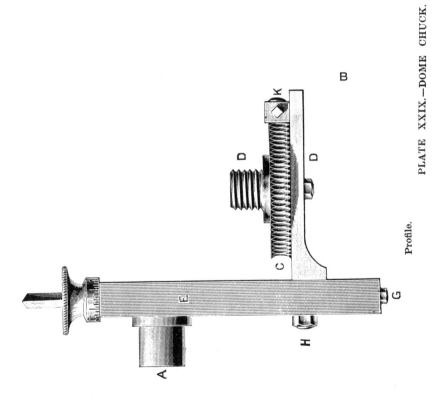

Profile.

PLATE XXIX.—DOME CHUCK.

the chuck away till it stands horizontally on the far side of the lathe, and while so held see if the tool, when advanced to the same degree as before, just touches what is to be the summit of the dome.

If such is the case the adjustment is complete; if not, raise or lower the slide until this result is obtained, or as nearly as can be managed. All is now prepared, and the cutting is to proceed as follows: Advance the tool very slightly, and move the chuck, as before, by hand, so as to pare off a thin slice, which, if the tool is well sharpened, it will do readily enough unless too deeply set. Next, by means of the tangent-screw, shift the work round a very little, and, repeating the action, take a second slice, and so continuously, until the entire hemisphere has been thus operated on. The form will thus be correctly hemispherical, unless very much out of shape when roughed out on the mandrel, when another series of cuts will be necessary to complete the form.

The process here described is evidently a somewhat slow one, yet not so much so as would be supposed, and with a sharp tool the several cuts will be cleanly made. Thus far we have only formed a perfectly plain dome, and if such were the sole use of the chuck it might be dispensed with, because an equally accurate hemisphere can be made on the mandrel by hand alone; but the main use of the chuck is to decorate rather than to form domes, and by this decoration the dome is to a great extent formed by the one operation Evidently the point, or round tool, will cut out grooves more or less deep, and at such equal distances apart as may be determined by using the division-plate of the worm-wheel. This is shown on the first drawing as a plain part at the bottom of the worm-wheel, and ought to have been drawn wider than it is, as the divisions are marked round the edge. The head of the tangent-screw is also generally graduated. A series of flutes or ribs which are spaced so as just to meet, whereby the rough material is cut entirely away, reduces the work to an ornamental dome at once, so that it is not necessary always to correct the form by one operation and then to decorate it by a second. Revolving cutters are used in this work as well as plain tools, and there is no more

difficulty than is found in decorating plain cylinders, because
the chuck, by its partial slow rotation, brings each individual
part consecutively under the action of the tools. For such
work, however, as beads or studs, it is evident that the material
must be held firmly in one position as each is being drilled.
For this, therefore, the division-plate on the mandrel is
brought into use exactly as if the work was mounted in its
normal position, without the intervention of the dome chuck.

FIG. 31.—FLUTED DOME AND DRILL.

Although I have thus far treated the matter as if the work
was to be the formation or decoration of a hemispherical surface,
such need not be the case. It may be desired, for example, to
finish a cylindrical column by a domed summit, the whole
being in one and the same piece. If the chuck is long enough
to enable the work to be lowered sufficiently to bring the
centre of the domed part in a line with the axis of the mandrel,
no difficulty can ensue, and the domed part can be cut.
as already described, just as if no cylindrical part existed,

Moreover, if the work is still further lowered a flatter dome than a hemisphere will result, as part of the material will miss contact with the tool at each cut. A few trials will very soon show the capabilities of the chuck, and render its use of easy application. A dome with projecting ribs (Fig. 31) is formed by using a fixed tool, or a drill, or a vertical cutter of which the edge is so shaped as to produce half a rib and half a hollow or which will cut a whole rib and hollow. The chuck must be moved gently round and a final cut at good speed taken, which ought, moreover, to be made with the tool freshly sharpened and polished. The tool shown is a quarter hollow drill, which does this work cleanly and satisfactorily. It is a difficult tool to sharpen well; but all the small drills and cutters which have hollows like this should be done upon a special apparatus, consisting of a brass cone, fed with emery and then with crocus, and running at high speed.

The dome chuck is used also for the formation of square and other flat-sided solids, which can be subsequently ornamented by revolving-cutters of the form, in reverse, of the various mouldings. The chuck holds the material, and it is shaped by the eccentric cutter. As the chuck has its own dividing wheel, it is easy to form polygons, squares, or triangles in this way, and for pedestals, forming the base of columns and other similar work, it is easier to use this chuck than to cut the same shaped articles upon the mandrel. The latter may, and often does, bring some part of the work into contact with the revolving-cutter, when by means of the dome chuck this may be prevented. As the work is held in a cup chuck, fitting either the dome chuck or mandrel, it can easily be tried upon both and shifted if necessary.

CHAPTER XVIII.

THE GONIOSTAT.

THIS is an essential apparatus for sharpening the cutters for ornamental turning if high-class work is undertaken. Such tools need to have *polished* as well as *sharp* edges and truth of angle, which is not possible to obtain by simple hand-work. The instrument in question, shown in Plate **XXX.**, is constructed to retain the tool at a given angle, whilst it is rubbed on a flat slab charged with abrasive material. There are usually three of these fitted into drawers of the case which contains the instrument, but sometimes all three slabs—one of oilstone, one of brass, and one of iron, are embedded in the same block, which also holds a slab of glass or hard wood upon which the legs of the instrument stand, and on which they can traverse while the grinding is carried on. An inspection of Plate **XXX.** will make the nature of the goniostat plain to the reader. It is reduced from one of my own drawings in "The Lathe and its Uses." A is a brass plate about $\frac{3}{16}$in. thick, with a semi-circular mortice, one edge of which is graduated. It is hinged at B to a horizontal plate, which has underneath two steel legs, nicely rounded to prevent them from grooving or injuring the glass or wood-slab upon which they work. The tool to be ground, C, clamped by screw D in a holder, forms a third leg when in place. By means of a graduated arc of steel, E, passing through a mortice in A, the plate can be raised to any angle, and clamped by the thumb-screw F. This will determine the angle at which the lower face or faces of the tool

PLATE XXX.—THE GONIOSTAT.

will be ground on the slab H. The side angles will depend on the position of the tool-holder, which is determined by the scale on the brass plate, the tool-holder being then clamped by a screw at the back. Thus a double-angle tool can be accurately ground on both facets. The slab, H, though shown separately, is in reality let in flush into a piece of hard wood, so that while the feet of the instrument rests upon the latter, the tool is in contact with the stone or metal surface. The other end of the steel arc E is fixed into the base plate.

SUBSTITUTES FOR THE GONIOMETER OR GONIOSTAT.—As the instrument costs more than many turners are able or willing to give—not less than £5—it is advisable to find, if possible, a substitute that a workman can make for himself. It is evident that we require such a holder as will place the tool in three positions. It must lean back to give the lower angle or angles, and sideways in either direction to give the side angles. In practice there are not a great many angles really necessary for the tools. For some designs the point may be more acute than for others, but unless the turner devotes his attention almost wholly to eccentric or geometric patterns, he will find it very unnecessary either to have a large assortment of cutters, or to give them more than two or three predetermined angles of cutting edge. I am indebted to a friend for a very simple goniostat of boxwood, costing absolutely nothing, and so effective in use that it will serve every purpose for flat-ended or pointed tools. Round-ended ones need a different and equally simple and inexpensive arrangement.

Plate XXXI. is the little wooden goniostat, the size of which is not material, but the one sketched here was 2½in. long and 1½in. square in the largest part before it was shaped. This gives plenty of finger-hold; but the size may, of course, differ either way, as some might prefer a somewhat larger block. The form is sufficiently shown in the drawing. An oblong block of box, or of any sound, hard wood, is first of all got up true, after which a groove is cut to take a tool-holder, which carries the short cutters in a square mortice at one end. This tool-holder, when in use is secured by two ordinary screws, or better still, by two nicely made screws of brass or iron tapped into the wood, because they have to be frequently screwed in and out, and will get loose if not nicely fitted. I may also suggest that the entire block might be cast in brass, and would then be as cheap and serviceable an instrument as the most enthusiastic amateur need desire. The block is cut away at the back so as to leave a projecting part, which is sloped off, and a hole bored to receive one of the wooden legs shown here, this back leg or strut determining the lower angle of the cutter. Another hole, made quite through the lower end at right angles to the first, receives another of the legs, which is inserted on either side, according as the right or left face of the tool is being ground. Of these wooden legs not more than two or three are likely to be needed, but to produce them only needs a few minutes work at the lathe.

THE VERTICAL CUTTER FRAME.—Mention has been made of this tool but no description of it has appeared, and as it is exceedingly simple and useful I now give an illustration of it in Plate XXXII., as it is made in both forms. The most approved is the second as it is thought to run more freely when the axle is thus supported by centres at each end. Probably one is as good as the other in practice, and the frame of No. 2 may be sometimes in the way, when the other may be free from this drawback. Fig. 32, however, is a design which, although in appearance more serviceable because it has no frame, is not satisfactory. The bearing is too short and the revolving cutter often sticks fast during work. I speak from personal experience, as I have one of this design, and have had to throw it aside as useless. The drawings will enable the reader to understand that the main shank, like that of the drill and eccentric cutter, is $\frac{9}{16}$in. square, fitting the receptacle of the slide-rest, and the cutter is driven like those instruments by a cord from the overhead. It must be understood that the part A of No. 1, Plate XXXII., is firmly fixed to the shank D, and is bored to receive a spindle running its whole length, B being an enlarged part of this spindle, and the driving-pulley C being attached to its other end. Steel collars are generally inserted, and the part just beyond B is made conical. The pulley being tightened by a small nut or central screw draws the conical end into its bearing and regulates the tightness of

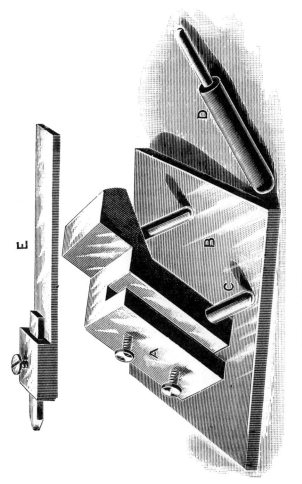

PLATE XXXI.—WOODEN GONIOSTAT.

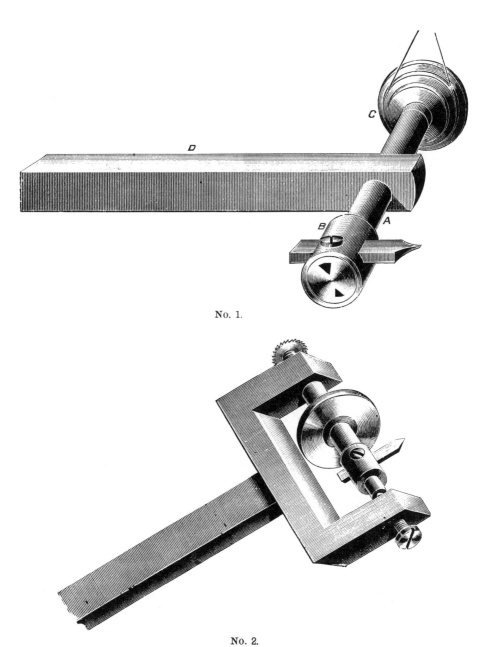

No. 1.

No. 2.

PLATE XXXII.—VERTICAL CUTTING FRAME.

fit, thus taking up wear. The vertical cutter forms patterns, like Fig. 33, its operation scooping out curved slices, which are usually placed side by side, alternating with those in the

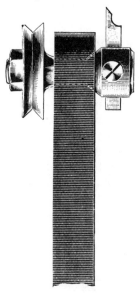

Fig. 32.—Badly Designed Vertical Cutter.

next row, so as to leave sharp-edged mouldings or projections. But much depends upon the form of tool used with the instrument, as one like Fig. 34 will produce rounded projections, while

Fig. 33.—Specimen of Work of Vertical Cutter.

Fig. 35 will make a series of angular channels. The division-plate of the mandrel is used to determine the number of cuts, and that of the slide-rest screw sets them side by side, either with intervals, in which the original surface appears, or close together, entirely cutting away such original surface. The first two cuts are made alternately, little by little, so as to enable the turner to judge of their proper depth, as it may be desired to bring the projections to sharp edges or to leave spaces between. When this is ascertained by actual trial the stop-screw is fixed, and it only remains to cut the entire series in succession to the depth thus determined. Infinite variety of pattern is produced by different spacing and different forms of tool edges and by using cutters of different widths. Such cutters are sold in cases of several dozen, and of which the widths varies by hundredths of an inch. This is nevertheless an expensive luxury, and a few well-selected sizes of flats, rounds, and hollows will enable a lot of very pretty and intricate work to be done.

Fig. 34.

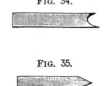

Fig. 35.

TOOLS USED IN CUTTER FRAME.

It will be understood with respect to this wooden affair, that the legs being of varied lengths any one of them may be used at pleasure, and the shorter it is the more will the instrument lie over towards that side, and an acuter angle on the tool will necessarily result. In the same way a long or short leg at the back will set the instrument more or less upright, and so regulate the lower angle of the tool. If preferred, however, the back leg may remain permanently of standard length, and the requisite alteration of angle may be made by drawing out the brass tool-holder, or pushing it further in, before clamping it by its two screws. The principle of this little instrument is exactly that of an orthodox goniostat; that is to say, it has two legs and the tool makes a third, and the result of grinding by its aid is the same, with quite as accurate a result. There is, moreover, no complication of parts, nothing to get out of order, and no expense incurred in its manufacture. By taking away the side leg and only inserting the back one a round-end tool can be ground very nicely, rolling it from side to side during the operation. The back leg insures the regularity of the angle of its cutting edge. When an eccentric chuck is used by itself the cutting tools have shanks long enough to lie in the bed of the slide-rest tool-receptacle, and they will thus lie in the slot of this goniostat without the intervention of the holder. This, however, is needed for the small cutters used in the eccentric cutting-frame, and in other similar apparatus herein described. There is no difficulty whatever in fitting up the slab on which to grind the tools, whether three separate ones are used or the three small squares of oil-stone, brass, and iron are let into a single base block of wood. Plates of metal are easily procurable, and they need not be more than about 3in. square. They must, however, be let in nicely into the wood-block, and should be fixed by cement. Turner's cement will answer well for this if the plate is heated and then pressed down firmly into place in its recess. The powders used are finest emery on the brass slab, and crocus or jewellers' rouge on the iron—this being an oxide of iron will give the tool a high polish. A little oil is used with it. Razor paste, sold in collapsible tubes, is the same and will do quite as well.

THE HORIZONTAL AND THE UNIVERSAL CUTTER.—These seem only a natural outcome of the vertical. It is evident, that as the shanks of such tools are square it is just as easy to place the vertical cutter on its side and so cause the cuts to assume a horizontal direction. But then comes the difficulty about the cord and driving-pulley, as the latter is now in the wrong position. This difficulty is, however, easily removed by adding a pair of guide-pulleys, or "fair leaders" D as they are sometimes called, which causes the vertical cutter to assume a form which is shown in Fig. 36 and renders it a horizontal instead of a vertical one. It then needed no great amount of ingenuity so to arrange the frame as to give it a movement round the square shank, A so that while the latter remains horizontal in the bed of the slide-rest the actual cutter frame may be fixed at any desired angle—vertical, horizontal, or otherwise. Thus arose the very useful modification called a universal cutter frame, answering all the purposes of the two first described, and being also capable of carrying the revolving tool at any angle that a design might need for its execution. This tool, therefore, will serve the purpose of the other two and render them unnecessary, and if only one can be afforded this may be selected as being of more extensive service. Like most combination tools it has, however, some defects, the chief of these consisting of the

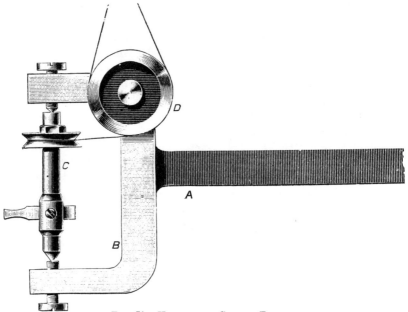

FIG. 36.—HORIZONTAL CUTTER FRAME.

fact that its frame is often in the way when the simpler tool may be made to work effectively. Theoretically, for instance, the vertical cutter, No. 2, Plate XXXII., against which I have warned the reader, is excellently suited to get into corners where the frames of the larger tool would prevent their use, but even if advanced very slowly, so as to take the lightest possible cuts, the strain of the driving band very soon causes the spindle to stick fast, even when it is well lubricated, as all such tools must always be. There are other patterns of all these tools, but on the whole, those shown are the most serviceable, and only those of ample means are at pains to provide a number of such appliances to meet every varying circumstance that may possibly occur. The better plan is to get one or two generally serviceable tools, and to suit the design to their capabilities, avoiding such intricate forms as would bring about difficulties such as I have suggested. If a design is first sketched, it will be readily seen whether, in carrying it out, the frame of the apparatus that is proposed to be used will come in contact with any of the projections. There is no need to give a special drawing of the universal cutter, as it can be readily understood. Suppose the shank A of the horizontal cutter frame to be separated at the point A from the remaining part, and the latter to have a round spindle attached at that point somewhat longer than the square shank and screwed at the end so as to take a nut. Then bore the square shank right through to receive the spindle. Evidently the rectangular frame which carries the revolving tool can then be set either horizontally, vertically, or at any intermediate angle. Such is the usual form of the universal cutter. The guide pulleys are mounted in a slightly different way so as to swivel round to suit the varying position of the cord, otherwise the description given is sufficiently explanatory, and gives a clear account of this very useful appliance in its usual and most simple form. Lathe-makers have indeed variously modified it and perhaps improved it, but one that I myself use, by a London lathe-maker, is similar to that which I have described, and no tool could do better work.

The selection of an ornamental lathe apparatus, herein described, will provide an amateur with all that he requires for general work. Of course, he may almost indefinitely extend the list until three figures will no longer express the necessary outlay. The intention of this little volume is not, however, so far-reaching as to form a guide to the use of the more complicated appliances now added to the lathe, the greater part of which, if purchased, would, in all probability, never be used at all. There are chucks, for instance, costing £60 or £70, which will trace the most exquisite patterns when once set going, and during the process the turner may put his hands in his pockets and a pipe in his mouth and watch the performance, having nothing to do but keep the treadle in motion. Such is to the writer a task of no interest whatever, and all the credit of the finished design is due to the chuck or its inventor.

THE ORNAMENTAL SLIDE-REST.—Nothing can be done with any of the ornamental turning appliances without a proper slide-rest, those already described for metal work not being suitable; the principle is the same, there being two slides at right angles to each other actuated by screws, but the details differ owing to the forms of tools to be used with them, and certain other special requirements of the ornamental turner.

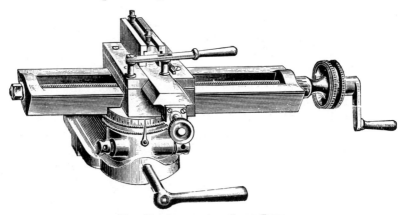

FIG. 37.—ORNAMENTAL SLIDE REST.

There is first of all a cradle, or gun-metal receptacle, fitted to the lathe-bed, which receives the sole of the rest and secures it absolutely at right angles to the lathe-bed. This is not always used, but saves a great deal of time and trouble, and may be considered essential. The sole of the rest and its socket is like that of an ordinary hand-rest, but is more carefully fitted, and has an addition or two belonging to it, as will be presently described in detail. Into this socket fits the stem or tenon of the main slide, which is from 12in. to 14in. long, and is very carefully planed and scraped to a true surface. This frame carries the top cross-slide and tool receptacle, and is made to traverse the frame from end to end by means of a screw of ten threads to the inch, which is actuated by a winch-handle. Instead of the design which has been sold for many years, I have here introduced a somewhat different one, made by the Britannia Company, of Colchester, which has some few novelties in its fittings. It is represented in Fig. 37, and the following is the description of it in the Company's catalogue :

" The above illustration represents our ornamental slide-rest constructed to suit a 5in. lathe, and embodying all the most material and useful improvements. It is arranged with a gun-metal cradle, planed to fit the lathe-bed and slide along it to any part, and planed at top to receive an eccentric socket at right angles to the bed. The socket is 12in. long, planed parallel at the sides to slide along the gun-metal cradle, and adjust to any distance from the axial line of centres. Within it is an eccentric shaft with eye and nut, a half-turn of which rigidly secures it to the lathe-bed. At its top end it is turned and screwed, and fitted with a gunmetal ring with milled edge to turn by thumb and finger, to adjust the height of the cutter. The longitudinal slide is 12in. long, made with a turned shank to fit into the socket of the eccentric slide, and swivel to any angle, its circular bottom being graduated to 50deg. each side of centre. Along its upper face are graduations in 10ths of an inch, and it is fitted with a steel draw-screw, having 10 threads per inch, with cones at each end to take up wear, and with a split gun-metal nut to adjust to take up backlash. On the collar of the screw are 20 divisions, to give an adjustment to 200ths of an inch, and it has a large milled-edged knob for thumb and finger adjustment, and is grooved for gut to enable it to be driven from overhead gear ; it also has a square at its end fitted with crank and handle. The top slide is made of gun-metal, fitted to the longitudinal slide by loose adjusting strips, with a transverse slide carrying tool-holder to suit $\frac{9}{16}$in. tools, and actuated by a milled-head thumbscrew and garter slide, screwed to 20 per inch, graduated by an ingenious contrivance to 25 divisions, giving an adjust-ment of the tool to the 500th part of an inch. The garter slide is instantly detachable, enabling the slide and tool-holder to be operated freely by lever. A stop screw is fitted to the tool-holder, and the face of the slide is graduated in 20ths of an inch. The whole instrument is well devised, very complete, and accurately and carefully made."

This rest having a tool receptacle of normal size, $\frac{9}{16}$in. square, will take any of the cutter frames and drills made by the leading makers, and which may frequently be picked up second-hand. It is essential in ornamental turning to be able at once to set the long or main slide of the rest at right angles to, or parallel with, the bed of the lathe, and this is done by two fixed stops underneath, which abut against a pair of adjustable screws, so fitted that the stops come into contact with them in either of these two positions of the main frame. A similar provision is made here by two slots or grooves in the pedestal into which the ends of the screws enter, which are seen just below the frame. The tool slide is here shown as actuated by a hand lever which is supplied

FIG. 38.—FLUTING STOP.

with all such rests, and was at one time almost constantly used for the purpose. There is, however, a screw which serves to advance or withdraw the tool slide when preferred, and which is here brought into action or the reverse by a slide, the end of which forms a bridle which embraces a groove cut round the end of the screw. Generally this bridle has to be removed and replaced by a little screw, which is liable to get lost. This sliding bridle is a decided improvement. When it is pushed forward so as to embrace the screw the latter comes into action to move the slide; when drawn back the slide is quite free and can be moved by the lever.

When the slide-rest is used for fluting work, in which it is necessary that all the grooves shall be of one length, it is not satisfactory to be obliged at each traverse of the tool to note the division on the main frame at which the tool slide stands. It is much better to have a pair of fluting-stops fitted to the frame, against which the tool slide will abut at the end of its traverse. These are made, like Fig. 38, so as to be detached readily when they are not needed. The horizontal screws which form the actual stops allow of very exact adjustment. These fluting stops may be replaced, if only a small amount of such work is to be done, by any simple temporary device, such as a couple of blocks of wood fitted inside the frame or made to fit on in the same way as these more expensive brass ones. So long as the purpose is served any simple plan may be adopted, but it is thought well to give the orthodox pattern here as made by the tool shops. It is drawn to a somewhat larger scale than the rest to show its construction clearly. The one bevel has to be made detachable, and is secured by a steady pin and screw. The stops, of which there are a pair, go on the frame, one on each side of the tool-box, which therefore at each traverse will touch the horizontal screw and determine the length of flute to the greatest nicety.

CHAPTER XIX.

THE OVAL OR ELLIPSE CHUCK.

THE oval chuck, No. 1, Plate XXXIII., although it is by no means ordinarily found in the turner's workshop, is, even in its simplest form, a piece of apparatus of great use. For very high-class ornamental turning it becomes almost essential. The complicated curves that may be traced by its aid when used in conjunction with the eccentric chuck and eccentric cutter still further enhances its value, but into these it is not my present purpose to enter. The front of the oval chuck is identical in appearance with that of the eccentric chuck, and might at the first glance be taken for it. The movable plate, however, is not actuated by a screw, but is perfectly free to slide in either direction between its parallel guide bars, and attached to it by screws are two flat plates, at right angles to the slide and at the back of the chuck. Slots are, of course, cut in the foundation-plate to allow of this attachment. The slide can therefore move up and down freely for a short distance, its motion being restricted thus far only by the length of these slots. The actual traverse when in use is regulated by the position of a ring, or hoop of brass, No. 2, Plate XXXIII, affixed to the face of the headstock, this ring being embraced by the two cross arms or pallets attached to the slide. The form of this is clearly seen by the drawing annexed. If this ring is concentric with the axis of the mandrel it is evident that the pallets will simply revolve in contact with it, but that no effect will be produced on the slide to which they are attached. If, however, the ring is, by means of its screws, placed eccentrically, the pallets, which are in close

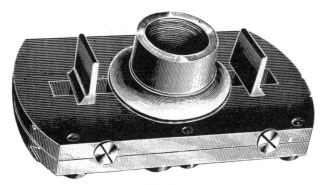

No. 1.

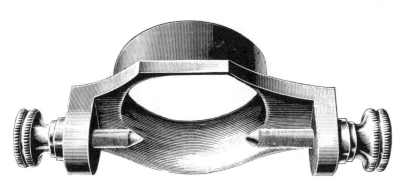

No. 2.

PLATE XXXIII.—THE ELLIPSE CHUCK.

contact with it, will compel the slide to accomodate itself to the position of the ring at every point of the revolution, and it will be found that a fixed tool on the slide-rest will trace an ellipse upon a disc of wood or other material mounted on the nose of the chuck. A larger or smaller ellipse will result according to the distance of the tool from the Lathe centre, but the character or proportion of the ellipse will depend upon the eccentricity given to the ring. This eccentricity can be exactly determined by a scale, which is engraved upon a flattened part of the frame which forms a part of the fitting of the ring, and is cast in one piece with it. This scale just comes level with the top of the headstock, and is read by a line engraved upon the same. To understand the precise action of this chuck needs a good amount of mathematical knowledge, and it would unduly lengthen this final chapter to add the necessary demonstrations; but a few words may be added in respect of the practical method of using it. The first essential (if ornamental work is to be done) is that, when the ring has no eccentricity, the chuck shall run perfectly true, so that the point of a tool in the rest, if brought to bear upon the centre, shall simply make a dot. This will be the case if the chuck and its ring have been truly and accurately fitted. In the next place, the motion of the ring when moved must be in a truly horizontal line, which will not be the case unless the two holes in the poppet, in which the ends of the adjusting screws take their bearing, are themselves in a horizontal line. If one is higher than the other, the ring will rise to a higher level as it passes sidewise in the act of setting it eccentrically. Such defects will cause the pallets to bind, besides causing defects in the traced patterns. For ornamental work again, the nose piece of the chuck must be fitted like that of the eccentric chuck, with a worm-wheel and tangent screw; the one illustrated being only intended for plain turning, such as cutting out oval frames and plain boxes, is not provided with this arrangement. The present chuck, therefore, although it is capable of cutting a series of concentric ellipses upon a surface, is incapable of placing a number of such ellipses radially, nor of executing patterns dependent upon such capability. It is, however, in conjunction with the eccentric

cutter, able to set interlacing circles upon elliptic outlines
instead of circular ones, which is a very pleasing variation of
an ordinary chain pattern, and is very suitable for a border
round an elliptic frame; but such circles will always fall more
and more closely together as they approach the foci, and
wider apart as they near the short diameter of the ellipse.
There is a special apparatus provided to eliminate this defect
—if defect it can be called—but it is very expensive, and
except for high-class work is not of great importance. In
turning elliptic work, it is first turned circular and a little
larger than it is intended ultimately to be. It is then transferred, chuck and all, to the ellipse chuck, which is mounted on
the mandrel, with its guide ring placed exactly central, and
its steady pin—the same as that of the eccentric chuck—in
its hole, so as to hold the two plates together and save the
sliding plate from all undue strain. The work is then trued
up to a correct form. If now the ring is set out a few degrees,
and the tool applied while the main slide of the rest is parallel
to the lathe-bed, as in ordinary cylindrical turning, it will be
found that the work comes with a good deal of shock against
the tool, which cuts in two places, i.e., on the ends of one diameter,
and misses the others; the latter being encroached upon,
however, more and more as the tool is set in further and further,
and the work attains more and more completely the elliptic
form. To avoid these shocks as much as possible the tool
must be advanced very gently, and light cuts only must be
taken, while the speed should also be reduced by putting the
lathe cord upon the slow-motion grooves of the flywheel and
mandrel pulley. The ring and pallets should also be lubricated.
But in all cases where it can be done, it is better to let the
tool act upon the face instead of side of the work until the
elliptical outline is completed, after which no shock will occur
as the work will be in contact with the tool without any
intermission. There is seldom any difficulty in working
upon the face in order to turn the circumference. All that
is necessary is to turn the rest across the face and set the tool
—round end or chisel—as if for hollowing out a box, only
allowing the edge to overlap the edge of the work as it
revolves. In this way it will very soon reduce it to an elliptical

form, after which the rest may be set parallel, and the cutting allowed to proceed exactly as in cylindrical turning.

This brief description must suffice for the present, as the ornamental work of which this chuck is capable, opens out too extensive a field, and it has already been fully treated by writers whose special object has been to treat of that more costly and elaborate lathe work, which would be of little practical use to the majority of our numerous readers.

CHAPTER XX.

A FEW HANDY RECEIPTS AND WRINKLES.

VARNISHES.—Eschew these utterly for all best work and ornamental turning and use French polish only, and for incised work, such as that produced by the eccentric and other cutters, even this must be avoided, or the appearance of the work will be spoiled. Eccentric cutting must depend for its brilliancy upon sharp and burnished tools only; any subsequent treatment will ruin it.

FOR TOOL HANDLES and similar articles, if the tools cut well, as they ought to do, nothing can beat a handful of shavings rubbed on while the Lathe is running at a good pace. This lays down the fine and almost invisible fibres, and makes a good, hard surface, which is bright and permanent.

BEESWAX AND TURPS.—A little of this, rubbed on with a bit of cloth or flannel before the shavings are used, will improve the appearance in the case of woods of more open grain. The wax is dissolved in turps by the aid of heat. Shave some wax, either bleached or the ordinary beeswax, and set it in a gallipot on the hob or near the fire, adding turps enough to produce a creamy infusion.

HARDWOOD LACKER.—This is another name for French polish. Its use and the method of applying it has been repeated so often in books and magazines that it is almost superfluous to repeat it. Hardwood lacker is a solution of one or more gums, of which shellac is the chief, in spirits of wine. It can be bought ready prepared at any oil and colour shop, or in small quantities at the cabinet makers. A wad is made by rolling up a strip of list, or by a handful of cotton wool, which is covered with a piece of rag and pinched up, or, better still, tied round, to form a soft, smooth ball, the ends forming a handle. For general lathe work it need not be bigger than a walnut, or for larger work, such as a table-leg, the size of a hen's egg. The lacquer is poured upon this, or it is charged by holding it to the mouth of the bottle and turning the latter bottom upwards for a second; and while the lathe is running at a fair pace the ball of polish is held against it and moved about constantly, never letting it rest in any one spot. As, however, it is liable to stick if applied without precaution, the ball is, after being charged, covered with another bit of soft, old linen, which is touched with a few drops of linseed-oil (raw, not boiled), and this is repeated after every renewal of the polish. Gradually, as the lacquer is absorbed the work assumes a brilliant appearance, and soon cheats the amateur with a pleasant idea that his work is done. Not a bit of it! Let it stand a few hours and its brilliant face will fade, and give place to cloudy dullness of a most unsatisfactory character. The polish, however, has merely sunk into the pores of the wood, and needs renewal. The process is therefore repeated, and, unless the wood is very absorbent, which most hard woods are not, a fresh and more brilliant surface is soon produced. When this seems dry a clean rag is taken and is just moistened with spirits of wine, and a quick application of it to the work as it revolves *should* efface any cloudiness and bring up the surface to a pitch of uniform brilliancy. I do not say that it *will*, because there is a little knack in putting on this finish. Too much spirit will undo what has been accomplished, and too little will do nothing. Lightness of hand is also necessary and quickness, but it is all a matter of practice, and if the result is not very tip-top as a performance it will very likely turn out presentable. For porous woods it is a common practice to use what is known as a filler to stop up the pores before the polish is laid on. This saves much labour and is no detriment to the work, but with hard woods, like ebony, black wood, camwood, and cocus, it is never needed. Moreover, even for such woods as beech or elm a good face can be got up by polish alone, if the several coats are allowed to sink in and dry. The polish then becomes its own filler.

FILLERS FOR SOFT WOOD.—The most commonly used of these is plaster of Paris made into a cream with water or oil, and this is rubbed well into the wood and left a short time to dry. The surplus is then wiped off, and the material re-surfaced with the finest sand-paper, after which the hard-wood polish may be used as it will not now sink into the wood. If the latter is not white, such as deal or beech, the filler may have some colouring matter mixed with it, such as dragon's blood, for mahogany, turmeric for yellow deal or satin wood— or lamp black if it is intended to ebonise the work. Another very usual filler is ordinary thin glue, brushed in well and allowed to dry very thoroughly. The sand-paper is then used to clean off the surface.

EBONISING.—The ebonised furniture, as it is called, has taken a strong hold on the public taste, especially when gold is used to pick out the edges and mouldings. There are many *varnish* black paints sold under various names, but they are far from satisfactory, and if laid on at all thickly so evidently declare themselves a cheat that they should only be used upon the more common articles of turning. Far better is it to stain the wood a dull black and to polish it afterwards, and I myself have a great partiality for Harger's black stain, which *is* a *stain* and in no sense a *varnish*. The still older and to a great extent trade method is to brush over the work a *hot* solution of logwood in water, followed when this is dry by a solution of sulphate of iron. If both are strong infusions, the result will be a deep and per-manent black, which is often still further deepened by a coat of vinegar, in which rusty bits of iron have been steeping. This, however, is after all, much the same as giving a second coat of sulphate solution. This ebony stain can be French polished, or varnished, or left dull, and merely finished by rubbing with very finely-powdered and sifted charcoal, such as is used by artists. A very nice dull polish is thus obtained.

CEMENTS.—These are not much used by turners, who prefer to join the several parts of turned work by cutting screws upon

them with the hand chaser or traversing mandrel, or to unite the
parts by turning tenons on the one and fitting it into holes bored
for their reception, in which case ordinary glue is used. Sometimes, however, especially for ivory, another kind is needed,
which is colourless, and then diamond cement, or Kaye's coaguline, or other such cements that any chemist will supply, is
preferable. The original diamond cement was a spirituous
solution of gum mastic. Kaye's coaguline, sold under various
titles, is isinglass dissolved in acetic acid, and a very useful
cement it is.

ANOTHER POLISH FOR TURNERY.—The following is recommended in some books and will be recognised as practically
an admixture of two others already mentioned. No doubt it
will be found serviceable : 1 pint of spirits of wine, 2oz. gum
sandarac, 2oz. orange shellac, dissolved by heat, add the
beeswax and turpentine mixture, and apply as directed on
flannel or cloth while the work is running in the lathe.

VARNISHES.—I give no recipes for making these, as it is a
dangerous process, and there is no sort of difficulty in procuring
them. Some of them are made with turps and some with
spirits of wine, and are light or dark. They are all brushed
on with a flat hog-hair tool, and the great secret is to lay it
on quickly, thinly, and evenly, in a warm, dry atmosphere, and
never to touch it till dry and hard, when a second coat may
be given, the first having been rubbed down with very fine or
worn glass-paper. As long as varnish is the least sticky or
tacky it must be left alone. The longer it is left to dry the
better. Very often no second coat will be needed, and there
is a varnish that dries so quickly that it has to be laid on
with great speed and dexterity. It is probably made with
pure alcohol or ether instead of spirits of wine or turpentine.

INDEX.

1896.

No. 6 CATALOGUE

ENGINEERS' TOOLS

ETC.

PRICE SIXPENCE

BRITANNIA COMPANY

WAREHOUSES:

100 & 101, HOUNDSDITCH, LONDON

ALL CORRESPONDENCE TO

BRITANNIA WORKS, COLCHESTER, ENGLAND

MAKERS OF ENGINEERS' TOOLS TO THE
BRITISH GOVERNMENT

PRICES ARE SUBJECT TO ALTERATION WITHOUT NOTICE

INDEX.

THE LATEST ·IMPROV·ED
PETROLEUM OIL ENGINE
THE "FACILE"
(GIBBON'S PATENT),

SO CALLED BECAUSE IT IS

Easy to Start. *Easy to Clean.* *Easy to Manage.*

ADVANTAGES.

ONLY **ONE** valve—**no lamp** (except a few minutes at starting).

No heating tube. No electricity. No vaporiser. A **separate explosion** chamber prevents the cylinder being unduly heated.

No dangerous oil or spirit used. **No blowing of fans**

The **most economical** engine yet invented. The oil is injected **directly into the cylinder.**

The **one valve**, which is used **can be taken out, cleaned and replaced in ten minutes**—this is a **special** feature.

Every part is **easily** detached **without displacing** other parts. The time required for cleaning is **reduced to a minimum.**

After starting. the **ignition is automatic,** and the Engine will run for many hours without attention.

It can be **started in six minutes.** The cheapest Petroleum can be used. Cost **about a half-penny** per horse-power per hour.

The **waste heat is utilized** to heat the ingoing charge, thus ensuring economy and reducing the quantity of water required to keep the Engine cool—an important advantage in Portable Engines.

GUARANTEE:—We undertake to replace or repair any part of these Engines within six months after date of delivery unless such wear or breakage is caused by careless or improper treatment.

TERMS:—One-third cash with order, One-third on delivery, and the balance in 28 days.

Packing for Shipment 5 per cent. extra.

Packing for Great Britain $2\frac{1}{2}$ per cent., two-thirds of which is allowed if package be returned promptly.

Terms for Foreign Orders:—One-third cash with order and balance with Bills of Lading in England.

☞ AGENTS ARE BEING APPOINTED. ☜

SOLE MAKERS—
BRITANNIA CO., COLCHESTER, England.

THE "FACILE"
PORTABLE PETROLEUM OIL ENGINES
(GIBBON'S PATENT.)

For 'Advantages' of this new patent Engine, see page I. And for Prices and Press Notices, see page 3.

FOR CONTRACTORS, FARMERS, &c.

(From a photograph of a 16 B.H.P. Portable Engine.)

BRITANNIA CO., COLCHESTER, England.

London Showrooms—100, Houndsditch.. All Letters to Colchester.

THE "FACILE"
PORTABLE PETROLEUM OIL ENGINES
(GIBBON'S PATENT.)

(For Advantages see page 1 and for Illustration see page 2).

PRICES

Actual Brake Horse Power	4	7	12	16	20
Revolutions	250	225	200	200	180
Price Complete	£135	£170	£265	£300	£325

These Engines are perfectly self-contained, and do not require any Tanks, or other fittings.

The Prices include everything necessary for running, including chocks and spare parts. The frames are exceptionally strong, and built for hard work. They are fitted with cooling apparatus which reduces the water used to a very small quantity. Driving Pulley and Shafts extra.

A cheaper form of Portable can be made in the smaller sizes (having a separate water tank), for which special quotations will be given.

"THE ENGINEER," July 5th, 1895.

"The governor acts on a cam, which leaves a trip finger more or less time in contact with the rod it pushes. The system of the Engine is one which combines the features of some others already known, as will be gathered from the engraving. . . . . In it one valve, like a large safety-valve with a piston body instead of wings, is employed as both main air valve and exhaust valve. The air, in passing into the cylinder, helps to keep this valve cool. The Engine is of the internal vaporiser type, the vaporiser also forming the ignition. . . . . . A shield is placed around the portion of the vaporising chamber and igniter within the combustion chamber, but with an intervening annular space, for the purpose of preventing the air entering the combustion chamber from impinging against the walls of the chamber and cooling it."

"ENGINEERING," June 28th, 1895.

"The new Engine made and shown by the Britannia Company is of the portable type. It has no separate igniting tube, the heat of the vaporising chamber firing the charge when the compression is complete. . . . . The oil is pumped directly into the base of the vaporising chamber. the amount being under the control of the governor, which actuates a trip gear, by which the throw of the pump is either reduced or prevented, according to the work upon the engine. At moderate loads the engine still explodes at each cycle, but with reduced charges. By this arrangement the combustion chamber is always kept hot."

BRITANNIA CO., COLCHESTER, England.

London Showrooms—100, Houndsditch.   All Letters to Colchester.

THE "FACILE"
(GIBBON'S PATENT).

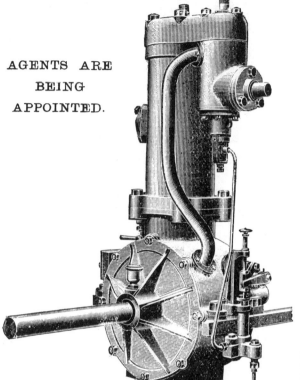

*AGENTS ARE
BEING
APPOINTED.*

REVOLUTION

IN

LAUNCH

ENGINES

These Engines can be fitted with cast iron bed plates and governors to be used as fixed engines.

* For Prices see opposite page.

The first practical Oil Motor for Launch and small boat work. The simplest in appearance and management yet invented.

ADVANTAGES.

No mechanically worked valves. Perfectly cased in, preventing escape of vapors or oil. **Cleaner than steam. No Coal or Boiler** room required. **No heating tube. No electricity. No vaporiser. A separate explosion** chamber prevents the cylinder being unduly heated. **No dangerous oil** or spirit used. **No blowing of fans.** The **most economical** engine yet invented. The oil is injected **directly into the cylinder.** Every part is **easily** detached **without displacing** other parts. The time required for cleaning is **reduced to a minimum.** After starting, the **ignition is automatic,** and the Engine will run for many hours without attention. It can be **started in six minutes.** The cheapest Petroleum can be used. The **waste heat is utilized** to heat the ingoing charge, thus ensuring economy and reducing the quantity of water required to keep the Engine cool—an important advantage in Launch Engines.

GUARANTEE:—We undertake to replace or repair any part of these Engines within six months after date of delivery, unless such wear or breakage is caused by careless or improper treatment.

TERMS:—One-third cash with order, one-third on delivery, and the balance in 28 days. Packing for Shipment, 5 per cent. extra. Packing for Great Britain, 2½ per cent., two-thirds of which is allowed if package be returned promptly.

Terms for Foreign Orders:—One-third cash with order and balance with Bill of Lading in England.

BRITANNIA CO., COLCHESTER, England.

London Showrooms—100, Houndsditch.   All Letters to Colchester.

BRITANNIA COMPANY'S
PATENT OIL ENGINES
FOR LAUNCHES, BARGES, OR OTHER BOATS.

PRICES OF LAUNCH ENGINES.

Actual brake horse power.	Approximate height.	Approximate breadth.	Approximate length.	Approximate weight.	Price of Engine only.	Price of Engine with governors.	Fitted with governor and bed plates for use as stationary engines.	Price of reversing gear or reversing propellor, stern tube & shafting.	Sheet iron cover for engine.
	ft. in.	ft. in.	ft. in.		£	£	£ s. d.	£ s. d.	£ s. d.
1	2 0	1 0	1 0	100 lbs.	40	45	*48 0 0	15 0 0	8 0 0
2	2 6	1 4	1 0	210 lbs.	50	55	58 0 0	17 0 0	9 0 0
*3	2 6	1 4	1 9	230 lbs.	55	60	62 0 0	20 0 0	9 10 0
*4	2 6	1 6	1 9	350 lbs.	75	82	86 0 0	25 0 0	10 0 0
*5	2 6	1 6	2 0	350 lbs.	85	92	96 0 0	30 0 0	10 10 0
*6	2 6	1 6	2 0	400 lbs.	100	107	112 0 0	30 0 0	11 0 0

* Are double cylinder.   The **3** horse power is also made with single cylinder.

PRICES OF ENGINES AND BOATS.	Price in Pine.	Price in elm or mahogany.	Approx speed	Weight of boat complete.	Extra for iron cover to engine.
	£	£	Miles	cwt.	£ s.
16ft. Boat, 4ft. beam, clinker built, varnished bright—the colour of the wood, fitted with 1 B.H.P. Engine and reversing propellor, with tank for 4 hours supply	90	95	4½	6½	7 10
*18ft. Boat, 4ft. 6in. beam fitted with 1 B.H.P. Engine, ditto for 4 hours supply	118	125	3½	10	8 0
*20ft. Boat, 5ft. beam, fitted with 2 B.H.P. Engine, ditto for 10 hours supply	150	165	6	13	9 0
*22ft. Boat, 5ft. beam, fitted with 2 B.H.P. Engine, ditto for 10 hours supply	155	171	5½	14	9 0
*22ft. 6in. Boat, 5ft. 6in. beam, fitted with 3 B.H.P. Engine, ditto for 10 hours supply	198	215	6¼	19	9 10
*25ft. Boat, 5ft. 6in. beam, fitted with 3 B.H.P. Engine, ditto for 10 hours supply	208	225	6	21	9 10

* These Boats are fit for Yachts' Launches.   Engines can be made to lift out.

Each of the above are provided with pair of Oars and Boat Hook, and every boat is tried and tested before being sent out.

For larger Engines and Launches send details of size required and we will quote.   Prices subject to alteration without notice.

These Engines can be started in 6 minutes, and use less than A PINT of OIL per brake horse power per hour, costing under a half-penny.

BRITANNIA CO., COLCHESTER, England.

London Showrooms—100, Houndsditch.   All Letters to Colchester.

HORSELESS CARRIAGES

Important Notice.

THE "FACILE" CARRIAGE MOTOR.

BRITANNIA CO.,

COLCHESTER, ENGLAND.

MAKERS OF ENGINEERS' TOOLS, &c.,

Beg to announce that they are now making Petroleum Oil Motors, and draw attention to some

SPECIAL ADVANTAGES.

1st. **Ordinary** Petroleum Lamp **Oil** is used instead of the more dangerous **inflammable** spirit or essence required by other engines.

2nd. Oil for these engines can be obtained in any village, and the cost is **less than half the cost of spirit.**

3rd. **No constant** burning lamp nor ignition tube is required, nor any driving belts, which slip and break, and are **the cause of trouble.**

4th. Patent speed variation gear, by which the carriage can be made to travel **fast or slow** while the engine **runs at its ordinary speed.** This is **most important.**

5th. Self-acting governor to adjust the speed of engine on ascending or descending hills, so saving one handle and being automatic.

6th. The great feature of the Motor is **its simplicity** and the **few working parts,** thus making it **easy** to manage.

7th. Only two handles and one foot lever are required on this engine, and very many intricate parts are dispensed with, which other engines require.

*In fact **it is THE** "Facile" engine, and is in advance of all others, and is equally adapted for Launches.*

IT IS OF SPECIAL DESIGN AND DIFFERENT FROM ANY OTHER ENGINE.

BRITANNIA CO., COLCHESTER, England.

London Showrooms—100, Houndsditch.   All Letters to Colchester.

THE BRITANNIA COMPANY'S
"FACILE" MOTORS
(GIBBON'S PATENT.)

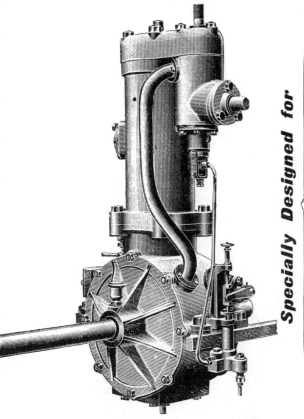

Specially Designed for

CARRIAGES

OMNIBUSES

TRICYCLES

LAUNCHES

TRAM CARS

LIGHT

RAILWAYS

APPROXIMATE PRICES OF CARRIAGES WITH MOTORS.

Three-wheel Carriage, fitted with a one-horse improved patent Motor, and improved gear for transmitting power to carry one person (or two in an emergency), estimated speed 2 to 10 miles per hour on level roads ... ... Price complete **£100**

Three-wheel Carriage, fitted with a two-horse improved patent Motor, and improved gear for transmitting power, to carry two persons side by side, estimated speed 2 to 14 miles per hour on level roads Price complete **£150**

Four-wheel Carriage, "Vis-a-Vis" style, fitted with a four-horse improved patent Motor and improved gear for transmitting power, estimated speed 2 to 15 miles per hour on level roads ... Price **£210**

The above prices are subject to alteration without notice.

FOREIGN PATENTS FOR THESE ENGINES AND CARRIAGES FOR SALE OR TO BE WORKED ON ROYALTY.

BRITANNIA CO., COLCHESTER, England.

London Showrooms—100, *Houndsditch*   *All Letters to Colchester.*

THE "FACILE"
PETROLEUM OIL ENGINES
(GIBBON'S PATENT).

(From a Photograph of a 12 B.H.P. Engine).

For prices see page 9, for description see page 1.

BRITANNIA CO., COLCHESTER, England.

London Showrooms—100, Houndsditch.   All Letters to Colchester.

THE "FACILE" PETROLEUM OIL ENGINES.

For illustration see opposite page.

Especially adapted for Electric Light, and suitable for every purpose for which power is required.

The economy is great compared with all others. The cost per Brake Horse Power is about one halfpenny per hour. The specific gravity of the Oil is ·8 upwards, the consumption is about one pint per hour per brake horse power; the running cost is therefore less than in Gas Engines or in any other Oil Engine.

Patented in England and abroad. Reward offered for infringements.

We are making a speciality of Pumps and Engines combined. Estimates and drawings supplied upon application.

PRICES.

Actual or Brake Horse Power.	Price.	Revolutions per Minute.	Approximate Weight of Engine.	Approximate Dimensions of Engine.	Prices of Water Tanks charged extra.	Usual size of Pulley charged extra.	Price of Pulleys.	Extra Flywheel.	Foundation Bolts.
1 Horizontal	£60	300	3¼ cwt.	2 ft. 3 in. × 3 ft. 3 in.	£1 10 0	9 in. × 3 in.	£0 6 0	£2 15 0	£0 5 0
2 ,,	75	260	9 ,,	4 ft. 7 in. × 2 ft. 1 in.	2 15 0	9 in. × 4 in.	0 6 0	3 15 0	0 7 6
3½ ,,	92	240	13½ ,,	5 ft. 9 in. × 3 ft. 0 in.	5 0 0	12 in. × 6 in.	0 9 0	4 15 0	0 10 0
5 ,,	110	230	18 ,,	6 ft. 0 in. × 3 ft. 3 in.	5 10 0	15 in. × 6 in.	0 10 0	5 15 0	0 10 0
7 ,,	130	220	24 ,,	7 ft. 0 in. × 3 ft. 6 in.	7 0 0	20 in. × 7 in.	0 18 6	6 10 0	0 12 6
12 ,,	175	210	30 ,,	8 ft. 0 in. × 4 ft. 0 in.	9 0 0	24 in. × 7 in.	1 3 6	Other sizes quoted for.	1 0 0
15 ,,	210	200	35 ,,	9 ft. 0 in. × 4 ft. 6 in.	10 0 0	30 in. × 7 in.	1 10 0		1 0 0
20 ,,	260	200	46 ,,	10 ft. 0 in. × 4 ft. 6 in.	12 0 0	30 in. × 8 in.	1 13 0		1 5 0
*24 ,,	300	200	64 ,,	8 ft. 6 in. × 5 ft. 6 in.	14 0 0	30 in. × 9 in.	1 16 0		1 10 0
*30 ,,	350	200	74 ,,	9 ft. 6 in. × 5 ft. 9 in.	21 0 0	36 in. × 12 in.	2 17 6		1 10 0
*40 ,,	400	200	83 ,,	10 ft. 6 in. × 6 ft. 0 in.	28 0 0	36 in. × 12 in.	2 17 6		1 10 0

* Are Double Cylinder.   NOTICE.—Prices are subject to alteration without notice.

The prices include exhaust box and everything necessary for running except pulley, water tank, cock, piping and foundation bolts. The fixing costs little, and the engine is entirely self-contained.

BRITANNIA CO., COLCHESTER, England.

London Showrooms—100, *Houndsditch.*   *All Letters to Colchester.*

HORIZONTAL BORING DRILLING, AND SURFACING MACHINE.

No. 42.

FOR LARGE WORK.

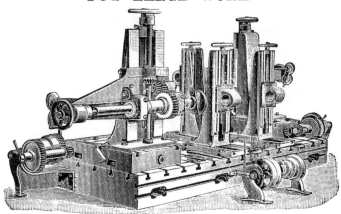

THESE machines are constructed with powerfully geared boring heads, having **steel spindles**, driven by strong spur and mitre gearing, with variable feed, **self-acting in either direction,** or stationary for surfacing; the heads are mounted on upright, **heavy, rigidly constructed** slides, with vertical adjustment by screw and hand-wheel, and transverse adjustment by rack and pinion. The upright bar rests are made with socket heads to carry the boring bar and bushes, one bar rest at each side of the work, and are also **adjustable vertically** by screws and hand-wheels. The driving cone pulleys have four speeds, and double gearing is fitted, giving **eight changes** of speed. The whole is mounted on a machine-planed **heavy foundation** bed-plate with T slots for bolting work to. The machine above illustrated has **steel spindles** $3\frac{1}{4}$ inches diameter, and is capable of boring holes up to **24 inches diameter** by 42 inches long, and has a **double set of boring heads** and bar rests, the foundation plate being 12 feet by 5 feet, but the machines are made **of all sizes to suit Purchasers' requirements; and estimates will be given on application.**

Price of above Machine on rails at Colchester with Top Driving Apparatus, &c., complete   ..   ..   **£200.**

Weight about 7½ tons.

Smaller machines driven by single gear, boring up to 12 inches diameter. made on similar principle—price with bed 13 ft. by 5 ft., to bore up to 12 in. hole, **£120.** Other sizes to order.

BRITANNIA CO., COLCHESTER, England.

London Showrooms—100, *Houndsditch.*   *All Letters to Colchester.*

HORIZONTAL BORING, DRILLING, AND FACING MACHINE.

No. 41.

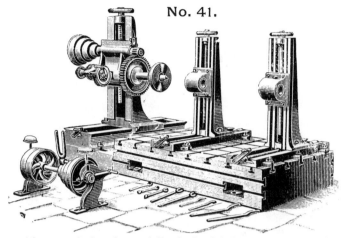

THESE machines are designed especially for boring heavy objects having several holes to bore parallel to each other, of which **any number can be bored at one setting,** as the boring head and rests for the boring bar are fitted with compound motion to adjust to the greatest accuracy, both vertically and horizontally, by screw and nut motion, with convenient handles.

The bed plate is a massive casting 9 feet long by 4 feet wide and 12 inches high, having T slots both longitudinally and transversely on its top face, and longitudinally on its side faces. The top, sides and long slots are all accurately planed parallel, and at one end of the bed plate is fixed, at right angles to its length, a truly planed V edged slide, carrying the vertical slide on which is mounted the saddle of the boring head.

The boring head is constructed with single geared motion, 4-speed cone pulley with pinion and spur gearing, feed motion by hand or self-acting by differential wheels, the wheel for hand feed being conveniently placed at the front, always accessible to the operator, particularly useful when starting the cut or facing work. The main spindle **is of steel**, and fitted in a sleeve revolving with the spur wheel keyed to it.

The pinion is thrown in or out of gear by a **clutch and lever to start and stop instantly** irrespective of the countershaft motion. The machine, as illustrated, is constructed to bore up to 24 inches in length and 12 inches in diameter ; and the general dimensions are as follows :—

Diameter of main steel spindle, $3\frac{1}{4}$ inches.
Diameter of gearing, $16\frac{1}{2}$ inches and $3\frac{3}{4}$ inches by 1 inch pitch
Diameter of speed cone, largest 13 inches, smallest 5 inches.
Width and number of speeds, 4 by $3\frac{1}{2}$ inches.
Maximum length and diameter to bore 24 inches by 12 inches.
Maximum and minimum height to bore from face of bed plate, 35 inches and $6\frac{1}{4}$ inches.
Maximum horizontal range of boring head, 46 inches.
Approximate weight, $3\frac{1}{4}$ tons.

Price complete, with Top Driving Apparatus, Spanners, Keys, &c. .. **£135**

Prices subject to fluctuations without notice.

BRITANNIA CO., COLCHESTER, England.

London Showrooms—100. *Houndsditch.*　　*All Letters to Colchester.*

VERTICAL BORING MACHINE,

No. 43.

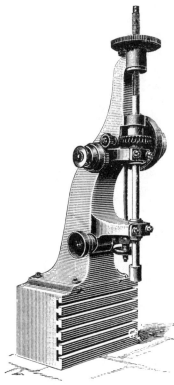

THIS machine is designed for boring **vertically** pump bodies, cylinders, or any similar work, the borings falling clear through the work. It is intended to be fixed on a bench, or may be mounted on a cast-iron box foundation base, with T slot (as illustrated), to which can be bolted the work, or an angle bracket can be attached, on which small work, as plummer blocks, &c., may be secured.

The dimensions are as follows:—

Steel spindle, 2½ inches diameter.

Driving cone, 4 speeds, 3¼ inches wide.

Diameters of largest and smallest speeds, 17½ inches and 7 inches.

Feed cones, 3 speeds, 1¾ inches wide.

Diameters of largest and smallest speeds, 7 inches and 4 inches.

Worm gearing, 2 inches pitch, double threads.

Feed wheels, 35 and 105 teeth, 7 pitch.

Diameter of driving shaft, 2⅛ inches.

Height, without base, 7 feet 6 inches.

Takes in diameter, 2 feet 4 inches.

Approximate weight, without base, 15 cwts.

Price, with Top Driving Apparatus complete, but without Base, **£50.**

BRITANNIA CO., COLCHESTER, England.

London Showrooms—100, *Houndsditch.*   *All Letters to Colchester.*

MILLING MACHINE, No. 1.

THIS is a very useful tool, capable of a large range of work, and will be found a great economiser of labour. From the illustration the principal features of the machine will be readily understood.

The bed is six feet long, with V Slide truly planed. The Traversing Table has also a vertical traverse of 12 inches, and horizontal of 9 inches.

The Headstock is back geared and with 4-speed cone pulley for $2\frac{1}{4}$ in. strap. The gearing is $1\frac{3}{4}$ in. by $\frac{5}{8}$ in. pitch, and is put in and out by an eccentric. The Spindle is of cast steel, running through, and with coned bearings. The neck of the Spindle is $2\frac{1}{4}$ in. diameter, and the nose bored conically 2 in. to 1 in. and screwed beyond to take mandrils for milling cutters. A strong adjustable arm traversing in a rest is used to support outer end of mandril when necessary, and can be readily removed when not required.

Table 36 in. long by 12 in. wide, longitudinal motion 36 in., vertical motion, 14 in., cross motion, 9 in., 6 changes of speeds, floor space occupied 84 by 54 in.

By using the arm, very wide cutters or a series of cutters can be used, for wide surfaces or any irregular form which may be required.

It is fitted with rack and pinion to work the saddle back quickly.

This tool has many advantages over planing machines in point of variety of uses to which it can be put, as well as its more rapid operation.

Price, Including Overhead Motion, one Mandril and Spanner, **£60.**

BRITANNIA CO., COLCHESTER, England.

*London Showrooms—*100, *Houndsditch. All Letters to Colchester.*

MILLING MACHINE, No. 10, SINGLE GEARED.

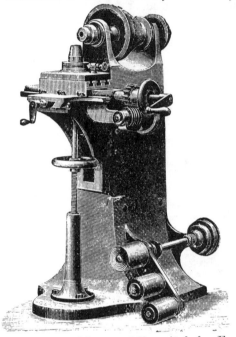

Improved Apparatus

for Sharpening Cutters,

£6 10 0.

———

Cutters made

to any shape to

order.

THIS is a machine specially suited for Engineers, Brass Finishers, Gun Smiths, Sewing Machine, Bicycle, and other small Machine Makers. It has a steel spindle with conical neck, steel lock nuts to take up wear and receive thrust in face work, and the nose is screwed and coned for chucks. It is fitted with longitudinal, transverse, and vertical slides; is self-acting in longitudinal by the most improved worm and wheel feed, and the vertical actuated by a convenient wheel and screw movement in front. A tray for tools is fitted at the side. An overhead motion with fast and loose, and cone pulleys, countershaft, hangers, and strap shifting gear is included in the price. When required for milling squares, hexagons, octagons, &c., as nuts or brass cocks and fittings, a very convenient dividing appliance can be supplied as shown on the illustration. The hollow body is fitted with a door and shelves for cutters, &c.

DIMENSIONS AND PRICES.

Extreme width, 2 ft. 8 in. ; extreme measure back to front, 3 ft. ; knee slide has a projection of 10 in. ; longitudinal slide, 20 in. long ; 3 changes of feed.

The Slides traverse Longitudinally .. .. .. 13½ inches.
,, ,, Transversely (*i.e.*, on knee slide) .. 4½ ,,
,, ,, Vertically .. .. 12 ,,

Work table is 11¾ in. by 6 in., with T grooves. Cone Pulley has 4 speeds for 2 in. belt. Total height is 3 ft. 7 in. Height to centre, 3 ft. 2 in. Approximate weight, 5½ cwt.

Price complete £24 0 0
Dividing Appliance 2 10 0
Parallel Vice to suit 2 0 0

BRITANNIA CO., COLCHESTER, England.

London Showrooms—100, Houndsditch. All Letters to Colchester.

SINGLE GEARED NO. 9
UNIVERSAL MILLING MACHINE.

This Machine has the table arranged to swivel to any angle and graduated to 45° either way, for spiral and angular milling.

It is fitted in all parts with great care and accuracy; the knee and horizontal slides are all scraped and fitted square and true, and with great precision for accurate work, and have loose adjusting strips to take up wear. All the hand adjustments are conveniently placed for the operator.

The long work table has planed T slots for attaching the work, and has a tray around it for catching the soap and water.

The main spindle is of steel, running in hard gun metal coned bearings, with adjustment for taking up wear, and is fitted with a chuck to receive the cutter mandrils.

It is fitted with improved telescopic self-acting feed, as well as quick hand feed, and with overhanging arm and adjustable centre to steady the outer end of long mandrils when using large cutters. The transverse and vertical motions are adjusted by hand wheels and screws. The self-acting feed has three changes of speed.

THE PRINCIPAL DIMENSIONS ARE AS FOLLOW:—

Longitudinal slide, 31 inches long.

Table, 24 inches long by 10 inches wide.

The traverses are—longitudinal, 15 in.; transverse, 7½ in.; vertical, 16 in.

Cone pulley has 4 speeds 2½ in. wide; largest, 10 in. diameter; smallest, 4½ in.

Height over all, 4 ft. 4 in.

Width, 3 ft. Depth, back to front, 4 ft.

Approximate weight, 14 cwt.

PRICE complete, with Top Driving Apparatus, Screw Keys, &c., &c. &55 0 0
Parallel Vice, with Swivelling Jaw, to suit 3 5 0
Spiral Appliance, as illustrated with the No. 13 Machine, with Dividing
 Head and Cut Change Wheels, &c., complete 22 0 0
Simple Dividing Appliance, with Tangent Worm and Wheel motion . 3 15 0

BRITANNIA CO., COLCHESTER, England.

London Showrooms—100, *Houndsditch.* *All Letters to Colchester.*

MILLING MACHINE, No. 12, DOUBLE GEARED.

£6 10s.

Improved Apparatus for Sharpening Cutters

Cutters made to any shape to order.

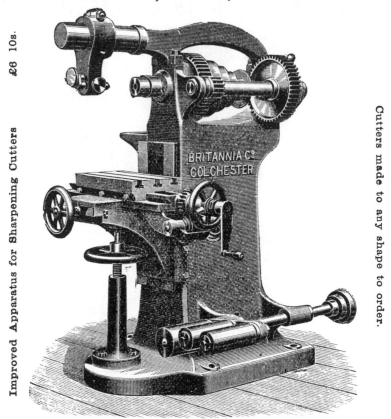

THE knee slide is accurately fitted to the front of the body or column, and rises and falls 14 inches, giving 15½ inches from top of work table to centre of spindle when at its lowest, and is adjusted by a vertical screw, and conveniently placed handwheel. The longitudinal slide is 24 in. long and 7½ in. wide, and has a transverse traverse, *i.e.*, parallel with axis of spindle of 7½ in., adjusted by handwheel and screw.

The work table is 24 in. long and 8½ in. wide, with T slots planed out for fixing the work, and has a longitudinal traverse of 18 in., self-acting by worm and wheel, and friction cone, and is provided with trough to catch soap and water. The belt cone pulley for self-acting feed, has three steps.

All the slides are accurately scraped and fitted, and have loose angle strips to adjust for wear. All traverse screws are steel, and all material is of the best. The whole is fitted and finished in a superior manner, and is a thoroughly reliable tool.

DIMENSIONS.—Height over all, 4 ft. 4 in. ; width, 3 ft. ; depth, 4 ft. ; diameter of main spindle, 1⅝ in. ; cone pulley has 4 speeds, 2¼ in. wide ; diameter of largest speed, 8½ in., and of smallest, 3¾ in. ; gearing is ⅝ in. pitch, and 2 in. on face ; diameters of gearing, 10 in. and 3¼ in. ; diameter of fast and loose pulleys, 10 in. and 3 in. wide ; eight changes of speed. Total weight about 12 cwt. with the back gearing.

	£	s.	d.
Price, including top driving apparatus, screw keys, &c., &c., complete ...	45	0	0
Parallel vice with swivelling jaw to suit	3	5	0
Dividing appliance with tangent worm and wheel for squares, hexagons, &c.	3	15	0

BRITANNIA CO., COLCHESTER, England.

London Showrooms—100, *Houndsditch.* All Letters to *Colchester.*

DOUBLE-GEARED MILLING MACHINE, No. 8.

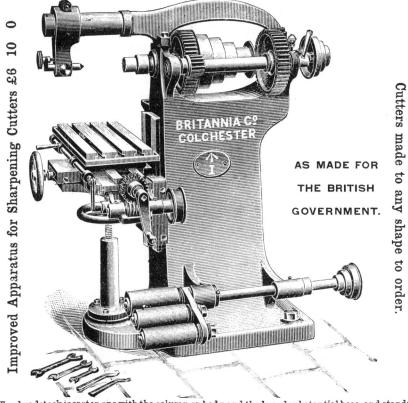

Improved Apparatus for Sharpening Cutters £6 10 0

BRITANNIA C?
COLCHESTER

AS MADE FOR

THE BRITISH

GOVERNMENT.

Cutters made to any shape to order.

The headstock is cast in one with the column or body and the broad substantial base, and stands firmly for its work. The body is a hollow box casting with door, and fitted inside with shelves for cutters and tools. A shelf or tray for tools and cutters is also fitted at the left-hand outside.

The spindle of headstock is steel with conical neck running in hard gun-metal bearings, and constructed with loose back cone to take up wear, and the front is coned and screwed internally for fitting and holding very firmly the chucks and cutter mandrels, and is fitted with a cone pulley having four speeds of 2¼ wide, and which, with the powerful back gearing, gives eight changes of speed, and great capacity for work.

The back gearing is put in and out of gear by eccentric motion.

The headstock is also fitted with a top arm (which is removable at pleasure) carrying an adjustable centre, to steady the end of a long cutter mandrel when using extra large, or groups of cutters.

The knee-slide is accurately fitted to the front of the body or column, and rises and falls 16 inches, giving 15½ inches from top of work table to centre of spindle when at its lowest, and is adjusted by a vertical screw and conveniently placed hand-wheel. The longitudinal slide is 31 inches long and 7½ inches wide, and has a transverse traverse, *i.e.* parallel with axis of spindle, of 7⅛ inches, adjusted by handle and screw.

The work table is 24 inches long, 10 inches wide, with T slots planed out for fixing the work, and has a longitudinal traverse of 15 inches, self-acting by worm and wheel and clutch, and has a trough around it to catch the soap and water. The belt cone pulley for self-acting feed has three steps, which give three changes of feed.

The work table is also fitted with adjustable automatic stop arrangement, enabling the feed to be disengaged at any desired position.

All the slides are accurately scraped and fitted, and have loose angle strips to adjust for wear. All traverse screws are steel, and all material is of the best. The whole is fitted and finished in a superior manner, and is a thoroughly reliable tool.

DIMENSIONS.

Height over all, 4ft. 4in. ; width, 3ft. ; depth, 4ft.	Diameters of gearing, 10 in. and 3¼ in. [wide.
Diameter of main spindle, 1⅝ in.	Diam. of fast and loose pulleys, 10 in. and 3 in.
Cone Pulley has 4 speeds, 2¼ in. wide. [3¾ in	Eight changes of speed.
Diameter of largest speed, 8½ in. wide, and of smallest,	Three changes of feed.
Gearing is ⅝ in. pitch and 2 in. on face.	Total weight, about 12 cwt.

PRICE, including Top Driving Apparatus, Screw Keys, &c., &c. (complete) ..	£51	0	0
Parallel Vice with Swivelling Jaw to suit	3	5	0
Dividing Appliance with Tangent Worm and Wheel for Squares, Hexagons, &c.	3	15	0

BRITANNIA CO., COLCHESTER, England.

*London   Showrooms—*100, *Houndsditch.   All Letters to Colchester.*

UNIVERSAL DOUBLE GEARED MILLING MACHINES, No. 13.

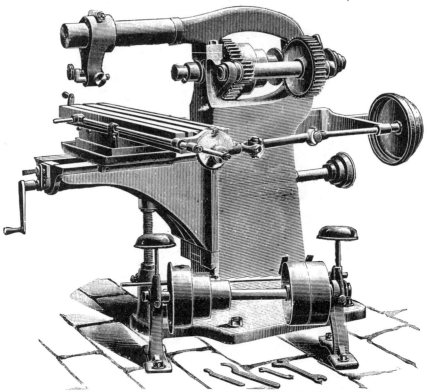

This Machine is of similar construction to the No. 12 Machine, but it is much heavier, and the slides are all much longer, giving a far greater range of work, and it is also fitted with the Universal Swivelling Arrangement, which, with the suitable appliance and wheels, enables skew gearing, spirals, and twist drills to be cut.

The longitudinal slide is also fitted with an automatic stop arrangement, to **stop at any given distance** the machine is set to. The self-acting feed is constructed on the most improved method by means of **universal swivelling** joints and telescopic shafts The machine is most accurately and carefully constructed, and is highly recommended for milling all kinds of fittings where **great precision and accuracy** are desired, and by its self-acting arrangements great economy of labour is effected, **as one man can attend to two or more machines.**

THE GENERAL DIMENSIONS OF THE MACHINE ARE AS FOLLOW:—

The Knee Slide has a projection of 20 inches and rises and falls by hand wheel and vertical screw through a range of 16 inches.

The Longitudinal Slide is 12½ inches long having a transverse traverse on the knee side of 8 inches.

The Work Table is 3 feet by 9 inches wide with planed T slots for securing the work, and has a longitudinal traverse either by hand or self-acting of 1 foot 9 inches.

The Cone Pulley has 3 speeds 3 inches wide, the largest being 10 inches in diameter and the smallest 6½ inches.

Six changes of speed.

The Gearing is ⅝ inch pitch 2 inches on face, the diameter of the large gear 11 inches and small 6½ inches.

Diameters of Pulleys on countershaft 11½ inches by 3 inch face.

Total height of machine 4 feet 4 inches, width 4 feet 4 inches, and depth 6 feet.

Approximate weight 22 cwt.

	£	s	d
Price with top Driving Apparatus, Screw Keys, Spanners, &c Complete ...	77	10	0
Parallel Vice with swivelling jaw to suit	3	5	0
Ditto ditto with swivelling bottom and very strong make	5	10	0
Simple Dividing Appliance with tangent worm and wheel motion giving divisions of 48 and its multiples	3	15	0
Improved Dividing Appliance	14	10	0
Spiral Appliance for Milling Twist Drills, &c., with change wheels for various pitches,	22	0	0

BRITANNIA CO., COLCHESTER, England.

London Showrooms—100, Houndsditch.   All Letters to Colchester.

SPIRAL MILLING

BY

No. 13 UNIVERSAL MACHINE.

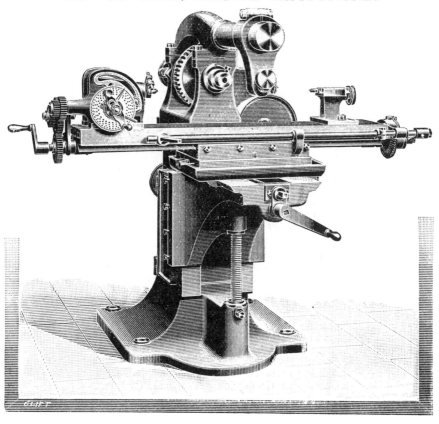

THE illustration shows our No. 13 Milling Machine, but fitted with the spiral attachment constructed for grooving twist drills, cutting spiral gearing, cutters, &c.

The appliance is arranged to fit on the longitudinal slide of the machine, the headstock having a steel mandril with carrier for driving the work, and to be used either in a horizontal position or vertical, or at any angle between, and geared up by mitre gears and change wheels to revolve at any required pitch of spiral, from 1 inch to 40 inches, and is further fitted with worm-wheel and worm, which, in conjunction with the division plate and index and sextant fitted to the worm shaft, will divide drills, gear wheels, &c., up to 360 divisions.

The spiral movement can be given to the mandril at any angle.

The price includes eight change wheels and necessary keys, spanners, &c.

	£	s.	d.
Price of Spiral Appliance for No. 13 Milling Machine	22	0	0
„ of No 13 Milling Machine with Spiral Appliance, Top Driving Appliance, Screw Keys, Spanners, &c. (complete)	99	10	0
,. of Parallel Vice with Swivelling Bottom, and very strong pattern	5	10	0

BRITANNIA CO., COLCHESTER, England.

London Showrooms—100, *Houndsditch.*   *All Letters to Colchester.*

APPLIANCE FOR SHARPENING CUTTERS FOR MILLING MACHINES, &c.

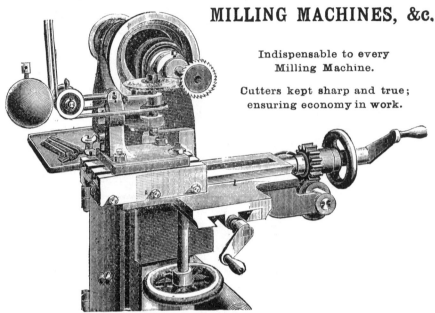

Indispensable to every Milling Machine.

Cutters kept sharp and true; ensuring economy in work.

THE above appliance, illustrated as in use on a Milling Machine, is designed as a handy device to fit on the table of an ordinary Milling Machine, to sharpen its cutters. It is intended to be driven from the countershaft of the machine, and adjusted to correct position for grinding by the slides of the machine, the cutter to be sharpened being meantime held in its usual position as for cutting in the mandril of the headstock, the driving belt of the latter being, of course, thrown off for the time.

The appliance is constructed with a firm base to bolt to machine table, and has a swivelling head carrying a steel spindle with driving pulley fitted, and arranged to hold an emery wheel at its end.

It has a pair of guide pulleys which swivel and slide upon a hinged lever, with a heavy weight at its end to keep the driving gut tight.

When in operation the emery wheel is brought into contact with the cutter, and the latter is turned by moving the cone pulley by hand, bringing each successive tooth in contact with the emery wheel.

The latter being fitted to swivel can be arranged to suit cutters having teeth cut square across or obliquely, and can also be used with a square-edged emery wheel, to run in a vertical direction, and sharpen the cutter by grinding the tops of the teeth, which is sometimes preferable.

It is useful also for backing off taps and reamers, flute drills, &c.

Price of the Appliance	..	..	..	£4 0 0
Or with Overhead for driving it independently		..		6 10 0

BRITANNIA CO., COLCHESTER, England.

London Showrooms—100, *Houndsditch.*   *All Letters to Colchester.*

DIVIDING APPLIANCE

FOR MILLING AND SHAPING.

Price £14 10s.

AS SUPPLIED TO THE ROYAL ARSENAL.

ENGINEERS' VICE

(STRONG PATTERN, WITH SWIVEL BOTTOM),

FOR MILLING AND PLANING.

Price   -   -   -   £5 10s.

STRONG ORDINARY PATTERN PLANER VICES

With one Jaw to swivel to grip parallel or taper work.

Width of Jaw	3 in.	4½ in.	5 in.	6 in.	7 in.
To take in -	4 in.	6 in.	7½ in.	9 in.	12 in.
Price -	40/-	56/·	72/·	90/-	115/-

DRILLING MACHINES

IN GREAT VARIETY AND ALL PRICES.

PLANING MACHINES, SHAPING MACHINES, SLOTTING MACHINES
MILLING MACHINES AND ENGINEERS' TOOLS

Of every description.

☞ TOOLS DESIGNED, OR MADE TO DRAWING
For Special Work.

BRITANNIA CO., COLCHESTER, England.

London Showrooms—100, *Houndsditch.*   *All Letters to Colchester.*

IMPROVED
SELF-ACTING PLANING MACHINE

THESE planers are constructed with the recent improvements. Self-acting in horizontal, vertical and angular cuts, with quick return. The slides are fitted with oil cups. They are adapted for hard and accurate wear. Spanners are included.

Height.	Width.	Length.	Price.	Approximate Weight.	Extra per foot long.
2 ft. 0 in.	2 ft. 0 in.	4 ft.	£	31 cwt.	£
2 ft. 6 in.	2 ft. 6 in.	6 ft.		55 cwt.	

POWERFULLY GEARED
SELF-ACTING PLANING MACHINE

THIS is a newly designed planer, embracing the latest improvements. It is self-acting in vertical, horizontal and angular cuts, self-oiling lubricators. The material and workmanship is guaranteed, and the gearing is strong and accurate. Spanners, &c., are included.

Height.	Width.	Length.	Price.	Approximate Weight.	Extra per foot long.	For Extra Tool Box.
3 ft. 3 in.	3 ft. 3 in.	10 ft.	£	95 cwt.	£	£

BRITANNIA CO., COLCHESTER, England.
London Showrooms—100, *Houndsditch.*   *All Letters to Colchester.*

IMPROVED PLANING MACHINE,

No. 8.

8 ft. by 3 ft. by 3 ft.

WITH ONE OR TWO TOOL BOXES.

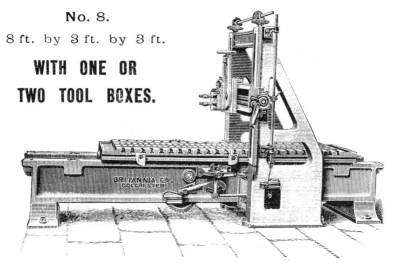

NEW and improved type, massive and rigid construction. The bed well ribbed with box ribs, V Slides, oil channel and four lubricating wells and spring action rollers on each side, and waste oil wells at each end. The Table very massive, accurately scraped to bed, and driven by intermediate spur gearing, giving a larger pinion to gear into the rack, thus gaining power by the longer leverage, and less liability to break teeth, because more teeth are engaged with the rack in driving. It has quick return movement. The feed is arranged on a novel and ingenious method, absolutely certain in its action, and giving only the exact movement to the belt fork to shift the belt from the forward to the backward pulley, or to the loose for stopping, and under the perfect control of the operator. It is self-acting in all cuts.

The bevil pinions giving motion to the self-acting vertical and angular feeds in the machine fitted with two Tool Boxes, are carried on slides, and made to engage by an eccentric movement. The Tool Boxes are constructed with a lip at lower end to take the thrust of the cut, relieving the swivelling pin and giving increased durability to the machine. The tool is constructed throughout with the greatest care, of the best materials and workmanship, and is complete with spanners and keys.

The chief dimensions are as follows—

The machine admits and will plane 8 ft. by 3 ft. by 3 ft. The Bed is 12 ft. long by 25 in. wide by 15½ in. deep.

GEARING—1st Motion. Spur wheel 14¾ in., pinion 5¾ in., 3 in. face, and 1 in. pitch.

2nd Motion. Spur wheel 20½ in., pinion 6½ in., 3½ in. face, and 1⅛ in. pitch.

Rack Gear. 5 in. face and 1¼ in. pitch, intermediate wheel, 17 in. diam., pinion 6¼ in. diam.

Pulleys—20 in. diam. by 4 in. wide. Approximate Weight—5 Tons.

	£	s.	d.
Price complete, with One Tool Box	120	0	0
Extra for Two Tool Boxes	11	10	0
Extra per foot for longer Table and Bed	5	10	0

BRITANNIA CO., COLCHESTER, England.

London Showrooms—100, *Houndsditch.* *All Letters to Colchester.*

SELF-ACTING PLANER, FOR HAND AND STEAM POWER.

THIS Machine is fitted with rack and pinion, 3 pulleys, and flywheel with 4 handles, quick return motion, self-feeding in the longitudinal motion.

Number		1	2	3
Take in length		16in.	24in.	32in.
Do. width	..	12in.	16in.	18in.
Do. under tool box		8in.	12in.	16in.

Number	1	2	3
Price	£21 5s.	£31 5s.	£41 5s.
Weight	5½ cwt.	10 cwt.	14 cwt.

BRITANNIA CO., COLCHESTER, England.

London Showrooms—100, Houndsditch.   All Letters to Colchester.

IMPROVED SLOTTING MACHINE.

THE annexed engraving illustrates a machine with the following advantages:—

The table cants over for cutting taper key ways, &c , &c.

It has longitudinal, transverse and circular motions, each can be disengaged independently, and are self-acting.

The ram is made with long bearings and compensation balance lever which acts in any position with the ram.

The end of the lever is slotted and carries a sliding block from crank pin, which gives an adjustable stroke and quick return.

The link is fixed at the extreme end of lever of ram, thus giving a direct thrust without side strain, and so avoiding considerable wear and friction.

The bearings of the ram are long, thus ensuring firmness and accuracy of stroke.

A long or short stroke can be given, either close to the table, or at the extreme end.

The adjusting screw for regulating height of ram is in front, but all movements of tables and slides are on the side where the man stands, thus saving much inconvenience, all being within reach of the workman. This is a contrast to other similar machines which require the man to mount the table and to move from one side of the machine to the other, to adjust the various movements.

The cone is *parallel* to the shafting and enables the machine to be fixed near the shafting and not at right angles. It is fitted with top driving apparatus, screw keys, &c.

				12in.	14in.	18in.
Length of Stroke	...	...	...	12in.	14in.	18in.
To admit { In diameter		...	...	4ft.	5ft.	6ft.
In depth	...	...	...	1ft. 8in.	2ft. 4in.	3ft. 0in.
Traverse of Table Slides { Longitudinally				2ft. 4in.	3ft. 0in.	3ft. 6in.
Transverse		...		2ft. 2in.	2ft. 6in.	3ft. 0in.
Approximate Weight	...	...	...	55cwt.	70cwt.	140 cwt.
Price	...	...	...	£	£	£

BRITANNIA CO., COLCHESTER, England.

London Showrooms —100. *Houndsditch.*   *All Letters to Colchester.*

8in. STROKE SLOTTING MACHINE,
No. 57.

POWERFUL single-geared machine of neat design and improved construction. The ram has a long continuous bearing with adjustable strip, and arranged with quick return motion controlled by slotted lever actuated by block on crank pin. It is also fitted with a compensating balance weight, which acts in any position with ram. The crank disc runs in a recess bored out in body casting, and its wear is taken up by means of an adjustable block at top. The stroke is altered by means of square thread screw in crank disc the position of stroke being regulated by screw and hand wheel at top. Compound Slides fitted with circular table having horizontal, transverse, and circular, self-acting feed motions varied and adjusted independently of each other, and actuated by cam on crank shaft.

DIMENSIONS.

Cone pulley, 4 speeds 3½in. wide, largest 17in. diam., smallest 8¼in. diam.
Gearing, 1¼in. pitch 3¾in wide, wheel 33½in. diam., pinion 5½in. diam.
Circular Table 24in. diam.

Longitudinal Traverse of 17in.
Transverse Traverse of 13in.
Admits work up to 3ft. diam. by 14in. deep.
Approximate Weight 2¼ tons.

PRICE .. .. £

BRITANNIA CO., COLCHESTER, England.
London Showrooms—100, Houndsditch.   All Letters to Colchester.

IMPROVED 4½ in. SLOTTING MACHINE, No. 55

A COMPACT and most convenient tool for small work. It is single geared, with adjustable stroke up to 4½ inch, and adjustable in the ram to any position to suit the varying depth of work, and the length of stroke is adjustable by block and stud in a slotted disc. It is fitted with compound slides and a circular table, all fitted with self-acting feeds varied and adjusted independently of each other, and actuated by heart cam on main shaft.

The ram works in long slides, accurately scraped and fitted, and with loose strip for taking up wear. The belt cone has two speeds of large diameter

Admits work up to 18 in. diam. by 7 in. deep. Traverse of Slides, 8 in., both directions. Diameter of Turned Hand Flywheel 26 in. Approximate weight 12⅜ cwt.

The principal dimensions are as follow:—

Total height, 5 ft. 6 in. Width, 2 ft. 9 in. Depth from back to front, 4 ft. 6 in.
Cone pulley, 2 speeds, 2⅜ in. wide, 17 in. and 14 in. diam.
Circular Table, 12 in. diam.

Price complete, with Top Driving Apparatus, Screw Keys, &c., £

BRITANNIA CO., COLCHESTER, England.

London Showrooms—100, *Houndsditch.*   *All Letters to Colchester.*

BRITANNIA COMPANY'S
IMPROVED PATENTED SHAPING MACHINE.

(Patented No. 7,697.)

As made for DAVEY, PAXMAN & CO.

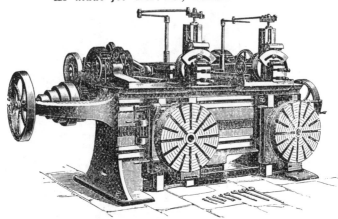

THIS is a most handy Machine for general Engineers or Machinists' Shop, enabling a piece of work with several planed faces, as valve or bracket seatings, to be shaped on all sides at one setting, the immense advantage of which, by ensuring accuracy, and as an economiser of time and labour will at once commend itself to every practical engineer.

The machine is constructed with a strong circular work table, having its face vertical, and with radial T slots for securely bolting the work to, which is capable of being easily rotated on its centre, and readily adjusted by slides both vertically and horizontally, so that any part of a piece of work fixed to it, can be brought quickly under the operation of the tool on the ram-head.

The circular motion is by worm and wheel gearing (and at a small extra cost can be made self-acting if desired) by which means cylinder flanges, cross-heads, ends of connecting rods, and other circular work can be done. The vertical adjustment is by worm or mitre gearing and elevating screw.

The machine is fitted with the most recent improvements, the gearing is on the saddle, conveniently under the control of the operator without having to move from his job, and is self-acting in both horizontal, vertical, and angular cuts.

The machine illustrated is a double machine of large size, having a stroke of 24 inches, and is fitted with two heads and two tables, acting independently of each other, but the same patented arrangement can be fitted to any of our smaller machines.

These machines can also be supplied with a loose angle bracket or table, to attach to the vertical faced circular table, forming at once an ordinary shaping machine, when circular or multiple faced work is not required to be done.

Specification of dimensions, &c. of the machine illustrated.

Length of stroke 24-in.	Pitch, width on face, and diameters of gearing :—
Length of bed 9-ft.	First pair 1½-in. by 4-in., pinion 9-in. spur
Height of face of bed from floor 4-ft.	wheel 18-in.
Width of face of bed 2-ft. 4-in.	Second ditto, 1½-in. by 4⅚-in., pinion 10½-in.,
Traverse of heads 3-ft. 6-in.	spur wheel 24-in.
Vertical adjustment of work table 16-in	Pitch of feed gearing ½-in. by 1½-in. on face.
Diameter of circular work table 30-in.	Approximate weight 11½ tons.
Extreme length of machine 15-ft., width	
5-ft. 4-in., height 7-ft.	

Price on rails at Colchester .. .. **£265.**

A similar machine, with 1 head, and with 1 or 2 tables—Price on application.

The above Tool is patented in England and abroad. Information of infringements will be paid for.

BRITANNIA CO., COLCHESTER, England.

London Showrooms—100, Houndsditch. *All Letters to Colchester.*

Extra Heavy Shaping Machine, No. 36

TWELVE-INCH STROKE.

AS MADE FOR THE BRITISH GOVERNMENT FOR INDIAN STATES RAILWAYS.

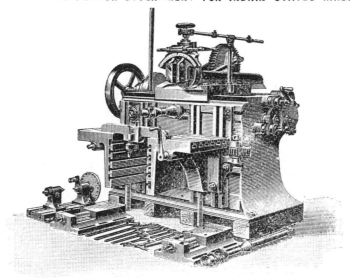

This is a powerful machine, designed for heavy railway work, and by its great weight and strength will save its extra cost in the rapidity of its work by heavy cuts.

It is made self-acting in all cuts, and is arranged for horizontal, vertical, angular, circular and curvilinear motions, the latter being adjustable for internal curves from a radius of 10 inches to nothing.

The cutting motion is given by an improved arrangement of adjustable stroke plate, by which the return motion retains its relative quickness, whether the machine be cutting a long or short stroke.

The tool holder is cut out of a solid block of forged steel, all other parts equally strongly constructed ; worms are forged steel, worm and feed gearing machine cut out of solid.

It is made with two tables, and the principal dimensions are as follows :—

Length, depth, and width of bed, 4 ft. 6 in. by 3 ft. 1 in., and 1 ft. 10 in.
Traverse of head along the bed, 2 ft. 3 in.
Maximum stroke, 12 in.
Size of table, 17 in. by 17 in. by 9 in.

Driving cone, 4 speeds, 3¼ in. wide, largest being 17½ in. and smallest 7 in. diameter.
Fly wheel, 24 in. diameter.
Driving gear, 14 teeth to 55 teeth, 1 in. pitch 3 in. face.
Approximate weight 3 tons 18 cwt.

Price, complete with top driving apparatus, screw keys, 2 vices, &c , but without dividing appliances £160 0 0

Dividing appliance, extra 7 10 0

BRITANNIA CO., COLCHESTER, England.

London Showrooms—100, Houndsditch.   All Letters to Colchester.

IMPROVED SELF-ACTING SHAPING MACHINE,

With Central Action, No. 33.

12 in. STROKE.   3 ft. 6 in. BED.

(AS MADE FOR THE BRITISH GOVERNMENT).

THESE machines are driven by direct motion of the link on the **centre** of the interior of the ram, obviating the usual connecting rod attached to the **side** of the ram, thus giving to the cutting tool a more direct and effective thrust.

All the feed motions are self-acting by cam and lever, and the vertical and angular feeds are very neatly and compactly contrived by tappets and rod at side of the ram, and the circular motion by worm and wheel gearing.

The tool holder swivels on the ram head, and is graduated to set to any angle, and the tool box is made with worm and quadrant for shaping internal curves. They have quick return motion. Table adjusts in both directions. Traverse of head along the bed is 24 inches. Size of Table, 16 in. by 14½ in.

Approximate weight, 26 cwt.

Price, complete with overhead motion, screw keys, &c., &c., **£64.**

BRITANNIA CO., COLCHESTER, England.

London Showrooms—100, Houndsditch.   All Letters to Colchester.

IMPROVED POWERFUL SHAPING MACHINE,

No. 32.

THESE machines are designed and constructed on the most approved principles, with the gearing for longitudinal traverse on the head or carriage, thus enabling the operator to set the cut without having to go to the end of bed, as heretofore. The above machines are made throughout with the greatest precision.

They are self-acting in horizontal and circular motion, the ram is indexed, and tool box provided with slides for vertical or angular cuts, and worm and quadrant for internal curves. The tables are adjustable on the bed, and are raised and lowered by handle in front. They are fitted with quick return motion by link arrangements. Overhead motion and screw keys complete.

Length of bed.	Stroke.	Traverse of Head,	Size of Table.	No. of Tables	Approximate Weight	Price.	Extra per Foot of Bed.	Additional Table.	Additional Head.
4 ft.	13 in.	2 ft. 8 in.	16 in. by 14½ in.	1	25	£60	£2 10	£8	£30

NOTE.—If made self-acting in vertical and angular cuts, extra, £

ABOVE AS SUPPLIED TO THE BRITISH GOVERNMENT.

BRITANNIA CO., COLCHESTER, England.

London Showrooms—100, *Houndsditch.*   *All Letters to Colchester.*

IMPROVED SHAPING MACHINE.

No. 29.

THESE are first-class tools, with longitudinal motion on the carriage, quick return by link motion. They are self-acting in circular and surfacing cuts. The tool box is fitted with slides for vertical and angular cuts.

Parallel vice, overhead motion, and screw keys are included.

Length of Bed	..	..	3ft.
Stroke	..	..	9in.
Traverse of Head	..		1ft. 10in.
Approximate Weight			14½ cwt.

Price	..	..	**£37 10**
Extra per Foot of Bed		..	**35s.**
Additional Table	..	..	**£6**

IMPROVED POWERFUL SHAPING MACHINE.

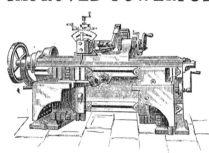

THESE machines are designed and constructed on the most approved principles, with the gearing for longitudinal traverse on the head or carriage, thus enabling the operator to set the cut without having to go to the end of bed, as heretofore. The above machines are made throughout with the greatest precision.

They are self-acting in horizontal and circular motion, the ram is indexed, and tool box provided with slides for vertical or angular cuts, and worm and quadrant for internal curves. The tables are adjustable on the bed, and are raised and lowered by handle in front. Overhead motion and screw keys complete.

They are fitted with quick return by link arrangements.

			6 ft.	8 ft.
Length of Bed	..	..	6 ft.	8 ft.
Stroke	..	..	14 in.	18 in.
Traverse of Head	..	..	4 ft. 6 in.	5 ft. 10 in.
Size of Table	..	..	20½ by 14¼	23½ by 16¼
No. of Tables	..	..	2	2
Approximate Weight		..	36 cwt.	60 cwt.
Price	..	..	**£**	**£**
Extra per Foot of Bed		..		
Additional Table	..	..		
Additional Head	..	..		

NOTE.—If made self-acting in vertical and angular cuts, extra, **£**

AS MADE FOR THE BRITISH GOVERNMENT.

BRITANNIA CO., COLCHESTER, England.

London Showrooms—100, Houndsditch.   All Letters to Colchester.

SELF-ACTING SHAPING MACHINE

For Hand or Steam Power, No. 31.

SIX-INCH STROKE.

(AS MADE FOR THE BRITISH GOVERNMENT).

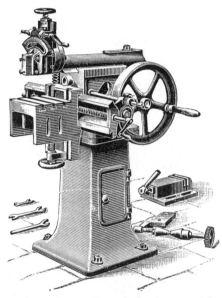

THIS is a handy machine for small work, having a quick action, and under ready control. It is made to be used either on a bench, or mounted on a cast iron box column as illustrated, the latter made with a door, and fitted with shelves as a cupboard for tools, &c.

It has an adjustable stroke up to 6 in. long.

The table is 9 in. by 9 in. by 8 in., and rises and falls by screw and hand wheel a distance of $7\frac{1}{2}$ in., and has a traverse along the bed of $25\frac{1}{2}$ in., either by hand or by self-acting feed. It is made with or without a self-acting circular motion, and is fitted with a parallel vice.

The tool box is made to swivel on ram head to any angle. The driving shaft is fitted with hand fly wheel, and with 3-speed cone pulley, for power driving. Approximate weight with pedestal complete, 8 cwt. 3 qrs.

Price,	with vice complete, as a bench tool	£25	0	0
,,	if fitted with self-acting circular motion, extra ..	2	10	0
,,	mounted on box pedestal, as illustrated, extra ..	3	5	0
,,	of complete top driving apparatus for power, extra	2	10	0

BRITANNIA CO., COLCHESTER, England.

London Showrooms—100, *Houndsditch.*   *All Letters to Colchester.*

B

SELF-ACTING SHAPER, FOR HAND OR STEAM POWER.

No. 30.

HAS a traverse of 12 inches and a 5-in. stroke. Rising and falling table fitted with T slots, and it is fitted with a 5-inch steel-jawed parallel vice, with cone and fly-wheel, for hand and steam power. It has self-feeding motion, and substantial hollow pedestal stand. Approximate weight complete, 5 cwt.

Price,	with Vice complete, as a bench machine	..	..	£19	0	0
,,	mounted on pedestal as illustrated ..	..	..	22	5	0
,,	if fitted with circular movement, extra	..	..	2	10	0
,,	of overhead motion for power, extra	..	..	2	10	0

BRITANNIA CO., COLCHESTER, England.

London Showrooms—100, Houndsditch.   All Letters to Colchester.

No. 27 STUD CHASING LATHE.

THE above illustration represents our improved hollow and open-sided spindle Lathe with Capstan Rest, for **quickly** and **cheaply** producing screwed studs, joint pins, and small fittings of all kinds, usually done in a Lathe. By means of this tool these can be made **uniformly,** far **quicker,** and by **cheap labour,** so that the tool soon **repays its cost.** It will turn, point and chase studs at one operation by means of the Capstan Rest.

The Headstock is constructed of two parts, accurately fitted to slide one over the other to adjust for taking up wear of spindle, the latter being made of steel, with hardened conical neck, with hole through its length to take long rods, and its sides open to enable headed bolts to be inserted for screwing, and its nose fitted with a coned chuck, and gripping dies for 9 sizes of tools and rods—$\frac{1}{4}$ in. to 1 in. diam.

The saddle is arranged with traverse slide, carrying a **Capstan tool holder,** fitted with five tools, adapted for sliding, rounding points, surfacing, parting, &c.

On the saddle is mounted the screwing arrangement with die box and adjustable dies for screwing $\frac{1}{4}$ in., $\frac{5}{16}$ in., $\frac{3}{8}$ in., $\frac{7}{16}$ in., $\frac{1}{2}$ in., $\frac{5}{8}$ in., $\frac{3}{4}$ in., $\frac{7}{8}$ in., and 1 in., and hinged to throw back out of the way when not screwing.

☞ The saddle is also fitted with **quick traverse** by rack and pinion, also **self-acting traverse** by fine thread leading screw with convenient disengaging nut.

The bed is of trough section to catch the soap and water, and constructed to conveniently draw it off.

The whole is of best materials and workmanship, and of the following dimensions. Complete overhead motion with reversing motion, soap sud can and stand, screw keys, spanners &c., are included in the price.

Height of centre ... 7 inches	Feed cones ... 3 speeds 1$\frac{1}{2}$ inches wide
Length & width of bed .. 5 ft. by 12$\frac{1}{2}$ in.	Overhead Pulleys, 13$\frac{1}{2}$ in. and 10 in. diam.
Driving cone 4 speeds 2$\frac{3}{4}$ inches wide	Approximate Weight .. ... 15 cwt.
Largest ... 13 in diam. ... Smallest, 7 in.	Price, complete ... £62 10 0

BRITANNIA CO., COLCHESTER, England.

London Showrooms—100, Houndsditch. *All Letters to Colchester.*

BRITANNIA COMPANY'S
NEW PATENT SCREWING MACHINES
(McILQUHAM'S PATENT, No. 15,982).

A Reward will be paid for information of Infringers.

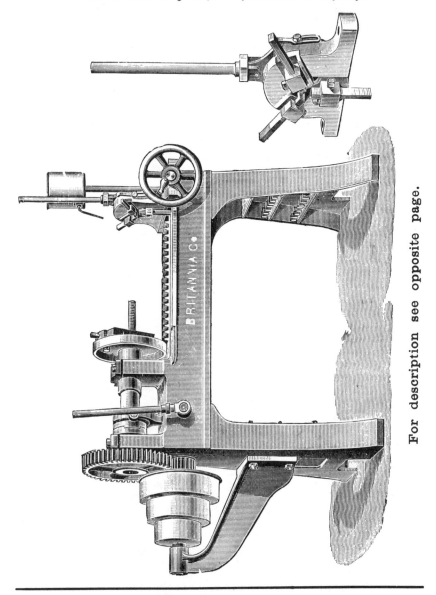

For description see opposite page.

BRITANNIA CO., COLCHESTER, England.

London Showrooms—100, Houndsditch.   All Letters to Colchester.

PATENT SCREWING MACHINE.

(For illustration see opposite page.)

THESE Machines are constructed on **improved and very simple principles,** greatly advantageous to users in point of economy, both in working and maintaining in repair.

The headstock is constructed with a **hollow spindle** to take rods or tubes of **any length** and with a **self-centring die chuck** for gripping rods. tubes, or bolt heads. A clutch and lever enables the machine to be started and stopped instantly and **independently of the counter-shaft.**

The Spindle is driven by a 3-speed cone pulley and powerful gearing.

The Bed is machine-planed, of trough section to catch the soap and water used in screwing, and is fitted with a tap to draw off.

Fitted to the bed is a Saddle to slide along, and moved by racks and pinions and hand wheel, and carries the Screwing Head. This is fitted with three tool boxes, carrying tools similar to ordinary chasers and so constructed as to be held firmly in position by one set screw to each. These are closed and opened by lever and eccentric cam, and the top face of the screwing head is **graduated and fitted with a stop** to **adjust** the depth of cut.

The **important feature** of this screwing head is the **simplicity of the dies,** which are **simply pieces of steel cut off the bar,** put into the tool holder and secured by set screws. In this machine they can then **be cut up by the master tap** and hardened and are finished ready for use ; **no expensive fitting** for length or in any other respect is needed, but treated as an ordinary turning tool is put in the slide rest of a lathe.

The advantages of this machine may be thus summarised :

The thread is completed at a **single cut.**

The Screwing Dies are as easily sharpened **by grinding the face** as ordinary lathe chasers, and hence do ten to twelve times the work of the many complicated systems in the market.

The Screwing Dies, when at last fairly worn out, are cheaply replaced **by any ordinary mechanic,** by merely cutting off from a bar of steel, fixing in their places by set screws as an ordinary lathe tool, and cutting the thread by the master tap supplied, **in their own machine.**

The method of holding the Dies is so arranged that the **strain comes on the rest or holder,** instead of upon the Dies, which thus endure so much more work.

The arrangement of the Screwing Head and Dies enables the cutting edges to be **plainly seen,** and these are clear for work and cannot get choked by cuttings.

The **Clutch** arrangement enables the machine to be **stopped instantly,** in case of accident or necessity.

The whole is so simple that there is nothing to get out of order by ordinary fair use, and if breakage occurs by any mishap, **parts can be easily replaced.**

Each Machine is sent out complete with Master Taps and Dies for $\frac{1}{2}$ in., $\frac{5}{8}$ in., $\frac{3}{4}$ in., $\frac{7}{8}$ in., and 1 in., Reversing Overhead Motion.

DIMENSIONS—Bed 4 ft. long ; 10 in. on face ; 6 in. deep ; Cone Pulley, 3 speeds, 3 in. wide, largest 12 in. diameter, Gearing $\frac{3}{4}$ in. Pitch, 2 in. face ; Spur Wheel 12$\frac{1}{2}$ in. diameter and Pinion 4$\frac{1}{2}$ in. ; Spindle bored with 1$\frac{3}{4}$ in. hole.

Approximate weight, 8 cwt.   Price complete, £35. To screw up to 1$\frac{1}{2}$ inch, Price complete, £45.

The Patented Screwing Head can be fixed to existing machines, or to the Saddles of ordinary Lathes.

ESTIMATES ON APPLICATION.   OTHER SIZES IN PREPARATION

BRITANNIA CO., COLCHESTER, England.

London Showrooms—100, Houndsditch.   All Letters to Colchester.

THE BRITANNIA COMPANY'S
HORIZONTAL RADIAL DRILL
No. 9.

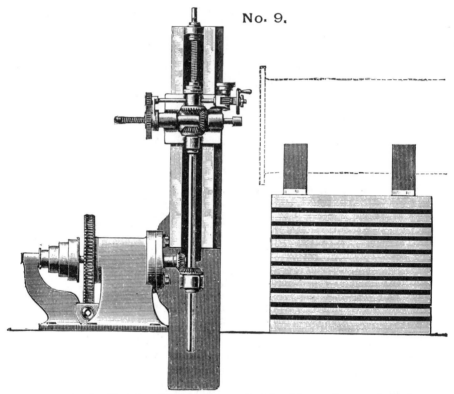

A VERY handy Tool for drilling flanges at ends of long pipes, or holes in any position in the vertical sides of machines or machine frames, as spindle holes, &c., which can all be done at once setting by rotating the arm and moving the saddle along it. The Radial Arm is counterbalanced, and is rotated by worm and wheel gearing to any position, and would revolve through an entire circle but for the floor. The feed is self-acting, with 3 changes of speed, and hand feed is also provided. The Table for holding the work is truly planed, and has T slots on top and one side, and carries a pair of V blocks for holding pipes up to 24 in. diameter.

DIMENSIONS.

Radial Arm is 5 ft. long from centre. Traverse of Saddle on it is 3 ft. 8 in. Will Drill a hole 1½ in. in diameter by 9 in. deep and 4 ft. 6 in. from centre. Steel Spindle is 1½ in. diameter. Vertical Driving Shaft, 1½ in. diameter. Bevil and Mitre Gearing, ¾ in. pitch. Worm Wheel, 22 in. diameter and ¾ in. pitch. Cone Pulley has 4 Speeds 2½ in. wide; largest Speed, 10 in. diameter; smallest, 4½ in. Approximate total weight, 2½ tons. Table is 3 ft. high by 3 ft. wide by 4 ft. long.

Price, with Table and V Blocks, as illustrated .. **£81 10 0**
   ,,   of Drill only, without Table and Blocks .. **£65 10 0**

BRITANNIA CO., COLCHESTER, England.
London Showrooms—100, *Houndsditch.*   *All Letters to Colchester.*

IMPROVED RADIAL DRILLING MACHINE,

With instantaneous reversing and slow or quick motions for tapping, &c

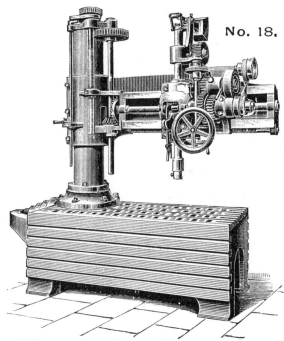

No. 18.

THIS is an improved Drilling Machine, of special design, strongly constructed, embodying many new features. It has a heavy foundation table of box form truly planed, and with planed T slots on top face and each side for securing the work, mounted on which is a turned column, firmly fixed and carrying within it the vertical driving shaft, geared up with mitre gearing, and around which revolves a strong truly bored and turned external column, accurately fitting it. The latter carries a radial arm, made to rise and fall by self-acting arrangement by power, fitted to the arm, and accurately scraped and gibbed to fit a planed parallel slide, is a saddle carrying the drilling spindle, which is fitted to drive by single or double gear, and with reversing motion to drive right or left, or remain stationary, without stopping the machine, which enables tapping and studding to be efficiently and rapidly done by the machine, and also permits the drill to be quickly withdrawn from the hole, and the spindle is also counterbalanced by weight and lever, and fitted with self-acting feed motion by rack and pinion, with engaging clutch. The horizontal driving shaft, fitted into the foundation bed, carries a driving cone having five speeds, giving, with the double gear, ten changes of speed.

The machine is strongly built in all parts, truly machined, accurately fitted, materials and workmanship of a high class.

The spur gearing is machine-cut out of the solid, the smaller gears cut out of mild steel, the mitre gearing is of crucible steel castings, the spindle and shafts and screws are all of steel.

The dimensions are as follows :—

Foundation bed, 6 ft. 4 in. long by 3 ft. 2 in. wide by 2 ft. 6 in. high.
The external rotary column, 12 in. diameter.
Length of arm, 6 ft. 4 in.
Vertical traverse of arm, 2 ft. 4 in.
Drills through a maximum radius of 5ft.
Drills out of solid up to 2 in. diameter.
Bores up to 9in. diameter and 12in. deep.

The steel spindle is $2\frac{1}{2}$ in. diameter.
Driving shafts, $2\frac{1}{8}$ in. diameter.
Bevel gearing, $1\frac{1}{4}$ in. pitch.
Machine-cut spur gearing, 1 in. pitch.
Speed cone, 5 speeds, $3\frac{1}{2}$ in. wide.
Largest speed, 17 in. diameter, smallest 6 in. diameter.
Approximate weight, $4\frac{1}{2}$ tons.

Price .. .. £137.

BRITANNIA CO., COLCHESTER, England.

London Showrooms—100, Houndsditch. *All Letters to Colchester.*

SELF-ACTING DOUBLE-GEARED RADIAL DRILL.

No. 19.

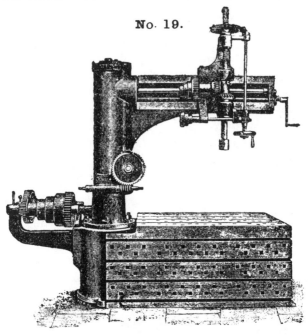

This is a modern designed Radial Drill, which dispenses with the over hanging top shaft and permits the arm to revolve through an entire circle and can be used in any position.

The massive Base is made with through bolt holes and T slots, planed out of solid, and measures 6 ft. 2 in. long by 3 ft. wide and 2 ft. 3 in. high.

Distance from centre of Pillar to end of Arm is 5 ft.

Arm rises and falls by worm gearing and Rack and Pinion 16 in.

The Steel Drill Spindle is $2\frac{1}{2}$ in. diameter. It will drill $12\frac{1}{2}$ in. deep and bore 10 in. diameter.

Radius of Spindle	4 ft. 6 in.
Traverse of Drill Head on Arm	2 ft. 10 in.
Will admit on Top of Base	3 ft. 7 in.
Will admit from floor	5 ft. 10 in.

Cone Pulley, 4 speeds, 3 in. wide.

Largest 12 in. diameter.　　　Smallest, $4\frac{1}{2}$ in. diameter.

Gearing $2\frac{1}{2}$ in. wide on face, $\frac{7}{8}$ in. pitch.

Large wheel 13 in. diameter.　　　Pinion, 4 in.

Approximate weight, $2\frac{1}{2}$ tons

Price complete, with Spanners and Keys, £

BRITANNIA CO., COLCHESTER, England.

London Showrooms—100, *Houndsditch.　　All Letters to Colchester.*

NEW PORTABLE RADIAL
DRILLING MACHINE, No. 6.

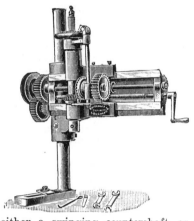

THIS machine has been specially designed to take the place of the old ratchet brace, and is adapted for bolting to locomotive frame plates or similar work for drilling and rimering holes up to 1½ in. diameter by 4 in. deep.

It consists of a **strong steel tubular** pillar forged on to a wrought iron slotted foot, and is capable of being turned to **any desired angle,** and when bolted in position is capable of drilling all holes within a radius of 18 in. from centre of pillar. The spindle is of **steel** 1½ in. in diameter, driven by strong gearing, and arranged to drive from either a swinging countershaft, as used in locomotive shops, or from a fixed countershaft if desired. The spindle has a **variable self-acting** and also hand feed. The drill will rise and fall on the pillar through a range of 18in. The bevel and driving gear is ⅝in. pitch. Approximate weight, 4cwt.

Price complete, if for swinging countershaft	..	£22	0 0
,, ,, if for fixed countershaft ..	..	27	0 0
Countershaft to suit, if required ..	..	..	2 10 0

A FOUNDATION BOX PLATE,

PREPARED to receive the wrought iron slotted foot of the drill, and accurately planed on top and one side, with planed T slots for bolting work to, can also be supplied, thus enabling the drill to be used (when desired) as a small but complete fixed radial drill.

Dimensions of base. 2 ft. 6 in. by 1 ft. 6 in., by 12 in. high.
Approximate weight of base, 4 cwt.

Price extra of base £6 10 0

BRITANNIA CO., COLCHESTER, England.

London Showrooms—100, *Houndsditch.* *All Letters to Colchester.*

POWERFUL VERTICAL DRILLING MACHINE,
No. 12.

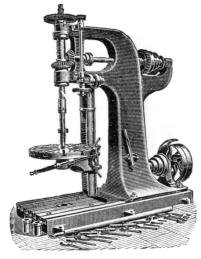

This is a back-geared machine of powerful build, having a heavy box section body, machine planed at bottom and securely bolted to a machine-planed heavy foundation plate, and with a turned pillar at one side to carry the strong arm which supports the table, which can thus be swung away for large work on the foundation plate, the latter being prepared with T slots for securing the work, and fork-shaped at front with filling piece fitted in.

The main spindle is of steel, and fitted with conical gun metal bearings, made to adjust by lock nuts to take up wear. All bearings are truly bored and bushed with gun metal. It has a self-acting screw feed by worm gearing, and the nut of feed screw is made to adjust to take up wear. The table elevates on the pillar by rack and pinion with worm and wheel purchase gear.

The steel pinion is coned to receive a 2-in. taper shank twist drill. The countershaft is self-contained in the frame of the machine, and is provided with convenient striking gear. It will drill out of solid 2 in. diameter by 12 in. deep, with a feed of 90 per inch and bore up to 9 in. diameter. Admits 48 in. diameter, and has a maximum depth of 39 in. between nose of spindle and the circular table, and of 58 in. between spindle and foundation plate.

Diameter of spindle, 2½ in.
Diameter of table, 36 in.
Diameter of pillar, 8 in.
Cone pulley, four speeds, 3¼ in. wide.
Largest and smallest diameters, 13 in. and 5 in.
Back gear, 13 T and 42 T, 1 in. pitch, 3 in. face.

Feed gear, 1⅜ in face, ½ in. pitch.
Fast and loose Pulleys, 24in. by 4in.
Total height, width, and length, 9 ft. 8 in. by 4 ft. 5 in by 9 ft. 3 in.
Approximate weight, 4 tons 7 cwt.

Price, complete with spanners, nut keys, &c., **£110.**

Above was designed & made for the British Government for Indian States Railways.

BRITANNIA CO., COLCHESTER, England.

London Showrooms—100, Houndsditch.   All Letters to Colchester.

43

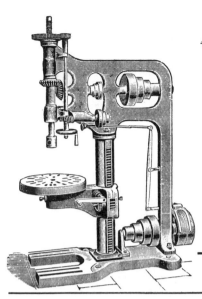

SINGLE SPEED
PILLAR DRILL,
No. 15.

WORMS for feed motion and rising of the table are wrought iron and case hardened. The screw at top is wrought iron, steeled at both ends and hardened. Frame and pillar are bolted to a planed bed with T Slots.

Takes in 30 inch diam.
Drills 10 inch deep
Steel Spindle 1¾ inch diam.
Bevel Gear ¾ inch pitch
4 Speed Cones 10½ inch diam., 2¾ inch wide
Table 22 inch diam.
Pillar 6 inch diam.
Weight about 14 cwt.

Price, £

POWERFUL DOUBLE GEARED
PILLAR DRILL,
No. 13.

WORMS for feed motion and rising of the table are wrought iron and case hardened. The screw at top is wrought iron, steeled at both ends and hardened. Frame and pillar are bolted to a planed bed with T Slots.

Takes in 30 inch diam.
Drills 10 inch deep
Steel Spindle 2 inch diam.
Bevel Gear ¾ inch pitch
4 Speed Cones 10½ inch diam., 2¾ inch wide
Gear Wheels 11¾ inch diam., ¾ inch pitch
Table 22 inch diam.
Pillar 6 inch diam.
Weight about 16 cwt.

Price, £

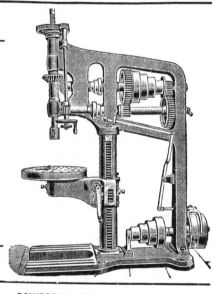

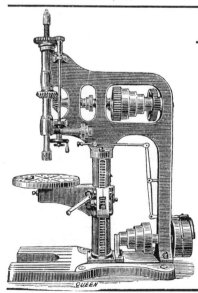

POWERFUL DOUBLE GEARED
PILLAR DRILL,
No. 11.

WORMS for feed motion and rising of the table are wrought iron and case hardened. The screw at top is wrought iron, steeled at both ends and hardened. Frame and pillar are bolted to a planed bed with T Slots.

Takes in 36 inch diam.
Drills 12 inch deep
Steel Spindle 2½ inch diam.
Takes in from spindle to Bed 3 ft 8 in.
Bevel Gear 1 in. pitch, 2⅝ across tooth
Spur Gear ⅞ pitch, 2¾ across tooth
Largest Speed 12 in. diam, smallest 5 inch diam., 3 inch wide
Table 26 inch diam.
Pillar 7¼ inch diam.
Weight about 1 ton 4 cwt.
Pulleys 14 inch diam., 3 in. wide

Price, £

BRITANNIA CO., COLCHESTER, England.
London Showrooms—100, Houndsditch. All Letters to Colchester.

DOUBLE GEARED PILLAR DRILL.

No. 16.

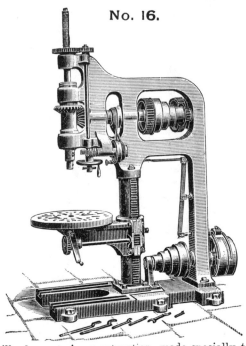

THIS is a Drill of a superior construction, made specially to a specification of one of the Government departments, and can be highly recommended as a durable and efficient tool. The bearings for shafts and spindle are bushed with gun metal, and the steel drill spindle is made adjustable by being fitted in a long conical sleeve running in gun metal bearings, and arranged with steel lock nuts above to take up wear. The feed is arranged with screw and hard steel thrust collars, the nut being carried in a bracket at top, and is made self-acting by worm and wheel and spur gearing, with friction cone, or operated by hand with wheel and handle.

The principal dimensions are as follows:—

Diameter of steel spindle	..	2in.	Diameter of largest & smallest		
Drills up to	..	2in.		10in. and 4½in.
Drills in depth	..	10in.	Diameter of pillar ..	..	6in.
Admits in diameter ..	..	30in.	Pitch of bevel gear ..	..	1in.
Diameter of table ..	..	24in.	Pitch and face of double gear ¾ × 2¼in.	
Table rises and falls ..	..	29in.	Diameter of large and small		
Cone pulley has 4 speeds, width	2½in.	gear	11 and 3¾in.	
Total height	..	8ft.	Diameter and face of driving		
			pulleys	12 × 3in.	

Approximate weight complete, 21 cwt.

PRICE—Complete with Spanners, Nuts, Keys, &c. .. £

BRITANNIA CO., COLCHESTER, England.

London Showrooms—100, Houndsditch.   All Letters to Colchester.

No. 1. STRONG

PILLAR DRILLING MACHINE.

THIS is a very useful machine, strongly built for its size. The main body is a box casting, faced and truly fitted on to a turned pillar, and securely bolted on to a planed foundation plate, having T slots for bolting large work to. The turned circular table is **made to swivel on its centre, and to swing around the turned pillar, and is raised and lowered by rack and pinion with worm gearing.**

The driving apparatus is self - contained, making the machine very compact.

The steel spindle is driven by strong bevel gear, and has both hand and self-acting feed by worm wheel and screw and friction cone.

All motions are arranged so as to be conveniently accessible to the operator, and all material and workmanship are of the best.

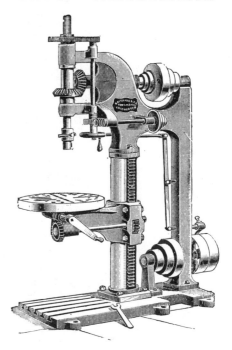

DIMENSIONS, &c.

Diameter of Steel Spindle	..	1¾in.	Cone Pulley, 3 speeds width		2¼in.
Drills up to	..	2 in.	Diameter of largest is	..	9 in.
Drills in depth	..	7 in.	Diameter of Pillar	..	6 in.
Admits in diameter	..	2¼ in.	Pitch of Bevel Gear	..	¾in.
Diameter of Table	..	2) in.	Pitch of Rack and Pinion	..	¾in.
Table rises and falls	..	27 in.	Total height	..	6ft. 6in.

Approximate Weight   ..   ..   12 cwt.

Price complete, **£26 10s.**, or with Double Gearing, **£31.**

For larger sizes send for quotations.

AS SUPPLIED TO THE BRITISH GOVERNMENT.

BRITANNIA CO., COLCHESTER, England.

London Showrooms—100, *Houndsditch.*   *All Letters to Colchester.*

SINGLE-GEARED DRILLING MACHINE,

No. 17.

A STRONG, durable, and handy machine, made with spindle to reverse by clutch and lever without stopping the machine, double arm, counter-balancing itself, having a revolving circular table at one end and a parallel vice at the other, and swinging entirely around the turned pillar, on which it is made to elevate by worm and wheel gearing with rack and pinion. The main body of the machine is a strong box casting, and the turned pillar, cast in one piece with the body, is securely bolted to the planed foundation plate, which has T slots for securing large work.

The steel spindle and shaft run in gun metal bearings. The bevel gearing is cast steel. Driving cone has three speeds. The machine has both hand and self-acting variable feed by three-speed cone pulley with worm and wheel gearing and friction cone.

The dimensions are as follows :— Steel spindle, 1¾ in. diameter. To drill up to 1½ in. diameter. To drill to a depth of 7 in. Admitting in diameter 20 in. Table rises and falls, 21 in. Total height, 6 ft. 6 in. Cone pulley three speeds, 2¼ in. wide. Diameter of largest, 9 in. Diameter of pillar, 6 in. Pitch of bevel gears, ¾ in. Pitch of rack and pinion, ¾ in. Approximate weight, 12 cwt.

Price, with complete Overhead Motion, &c. **£32**

ABOVE WAS DESIGNED AND MADE FOR THE BRITISH GOVERNMENT.

BRITANNIA CO., COLCHESTER, England.

London Showrooms—100, *Houndsditch.*   *All Letters to Colchester.*

Nos. 2 and 3 Strong Single Gear Pillar Drilling Machines

AS SUPPLIED TO THE BRITISH GOVERNMENT.

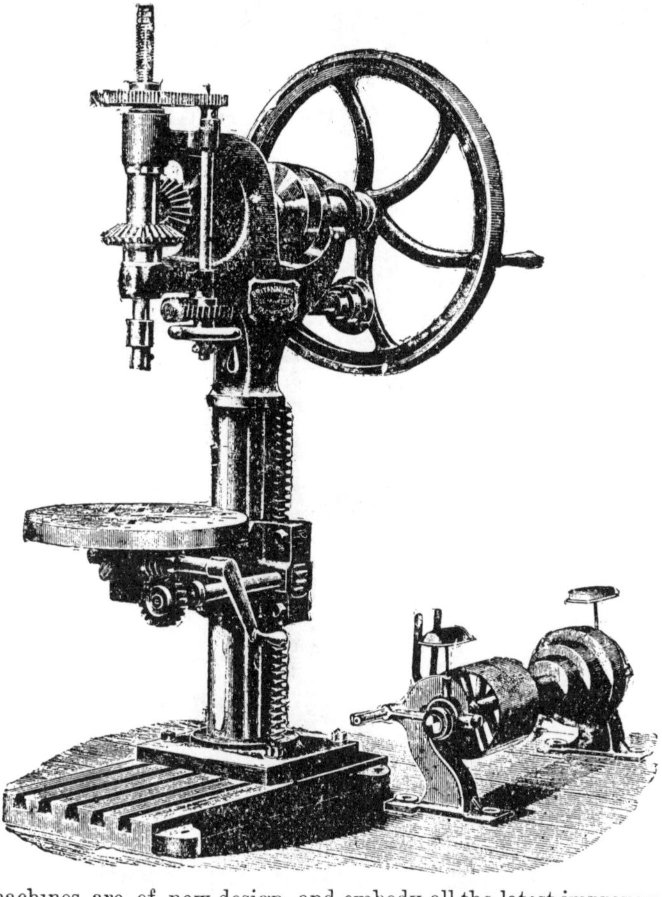

MULTIPLE DRILLING MACHINES MADE TO SUIT ANY WORK.

THESE machines are of new design, and embody all the latest improvements in small Drills. They have strong box casting for the body, pillar and base in one piece, the pillar being turned bright, and the base firmly bolted on to a planed foundation plate with T slots for larger work. The spindle is of steel, driven by strong bevel gearing; hand and self-acting feed by worm wheel and screw, engaging by friction cone. The circular work table will swivel on its centre, and also swing entirely round the pillar, and is raised and lowered by worm and wheel, with rack and pinion gearing. The fly-wheel has truly turned bright rim, and fitted with wood handle for driving by hand when it is desired. A complete top driving apparatus for steam power. and necessary keys and wrenches are included in the price. They are of the best materials and workmanship.

DIMENSIONS, &c.

	No. 2	No. 3		No. 2	No. 3
Steel Spindle, diameter ...	$1\frac{1}{8}$in.	$1\frac{3}{8}$in.	Cone Pulley, 3 speeds, width	$2\frac{1}{4}$in.	2in.
Drill up to	$1\frac{1}{2}$in.	$1\frac{1}{4}$in.	Diameter of largest speed ...	9in.	$7\frac{1}{2}$in.
Drill in depth	7in.	6in.	Diameter of Pillar	6in.	5in.
To admit in diameter ..	24in.	24in.	Pitch of Bevel Gearing ..	$\frac{3}{4}$in.	$\frac{5}{8}$in.
Diameter of Table... ...	20in.	20in.	Pitch of Rack and Pinion ...	$\frac{3}{4}$in.	$\frac{3}{4}$in.
Table rises and falls ...	21in.	18in.	Total Height	5ft. 6in.	4ft 11in
			Approximate Weight ...	11 cwt.	$8\frac{1}{2}$ cwt.

Price, complete with Countershaft, &c. No. 2, **£25**; No. 3, **£22 10s.**

BRITANNIA CO., COLCHESTER, England.

London Showrooms—100, *Houndsditch.* *All Letters to Colchester.*

QUICK-RUNNING
SENSITIVE DRILLING MACHINE,

No. 21.

DESIGNED FOR THE BRITISH GOVERNMENT.

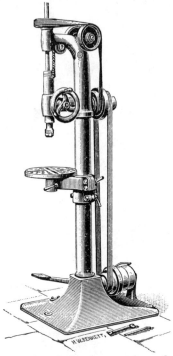

THIS machine is specially designed for fine work, and is strongly recommended for Electrical Engineers, Cyclists, and all kinds of light trades requiring large quantities of small holes accurately and quickly drilled.

The machine is made with counter-balanced steel spindle, working through the driving pulley and sleeve, and having its nose fitted with a patent scroll chuck, to take up $\frac{9}{16}$ in. The feed is arranged by hand wheel or lever and pinion, engaging with a rack on the sleeve, and is under perfect control, and only the necessary pressure need be applied. There are no gears—all revolving parts are turned to balance truly, and are driven by flat belt. The machine is started by treadle lever, and stops on removal of the foot. The workmanship throughout is of a high class, and material of the best.

DIMENSIONS.

Diameter of spindle, $1\frac{5}{16}$ in. Depth of feed, 6 in. Drills up to $\frac{5}{8}$ in. Distance from centre to frame, $7\frac{1}{2}$ in. Countershaft pulleys, 6 in. × $2\frac{1}{4}$ in. Cone pulleys, 4 speeds, $1\frac{1}{4}$ in. wide. Largest, $7\frac{1}{2}$ in. diameter. Smallest, 3 in. Total height, 6 ft. 6 in. Approximate weight, $5\frac{1}{4}$ cwt. Speed, 400 revolutions per minute.

| Price | ... | ... | ... | £17 10s. |

BRITANNIA CO., COLCHESTER, England.

London Showrooms—100, Houndsditch.   All Letters to Colchester.

No. 25 LIGHT PILLAR DRILL

For either Foot, Hand or Power.

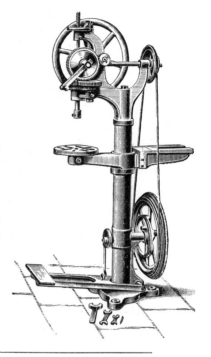

THE body is of strong web section, turned to fit on the top of the pillar, secured to it by strong bolt and nut, and can be swivelled around to any angle, very handy for drilling holes in large articles. The pillar and base are cast in one, pillar is truly turned and fitted with a bracket carrying a circular work table.

The spindle is fitted for both single and double gearing to suit small or large holes, and the feed self-acting or by hand.

It has two driving shafts, that for the treadle or power running to the back, and that for the hand motion to the right side, and these drive the spindle by bevel and spur gearing, which by an ingenious contrivance and combination with the Fly wheel give an immense impetus to the motion and greatly facilitate the work.

The treadle wheel has four speeds, and with the double gearing gives 8 variations of speed.

DIMENSIONS AND PRICES.

Diameter of Spindle	$\frac{7}{8}$ in.
Drilling holes up to	$\frac{3}{4}$ in. diam. by 5 in. deep
Turned Pillar	4 in. diam.
Distance from Drill Point to Pillar	9 in.
Diameter of Fly Wheel	18 in.
Diameter of Treadle Wheel	20 in.
Diameter of Circular Table	10 in.
Table will rise and fall on pillar	$20\frac{1}{2}$ in.
Approximate Weight	$3\frac{1}{2}$ cwt.
Price as Hand and Treadle Drill	£9 10 0
Price extra for Countershaft for Power	2 0 0
Price for Planed Square Table (as shown in illustration), in addition to the Circular one	0 15 0
Price for Adjustable Vice to fit on last attachment	1 0 0

BRITANNIA CO., COLCHESTER, England.

London Showrooms—100, *Houndsditch.*   *All Letters to Colchester.*

No. 5 BENCH DRILLING MACHINE.

(For particulars see opposite page).

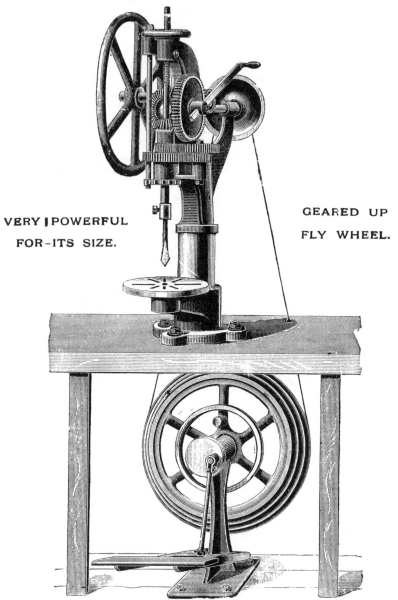

VERY POWERFUL
FOR-ITS SIZE.

GEARED UP
FLY WHEEL.

BRITANNIA CO., COLCHESTER, England.

London Showrooms—100, Houndsditch.   All Letters to Colchester.

No. 5 BENCH DRILLING MACHINE.
IMPROVED STYLE.

(For illustration see opposite page.)

THIS is a handy drill for light work ; made to drive by hand or treadle, or by both, and can also be driven by power if desired. It is constructed with a web-section body, turned to fit on to and swivel around a stiff turned pillar, secured by a nut at any angle, and by loosening which the drill can be brought to any position in its radius, and is thus **very handy for drilling holes in large objects.**

The pillar is cast in one with a strong foot, to bolt on to the bench, and carries a bracket which swivels entirely round it, carrying a circular work-plate which also swivels on its own centre, giving every faciilty for adjusting the work bolted to it under the drill. It has two driving shafts, that for the treadle or power running to the back, and that for hand motion to the right side, and these drive the spindle by bevel and spur gearing. **It is constructed with a specially ingenious contrivance of spur gearing in combination with a flywheel, which gives immense impetus to the motion, and greatly facilitates the work.** It has also **single and double gearing for small and large holes,** and has both self-acting and hand feed.

The treadle driving gear is made independent of the machine, to fix under the bench, the wheel having four speeds to drive the speed cone fitted to the driving shaft, thus giving with the double gearing eight changes of speed.

By the combination above named, this drill is more effective than much larger tools of the usual pattern.

DIMENSIONS AND PRICES.

Diameter of spindle	$\frac{7}{8}$ in.
Drilling up to $\frac{3}{4}$ in. diameter, by 5 in. deep	
Pillar 4 in. diameter by 11 in. high	
Distance from drill point to pillar	9 in.
Diameter of driving shaft	$\frac{7}{8}$ in.
Diameter of flywheel	18 in.
Diameter of driving wheel of treadle motion	20 in.
Diameter of circular work table	10 in.
Table will rise and fall on pillar	$6\frac{1}{2}$ in.
Extreme distance between nose of spindle when at its highest point, and the top of table when at its lowest point ...	$9\frac{1}{2}$ in.
Approximate weight	$2\frac{1}{2}$ cwt.
Price complete, as hand drill only	£6 10 0
,, complete, as hand and treadle drill	8 0 0
,, of top driving apparatus for power driving, if desired	2 0 0

BRITANNIA CO., COLCHESTER, England.

London Showrooms—100, *Houndsditch.* *All Letters to Colchester.*

No. 140 PILLAR DRILL.

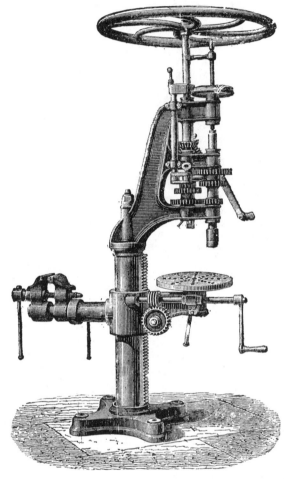

THIS Drill is self-acting, treble geared, for hand and power, with parallel vice and table to swivel round.

Will drill up to 2 inches diameter. Fly wheel 43 inches. Admits about 28 inches diameter. Weight about 9 cwt. Height 6 feet 6 inches.

Price for Hand Power	**£20 0s.**	
,, for Hand and Steam Power	**20 15s.**	
Extra for Gun Metal Bushed Bearings,	**£1 10s.**	
Price of Top Driving Apparatus ...	**2 10s.**	

BRITANNIA CO., COLCHESTER, England.

*London Showrooms—*100, *Houndsditch.* *All Letters to Colchester.*

No. 340 PILLAR DRILL.

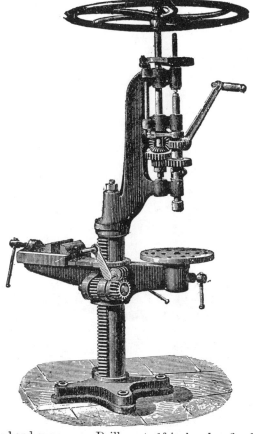

No. 340.—For hand or power. Drills up to 1⅜ inches, has flywheel 38 inches. Admits 24 inches diameter. Weight 6½ cwt. Height **6** feet 6 inches.

Price £15 10s.   For Steam, **15s**. extra.

No. 350.—Drills up to 1⅝ inches diameter. Flywheel 38 inches. Admits 28 inches. Weight 7 cwt. Height 6 ft. 8 inches.

Price £17.   For Steam, **15s**. extra.

No. 360.—Drills up to 1¾ inches. Diameter of flywheel 40 inches. Admits 30 inches diameter. Weight 8 cwt. Height 7 feet.

Price £18 10s.   For Steam, **15s**. extra.

Countershaft to suit either of above, **£2 10s**.

BRITANNIA CO., COLCHESTER, England.

London Showrooms—100, Houndsditch.   All Letters to Colchester.

ELECTRICAL ENGINEERS' DRILLS.

No. 8.

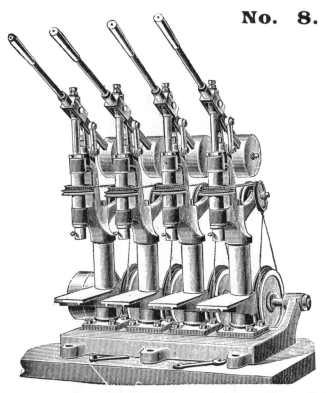

THE above illustration represents a gang of four quick speed drilling machines, mounted on a cast-iron base, for rapidly drilling small holes of equal or varying sizes, or countersinking, recessing, &c.

They are driven by countershaft at back, fitted with one pair of fast and loose pulleys, and a cone pulley for each drill, and are designed to be driven by power.

They are made with hard steel spindles, running in hard steel bearings, and are fed by hand lever and link motion, with balance weight to bring up the spindle, the latter having a steel swivel at top. They have turned pillars, with tables to rise and fall, or swivel around.

DIMENSIONS, PRICE, &c.

To drill holes up to $\frac{3}{8}$ in diameter, and $3\frac{1}{2}$ in. deep.
Diameter of steel spindle, $\frac{7}{8}$ in.
Turned Pillar $2\frac{1}{2}$ in. diameter by 9 in. high.
Table rises and falls $6\frac{1}{2}$ in.
Distance between centres of drills 6 in.
Size of cast-iron base for four drills, $26\frac{1}{2}$ in. by 10 in.
Total height from base to lever, 26 in.

Price, for gang of four drills, as illustration   ..   £37 10s.
Single drills, made as above   ..   ..   each   9 10s.

BRITANNIA CO., COLCHESTER, England.

London Showrooms—100, Houndsditch.   All Letters to Colchester.

No. 4 BENCH DRILL.

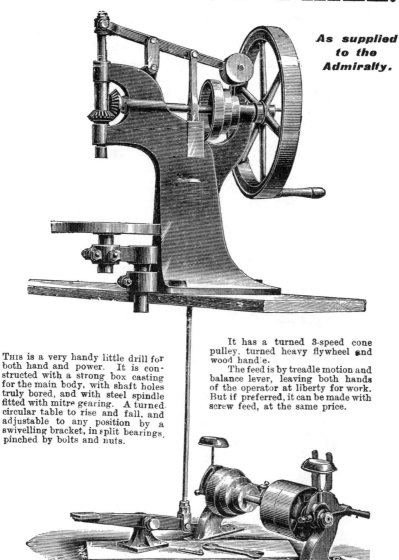

As supplied to the Admiralty.

This is a very handy little drill for both hand and power. It is constructed with a strong box casting for the main body, with shaft holes truly bored, and with steel spindle fitted with mitre gearing. A turned circular table to rise and fall, and adjustable to any position by a swivelling bracket, in split bearings, pinched by bolts and nuts.

It has a turned 3-speed cone pulley, turned heavy flywheel and wood handle.

The feed is by treadle motion and balance lever, leaving both hands of the operator at liberty for work. But if preferred, it can be made with screw feed, at the same price.

DIMENSIONS AND PRICE.

Steel Spindle ... ... 1¼ in. diameter
Cone Pulley, 3 speeds ... 1⅜ in wide
Diameters ... Largest 9 in., Smallest 5 in.
Circular Table ... ... 16½ in. diameter
Distance between Spindle & Table, 12 in.
Will take in a diameter of ... ... 17½ in.
Will Drill a hole ¾ in. dia. by 4½ in. deep

Base of Body measures ... 18 in. by 14 in.
Fly wheel ... 26 in. diameter, 2¾ in. face
Total ht. from bench to top of Drill, 40 in.
Approximate Weight ... ... 4¾ cwt.
Price complete, including countershaft
for power ... ... **£12 0s.**
With hardened steel spindles, **£16 10s.**

BRITANNIA CO., COLCHESTER, England.

London Showrooms—100, Houndsditch. *All Letters to Colchester.*

IMPROVED BENCH PILLAR DRILLING MACHINES.

For Hand or Steam Power.

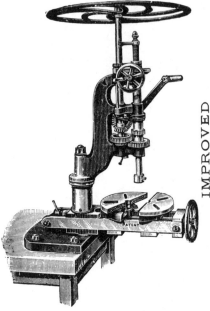

Numbers of Machines.	To drill holes up to diam.	Diameter of Flywheel	Diameter of Patent Circular Vice Plate	Distance from spindle to frame or Pillar	Total Height	Weight in cwts. Approx.	Price for Hand	Price for Hand and Steam	Price with Overhead Motion
48	1 in.	36 in.	14 in.	12 in.	54in.	4½ cwt.	225/-	240/-	290/-
49	1¼ ,,	38 ,,	15 ,,	12½ ,,	60 ,,	5½ ,,	280/-	275/-	335/-
50	1½ ,,	40 ,,	15 ,,	13 ,,	65 ,,	6½ ,,	290/-	305/-	390/-

☞ Set of Improved Tubular Dogs on Face-plate, 50/-

Set of 6 Drills, No. 48   49   50

15/- 18/- 20/-7in long Best Cast Steel.

The above are fitted with patent parallel vice and revolving chuck-plate.

IMPROVED PILLAR DRILLING MACHINES.

For Hand or Steam Power.

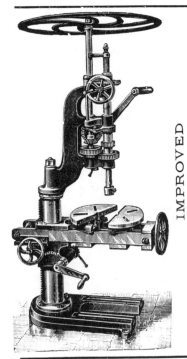

Numbers of Machines	To drill holes up to diam.	Diameter of Flywheel	Diameter of Patent Vice Plate	Distance from spindle to frame or pillar	Total Height	Weight in cwts. Approx.	Price for Hand	Price for Hand and Steam	Price with Overhead Motion
51	1 in.	36 in.	14 in.	12 in.	72in.	6 cwt.	290/-	305/-	355/-
52	1¼ ,,	38 ,,	15 ,,	12½ ,,	76 ,,	7 ,,	340/-	355/-	415/-
53	1½ ,,	40 ,,	15 ,,	13 ,,	86 ,,	8½ ,,	375/-	390/-	465/-

☞ Set of Improved Tubular Dogs on Face-plate, 50/-

Set of 6 Drills, No. 51   52   53

15/- 18/- 20/- 7 in. long, Best Cast Steel.

BRITANNIA CO., COLCHESTER, England.

London Showrooms—100, Houndsditch.   All Letters to Colchester.

No. 410 AND 420 DRILLS.

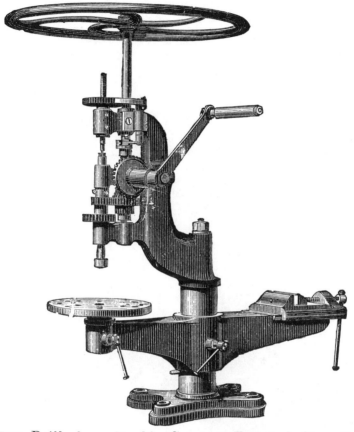

THESE Drills have Double Gearing, Fast and Slow Feed Motion, Fast and Loose Pulleys, or 3-speed Cone on Side, Circular Table, Parallel Vice to swing round under Drill. Table rises and falls on pillar 9 inches.

Nos. of Machines.	To Drill Holes diameter	Diameter of Flywheel	Will take in diameter	Height	Approximate Weight	Price for Hand only	Hand and Steam
410	$\frac{7}{8}$in.	27in.	24in.	4ft. 4in.	3 cwt.	£7 10s.	£8
420	1in.	30in.	26in.	4ft. 6in.	3½ cwt.	£8 15s.	£9 5s.

These can be raised on pillar so as to give 14in. more distance between spindle and table at an extra charge of **15/-**

BRITANNIA CO., COLCHESTER, England.

London Showrooms—100, Houndsditch. *All Letters to Colchester.*

BENCH DRILLING MACHINE

To be worked by Hand or Steam Power.

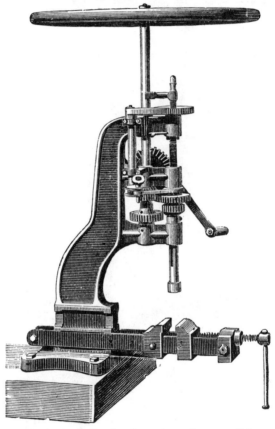

THIS pattern Machine is made in five sizes, has a solid cast-iron frame, powerful double gearing, strong self-feeding motion by pressure from the top, a large fly-wheel on top of inside spindle, an improved adjustable parallel vice sliding along the frame of machine, in grooves one above the other. The handle, and fast-and-loose pulleys or cone are on the right hand side. These machines are used largely amongst Coachbuilders and Wheelwrights.

Nos. of Machines.	Diameter of Fly-wheel.	To drill holes up to diam.	Distance from Spindle to frame.	Approximate weight.	Price for Hand Power.		Height.	
	in.	in.	in.	cwt.	£	s.	ft.	in.
290	20	$\frac{3}{4}$	8	1	4	0	3	1
370	32	1	10	2	5	15	3	3
380	36	$1\frac{1}{4}$	11	$2\frac{1}{2}$	7	0	3	6
390	38	$1\frac{1}{2}$	$12\frac{1}{2}$	3	8	0	4	4
400	40	$1\frac{5}{8}$	14	4	9	0	4	6

Arranged for Hand and Steam, **10s.** and **12s.** extra.

BRITANNIA CO., COLCHESTER, England.

London Showrooms—100, *Houndsditch.*   *All Letters to Colchester.*

BENCH DRILLING MACHINE

To be worked by Hand or Steam Power.

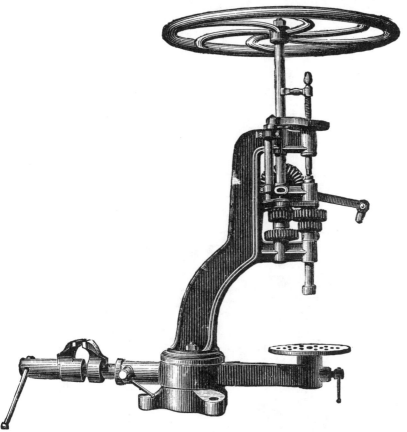

HAS strong solid cast-iron frame, strong double gearing, a slow and fast
self-feeding motion, by pressure from the top by screw and ratchet, handle,
fast and loose pulleys or 3-speed cone on the side ; a circular adjustable
plate, and patent wrought iron parallel sliding vice, 4 and 5 in. jaws, finished
bright, to swing completely round. The Machines revolve on their base by
loosening the nuts on the top thereon.

Nos. of Machines.	To drill holes up to diam.	Diameter of Flywheel.	Will take in diam.	Height	Approx. Weight.	Price for Hand only.	Diam. of Plates.
190	$\frac{7}{8}$ in.	28 in.	19 in.	3 ft. 9 in.	2 cwt.	£7 5s.	10 in.
200	$1\frac{1}{4}$ in.	36 in.	26 in.	4 ft. 8 in.	3½ cwt.	10 10s.	12 in.

For Steam Power, **10s.** and **12s. extra.**

BRITANNIA CO., COLCHESTER, England.

London Showrooms – 100, *Houndsditch.*   *All Letters to Colchester.*

NEW PATENT DRILLING MACHINES,

With Improved Chuck-plate, and Parallel Vice, Self-centreing.

FOR HAND OR STEAM POWER.

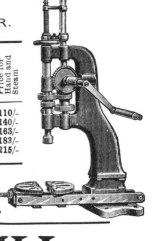

Numbers	To drill holes up to diameter	Diameter of Fly-wheel	Diameter admitted under Spindle	Diameter of Patent Vice Plate	Height over all	Weight, approx.	Price for Hand	Price for Hand and Steam
29 BB	¾in.	20in.	8 in	10in.	37in.	1½cwt.	100/-	110/-
37 BB	1 ,,	32 ,,	10 ,,	12 ,,	40 ,,	2¼ ,,	130/-	140/-
38 BB	1¼ ,,	32 ,,	10 ,,	14 ,,	46 ,,	3 ,,	158/-	163/-
39 BB	1½ ,,	38 ,,	12¾ ,,	14 ,,	52 ,,	3¾ ,,	178/-	183/-
40 BB	1⅝ ,,	40 ,,	14 ,,	15 ,,	54 ,,	4¼ ,,	200/-	215/-

Set of 6 Drills, No. 29BB 37BB 38BB 39BB 40BB
7/6   12/-   15/-   18/-   20/-

Hand Wheel and Gear for raising Drilling Spindles, 10/- extra.

No. 110 DRILL.

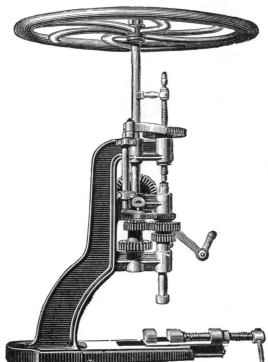

Will Drill Holes up to 1in.

Height, 3ft. 8in.

Diameter of Flywheel, 36in.

Distance of Spindle to Frame 11in.

Weight 2½cwt.

———

Price for Hand, £6 5s.

Price for Hand and Steam, £6 15s.

BRITANNIA CO., COLCHESTER, England.

London Showrooms—100, Houndsditch.   *All Letters to Colchester.*

No. 10 **LEVER TREADLE DRILLING MACHINE**

To Drill holes up to $\frac{5}{16}$ in. diameter by foot or steam.

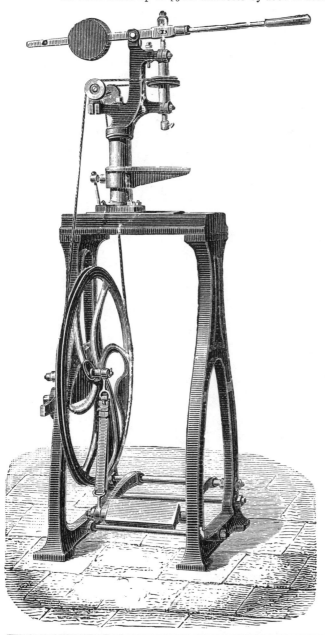

Speciality for drilling small holes high speed ; well fitted, suitable for Bicycle makers and others.

Price, for foot and steam, **150/-**

Price, for foot, **135/-**

BRITANNIA CO., COLCHESTER, England.

London Showrooms—100, *Houndsditch.*   *All Letters to Colchester.*

No. 120 'UNION' PATENT BENCH DRILL

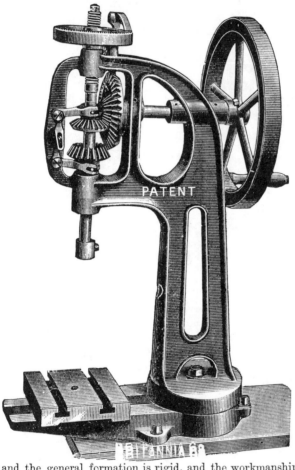

THIS Tool has two rates of speed obtained by means of two sets of bevel wheels, the pinions of which are caused to be in or out of gear alternately by turning the eccentric lever controlling them.

The table is carried on a slotted arm and can be revolved so that any part of the table can be brought under the point of the drill. The standard is made to move radially on the base. These movements give great scope and convenience, and will be found valuable in use.

It is self-acting in its feed and the general formation is rigid, and the workmanship and material good.

It is also made single speed, with or without self-acting feed, and a drilling vice is supplied when desired. Will drill up to $\frac{7}{8}$ in., take in $19\frac{1}{2}$ in. diameter, and is 2 ft. 7 in. high. Weight about 1 cwt.

PRICES.				£	s.	d.
Double Speed, Self-Acting Feed	...	...	...	4	5	0
Single ,, ,, ,,	...	...	...	3	17	6
,, ,, (not Self-Acting)	...	...	...	3	15	0
Vice (large)	...	...	...	1	0	0
,, (small)	...	...	...		12	6

BRITANNIA CO., COLCHESTER, England.

London Showrooms—100, *Houndsditch.* *All Letters to Colchester.*

DRILLING MACHINE FOR LATHE.

No. 160.

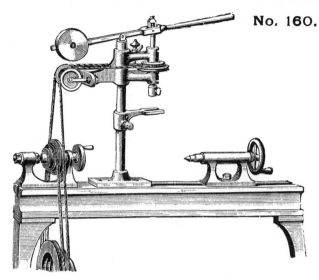

THIS can be used on any ordinary Lathe, and driven either from below of a treadle lathe or from an overhead. This is a useful tool. Price £2 2 0

BENCH DRILL.

No. 150.

Size A.

Weight 25 lbs. ... Drill $\frac{5}{8}$ holes,
30/-

Size B.

Weight 80 lbs. ... Drill $\frac{3}{4}$ holes,
45/-

Size C.

Weight 150 lbs. ... Drill $1\frac{1}{2}$ holes,
80/-

BRITANNIA CO., COLCHESTER, England.

London Showrooms—100, Houndsditch. *All Letters to Colchester.*

No. 130 BENCH & BREAST DRILL.

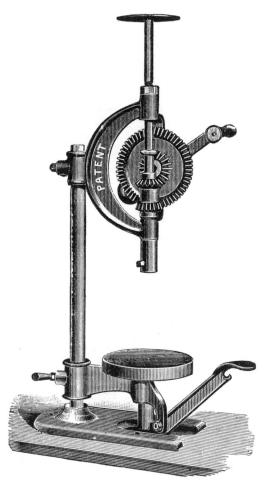

CAN also be used as a BRACE by taking it off the Pillar. By pressing the Lever at foot the Table is raised.

Price 30s.

"A very useful tool in any shop."

BRITANNIA CO. manufacture a large number of Drilling Machines for Hand or Steam Power.

Special attention is requested to the Quality of our Drills.

BRITANNIA CO., COLCHESTER, England.

London Showrooms—100. *Houndsditch.*   *All Letters to Colchester.*

HANDY DRILLING POSTS.

Nos. 170 and 180.

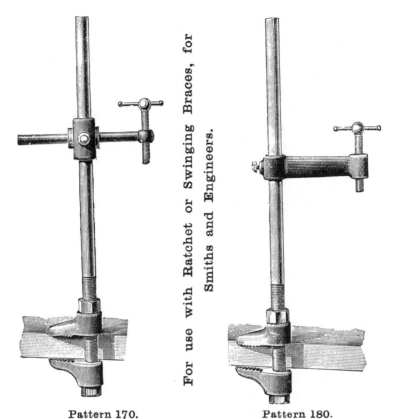

Pattern 170.   Pattern 180.

MADE with bright turned pillars, 1⅜in. diameter, about 36in. high, strongly fitted to cast-iron foot, with loose clamping jaw and nut, to attach to bench. Made in two patterns, 170 and 180, the former having a wrought iron adjustable and swivelling arm, and the latter with a fixed centre cast-iron swivelling arm.

Feed Screws with hardened female centres.

Prices—Pattern 170, £2 0 0:   Pattern 180, £1 15 0

BRITANNIA CO., COLCHESTER, England.

London Showrooms—100, *Houndsditch.*   *All Letters to Colchester.*

C

PLATE FLANGING MACHINE,

No. 40.

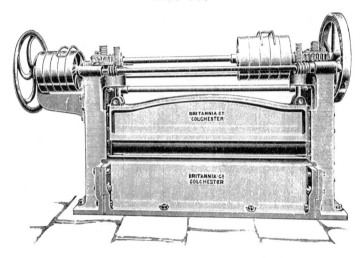

THIS is a very heavy and strongly constructed machine, consisting of two end uprights rigidly braced together by box stay casting at bottom, and wrought iron stay rod at top. In these uprights are sliding blocks carrying the flanging roll (9in. diam.) which is raised and lowered by powerful worm gearing and screws. The Clamping Girder for gripping plate is raised and lowered in a similar manner. Both of these operations are driven by power by open and cross belts. The whole machine is arranged in a rigid manner, and capable of flanging plates up to $\frac{3}{8}$in. thickness by 6ft. wide.

Flanging roll driving pulleys 18in. by 4in., Fly Wheel 3ft. diam., 3in. face.
Clamping girder driving pulleys, 15in. diam. by 2¾in.
Flanging roll worm gearing, 1½in. pitch, 11in. diam., 3in. face.
Clamping girder worm gearing, 1in. pitch., 8in. diam., 2in. face.
Approximate Weight, 4¼ tons.

PRICE   ..   ..   ..   £

BRITANNIA CO., COLCHESTER, England.

London Showrooms—100, Houndsditch.   All Letters to Colchester.

No. 37, IMPROVED DOUBLE-ENDED

PUNCHING & SHEARING MACHINE,

With Double Gearing and driven by Self-Contained Engine.

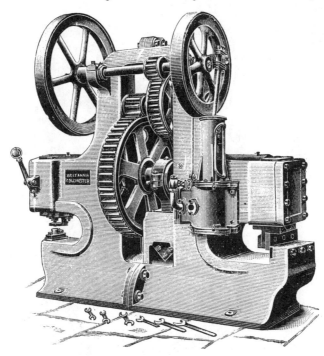

To Punch $\frac{7}{8}$ in. hole through $\frac{7}{8}$ in. plates, and shear $\frac{7}{8}$ in plates—and with Angle Iron Shears for $4\frac{1}{2}$ in. by $4\frac{1}{2}$ in. by $\frac{5}{8}$ in. Depth of Gullets each 18 in. Shear Blades 12 in. wide, and set at an angle for shearing long bars. Disengaging motion to punch and angle shears, and, if required, to straight shears also. Flywheel is 3 ft. 3 in. diam. and 4 in. wide on face. Gearing is first pair, pinion $7\frac{1}{4}$ in. diameter, wheel $22\frac{1}{2}$ in. diameter, $1\frac{1}{2}$ in. pitch, $4\frac{1}{4}$ in. face—second pair, pinion $8\frac{1}{2}$ in. diameter, wheel 41 in. diameter, $2\frac{1}{4}$ in. pitch, 6 in. face. All gearing shrouded on both sides to pitch line. Diameter of Steel Eccentric Shaft $5\frac{3}{8}$ in. Dimensions of Engine—cylinder 7 in. diameter, stroke 10 in., Engine flywheel 32 in. diameter, 4 in. face, length of Machine over all 8 ft. 8 in., height of Machine over all 8 ft. 3 in., approximate weight 6 tons.

					£	s.	d.
Price, with Engine	..	..	..		145	0	0
,, without Engine	..	..	..		133	0	0

BRITANNIA CO., COLCHESTER, England.

London Showrooms—100, *Houndsditch.*   *All Letters to Colchester.*

IMPROVED PUNCHING
AND SHEARING MACHINES.
No. 36.
(AS MADE FOR THE BRITISH GOVERNMENT.)

THE illustration represents a very handy punching and shearing machine of improved construction, powerfully geared, single ended, shearing above and punching below. The body is a strong box casting, with thick beads round the gullets, and fitted with slide, accurately scraped in, carrying the shear blade and punch, the former being set at an angle for shearing long bars.

Steel main shaft, strong gearing, heavy turned flywheel, with handle for working by hand. The machine can be mounted on four strong wheels for moving about the yard, or made with fast and loose pulleys for power driving, and without transport wheels, if desired.

Gearing $3\frac{3}{4}$-inch face by $1\frac{1}{4}$-inch pitch; large wheel 32 inches diameter; pinion 6 inches diameter flywheel 48 inches diameter; fast and loose pulleys $15\frac{1}{2}$ inches diameter, 3-inch face.

No.	To punch in diam.	Thickness of plate to punch	Thickness of plate to shear	Depth of gullets to punch	to shear	Approx. weight.	Price for hand power only.	Price for hand and steam power.
PS 36	$\frac{3}{4}$-in.	$\frac{1}{2}$-in.	$\frac{1}{2}$-in.	10-in.	11-in.	25 cwt.	£32	£33 10s.
PS 2	$\frac{3}{4}$-in.	$\frac{5}{8}$-in.	$\frac{5}{8}$-in.	12-in.	9-in.	36 cwt.		
PS 3	$\frac{3}{4}$-in.	$\frac{3}{4}$-in.	$\frac{3}{4}$-in.	12-in.	11-in.	40 cwt.		

For larger or smaller sizes send for quotations.

BRITANNIA CO., COLCHESTER, England.
London Showrooms—100, Houndsditch.   All Letters to Colchester.

No. 18 Punching & Shearing Machine

For Hand and Steam Power.

WILL punch by hand $\frac{5}{8}$-in. diameter holes through $\frac{3}{8}$-in. plates, and shear $\frac{3}{8}$-in. sheets 6 in. from edge, and square or round bars $\frac{3}{4}$ in. diam.

Has top gear machined out of the solid : stop motion in front, adjustable sliding die holder to punch holes in keg ends, angle and H iron : fitted with fast and loose pulleys, large flywheel and handle. Weight of Machine, $9\frac{1}{2}$ cwt.

Price   -   -   -   £22 10 0

For larger sizes, send for quotations.

BRITANNIA CO., COLCHESTER, England.

London Showrooms—100, Houndsditch.   All Letters to Colchester.

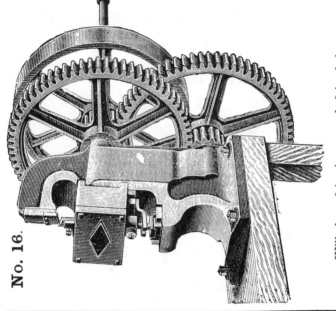

SHEARING AND PUNCHING MACHINES.

No. 16.

Will shear $\frac{3}{8}$-in. iron, punch $\frac{5}{8}$-in. holes.

Price - - - £18

No. 15.

Will shear iron $\frac{1}{4}$-in. in thickness, and will punch $\frac{3}{8}$-in. holes through $\frac{1}{4}$-in. iron.

Price - - £6 10s.

LEVER SHEARING MACHINE.
No. 11.

To cut sheet iron up to $\frac{1}{8}$-in. × $3\frac{1}{2}$-in. wide, round or square bars up to $\frac{3}{16}$-in.

Has a solid casting and guide; will cut through the middle of sheet iron.

Weight	...	...	60 lbs.	Length of Blades	...	6 in.
Price	...	...	**45s.**	Extra Shears	...	**7s.**

BRITANNIA CO., COLCHESTER, England.

London Showrooms—100, *Houndsditch.*   *All Letters to Colchester.*

PUNCHING AND SHEARING MACHINES,

Of new design with lever at back. Box casting for body. To punch at bottom and shear at top. In five sizes as under :—

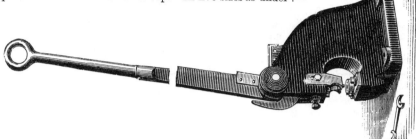

Number	21	22	23	24	25
Largest diameter to punch ...	$\frac{3}{16}$	$\frac{1}{4}$	$\frac{5}{16}$	$\frac{3}{8}$	$\frac{1}{2}$
Thickness ,, ...	$\frac{3}{16}$	$\frac{1}{4}$	$\frac{5}{16}$	$\frac{3}{8}$	$\frac{1}{2}$
Width and thickness to shear	$\frac{3}{4} \times \frac{3}{16}$	$\frac{3}{4} \times \frac{1}{4}$	$1 \times \frac{5}{16}$	$1\frac{3}{16} \times \frac{5}{8}$	$1\frac{3}{8} \times \frac{1}{2}$
Distance from body to punch	$1\frac{1}{2}$	$2\frac{1}{4}$	3	$3\frac{1}{8}$	$3\frac{1}{2}$
Approximate weight ...	28 lbs.	50 lbs.	90 lbs.	154 lbs.	190 lbs.
Price	**35/-**	**45/-**	**60/-**	**75/-**	**100/-**

LEVER PUNCHING MACHINES

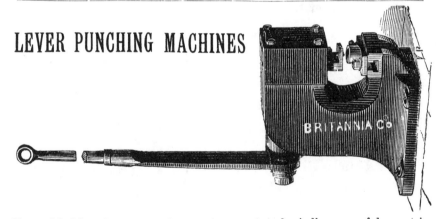

These Machines have strong box castings, cast steel spindles, powerful eccentric levers on the sides, punches and dies set to punch angle and ⊥ iron. Work easily and efficiently.

Number of Machines	4	1	2	20
Will punch diameter	$\frac{1}{4}$ in.	$\frac{3}{8}$ in.	$\frac{1}{2}$ in.	$\frac{5}{8}$ in.
Through plates	$\frac{1}{8}$ in.	$\frac{1}{4}$ in.	$\frac{3}{8}$ in.	$\frac{3}{8}$ in.
Depth of gap	$1\frac{1}{2}$ in.	3 in.	4 in.	$4\frac{1}{2}$ in.
Weight	28 lbs.	1 cwt.	2 cwt.	3 cwt.
Price	**35/-**	**85/-**	**120/-**	**200/-**

No. 4—A speciality for Hoop Iron.

BRITANNIA CO., COLCHESTER, England.

London Showrooms—100, *Houndsditch.* *All Letters to Colchester.*

IMPROVED LEVER PUNCHING AND SHEARING MACHINE.

HAS strong box casting, with lever on the side, with top blade fitted against same, cast steel spindle and eccentric, punch and die holder set to punch ∟ and ⊥ iron. Guide, punch and die, of largest diameter the Machine will punch.

Numbers of Machines.	0	00	000
To punch holes diameter ...	$\frac{5}{16}$ in.	$\frac{3}{8}$ in.	$\frac{1}{4}$ in.
Through plates diameter ...	$\frac{3}{16}$ in.	$\frac{1}{4}$ in.	$\frac{1}{8}$ in.
Shears bars thick	$\frac{3}{16}$ in.	$\frac{1}{4}$ in.	$\frac{1}{8}$ in. hoops
Admitted at gap	$2\frac{3}{8}$ in.	$3\frac{1}{8}$ in.	$1\frac{5}{8}$ in.
Weight	$\frac{1}{2}$ cwt.	1 cwt.	30 lbs.
Price	55/-	95/-	40/-
Extra punches and dies, per pair	2/2	2/6	2/2
Extra pair of blades	5/-	7/-	4/-

No. 12,
LEVER SHEARING MACHINE.

HAS a solid casting, a forged upper jaw, with guillotine at one end, and guide. Will cut through the middle of sheet iron.

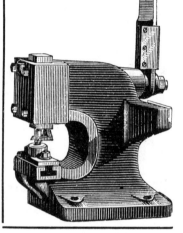

Weight	$2\frac{1}{2}$ cwt.
Length of Shears ...	8 in.

Price	**150/-**
Extra Shears	**12/-**

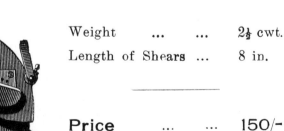

BRITANNIA CO., COLCHESTER, England.

London Showrooms—100, Houndsditch. All Letters to Colchester.

IMPROVED
LEVER SHEARING MACHINES,

Specially designed and constructed for shearing plate iron through the middle or any part.

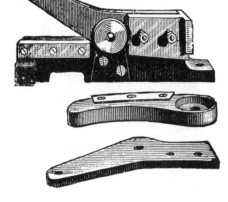

DETAILS.

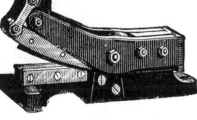

BACK.   FRONT.

Number.					26	27	28
Thickness to Shear	..	..	..		$\frac{3}{16}$	$\frac{1}{4}$	$\frac{3}{8}$
Length of Blades	..	..				$8\frac{1}{4}$	10
Approximate weight	..	..	..		80 lbs.	150 lbs.	590 lbs.
Price	..	..	..	..	**£6**	**£7 10s.**	**£18**

No. 28 has counterbalance weight.

BRITANNIA CO., COLCHESTER, England.

London Showrooms—100, Houndsditch.   *All Letters to Colchester.*

SMALL HAND COLD-SAWING MACHINE,

Driven by Worm Gearing, Circular Saw 8 inch
diameter, with strong Parallel Vice, for gripping up to
2¼ inch.

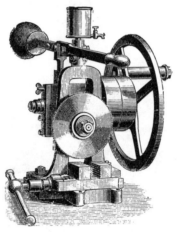

THE Machine is so arranged that it can be fixed on a bench
or table, and will cut round iron or steel $2\frac{1}{4}$ in. diameter,
and mill accurately faces of equal dimensions; it is,
therefore, a tool used not only for cutting off, but for
milling off as well.

It is admirably adapted for cutting off iron or steel
to exact gauge, tubes, &c., and for nicking screws, &c.

The Machine is chiefly supplied for hand power, but can
be fitted with pulleys also, as may be seen from sketch, but
the belt can only be put horizontally on the pulleys, as the
latter moves up and down with the slides.

Price, Complete with Parallel Vice and one Saw of 8 inches diameter
(without Pulleys), £9.

If with Fast and Loose Pulleys, £10 5s. 0d.

BRITANNIA CO., COLCHESTER, England.

London Showrooms—100, *Houndsditch.*   *All Letters to Colchester.*

TYRE BENDING MACHINES

For hand and steam power.

HAVE solid cast-iron frames and extra powerful gearing. The cylinders are of wrought iron, case hardened, the outside ones are fluted; pressure by screw underneath. Warranted to bend a bar to any desired sweep, by once going through. A welded tyre can be replaced in the machine for finishing, by drawing out the top spindle and removing the cylinder.

These machines are used all over the world, and are recommended to be durable and more efficient than any other machine of this kind; very little power required to work them.

NUMBER OF MACHINES ...	6	6a	7	8
Warranted to bend bars	$4\frac{1}{2}$in by $1\frac{1}{4}$in.	6in by $1\frac{3}{8}$in.	$5\frac{3}{4}$in. by $1\frac{5}{8}$in.	$6\frac{3}{4}$in. by $1\frac{3}{4}$in.
Weight	$3\frac{1}{2}$ cwt.	$3\frac{3}{4}$ cwt.	5 cwt.	6 cwt.
Price for hand ...	150/-	165/-	215/-	230/-
,, for hand & steam	165/-	180/-	250/-	245/-

BRITANNIA CO., COLCHESTER, England.

London Showrooms—100, Houndsditch.   All Letters to Colchester.

POWERFUL
TREBLE-GEARED FACING AND BORING LATHE.

(For description see opposite page.)

BRITANNIA CO., COLCHESTER, England.

London Showrooms—100, Houndsditch.   *All Letters to Colchester.*

POWERFUL TREBLE-GEARED FACING AND BORING LATHE.

WITH 12½ in. Centre Headstock mounted on strong box section pedestal, cast in one piece with a strong foundation plate, latter truly planed and with ⊤ slots on its face, on which is securely bolted, but adjustable in position, a circular pillar, planed at bottom and turned at top, and fitted with a Compound Slide Rest, with extra long slide.

The Headstock is fitted with a Steel Mandril with parallel necks, running in hard gun metal bearings; the front end forged with a broad flange truly turned, and having bolted securely to it a strong well ribbed Face Plate, with radial ⊤ slots and internal gear; and the tail end of mandril fitted with a slotted disc, carrying an adjustable stud and eye for self-acting overhead feed, the Slide Rest being provided with lever, pawl, and ratchet for that purpose.

PRINCIPAL DIMENSIONS.

Headstock, Mandril bearings—Front, 6½ in. long by 3½ in. diameter; Back, 4⅝ in. long by 2½ in. diameter.

Speed Cone, 4 Steps, 3⅞ in. wide; Largest, 16 in. diameter; Smallest, 7 in.

Gearing—Double, 17 in. and 5½ in., 3¼ in. face, 1⅛ in. pitch; Treble Pinion 6¼ in. diameter, Internal Wheel, 43 in. diameter, 3½ in. face, 1¼ in. pitch.

Face Plate, 48 in. diameter. Slide Rest arranged to bore 24 in. deep.

Foundation Plate, over all 7 ft. long by 3 ft. 4 in. wide.

Price complete, with Top Driving Apparatus, Keys and Spanners, &c. ...   . £85.

BRITANNIA CO., COLCHESTER, England.

*London Showrooms—*100, *Houndsditch.*   *All Letters to Colchester.*

POWERFUL DUPLEX BORING MACHINE,
No. 44.

(For description see opposite page.)

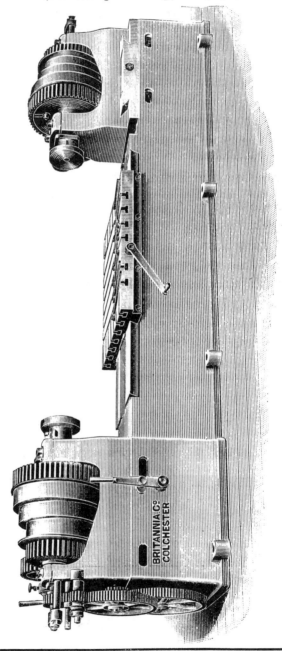

BRITANNIA CO., COLCHESTER, England.

London Showrooms—100, *Houndsditch*   *All Letters to Colchester.*

POWERFUL DUPLEX BORING MACHINE,

No. 44.

(For illustration see opposite page.)

THIS is a machine of very solid construction with the Bed cast in one piece, on which are mounted two very strong double-geared Headstocks, with cone pulleys of large diameter, giving great driving power, and steel spindles with flanges forged solid, and with parallel necks running in Gun Metal.

One Headstock is made adjustable transversely with Bed, to suit the varying centres of holes to be bored.

The Work Table is of large dimensions and arranged to move for feed by screw within the Bed, and automatically driven by spur gearing at the end through the gearing at back end of fixed head, and which can be reversed for feeding in either direction by sliding pinions.

Provision is made for quick return by hand through worm and wheel gearing and a handle at front of table. The rate of feed is altered by a lever conveniently placed in front of bed, and a clutch will disengage the feed for facing work.

DIMENSIONS.

Height of centres from Bed, 15 in.

   ,,   ,,   over Table, 12 in.

Bed is 12 ft. long by 24 in. wide by 21 in. high.

Traverse of Table along Bed, 4 ft.

Maximum distance between centres of holes to be bored, 12 in.

Steel Spindles Front Necks, $3\frac{3}{4}$ in. diameter by $6\frac{3}{4}$ in. long.

Back Necks, $2\frac{1}{2}$ in. diameter by $4\frac{3}{4}$ in. long.

Cone Pulleys, 3 speeds, $3\frac{1}{2}$ in. wide ; largest, 20 in. diameter ; smallest, 14 in.

Gearing, $3\frac{1}{2}$ in. face by $1\frac{1}{8}$ in. pitch.

Diameter of Wheels, 21 in. and Pinions, 6 in.

Feed Screw, $2\frac{1}{2}$ in. diameter by $\frac{1}{2}$ in. pitch.

Approximate weight, $3\frac{1}{2}$ Tons.

Price, with 2 Overhead Motions, Screw Keys, &c., &c., £

BRITANNIA CO., COLCHESTER, England.

London Showrooms —199, Houndsditch.   *All Letters to Colchester.*

DOUBLE HEADED LATHE

THE above represents our Double Headed Lathe made for long lengths of shafting, screws, &c., which is very handy in the General Engineer's Shop, where long work may only occasionally be wanted, when the Centre Head and one Poppet can be quickly removed, and the whole length of Lathe is then available, and both the Saddles and Rests can be used, one for roughing and the other for finishing; while for ordinary work of shorter lengths, both Heads and Rests are complete and ready for either two distinct jobs, or one can rough out or slide and other can finish or cut screws. The Lathe can thus be used economically and conveniently by one man, and a great deal of work turned out cheaply.

DIMENSIONS AND PRICE.

Height Centres, 10 in.
Bed, width and depth, 16 in. by 11 in.
  ,,   Length up to 40 feet.
Gap, $15\frac{3}{4}$ in. wide; $10\frac{1}{2}$ in. deep.
Leading Screw, $2\frac{1}{4}$ in. diameter, $\frac{1}{2}$ in. pitch.
Back Shaft, $1\frac{3}{8}$ in. diameter.   [5 in.
Cone Pulleys, 4 speeds, $3\frac{1}{4}$ in. wide; Largest, 13 in. diameter, smallest
Face and Pitch of Gearing, 3 in. by 1 in.
Diameters of ditto, 14 in. and $4\frac{1}{2}$ inch.
  ,,   Body and Nose of Spindles, $2\frac{1}{4}$ in. and $2\frac{3}{4}$ in.
Face and Pitch of Change Wheels, $1\frac{1}{2}$ in. and $\frac{7}{16}$ in.
Extreme length between Centres with 40 ft. bed 35 feet.
Approximate Weight, 5 Tons.

Price—as shown   ...   .
  ,,   with only 1 pair of heads   ...   .
Sliding, Surfacing only   ...   .
Sliding, Surfacing and Screwcutting ...   .
Sliding and Screwcutting only   ...   .
Poppets to set over extra   ...   .
Bed more or less per foot   ...   .

BRITANNIA CO., COLCHESTER, England.

London Showrooms—100, Houndsditch.   *All Letters to Colchester.*

Specification of No. 23, 14 in., and No. 33, 16 in. Centres.

SELF-ACTING, SLIDING, SURFACING, AND SCREW-CUTTING LATHES.

Fitted with double-geared headstock, steel spindle, conical necks, gun-metal bearings, reversing motion for cutting right and left-hand screws; the loose headstock is fitted with cylinder mandrel, and left-hand square thread traverse screw, bright turned hand-wheel, and can be made to set over by transverse slide motion for taper turning if desired. The saddle has a flush top and T grooves for bolting work to for boring purposes, compound slide rest, made to swivel to any angle for surfacing, and graduated for turning conical. The bed is accurately planed and surfaced, and provided with movable bridge piece for gap, box end at left hand, and firmly bolted to strong standard with planed faces at right-hand end. The metal is carefully distributed, so that the Lathe is quite rigid under the heaviest cutting strain; the leading screw is of steel, accurately cut, and extends full length of bed. It has a double clam gun-metal nut, actuated by eccentric movement to engage and release the saddle, the latter having also a quick hand traverse by rack, pinion, and double purchase gearing. The self-acting sliding and surfacing motions are arranged with backshaft and worm gearing. Any length of bed made to order.

The Lathe is fitted complete with back traversing stay, 22 change wheels, index plate, face plate, catchplate, and top driving apparatus complete, screws, keys, &c.

Dimensions, Prices, &c.	No. 23.	No. 33.
Height of Centres	14 inches.	16 inches.
Length, Width and Depth of Bed	20 ft. by 23 in. by 14½ in.	20 ft. by 27 in. by 16 in
Width and Depth of Gap	21 in. by 14½ in.	25 in. by 16 in.
Diameter and Pitch of Leading Screw	2⅝ in. by ½ in.	3⅛ in. by ½ in.
,, of Back Surfacing Shaft	1⅝ in	1¾ in.
Number of Speeds on Cone Pulley, and Width	4—4½ in.	4—5 in.
Diameters of Largest and Smallest Speeds	18 in. and 8½ in.	22½ in. and 9 in.
Width on Face and Pitch of Gearing	3½ in. by 1¼ in.	4½ in. by 1½ in.
Diameters of Large Wheel and Pinion	19⅜ in. and 6¼ in.	23¾ in. by 7½ in.
,, of Body and Nose of Steel Spindle	3 in. and 3½ in.	8⅞ in. and 4¼ in.
Width on Face and Pitch of Change Wheels	2 in. by ⅝ in.	2 in. by ⅝ in.
Extreme Length between Centres	13 ft. 6 in.	12 ft. 3 in.
Approximate Weight	5 Tons.	8½ Tons.
Price: Sliding, Surfacing, and Screw-Cutting		
Price: Sliding and Screw-Cutting only (no back shaft)		
Price: If with Poppet to set over for Taper Turning		
Price: Per Foot of Extra Length of Bed		

Can be made with parallel necks if preferred.

THESE LATHES ARE FITTED FOR HARD AND ACCURATE WORK, AND ARE SIMILAR TO THOSE SUPPLIED TO THE BRITISH GOVERNMENT.

BRITANNIA CO., COLCHESTER, England.

London Showrooms—100, *Houndsditch.* *All Letters to Colchester.*

Specification of No. 21, 10 in., and No. 22, 12 in.,

SELF-ACTING, SLIDING, SURFACING, AND SCREW-CUTTING LATHES.

FITTED with double-geared headstock, steel spindle, conical necks, gun-metal bearings, reversing motion for cutting right and left-hand screws; the loose headstock is fitted with cylinder mandrel, and left-hand square thread traverse screw, bright turned hand-wheel, and can be made to set over by transverse slide motion for taper turning if desired. The saddle has a flush top and T grooves for bolting work to for boring purposes, compound slide rest, made to swivel to any angle for surfacing, and graduated for turning conical. The bed is accurately planed and surfaced, and provided with movable bridge piece for gap, box end at left hand, and firmly bolted to strong standard with planed faces at right-hand end. The metal is carefully distributed, so that the Lathe is quite rigid under the heaviest cutting strain; the leading screw is of steel, accurately cut, and extends full length of bed. It has a double clam gun-metal nut, actuated by eccentric movement to engage and release the saddle, the latter having also a quick hand traverse by rack, pinion, and double purchase gearing. The self-acting sliding and surfacing motions are arranged with backshaft and worm gearing. Any length of bed made to order.

The Lathe is fitted complete with back traversing stay, 22 change wheels, index plate, face plate, catch plate, and top driving apparatus complete, screws, keys, &c.

DIMENSIONS, PRICES, &c.	No. 21.	No. 22.
Height of Centres	10 inches.	12 inches.
Length, Width and Depth of Bed	12 ft. by 16 in. by 11 in.	12 ft. by 19 in. by 13 in.
Width and depth of Gap	15¾ in. by 10½ in.	19½ in. by 12½ in.
Diameter and Pitch of Leading Screw	2¼ in. by ½ in.	2½ in. by ½ in.
" of Back Surfacing Shaft	1⅜ in.	1⅝ in.
Number of Speeds on Cone Pulley, and Width	4—3¼ in.	4—3⅞ in.
Diameters of Largest and Smallest Speeds	13 in. and 5 in.	16 in. and 6⅞ in.
Width on Face and Pitch of Gearing	3 in. by 1 in.	3¼ in. by 1⅛ in.
Diameters of Large Wheel and Pinion	14 in. and 4½ in.	17¼ in. and 6 in.
" of Body and Nose of Steel Spindle	2¼ in. and 2¾ in.	2½ in. and 2¾ in.
Width on Face and Pitch of Change Wheels	1½ in. by 7/16 in.	1½ in. by ½ in.
Extreme Length between Centres	7 ft. 3 in.	6 ft. 8 in.
Approximate Weight	2½ Tons.	4 Tons.
Price. Sliding, Surfacing, and Screw Cutting		
Price. Sliding and Screw Cutting only (no back shaft)		
Price. If with Poppet to set over for Taper Turning		
Price. Per Foot of Extra Length of Bed		

Can be made with parallel necks if preferred.

THESE LATHES ARE FITTED FOR HARD AND ACCURATE WORK, AND ARE SIMILAR TO THOSE SUPPLIED TO THE BRITISH GOVERNMENT.

BRITANNIA CO., COLCHESTER, England.

London Showrooms—100, *Houndsditch.* *All Letters to Colchester.*

SELF-ACTING, SLIDING, SURFACING, AND SCREW-CUTTING LATHE, No. 24, 9 and 10in.

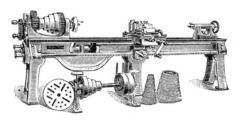

THIS Lathe is a stiff-built tool for heavy work, up to its capacity of size, and is strong enough to raise to 10 inch for lighter work. It is well proportioned in all parts and is constructed with gap bed, accurately planed and surfaced, and bridge piece fitted to gap; double-geared headstock, steel spindle, conical neck, gun metal bearings, reversing motion for cutting either right or left hand screws, loose head with cylinder barrel and left hand square thread traverse screw, and made to set over for taper turning if required; steel leading screw accurately cut, and extending full length of bed, with double clam gun metal nut clipping screw at top and bottom, saddle with long wings flush top, and grooved for bolting work to for boring, and with quick hand traverse by rack and pinion, compound slide rest to swivel to any angle, graduated for turning conical, &c., and steel draw screws; back surfacing shaft and worm gearing for sliding without the leading screw (saving wear of same) and for surfacing. The price includes back following stay, catch and face plates, 22 change wheels, index plate, overhead motion, screw keys, &c., complete. All materials and workmanship guaranteed.

DIMENSIONS, PRICES, &c.

Height of Centres	9 inches
Length, breadth, and depth of bed	12 ft. by 14½ in. by 10 in.
Length and diameter will swing in gap ...	... 15 in. by 38 in.
Diameter and pitch of Steel Leading Screw ...	... 2 in. by ⅜ in.
Diameter of Back Surfacing Shaft	1¼ in.
Number and width of Speeds on Cone Pulley ...	4—3 in.
Diameters of largest and smallest Speed ...	12 in. and 4½ in.
Width on face and pitch of Gearing	... 2½ in. by ⅞ in.
Diameters of large and small Gear	13 in. and 4¼ in.
Diameters of body and nose of Steel Spindle ...	.. 2 in. and 2½ in.
Pitch of the 22 Change Wheels	.. 7/16 in.
Extreme length between Centres	7 ft. 6 in.
Approximate Weight	55 cwt.

	9 in. Centre			10 in. Centre		
	£	s.	d.	£	s.	d.
Price with Leading Screw and Back Shaft ...						
,, ,, ,, only						
Poppet to Set over extra						
Extra length of Bed per foot ...						

BRITANNIA CO., COLCHESTER, England.

London Showrooms—100, Houndsditch.   *All Letters to Colchester.*

SELF-ACTING, SLIDING & SCREW-CUTTING LATHE,

No. 29, $7\frac{1}{2}$ in. Centre.

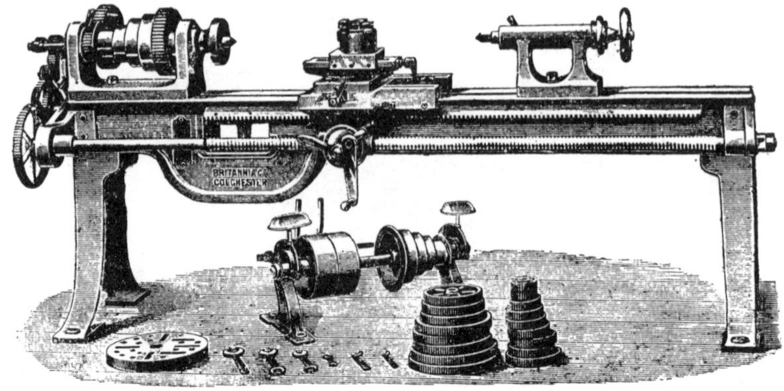

A good and useful Lathe for light work ; the bed is gapped with gap piece fitted and accurately planed and surfaced ; double geared headstock, steel spindle, conical necks, gun metal bearings, reversing motion for cutting either right or left hand screws, poppet head with cylinder barrel and internal left hand square thread screw, steel leading screw, accurately cut, and extending full length of bed, saddle with flush top and grooved for securing work for boring, and with quick hand traverse by rack and pinion, compound slide rest to swivel to any angle and graduated, steel draw screws, back following stay, catch and face plates, 22 change wheels, overhead motion, screw keys, &c., complete.

DIMENSIONS.

Height of centres	$7\frac{1}{2}$ in.
Length, breadth and depth of Bed	8 ft. × $10\frac{1}{4}$ in. × $7\frac{1}{4}$ in.
Gap will admit ...	$9\frac{1}{2}$ in. long × 29 in. diam.
Diam. and pitch of Leading Screw	$1\frac{5}{8}$ in. × $\frac{1}{2}$ in.
Diam. of Back Shaft	$1\frac{1}{8}$ in.
Number and width of speeds on Cone Pulley	4 × $2\frac{3}{16}$ in.
Diam. of largest and smallest Speeds	$7\frac{3}{4}$ in. and $3\frac{5}{8}$ in.
Width on face and pitch of Gearing	$1\frac{7}{8}$ in. × $\frac{5}{8}$ in.
Diam. of large and small Gear	$9\frac{1}{8}$ in. and $3\frac{1}{4}$ in.
Diam. of body and nose of Spindle	$1\frac{1}{2}$ in. and $1\frac{3}{4}$ in.
Pitch of 22 Change Wheels	$\frac{5}{16}$ in.
Extreme length between Centres	4ft. 8 in.
App oximate weight	15 cwt.

PRICE, complete as above ... ... £

,, if self-surfacing by back shaft ... ...

,, per foot of extra length bed ... .

BRITANNIA CO., COLCHESTER, England.

London Showrooms—100, *Houndsditch.* *All Letters to Colchester.*

SELF-ACTING, SLIDING, SURFACING, AND SCREW-CUTTING LATHE,

Nos. 25 and 20.

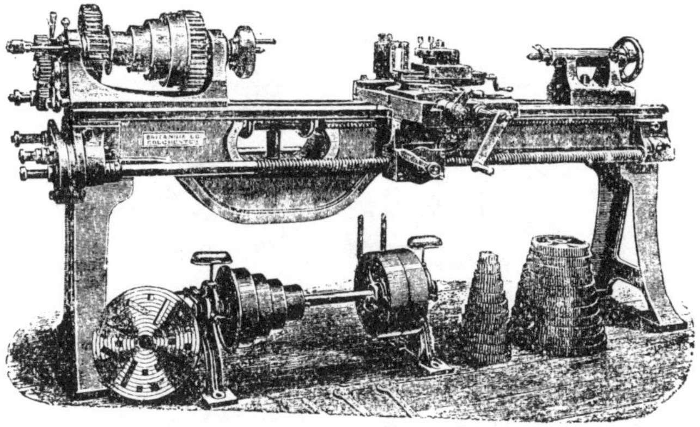

WITH gap bed, accurately planed and surfaced, and bridge piece fitted to gap ; double-geared headstock, steel spindle, conical neck, gun metal bearings, reversing motion for cutting either right or left hand screws, loose head with cylinder barrel and left hand square thread traverse screw, and made to set over for taper turning if required ; steel leading screw, accurately cut, and extending full length of bed, with double clam gun metal nut clipping screw at top and bottom, saddle with long wings, flush top and grooved for bolting work to, for boring, and with quick hand traverse by rack and pinion, compound slide rest to swivel to any angle, graduated for turning conical, &c., and steel draw screws, back following stay, catch and face plates, 22 change wheels, index plate, overhead motion, screw keys, &c., complete. All materials and workmanship guaranteed. These Lathes up to 10 feet have 2 standards, above 10 feet 3 standards.

DIMENSIONS.	No. 25 LATHE.	No. 20 LATHE.
Height of Centres	$7\frac{1}{2}$ in.	9 in.
Length, breadth, and depth of Bed ..	8ft. by $10\frac{3}{4}$ in. by 8 in.	10ft. by 13in. by $8\frac{1}{2}$ in.
Length and diameter will swing in Gap ...	11 in. by 31 in.	12 in. by 36 in.
Diameter and pitch of Steel Leading Screw ..	$1\frac{5}{8}$ in. by $\frac{1}{2}$ in.	$1\frac{7}{8}$ in. by $\frac{1}{2}$ in.
,, of Back Surfacing Shaft ...	$1\frac{1}{8}$ in.	$1\frac{1}{8}$ in.
Number and width of Speeds on Cone Pulley ..	4 by $2\frac{1}{4}$ in.	4 by $2\frac{1}{2}$ in.
Diameters of largest and smallest Speed ..	$8\frac{1}{2}$ in. and $3\frac{3}{4}$ in.	10 in. and $4\frac{1}{2}$ in.
Width on face and pitch of Gearing ...	$2\frac{1}{8}$ in. by $\frac{5}{8}$ in.	$2\frac{1}{4}$ in. by $\frac{3}{4}$ in.
Diameters of large and small Gear ...	10 in. and $3\frac{1}{4}$ in.	11 in. and $3\frac{1}{2}$ in.
,, of body and nose of Steel Spindle ...	$1\frac{1}{2}$ in. and 2 in.	$1\frac{3}{4}$ in. and $2\frac{1}{4}$ in.
Pitch of the 22 change Wheels	$\frac{3}{8}$ in.	$\frac{3}{8}$ in.
Extreme length between Centres	4 ft 6 in.	6 ft. 6 in.
Approximate Weight	16 cwt.	26 cwt.
Price with both Leading Screw and Back Shaft		
,, Leading Screw only		
Poppet to set over, extra		
Extra length of Bed per foot		
Beds to any length.		

These Lathes are made for the British Government.

THE WEARING PARTS ARE STEEL.

BRITANNIA CO., COLCHESTER, England.

London Showrooms—100, *Houndsditch.* *All Letters to Colchester.*

POWERFUL SINGLE GEARED HOLLOW MANDREL

TURRET SCREW-CUTTING LATHE

No. 46.

HEADSTOCK has steel hollow spindle, bored 2 inches the whole length, running in hard gun metal conical bearings of large diameter, and provided with hardened steel thrust collars. The cone pulley is arranged for 4 speeds 3 inches wide. The nose of mandril is screwed to receive chucks, &c. Bed is of very strong section and is mounted on two strong neat cast iron standards. The saddle is fitted with cross slide and compound slide rest, the top slide being fitted with turret (which is of mild steel) 8 inches diameter arranged to carry six tools. This slide may be actuated from a former fixed to the bottom of the cross slide, not shown in the illustration, but can be added if desired. Lathe is fitted with strong steel leading screw, complete set of change wheels and overhead motion consisting of cone speed, hangers, and two sets of pulleys for reversing.

DIMENSIONS:—

Height of centre, 10½in.
Bed, 4ft. 6in. or 5ft. long, 15in. on face, 10in. deep.
Cone Pulley, 4 speeds 3in. wide, largest 13¾in., smallest 7in.

Hole in mandrel, 2in. diameter.
Leading screw, 2¼in. diameter, ½in pitch.
Change wheels, ½ inch pitch.
Approximate weight, 25 cwt.

Price, with former, **£**   **Price,** without former, **£**

BRITANNIA CO., COLCHESTER, England.

London Showrooms—100, *Houndsditch.*   *All Letters to Colchester.*

Improved Chasing Lathe for Brass Finishers, &c.

THIS Lathe is offered to Brass Finishers and others as the best labour saving machine of its kind in the trade. It is constructed with a strong straight bed of wide and deep section, well ribbed, and with a fast headstock of heavy build, having a hollow steel mandrel, with conical necks, running in hard gun metal bearings, and arranged to adjust to take up wear, and made with either single or double gear. The belt cone has 4 speeds for 2 inch belt, and of large diameter. The loose head is made with slide to set over

No. 31.

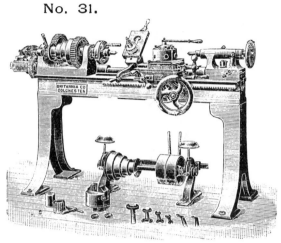

laterally for turning taper shafts. The saddle is made to traverse the bed by rack and pinion, with conveniently placed hand wheel, and is carefully and accurately fitted square with the bed, and carries a compound slide rest mounted with a revolving turret prepared for 6 tools, accurately adjusted to the centres of the heads, and the rest is made to swivel and is accurately graduated to turn or bore to any angle. The rest screws are all of steel and their handles are balanced.

A special advantage of this Lathe is the simple and efficient means provided for self-acting screw chasing, by a shaft at the back of the lathe fitted with levers and a tool holder and die, fitting into a "*former*" fixed at the back of the fast head, and driven from its mandrel by gearing as shewn. This die and former are engaged and disengaged by the lever with handle seen in the engraving laying across the face of the bed, and which carries at its back end the adjustable tool holder with chasing tools, as will be seen. This chasing apparatus can be swung completely out of the way leaving all clear when working the turret rest.

By this means skilled labour is no longer necessary for screwing as a boy can use this tool and produce quicker and more uniformly accurate work. The turret is arranged with locking levers to fix when adjusted and is moved along its slide by screw and by lever also if desired. The lathe is sent out with one former and die to suit, and one master tap to recut the die, and to cut 11 threads per inch or any other pitch preferred; and with complete top driving apparatus made to reverse; tool board, spanners, &c., &c.

The principal dimensions are as follows :—

Bed—length, breadth, and depth, 5ft. by 8¾in. by 6in.
Headstock—6¼in. centres. 16¼in. long.
Cone Pulley—4 speeds, 2in wide, largest 7½in diameter, smallest 3in.

Hole through spindle—1in. diameter.
Gearing (when fitted)—large 8½in. diameter, small 3in. by 1½in. face.
Holes in Turret—1¼in. diameter.
Approximate Weight—10¾ cwt.

PRICES.

	£	s.	d.		£	s.	d.
Complete, with Single Gear	42	0	0	Extra for additional Formers,			
Extra for Back Gearing ...	3	0	0	Dies and Taps, per set of 3			
„ for 2-jaw Chuck with				pieces	1	15	0
slip jaws ...	4	10	0	Per pair for Chasers for Rest	0	7	6
„ for Lever motion to				Each for Tool Holders and			
Turret, in addition to Screw	3	10	0	Tools for Turret ...	1	5	0

BRITANNIA CO., COLCHESTER, England.

London Showrooms—100, *Houndsditch.*   *All Letters to Colchester.*

HOLLOW MANDREL STUD LATHE.
No. 12.

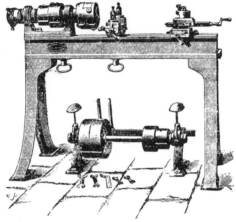

THIS is a tool of very substantial construction, designed for a heavy class of work (for its size and capacity), while its handiness and smoothness of working enables even light work to be efficiently produced. The Headstock is fitted with hollow steel spindle, ground absolutely true, and running in adjustable phosphor bronze bearings, and fitted with Gripping Chucks at both ends.

The illustration shews ordinary Compound Slide Rest, but a Capstan Rest is preferable, fitted with four or more tools and provided with Clamping Lever for fixing it absolutely rigid with the slide when doing heavy work. The Capstan is rotated by hand and is fitted with hardened and ground steel locking ring and adjustable bolt. The Cut-off Rest carries tools back and front, is fitted with tool adjustment for regulating the height, and provided with stops.

DIMENSIONS.

Height of centre ...	5 in.	Diameter of Cone Pulley
Length of Bed ...	5 ft.	6 in. and 4¾ in.
Admit through Spindle	2 in.	Diameter of Capstan ... 4¾ in.
Cone Pulley, 2 Speeds, 3 in. wide		Approximate Weight ... 6 cwt.

	£	s.	d.
Price of Lathe, with plain Cut-off Rest and plain Compound Slide Rest	£31	10	0
Price with Capstan Rest for 4 Tools	37	0	0
Extra for Automatically Revolving Capstan	3	10	0

BRITANNIA CO., COLCHESTER, England.

London Showrooms—100, Houndsditch. All Letters to Colchester.

TREBLE GEARED SCREW-CUTTING FOOT LATHE.

No. 18, 5in. No. 19, 6in.

DESIGNED specially for heavy work by foot power, where steam, gas, or water power is not available.

It is sufficiently strong to take a $\frac{1}{2}$ in. cut off a 2in. or 3in. shaft, or turn a 20in. or 24in. plate or wheel without chattering.

Care has been taken to distribute the metal so that strength is obtained without overloading the foot power.

The bed has a gap with loose bridge fitted, and is firmly bolted to substantial standards. The driving or fly wheel is counterbalanced to overcome the dead centre. The crank shaft has two dips, and runs in anti-friction roller bearings of the most improved design, boxed in so as to exclude all dirt, &c., &c.

The treadle is fitted with anti-friction rollers, and chain connections. The leading screw is steel, accurately cut to $\frac{1}{4}$ in. pitch, and has double clam gun metal nut. The carriage has a flat face and T slots for bolting work to for boring; it is provided with a jambing nut to fix in any position, and has quick return by rack and pinion. The slide rest is made to swivel, and is graduated to turn to any angle.

It is fitted with reversing motion for cutting right and left hand screws.

The head stock is fitted with treble gearing, disengaging by eccentric movement, and can be changed at pleasure to EITHER SINGLE, DOUBLE, OR TREBLE GEAR INSTANTLY. Steel mandrel with conical neck running in gun metal.

The poppet is made either in one casting or with loose bottom and planed sides to set over for turning taper. Steel barrel. Best cast steel centres. Full set of 22 change wheels. Travelling back stay. Face plate and set of steel spanners.

DIMENSIONS AND PRICES.

	No. 18. 5in. centre	No. 19, 6in. centre
Bed, length, depth, and face	5ft. 0in.	6ft. 0in.
	5$\frac{1}{2}$in. by 7$\frac{1}{4}$in.	6in. by 8$\frac{3}{4}$in.
Width, and depth of gap	9in. by 5in.	10in. by 6in.
Diameter of Leading Screw	1$\frac{1}{4}$in.	1$\frac{3}{8}$in.
Diameter of Crank Shaft	1$\frac{3}{8}$in.	1$\frac{1}{4}$in.
Diameter of Body of Mandrel	1in.	1$\frac{1}{8}$in.
Nose of Mandrel, Whitworth	1$\frac{3}{8}$in.	1$\frac{3}{4}$in.
Cone Pulley, 3 speeds	3in., 4$\frac{3}{4}$in., and 6$\frac{1}{2}$in. by 1$\frac{1}{4}$in.	4in., 6in., 8in., by 1$\frac{1}{4}$in.
Diameter of Gearing	6$\frac{3}{4}$in. by 2$\frac{1}{2}$in.	8$\frac{1}{4}$in. by 3in.
Face and pitch of Gearing	1$\frac{1}{4}$in. by 1$\frac{7}{16}$in.	1$\frac{1}{2}$in. by $\frac{1}{2}$in.
Face and pitch of Change Wheels	$\frac{1}{4}$in. by $\frac{3}{4}$in.	$\frac{5}{16}$in. by 1in.
Approximate Weight	10 cwt.	14 cwt.
PRICE—Complete	£36 0 0	£46 10 0
„ if Sliding and Surfacing by Back Shaft also	42 0 0	53 0 0
„ if Sliding and Surfacing only (no Leading Screw) ...	40 0 0	51 0 0
„ Extra for Poppet to set over	0 18 0	1 0 0
„ Less if with Overhead for Power instead of Treadle Motion	2 0 0	3 0 0
„ More or less of bed at per foot	1 10 0	2 0 0
The various Chucks and Fittings shown in the illustration can be supplied, if desired, at the following prices:—		
Extra large Face Plate, to Swing in the Gap	1 15 0	2 0 0
4-jaw Chuck	5 0 0	6 0 0
Fixed steady with 3 adjustable Jaws, top hinged	2 0 0	2 0 0
8-screw Bell Chuck	1 5 0	1 10 0
Angle Brackets to Bolt to Face Plate for boring, &c., 2 sizes ...	10/- & 15/-	12/6 & 17/6
Clement's Driver, as shown in illustration, instead of ordinary Catch Plate	£1 5 0	£1 5 0
Hand Rest and 4 Tees to fit on Saddle	0 15 0	1 0 0
Boring Collar	1 0 0	1 5 0
Soap Suds Can, with brass cock and stand with swivel to rise and fall	0 10 0	0 10 0

No. 18, with 5ft. Bed, is 3ft. 2in. between centres. No. 19, 6ft. Bed, 3ft. 6in. between centres.

THE ABOVE LATHES WERE DESIGNED FOR THE BRITISH NAVY.

BRITANNIA CO., COLCHESTER, England.

London Showrooms—100, Houndsditch. *All Letters to Colchester.*

SELF-ACTING, SLIDING, SURFACING, AND SCREW-CUTTING LATHE,

No. 17, 6 inch, 6 feet

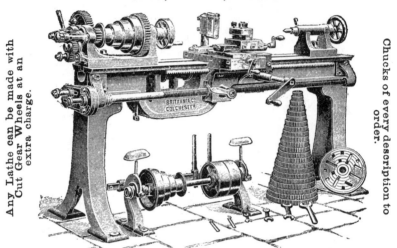

Any Lathe can be made with Cut Gear Wheels at an extra charge.

Chucks of every description to order.

WITH gap bed accurately planed and surfaced, and bridge piece fitted to gap, double-geared headstock, steel spindle with conical neck, gun-metal bearings, reversing motion for cutting right and left-hand screws. The loose head has cylinder barrel and left-hand traverse screw, and made to set over for taper turning, if required; steel leading screw accurately cut, and extending full length of bed, with double clam gun-metal nut gripping screw at top and bottom, saddle with long wings, flush top, and grooved for bolting work to when boring; quick hand traverse by rack and pinion, compound slide rest to swivel to any angle, graduated for turning conical, steel draw screws, back following stay, catch and face plates, twenty-two change wheels, index plate, overhead motion, screw keys, etc., etc.

All materials and workmanship guaranteed.

SPECIFICATION.

Height of Centre, 6 in.; breadth of Bed, $8\frac{3}{4}$ in.; depth of Bed, 6 in.; width of Gap, 10 in.; depth of gap, 6 in.; diameter of Leading Screw, $1\frac{1}{2}$ in.; pitch of Leading Screw, $\frac{1}{4}$ in.; diameter of Back Shaft, 1 in.; Change Wheels (22), $\frac{5}{16}$ in. pitch; Cone Pulley (4 speeds), 2 in. broad; Large Cone, $7\frac{3}{4}$ in. diameter; Large Gear, $8\frac{1}{2}$ in. diameter, $1\frac{1}{2}$ in. broad $\frac{1}{2}$ in. pitch; Body of Spindle, $1\frac{3}{8}$ in. diameter; Nose, $1\frac{3}{4}$ in. diameter. Approximate Weight, with 6 ft. bed, $13\frac{1}{2}$ cwt. Swing in Gap, 12 in.; admits between centres of 6 ft. Lathe, 3 ft. 6 in.

Price, Sliding and Screw-cutting ..	..	..	£37 16 0
Price for Self-acting Sliding, Surfacing, and Screw-Cutting (by Back Shaft) ..	..	..	44 2 0
Poppet to set over, extra	..	..	1 0 0
Extra Length of Bed, per foot ..	..	..	2 0 0

BRITANNIA CO., COLCHESTER, England.

London Showrooms—100, Houndsditch.   *All Letters to Colchester.*

SELF-ACTING SLIDING AND SCREW-CUTTING LATHE.

No. 16.   5 in. and 6 in. Centres.

WITH gap bed accurately planed and surfaced, and bridge piece fitted to gap; double geared headstock; steel spindle with conical neck; hard steel or gun-metal collars; reversing motion for cutting right and left-hand screws. The loose head has cylinder barrel and left-hand traverse screw, and made to set over for taper turning, if required; steel leading screw accurately cut, and extending full length of bed, with double clam gun-metal nut gripping screw at top and bottom; saddle with long wings, flush top, and grooved for bolting work to when boring; quick hand traverse by rack and pinion; compound slide-rest to swivel to any angle, graduated for turning conical and steel draw screws; back follow ng stay; catch and face-plates; twenty-two change wheels; index plate; treadle motion; screw keys, etc., etc. All materials and workmanship guaranteed. The 5ft lathe measures 2ft. 11in. between centres; 6ft. measures 3ft. 10in. between centres.

SPECIFICATION.

Breadth of Bed	...	... 7 inches	5 in. Cone Pulley, 3 speeds	1¼ in. broad	
Depth of Bed	...	... 5⅜ ,,	Large Cone, 6¼ in. diam., smallest. 3¼ in.		
Width of Gap	...	... 9 ,,	Width on face and	5 in. centre, 1¼ & ⅜	
Depth of Gap	...	... 5¼ ,,	pitch of gearing	6 in. ,, 1¼ & 7/16	
Diameter of Leading Screw	...	1¼ ,,	Diam. of large and	5 in. ,, 6⅜ & 2¼	
Pitch of ,, ,,	...	... ¼ ,,	small gear wheels	6 in. ,, 7⅜ & 2½	
Diameter of Back Shaft	...	1 ,,	Diam. of nose of	5 in. ., 1¼	
Change Wheels, 22 ...	... ¼in. Pitch		Steel Mandril ...	6 in. ,, 1⅜	
6 in. Cone Pulley, 3 speeds	1½in. broad				

Approximate Weight, with 6 ft. Bed, 10½ cwt; 5 ft., 9 cwt.

Price, Sliding and Screw-cutting, 5 in. Centre, 5 ft. Bed ...	£31	10	0
Ditto ditto 6 in. Centre, 6 ft. Bed ...	35	14	0
Extra Length of Bed, per foot	2	0	0
If made without Treadle, but with Overhead for Steam Power, 5 in. Centre, 5 ft. Bed	30	0	0
Ditto ditto 6 in. Centre, 6 ft. Bed ...	34	0	0
If Self-acting Sliding, Surfacing, and Screw-cutting (by Back Shaft and Leading Screw), extra	4	4	0
Poppet to set over, extra	1	0	0

BRITANNIA CO., COLCHESTER, England.

London Showrooms—100, *Houndsditch.*   *All Letters to Colchester.*

No. 15 LATHE.

With 4 or 5 ft. Beds.

Overhead Motions similar to that shown on Lukin Lathe can be fitted to any Lathe from £5 5s.

Ornamental Drill Spindle, £1 10s.

SELF-ACTING Sliding and Screw-cutting, with 4 ft. gap bed, back geared headstock, cast steel mandrel, conical necks running in hardened collars, steel lock nuts and back centre, cone pulley turned three speeds for gut band. fitted with reversing motion for cutting right or left-hand screws. Compound slide rest, with long bearings, accurately fitted to bed. The top slide is made to swivel, and is graduated to 50° each side of centre to turn cones to any angle. The tail stock has cylinder mandrel, square thread traverse screw, bright turned hand wheel.

The bed is accurately planed, and is 6¼ in. wide and 4¼ in. deep. The gap is 4¼ in. deep, 6 in. wide. Steel leading screw, 1⅛ in. diameter and ¼ in. pitch, the gunmetal nut for ditto is in halves to detach. The lathe is fitted with rack and pinion for quick return. It has a full set of 22 change wheels, is fitted with steel centres, face plate, catch plate, spanners, &c. Strong iron stand, with improved treadle motion, with adjustable outside crank and friction rollers. or with ordinary crank and pitman. The 4 ft. lathe measures between centres 2 ft. 6 in., swings 1 ft. 4 in., in gap. The flywheel is counterbalanced, and has 5 speeds. Weight of 4 in. lathe about 5 cwt.

These Lathes can be fitted with Overheads for Steam Power at 20s. less than as for Foot Power.

We can fit cut gear wheels to this or any other of our Lathes at an extra charge.

Price, 4 in. centre, **£25 4s.**; 4½ in., **£26 15s. 6d.**; 5 in., **£28 7s.**

If self-acting and surfacing by back shaft, extra **£4**. If with Flat Speed Pulleys, **21/-** extra. Set over Poppet, **20/-** extra. If with 5 ft. bed, **£2** extra. Quick withdraw motion to slide rest, extra **50/-**.

The 5 in. flat speed belt pulleys have 3 speeds, 3¼ in., 4⅜ in., 6¼ in. by 1 in. wide. Gearing, ⅞ in. face by 6¾ in. diameter, ₁⁶ in. pitch.

The 4 in. flat speed belt pulleys have 3 speeds, 2¼ in., 3¹³⁄₁₆ in., and 5⅞ in. by 1 in. wide. Gearing, ¾ in. face by 5⅝ in. diameter, ¼ in. pitch.

☞ **NOTE.—The Leading Screw and Wearing Parts are Steel.**

BRITANNIA CO., COLCHESTER, England.

London Showrooms—100, Houndsditch.   All Letters to Colchester.

No. 14 NEW AND IMPROVED
SELF-ACTING & SCREW-CUTTING LATHE.
3½-inch Centres. 3 ft. 6 in. Bed.

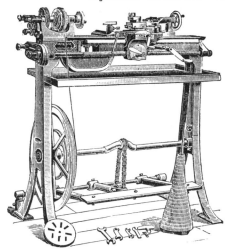

THIS is a self-acting sliding and screw-cutting Lathe of new design of 3½ inch centre and with 3 ft. 6 in. gap bed. The fast Headstock is well constructed with Back Gearing, machine cut out of solid hard steel mandrel, conical neck, adjusting cone at back end to take up wear, and running in hardened steel collars, three-speed cone pulley, for gut band and fitted with reversing gear to cut right or left-hand screws. The Poppet Head has a steel cylindrical Mandrel, a left hand square thread traverse screw, and bright turned hand-wheel; best steel centres, cone-fitted.

The Saddle is strongly made, with flush top and T grooves for bolting work to, for boring; well scraped and fitted to bed, with adjustable strip to take up wear, and carries a compound slide rest of modern design, swivelling and graduated to turn at any angle; improved tool-holder.

The Bed is cast-iron, V edges, all machine planed, 3 ft. 6 in. long, 4¾ inch on face, 3¾ deep, with gap 5 inch wide and 3¾ inch deep, with bridge piece properly fitted.

The leading screw is steel, accurately cut ¼ inch pitch and one inch diameter, with double gun-metal nuts, disengaging by eccentric motion, and the saddle is fitted with rack and pinion for quick return motion.

The Bed is planed at bottom and firmly bolted on to strong cast-iron standards, planed at top faces.

The Crank shaft and Treadle shaft run in self-adjusting, swivelling bearings. The Treadle is made with three cast-iron arms, and bright turned shaft, and connected with the bright turned crank shaft by anti-friction chain and roller. The driving wheel is 24 in. in diameter, bright turned, with three top speeds and a small speed for slow motion. A polished tool tray is neatly fitted between the standards, extending back and front to hold tools, small work, &c It has a full set of 22 Change Wheels, 14 pitch ⅝ inch face, Face and Catch Plates, Eccentric Hand Rest and 2 Tees, Spanners, Keys, &c., &c. It will admit 25 inch between Centres, 5¼ inch diameter over Saddle, 7 inch over Bed and 14¼ inch in the Gap. Height from Centre to floor is 3 ft. 8 in. Approximate Weight, 430 lbs.

Price .. .. .. £18 18s.
As Bench Lathe only .. 16 5s.

Cut Gear Wheels for this or any other Lathe at extra charge.
Quick Withdraw Motion to Slide Rest extra. 50s.
If with Cone Speed and Driving Wheel for Flat Belt, 21s. extra.
Ornamental Overhead Motion, similar to Lukin Lathe, £5 5s.
Drill Spindle for Ornamental Turning, 30s. extra.

BRITANNIA CO., COLCHESTER, England.

London Showrooms—100, Houndsditch. All Letters to Colchester.

LATHE No. 13.

Improved Self-acting, Sliding, and Screw-cutting Gap Bed Lathe, of superior finish, best material and workmanship.

SPECIFICATION.

THREE-INCH centre, 30 in. gap bed; the headstock is back-geared with cast steel spindle, conical necks, steel lock nuts and back centre, machine cut gearing, coned pulley, turned three speeds for gut band, fitted with reversing motion for cutting right and left-hand screws; compound slide rest on carriage with long bearings accurately fitted and scraped to bed, and well gibbed. The top slide is made to swivel, and is graduated to 50° each side of centre to turn cones to any desired angle; strong tool holder with steel screws and made to swivel; tail stock of good design, cylinder mandrel, square thread traverse screw. bright turned hand wheel. The bed (machine planed) is $3\frac{1}{2}$ in. on face, $2\frac{3}{8}$ in. deep with gap $2\frac{1}{4}$ in. deep, and $2\frac{7}{8}$ in. wide. The leading screw is $\frac{7}{8}$ in diameter, $\frac{1}{4}$ in. pitch, accurately cut; the gunmetal nut is in halves to detach, and lathe is fitted with rack and pinion for quick return motion. It has a full set of 22 change wheels; it is fitted with face plate, catch plate, steel centres, double spanner, and mounted on an iron stand, with polished wood top and drawer; flywheel 20 in. diameter, with four turned speeds, treadle motion, &c., complete. Measures between centres, 19 in., swings, $10\frac{1}{2}$ in. by $2\frac{7}{8}$ in. in gap, 6 in. over the bed, and $4\frac{1}{4}$ in. over the carriage. Total weight, about $2\frac{1}{4}$ cwt.

Price—Without Ornamental Overhead   ..   **15 Guineas.**

,,   with 3 ft. Gap Bed   16   ,,

,,   3 ft. 6 in.   ,, ...   17   ,,

Overhead Motion for Ornamental Turning, as illustration, **£3 15s.**

Drill Spindle, **30s.**

Extra Hard Mandrel and Collars, **30s.** extra.

Self-surfacing off Leadiug Screw, **£3 10s.** extra.

BRITANNIA CO., COLCHESTER, England.

London Showrooms—100, *Houndsditch.*   *All Letters to Colchester.*

THE LUKIN LATHE.

FOR ORNAMENTAL TURNING.

LATHES MADE TO ANY DESIGN.

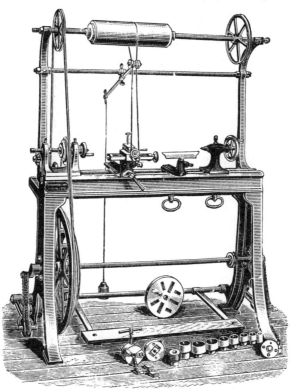

CONSTRUCTED TO THE DESIGN OF J. LUKIN, B.A.

It is fitted with Traversing Mandrel and Six Guides for Chasing Screws on Microscopes, Telescopes, and similar metal work, or on Box Lids and similar work in wood. A great variety of beautiful ornamental work may be done by suitable appliances.

Price of Lathe, 5 in. centre, 4 ft. bed, with Traversing Mandrel, Six formers ..	..	..	..	..	£22 10 0
Ornamental Overhead	..	..	..	..	..	7 10 0
Ornamental Slide Rest	..	..	..	..	..	15 15 0
Division Plate	..	..	..	..	..	2 10 0
Plain Slide Rest ..	..	..	..	..	..	5 0 0
Ornamental Drill Spindle	..	..	..	..	1 10 0

Price, extra, if bed be 4 ft. 6 in., 12/6; or 5 ft. long, 25/-. Price, extra, of bed with gap, 20/-.

Oval, Eccentric, Geometric, or any of the Chucks or Appliances in our list can be fitted at list price.

BRITANNIA CO., COLCHESTER, England.

London Showrooms—100, Houndsditch.   All Letters to Colchester.

IMPROVED FOOT LATHE,

No. 5.

This is a Lathe with a heavy Bed, Standards and Flywheel. Bed is 4 ft. long and 4½ in. on face. It has an Improved Treadle Motion, combining great power with ease of motion; the bright turned shaft on which wheel is keyed runs in Friction Rollers at each end. The Head is fitted with hard steel mandrel and collars. The Crank (as illustration shows) is *outside* the left-hand standard, and is slotted, in order that the driving stud may be adjusted to give more or less leverage to increase or decrease power at will of the operator. The Flywheel is counterbalanced to avoid dead centre. Approximate weight, 4½ Cwt.

Each Lathe is accompanied by Hand Rest with two Tees, Face, and Catch Plates, two plain Centres, and Spanners.

4 in. Centre ($\frac{3}{4}$ in. nose)	..	£11	0	0	Back Geared (1 in. nose)	£13	0	0
4½	.. ($\frac{7}{8}$,,) ..	11	10	0	,, ($1\frac{1}{4}$,,)	13	15	0
5	,, ($\frac{7}{8}$,,) ..	12	0	0	,. ($1\frac{1}{4}$,,)	14	10	0

Gap Bed, 20/- extra.   Slide Rests and Chucks as per list.

Extra Large Face Plate to suit Gap, 20/- extra.   5 ft. Bed, 20/- extra.

A similar Lathe, with 5 in. centre, heavier bed, 5½ in. on face, 5 ft. long, weight about 5½ cwt.—

Single Geared   ..   **£14.**   Back Geared   ..   **£16.**

If with 6 ft. bed, 20/- extra.   Gap Bed, 20/- extra.

Overhead, similar to the Lukin Lathe, £5 5. Ornamental Drill Spindle, 30/-

The above Lathes can be fitted with Hooks and Cranks instead of Chains.

The Lathes with 4 ft. Bed will admit about 2 ft. 4 in. between Centres.

BRITANNIA CO., COLCHESTER, England.

London Showrooms —100. Houndsditch.   All Letters to Colchester.

IMPROVED FOOT LATHE,

No. 4.

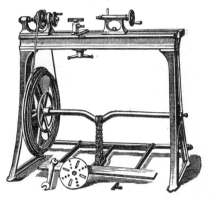

THIS illustration represents an excellent Foot Lathe especially suited for Gas Fitters, Jewellers, Dentists or Amateurs.

It has a machine-planed iron Bed, 3 ft. long, on strong iron standards, with 4-speed turned fly-wheel, and an easy, light-running treadle movement.

The single-geared headstock has a steel mandrel, with hard-coned neck running in hard collar.

The back-geared headstock has a hard steel mandrel. with reverse cones (adjustable to take up wear), and running in hard steel collars, steel-coned centre, 3-speed turned cone pulley.

The tailstock has cylinder mandrel, with square thread steel traversing screw and steel-coned centre. Each Lathe is accompanied by hand rest, with two tees, face and catch plates, two plain centres, spanner, and tool table. The 3 ft. Lathe takes 1 ft. 6 in. between centres.

Slide rests and chucks as per list.

Ordinary Tees, 4 in. and 9 in.; Extra long Tee, 12 in., extra **3/6**.

Strength and durability are obtained in a high degree, without clumsiness. Approximate Weight of 3 ft. 6 in. Lathe, 2 cwt. 3 qrs.

				£	s.					£	s.
$3\frac{1}{2}$ in. Centre,	$\frac{3}{4}$ in. nose			**8**	**0**	Back Geared,	1 in. nose			**10**	**0**
4 ,,	,,	$\frac{3}{4}$	,,	**8**	**10**	,,	1	,,	**10**	**15**
$4\frac{1}{2}$,,	,,	$\frac{7}{8}$	,,	**9**	**0**	,,	$1\frac{1}{4}$	,,	**11**	**10**
5 ,,	,,	$\frac{7}{8}$	,,	**9**	**10**	,,	$1\frac{1}{4}$	,,	**12**	**0**

3 ft. 6 in. Bed, **10/** - extra. 4 ft. **20/**- extra.

If with Gap Bed and Bridge, **20/**- extra.

Extra Large Face Plate, to use with Gap Bed, **20/**-

Fitted with overhead like the Lukin Lathe, **£5 5.**

Ornamental Drill Spindle, **30/**- extra. Division Plates to order.

BRITANNIA CO., COLCHESTER, England.

London Showrooms—100, *Houndsditch.* *All Letters to Colchester.*

D

NEW
SINGLE GEARED LATHE.
No. 8.

3½ in. Centres.   2 ft. 6 in. Bed.

WILL TAKE 16½ INCHES BY 7 INCHES BETWEEN CENTRES.

THE above is introduced to supply a demand for a Lathe coming between our No. 3 and No. 4 patterns. It is fitted with gun-metal mountings. and it can be recommended with confidence for general light turning, and for amateurs, clockmakers, etc.

It is thoroughly well made, and very light running. The fast head is fitted with best steel mandrel and best steel collar, both hardened, 4 speed turned cone pulley, nose ⅝ in. Whitworth: the loose head has steel cylindrical spindle, square thread traverse screw, best steel centres, hand rest and 2 tees, machine-planed cast-iron bed, 3¼ in. face, 3 in. deep, securely bolted to cast-iron standards; wrought-iron crank shaft and treadle, working on steel centres, turned speed fly-wheel. tool board, leather driving cord, driver chuck, drill chuck, etc., complete. Weight, 180 lbs.

Price   ..   .. **£6 10s.,** or with 3 ft. Bed. **£7.**

Slide rest, to suit, £3   Tools for both hand and slide rest kept in stock.
Any of the chucks in our general list can be fitted to any lathe.

BRITANNIA CO., COLCHESTER, England.

*London Showrooms—*100, *Houndsditch.   All Letters to Colchester.*

No. 10 CHEAP WOOD-TURNING LATHE.

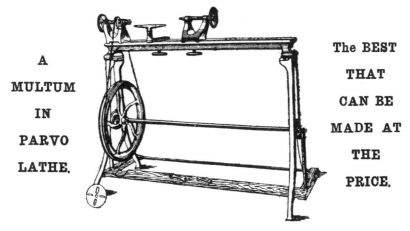

**A
MULTUM
IN
PARVO
LATHE.**

**The BEST
THAT
CAN BE
MADE AT
THE
PRICE.**

THE very great demand for a cheap but efficient Lathe for wood turning, with long bed and high centres suitable for pattern-makers, joiners and amateurs, has led us to introduce the above, and we fix the price so low as to bring it within the reach of the million.

It is entirely constructed of Iron and Steel except the treadle, which is of hard wood for quietness and lightness.

The planed cast iron bed is 4 ft. long 4 inches wide and 4 inches deep, iron standards, arranged with adjusting swivelling bearings for the steel wheel shaft. The driving wheel has two speeds, and is about 21 inches diameter. The parallel bearings of the Fast Head are split and fitted with screws to take up wear.

The steel mandrel is made with a collar forged on, with a ¾ in. nose screwed Whitworth standard, to which most of our ordinary chucks may be at any time fitted ; the tail end of this mandrel carries a balance wheel. The cone pulley has two speeds corresponding with driving wheel.

Turned steel centres with taper shanks to fit into spindles. Face plate 5 inches diameter, Fork driver Chuck, Hand Rest and 9 inch Tee, Spanner and Belt are sent with each Lathe.

Height from floor to top of Bed, 36in.	Extreme distance between Centres, 36in.
Height of Centres from Bed 5 in.	Total Weight .. .. 144 lbs.

Price complete .. .. .. £4 10s.

BRITANNIA CO., COLCHESTER, England.

London Showrooms—100, *Houndsditch.*   *All Letters to Colchester.*

BACK-GEARED LATHE,

No. 3.

A FIRST-CLASS, well-finished Lathe, with machine-planed iron bed, plain or with gap ; back-geared headstock, cast-steel mandrel, conical necks, tail pin running through; adjusting screw, and lock nuts to take up wear ; 3-speed bright turned cone pulley ; steel centres, tail-stock with cylinder mandrel, square thread traverse screw; eccentric hand rest and 2 tees and catchplate as shown. Weight, on Stand complete, 149 lbs.

Bed 30 in. long, and 3 in. centres, turning 18 in. by 6 in.

	£	s.	d.
Price–without stand, as Bench Lathe only, with back-geared headstock and plain straight back	4	0	0
Ditto, with back gear and gap bed	4	10	0
Ditto, with 3 ft. gap bed like No. 13 lathe, extra	1	0	0
Face Plate, to suit 5½ in. diameter	0	10	0
Slide Rest to suit	2	10	0
Foot Power Motion, to fix under Bench, with 4-speed turned fly-wheel, 20 in. diameter, treadle and frame complete as illustrated	1	10	0
Substantial Iron Stand complete, with polished wood top and tool drawer, 4-speed turned fly-wheel, 20 in. diameter, treadle, &c.	2	0	0
Ditto, of a heavier make, with very heavy fly-wheel, as shown in No. 13 Lathe	2	10	0
Lathes fitted with hard mandrel and collars, extra	1	10	0
Ditto, division plate and steel index	1	10	0

Can also be fitted with Fret Sawing Appliance, Circular Saws, Emery and Buff Wheels, Chucks, &c.

BRITANNIA CO., COLCHESTER, England.

London Showrooms—100, Houndsditch.   All Letters to Colchester.

Nos. 2 and 3 LATHES.

Suitable for Amateurs, Jewellers, Dentists,

OR ANY LIGHT USE.

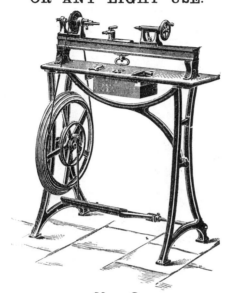

No. 2.

24 in. bed, 2½ in. centres, turning 14 in. long by 5 in. in diameter.

Price, without stand, as Bench Lathe only	£1 15 0
Or with Stand, Fly-wheel, and Treadle complete	3 10 0
Foot-power Motion, with Treadle and Frame, and 18 in. Fly-wheel, as illustration on page 100	1 2 0

Weight complete, 81 lbs.

No. 3.

30 in. bed, 3 in centres, turning 18 in. long by 6 in. in diameter.

Price without stand, as Bench Lathe only	2 5 0
Or with Stand, Fly-wheel, and Treadle complete	4 5 0
If with Gap bed, extra	0 10 0
Foot-power Motion, with 20-in. Fly-wheel, Treadle and Frame, as illustrated on page 100	1 10 0

Weight complete, 128 lbs.

First-class, well-finished Lathes, with machine-planed iron bed; headstock has steel mandrel with conical neck and adjusting screw and lock nut to take up wear; 3-speed bright turned cone pulley ; hardened centres, driver chuck, cylinder mandrel with square thread traverse screw to tail stock, hand rest and two tees. Substantial iron stand with polished wood top and tool drawer, turned speed fly-wheel, and easy treadle motion.

Circular Saws, emery and buff wheels, can be used in these Lathes.

Fret-sawing Appliance, to suit the No. 3 Lathe, which attaches very easily to bed and is driven by the Lathe, price £1 10s.

If fitted with hard Mandrel and Collar, 30s. extra.

BRITANNIA CO., COLCHESTER. England.

London Showrooms—100, Houndsditch.   All Letters to Colchester.

LATHE No. 6.

THIS Lathe has been designed to meet the demand for a lower priced tool than Nos. 2 and 3 Lathes.

It has a planed iron bed, 20 in. long; $2\frac{1}{2}$ in. centre heads, which can easily be blocked up to 4 in. for wood turning; will admit 11 in. between centres. It is fitted with a well-designed stand with a turned fly-wheel, 18 in. diameter. Each Lathe has a spanner, hand rest, and two tees, driver chuck and centres, drill chuck, and fork centre for wood. Weight complete, 78 lbs.

The "catch-plate" shown in illustration has been replaced by a more convenient "driver chuck."

Price, complete   -   -   -   £2 15s.
Slide Rest to suit, £2.

Even this, our Cheapest Lathe, has a Conical Mandrel.

Beware of so-called Cheap Lathes, which have no provision for taking up wear.

BRITANNIA CO., COLCHESTER, England.

London Showrooms—100, *Houndsditch.*   *All Letters to Colchester.*

LAPIDARY'S LATHE.

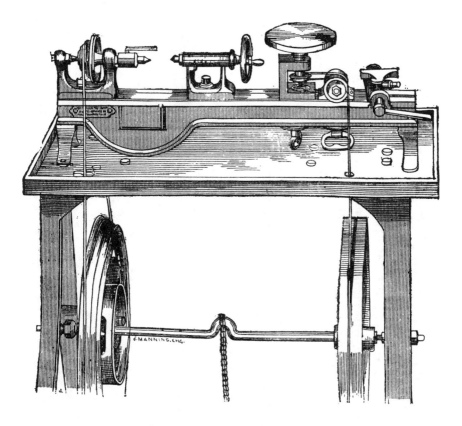

ABOVE illustration shows a very useful lapidary attachment, which can be fixed to any Lathe. By its use stones can be ground and polished upon the horizontal plate by emery or other cutting powders.

Price of the Apparatus without Lathe, from £6.

BRITANNIA CO., COLCHESTER, England.

London Showrooms—100, *Houndsditch.*   *All Letters to Colchester.*

BRITANNIA CO.'S
Combined Epicycloidal, Rose-Cutting, Eccentric-Cutting, Drilling, Fluting & Vertical-Cutting Appliance.

(Also easily adapted for cutting spirals on the cylinder.) Beddow's Patent, No. 23,743, of 1893.

For description and samples of work see pages 105 to 107.

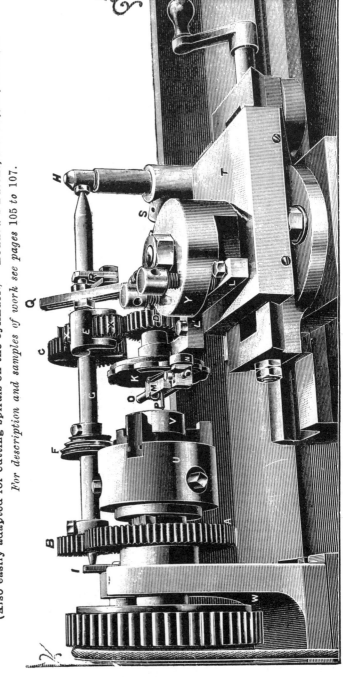

BRITANNIA CO., COLCHESTER, England.
London Showrooms—100, Houndsditch. *All Letters to Colchester.*

BRITANNIA CO.'S

Combined Epicycloidal, Rose-Cutting, Eccentric-Cutting, Drilling, Fluting & Vertical-Cutting Appliance.

For illustration see page 104.

THIS apparatus meets a long-felt want, viz., that of a **cheap** and **efficient** appliance for performing in the handiest manner, and by an **entirely new method,** a singular variety of ornamental work in the Lathe, some of it entirely new, and the rest hitherto out of the reach of most amateurs owing to the prohibitive prices of the various instruments, each doing one special kind of work only. The surface designs which may be produced, are absolutely unlimited in number and variety, and their character again is entirely altered when deep cuts to show facets, with, say, a broad round-nosed cutter. Any epicycloidal pattern, having a decided loop, may be cut in this manner.

All manner of the most beautiful work may also be executed with this appliance on the cylinder.

It can be used in any Lathe that is provided with a slide-rest and an ordinary jaw chuck. The only fitting or alteration required being a wheel fitted to the chuck (or mandrel), and a moveable bracket bolted to the mandrel-head. (For vertical cutting a plain spindle with no graduated arm, but a hole and a set-screw to take the cutters is preferable, and for spiral work on the cylinder a fixed collar and a wheel added to the slide-rest is also required.)

For the epicycloidal and compound geometric work no overhead motion, or division plate and index, is required, and if the slide-rest is not an ornamental one, any graduation required on it is easily done by the aid of the instrument itself.

Its strength and simplicity are notable points, and there is little doubt when its capabilities become known and are realized, that it will form an indispensable adjunct to the Lathe, as it is not a toy, but a really useful tool for a great variety of purposes.

The engraving on page 100 shows the apparatus as fixed in an ordinary Lathe ready for surface cutting. T is an ordinary slide-rest, in which is clamped the frame L, L, carrying a revolving spindle (called the tool spindle), on which is fixed by a set-screw the wheel D, the boss being to the left and close to the frame, which prevents the spindle from moving to the right or left. This wheel is connected with the wheel C on shaft G, by means of the carrier wheels X. X, fixed in the frame E, which is in turn fixed in any desired position by means of a screw and nut to the adjustable arm Q. This arm is centred upon one of the steel collars in which the tool spindle works. so that in whatever position it is fixed the carrier wheels always remain in gear with wheel D. Similarly, by means of the jointed arm R, they may be kept in gear with wheel C. so that by slackening the set-screw, which retains the arm Q in any desired position, the slide-rest may be advanced to or from the centre of the work V to be ornamented, all the wheels remaining in gear and with exactly the same play between the teeth.

By fastening a spring at one end of bar, and attaching to it a glass pen or a pencil, designs may be traced on paper instead of being cut. with, however, some slight and unavoidable loss of accuracy as compared with the fixed cutter.

BRITANNIA CO., COLCHESTER, England.

London Showrooms—100, Houndsditch.   *All Letters to Colchester.*

THE SPIRAL CUTTING APPLIANCE.

For spiral and twist cutting on the cylinder the cutters are fixed in the spindle used for vertical cutting, and revolved in a similar manner, *i.e.*, direct by the overhead motion. The bracket **I** is bolted on the front part of the mandrel head (or if sufficiently long, and curved, in the same position as described), and the hand-rest containing the pillar **H** is brought forward so that the shaft **G** is in front of the work to be ornamented instead of behind it as before. This new position obviates the necessity of using very large wheels, and also allows of the poppet-head being advanced to support the work if desired.

A collar is fastened to the slide-rest, and centred on the handle, and on this collar the arm **Q** works, just as on the projecting collar of the frame, the carrier wheels being bolted on the right-hand side of it instead of on the left. These wheels gear with a small wheel fixed on the handle of the rest (the latter traversing the tool during the cutting of the twist) and with the wheel **O** on the shaft **G** as before. Wheel **B** gearing with wheel **A** on this side of it, instead of at the back as previously directed.

By using wheels of various sizes, the twist or spirals will be varied accordingly.

Full directions are sent with each appliance.

PRICES OF

Beddow's Patent Lathe Appliance.

Malleable iron with steel spindle revolving in same, set of cast change wheels, 10 in number, cast iron radial arm and reversing gear, iron sling, and spindle to carry change wheels	£10	0 0
Rosette attachment with one brass rosette, metal arm, and roller rubber	1	12 6
Extra spindle for drills	1	0 0
Drills and cutters, per dozen	1	1 0
	£13	13 6
A superior highly finished instrument composed of gun metal frame with hardened steel collars, cast steel spindle with eccentric arm, steel radial arm, gun metal frame for reversing and connecting gear, full set of 10 machine-cut cast iron change wheels, nett ...	£15	15 0
Rosette attachment in 2 brass rosettes, steel arms, and roller rubber, oscillating spindle mathematically divided, and grooved to retain the rubber rigidly in its place	2	12 6
Extra spindle for drill	1	1 0
Spiral attachment	2	2 0
Drills, cutters, &c., per dozen	1	1 0

BRITANNIA CO., COLCHESTER, England.

London Showrooms—100, Houndsditch. All Letters to Colchester.

SAMPLES OF WORK DONE
ON
Britannia Co.'s Ornamental Appliance.

Fig. 23.

Fig. 27.

Fig. 20.

Fig. 33.

Fig. 34.

Fig. 20.—Seven Cuts of Fourteen Loop Combination, Circulating, External.
,, 23.—Examples of Twelve Loop Combination, Direct.
,, 27.—Two Cuts of Fifteen Loop Combination, Circulating.
,, 33 and 34.—Examples of Eccentric Circle Cutting.

BRITANNIA CO., COLCHESTER, England.
London Showrooms—100, *Houndsditch.*   *All Letters to Colchester.*

APPLIANCES FOR LATHES.

MOST of the foregoing LATHES can be made with Hollow Mandrels drilled about 5 inches up, if desired, at from **10/-** extra ; or hole quite through, from **20/-** extra.

If with extra hardened finished Mandrels and collars, extra, **30/-**

SELF-ACTING SCREW-CUTTING LATHES. can be fitted for Self-acting Surfacing also, either from the Leading Screw (in small sizes) or by Back Shaft (in larger sizes), at from £3 **10s.** extra.

BORING-COLLARS.

	For 3 in.	4 in.	4½ in.	5 in.	6 in.	7½ in.	9 in.	10 in.	12 in. centre.
Price,	15/-	17/6	20/-	25/-	30/-	37/6	45/-	50/-	55/-
BACK STAYS	10/-	12/6	12/6	12/6	15/-	20/-	25/-	30/-	35/-

DIVISION PLATES can be fitted to any of the foregoing Lathes, either to Single or Double Geared Headstocks, and with one, two, three, four or more circles of holes, including Spring Index Point, at from **10/-** to **60/-** extra, about **5/-** per hundred holes.

ORNAMENTAL SLIDE RESTS, from £6 **10/-** each.

    ,,   **TOOL CUTTER RECEPTACLE,** 15/- Cutters, 1/6 each.

ECCENTRIC CUTTING INSTRUMENTS, from £3 **10/-** each.

ORNAMENTAL CUTTERS for above, **18/-** to **24/-** per dozen.

DRILLING INSTRUMENT, for Ornamental Work, from £1 **10/-**

ORNAMENTAL DRILLS, for above, **1/6** and **2/-** each.

VERTICAL CUTTING INSTRUMENT, for Wheel Cutting, Fluting Slotting, Nicking Heads of Screws £4 **4/-** Cutters for ditto, **10/-** each.

ECCENTRIC CHUCKS, with Ratchet Wheel and Detent, Rectilinear Slide and Screw, Ratchet Nose, at £8, £12 and £15, according to size and construction.

OVAL CHUCKS, at £9, £12 **10/-** and £16, according to size and construction.

GEOMETRIC CHUCKS, from £25 to £90.

ORNAMENTAL OVERHEADS, as No. 13, from £3 **15/-**

    ,,   **DRILL SPINDLES** from **30/-**

Metal Spinning can be done on almost all our Lathes. See our Lathe Book, page 139.

SURFACE PLATES, cast from specially prepared close grained iron, carefully planed and scraped perfectly true ; well-ribbed, thick and heavy, turned handles, 15 in. by 9 in. £2 **15/-** 18 in. by 14in. £4 **15/-** Other sizes in proportion.

LATHE HEADSTOCKS.

Of superior quality, new designs, as shown on our Lathes. Complete with Face and Catch Plates, Hand Rest, and Two Tees.

(Face Plates are not included in the 2½ in. and 3 in. sizes.)

Price,	2½ in.	3 in.	3½ in.	4 in.	4½ in.	5 in.	6 in.	7½ in.	9 in.	10 in.	12 in.
Single geared for gut or flat band	25/-	35/-	70/-	80/-	90/-	100/-	120/-	160/-	200/-		
Back geared for gut	70/-	110/-	125/-	140/-	150/-	190/-					
Extra strong for flat band							260/-	290/-	330/-	450/-	600/-

Extra hard steel mandrel and collars from **30/-** extra.

Back geared Headstocks for flat band, 6 in. and under, **21/-** extra.

BRITANNIA CO., COLCHESTER, England.

London Showrooms—100, Houndsditch. All Letters to Colchester.

LATHE CASTINGS IN ROUGH OR PART FINISHED.

LATHE BEDS, STRAIGHT AND GAP.

Cat. No.	Length.	Face.	Depth.	Price of Castings in rough	Price, Machine Planed	Gap Beds in the rough.	Gaps fitted in and planed
	ft. in	in.	in.	£ s. d.	£ s. d.	£ s. d.	£ s. d.
6	0 20 ×	2 ×	2	0 3 6	0 5 6	—	—
2	2 0 ,,	2 ,,	2	0 6 0	0 9 0	—	—
3	2 6 ,,	2½ ,,	2⅛	0 7 6	0 11 6	0 10 6	1 1 0
4	3 0 ,,	4⅜ ,,	3⅝	0 13 0	1 6 0	0 18 0	2 0 0
4	3 6 ,,	4⅜ ,,	3⅝	0 15 0	1 10 0	1 0 0	2 5 0
5	4 0 ,,	4⅝ ,,	4¾	1 0 0	1 17 0	1 7 6	2 15 0
5	5 0 ,,	5¼ ,,	5½	1 10 0	2 15 0	2 0 0	3 15 0
5	6 0 ,,	5¼ ,,	5½	1 15 0	3 2 6	2 5 0	4 5 0

SCREW CUTTING LATHE BEDS, WITH GAPS.

Catalogue No.	Length.	Face.	Depth.	Price of Castings in the rough.	Price with Gaps fitted in & planed.
	ft. in.	in.	in.	£ s. d.	£ s. d.
13	2 6 ×	3½ ×	3	0 18 0	2 0 0
13	3 0 ,,	3½ ,,	3	1 0 0	2 5 0
15	4 0 ,,	6¼ ,,	4⅜	1 10 0	3 0 0
16	5 0 ,,	7⅛ ,,	5½	2 5 0	4 10 0
16	6 0 ,,	7⅜ ,,	5½	2 12 6	5 5 0
17	6 0 ,,	8¾ ,,	6	3 7 6	6 0 0
17	7 0 ,,	9 ,,	7	4 7 6	8 0 0

Larger Lathe Beds to any size to order.

LATHE DRIVING WHEEL CASTINGS.

	For Gut.						For Flat Belt.			
Diameter, inches	14	18½	20	20	24	27	27 × 1¼	27 × 1¼	27 × 1½	27 × 2
Weight, lbs. ...	17	28	36	59	82	124	113	130	125	183
No. of Speeds...	3	2	4	4	4	5	3	4	3	4
Price in rough	3/-	4/9	6/-	10/-	14/6	21/-	19/-	22/-	21/-	30/6
Bored and turned	7/-	9/-	12/6	17/6	25/6	34/-	32/6	35/6	33/6	52/-

LATHE CRANK SHAFTS.

Single Throw.

	Double Throw.			

For Lathes of Length Bed	2ft. 6in.	3ft.	3ft.	4ft.	4ft.	5ft.	6ft.	7ft.
Rough forgings	4/-	4/3	7/6	8/6	12/6	16/6	18/6	21/-
Shaft and Dips turned bright	8/-	9/-	14/-	17/-	22/-	28/-	32/-	36/-

Anti-Friction Roller Bearings for Crank Shafts, 17/6 per pair.

CHANGE WHEELS FOR SCREW CUTTING LATHES.

No.	14	12	10	8	7	6
Pitch ... ... inch	$\frac{3}{16}$ full	¼ full	$\frac{5}{16}$	⅜	$\frac{7}{16}$ full	½ full
In Rough	12/6	16/6	30/-	50/-	70/-	95/-
Bored, turned and key ways cut	30/-	37/-	51/-	67/-	85/-	108/-

Special quotations for Bevel and Mitre Wheels, Racks, etc.

Machine Cut Gearing of all kinds.

COMPOUND SLIDE REST CASTINGS.

For Lathes of Height Centre	2	2½	3	3½	4	4½	5	6	7	8	10 in.
Price, Rough	2/3	2/3	2 9	4/-	5/6	6 9	11/-	13/-	19/-	22/-	40/-
,, Planed	6/-	6/-	9/-	11/6	16/-	18/6	22/-	30/-	38/-	60/-	100/-

BRITANNIA CO., COLCHESTER, England.

London Showrooms—100, Houndsditch.   *All Letters to Colchester.*

Castings for Lathe Headstocks and Rests.

Catalogue No.	Height of Centres. Inches	Component Parts of Sets.	Price in the rough.			Do. Heads Bored and Planed.		
			£	s.	d.	£	s.	d.
		SINGLE GEARED.						
2	2½	Headstock, Cone Speed, Driver Chuck, Poppet, Hand Wheel, Cap, Barrel and Screw, Mandrel, Cast Steel for Centres, Holding down Plates, Hand Rest and two Tees	0	10	0	0	14	0
3	3	Ditto and Locking Handle	0	12	0	0	17	0
4	3½	Ditto and Face and Catch Plates	1	5	0	1	14	0
4 or 5	4	Ditto ditto ...	1	7	6	1	17	6
4 or 5	4½	Ditto ditto ...	1	10	0	2	1	0
4 or 5	5	Ditto ditto ...	1	15	0	2	7	0
5	6	Ditto ditto ..	2	5	0	2	19	0
		BACK GEARED.						
3	3	Headstock, Cone Speed and Pinion, two Gear Wheels and Pinion, Catch Plate, Poppet, Hand Wheel and Handle, Cap, Barrel and Screw, Back Cone, Locking Handle, Gear Knob and Bolt, Mandrel, Tail Pin, Cast Steel for Centres and Back Shaft	0	15	0	1	1	6
4	3½	Ditto and Face Plates and Steel for Bushes	1	10	0	2	0	0
4 or 5	4	Ditto ditto ...	1	15	0	2	7	0
4 or 5	4½	Ditto ditto ...	2	0	0	2	13	0
4 or 5	5	Ditto ditto ..	2	5	0	2	19	0
16	5	Ditto Gut Speed	3	3	0	3	19	0
16	6	Ditto ditto ...	3	7	6	4	3	6
16	5	Ditto Flat Speeds with Eccentric Back Barrel and Shaft	3	7	6	4	4	0
16	6	Ditto with ditto	3	10	0	4	6	6
17	6	Ditto ditto ...	5	17	6	7	7	6
17	7	Ditto ditto ...	6	10	0	8	2	0

BRITANNIA CO., COLCHESTER, England.

London Showrooms—100, Houndsditch. *All Letters to Colchester.*

USEFUL LATHE CHUCKS, &c.

No.		£	s.	d.
1 Pronged Chuck, for wood, ⅝ in. shank		0	2	6
2 Cross or Four-blade Chuck, for hard wood, ⅝ in. shank ...		0	3	0
3 Square tapered-hole Chuck, to suit ordinary brace bits, ⅝ in. shank		0	3	0
4 Solid Gunmetal Chuck, ⅝ in. shank, face left solid and plain to turn to requirements		0	1	6
5 & 6 Main Chuck, turned and tapped to fit nose of mandrel, and with ⅝ in. hole at other end to receive the "Essex" or other small Chucks ... ... 5/- and		0	7	6

	£	s.	d.
7 Flange Chuck, 2 in. diameter, with taper screw for wood	0	6	0
Ditto 4 in. diameter	0	7	6
8 Flange Chuck for attaching flat wood to, bored and tapped to fit mandrel nose, and drilled, countersunk at back, 3 in diameter	0	5	0
Ditto, ditto, 6 in. diameter	0	7	6
9 Mandrel with screw collars for holding saws or { 6/-, 8/-, 10/6, 12/6 emery wheels ... ... { 6, 8, 10, 12 ins.			
10 Driver Chucks ... ... 10/- and	0	12	6

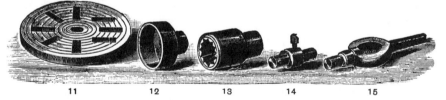

11 Face Plates, 6 in. **10**/-; 8 in. **15**/-; 12 in. **20**/-; 16 in. **30**/-; 18 in. **35**/-

12 Gunmetal Cup Chucks, of various diameters ¾ in., **2/6**; 1 in. **3**/-; 1¼ in., **4**/-; 1½ in., **5**/-; 2 in., **6/6**; 2½ in., **8**/- ; and 3 in., **10**/- each   ... ... The set   **1 19 0**

13 Self-centring Chuck for wood, with conical hole, ribbed longitudinally   ... ... **5**/- and   **0 7 6**

14 Drill Chuck, ⅜ in. hole, with set screw and extra plug for small drills, ⅝ in. shank **0 4 6**

15 Lathe Carriers, Steel screws, Turned Shanks, ⅜ in. **1/4**; ½ in. **1/8**; ¾ in. **2**/-; 1 in. **2/6**; 1¼ in. **3**/-; 1½ in. **3/6**; 1¾ in. **4/6**; 2 in. **5**/-.

Square, Half-Round and Female Centres from **1/6** to **2/6** each.

Grindstones, with troughs, for fixing on No. 9 Mandrels, 4 in. **3/6**; 5 in. **4**/-; 6 in. **5**/-.

BRITANNIA CO., COLCHESTER, England.

*London Showrooms—*100, *Houndsditch.*   *All Letters to Colchester.*

USEFUL LATHE APPLIANCES.

BELL CHUCKS.

Outside diameter. Inches—	2	3	4	5	6	7	7½	10
Four Screws	14/-	15/-	17/6	22/6	25/-	32/6	38/-	50/-
Eight Screws	14/-	18/-	22/-	25/-	30/-	38/-	45/-	60/-

Oval, Eccentric, and Ornamental Chucks made to order.

Ornamental Rests, Drill Spindles. Cutters, etc.

Turning Tools for Wood or Metal, for Hand, 1/-, 1/6, and 2/- each. Ditto, for Slide Rests, $\frac{3}{8}$ in., 1/- ; $\frac{1}{2}$ in., 1/3 ; $\frac{5}{8}$ in., 1/6 ; $\frac{3}{4}$ in., 1/9.

Screw Chasing Tools, internal and external, price per pair, Handled, from 40 to 12 threads per inch, 3/- ; from 11 to 6 threads per inch, 4/-.

Metal Spinning Tools, 2/- each. Milling Wheels, handled, 2/- each.

Taps, Taper, Second or Plug.

Size	$\frac{1}{4}$	$\frac{5}{16}$	$\frac{3}{8}$	$\frac{7}{16}$	$\frac{1}{2}$	$\frac{5}{8}$	$\frac{3}{4}$	$\frac{7}{8}$	1	$1\frac{1}{8}$	$1\frac{1}{4}$ inch.
Price	2/-	2/-	2/-	2/6	2/6	3/-	4/-	5/-	7/-	8/-	9/- each.
Boring Bars ..		2/6	3/-	3/-	4/-	5/- each.		Cutters. 6d. each.			
Swivel Cutter Bars	4/6	5/6	5/6	7/-	8/6 ,,		,,	,,			

Plain Drills, 2d., 3d., 4d., and 6d. each.

Circular Saws : 3 in., 3/- ; 4 in., 4/- ; 5 in., 5/6 ; 6 in., 7/- ; 7 in., 8/- ; 8 in., 9/6 each.

Platforms for ditto, with adjustable tables, 6 in. by 8 in., 12/6 ; 8 in. by 12 in., 15/-

Emery Wheels, 3 in., 3/- ; 4 in., 4/- ; 6 in., 4/6.

Buff Wheels, 3 in., 1/- ; 4 in., 2/-. Polishing Brushes, 1/- each.

Wire Brushes, 2/6, 2/-, and 1/6 each. Polishing Bobs, 2/- each.

Chucks listed are all cut to Whitworth standard pitches. Odd threads and pitches will be charged extra.

BRITANNIA CO., COLCHESTER, England.

London Showrooms—100, *Houndsditch.* *All Letters to Colchester.*

SLIDE REST TOOLS

IN GREAT VARIETY, MADE OF THE VERY BEST STEEL.

The Patterns most generally used are: No. 1 to No. 19.

SOLD SINGLY, OR IN SETS.

	$\frac{3}{8}$	$\frac{7}{16}$	$\frac{1}{2}$	$\frac{5}{8}$	$\frac{3}{4}$	$\frac{7}{8}$	1 inch.
	1/-	1/2	1/3	1/6	1/9	2,6	3/- each.
		$\frac{3}{8}$	$\frac{7}{16}$	$\frac{1}{2}$	$\frac{5}{8}$	$\frac{3}{4}$	$\frac{7}{8}$	1 inch.
No. 20	{	4/6	4/9	5/-	6/-	7/-	8/-	9/- each.
No. 21	{	$\frac{3}{8}$	$\frac{7}{16}$	$\frac{1}{2}$	$\frac{5}{8}$	$\frac{3}{4}$	$\frac{7}{8}$	1 inch.
No. 22	{	2/6	2/9	3/-	4/-	5/-	6/-	7/- each.

In sets of 12 with block.
$\frac{3}{8}$ in. **13/-**, $\frac{7}{16}$ in. **15/-**, $\frac{1}{2}$ in. **16/-**,
$\frac{5}{8}$ in. **19/6**, $\frac{3}{4}$ in. **22/9**,
Made of special tool steel.

In sets of 9 with block.
Made of very best steel.
$\frac{3}{8}$ in. **10/-**, $\frac{7}{16}$ in. **11/6**, $\frac{1}{2}$ in. **12/6**,
$\frac{5}{8}$ in. **15/-**, $\frac{3}{4}$ in. **17/6**.

BRITANNIA CO., COLCHESTER, England.

London Showrooms—100, *Houndsditch,*   *All Letters to Colchester.*

LATHE TOOLS.

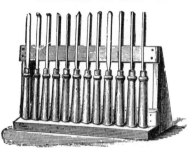

Hand Turning Tools in great variety, **1s.** each, **10s.** per dozen.

Larger sizes, **1s. 3d., 1s. 6d.,** and **2s.** each.

Long Handles if specially ordered.

Stands to hold Tools, from 2/6 each.

CARVING TOOLS.

Set of 3 with applewood handles, 3½ in. blade ... **4/-**
Set „ 6 „ rosewood „ 2⅓ in. „ ... **5/-**

SELF-ADJUSTING, SELF-GRIPPING AND SELF ACTING

LINK SPANNER & PIPE WRENCH,

For Bolts, Nuts, Tubes, Gas Pipes, &c., &c.

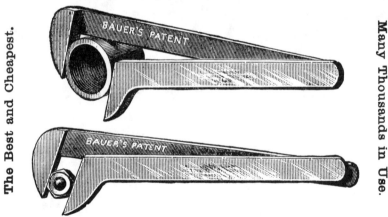

The Best and Cheapest.

Many Thousands in Use.

5 in., **1/8** ; 8 in., **2/8** ; 12 in., **4/-**; 15 in., **5/-**; 18 in., **6/-**; 24 in., **8/-**

IT is made entirely of steel and acknowledged to be the best shifting spanner ever seen ; also the best pipe wrench, as it grips from the smallest to the largest size instantly.

BRITANNIA CO., COLCHESTER, England.

London Showrooms—100, Houndsditch.   All Letters to Colchester.

THE ESSEX CHUCK.

To take up to $\frac{1}{4}$ in. Drills	**10/-**
Size larger, to take $\frac{1}{2}$ in. Drills	**25/-**

Made of Steel throughout.

A CHEAP AND DURABLE CHUCK.

THE J. K. P. CHUCK.

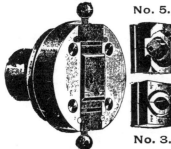

No. 5.

This is a very useful Chuck, with independent Jaws, to chuck either concentric or eccentric.

———

It holds tighter than many others, and takes irregular shaped articles, and has five different forms of Jaws.

No. 3.

Price, with Back Plate and one set of Jaws .. **50/-**

Extra Jaws, per pair, **10/-** as under:

No. ..	1	2	3	4 (V SHAPED)	5 (STEPPED)
Holds from	$\frac{1}{4}$ to $\frac{3}{8}$	$\frac{1}{2}$ to $\frac{3}{4}$	$\frac{3}{4}$ to 1 in.	$\frac{5}{64}$ to $\frac{27}{64}$	$1\frac{1}{16}$ to $1\frac{11}{16}$

NEW CHEAP DIE CHUCK.

Is Simple, Durable, and Remarkably Cheap!

Unlike Scroll Chucks, they can be used either concentric with or eccentric to the Lathe centre. They have back plates with plain hole, ready for screwing to fit any Lathe. They have a wide range of work, and, from their simplicity of construction, are free from liability to get out of order.

Diameter.	Size of Lathe, to suit.	Range.	Price.
$2\frac{1}{4}$ inch	$2\frac{1}{2}$ inch to $3\frac{1}{2}$ inch	$\frac{3}{16}$ inch to $\frac{1}{2}$ inch	**10/-**
$4\frac{1}{2}$,,	4 ,, to 6 ,,	$\frac{1}{4}$,, to 1 ,,	**15/6**

Fitting to Lathe, extra, **2/6.**

BRITANNIA CO., COLCHESTER, England.

London Showrooms—100, Houndsditch.   All Letters to Colchester.

INDEPENDENT REVERSIBLE 4 JAW CHUCKS.

6 inch	..	..	..	**60/-**
8 ,,	..	..	..	**80/-**
9 ,,	..	..	..	**90/-**
10 ,,	..	..	..	**100/-**
12 ,,	..	..	..	**120/-**

Larger sizes up to 20 inches diameter, per inch, **10**/- 22 inch, to 60 inch, per inch, **12/6**.

These Chucks are strongly made, with heavy plates and forged steel case hardened jaws, made reversible; the screws of mild steel with square thread, bearing necks case hardened. Plates are cut to Whitworth standard pitches but can be specially made to any pitch at same prices.

THE JEWELLER'S CHUCK

Is a valuable appliance to the mechanic or amateur. It carries drills, circular saws. and polishing brushes and bobs. It is made with $\frac{5}{8}$ in. shank to suit any main chuck.

Price **5**/-; Saws to suit **2/6**; Polishing Brushes. **1/6**; Emery Wheels, **2** - each.

WHITON'S "1883" DRILL CHUCK

These Chucks are easily attached to any Lathe or Drill by a taper plug or screwed direct. All the parts are of steel, and thoroughly made.

No. 1, 2 in. diameter holds Drills from, 0 in. to $\frac{9}{16}$ in., **17/-**

No. 2, 2½ in diameter, holds Drills from $\frac{1}{64}$ in. to $\frac{3}{4}$ in., **21/-**

BRITANNIA CO., COLCHESTER, England.

London Showrooms—100, Houndsditch. *All Letters to Colchester.*

WHITON'S PATENT GEARED SCROLL CHUCK.

Diameter	Weight About	Price		Diameter	Weight About	Price	
2½ inches	2 pounds	30s.		6 inches	12¾ pounds	71s.	The outer shells of all chucks up to and including 5 in. are of malleable iron, and the jaws, scrolls, pinions, &c., of all sizes are of steel. The workmanship is first-class throughout. Price list includes keys and bolts. Unless otherwise ordered, these chucks are always supplied with lathe jaws. Add 10 per cent. for chucks having four jaws. Add 20 per cent. for chucks having two sets of jaws (lathe and drill).
3¼ ,,	3 ,,	42s.		7½ ,,	20 ,,	80s.	
4⅛ ,,	6 ,,	50s.		9 ,,	35 ,,	92s.	
5 ,,	8½ ,,	59s.		12 ,,	60 ,,	125s.	

WHITON'S IMPROVED LEVER CHUCKS.

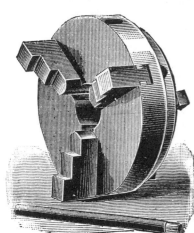

A HEAVY band of wrought iron is shrunk firmly around the front plates of the larger sizes, which are thus greatly strengthened. The holes in the scroll for receiving the lever are drilled into bosses cast for the purpose, while the outer rim of the scroll between these bosses is much lighter than formerly; thus the parts of this chuck receiving the heaviest strains are made stronger than in other chucks of this class, without making them inconvenient from over weight.

The front plates of the 3 in., 4 in., and 6 in., sizes are of malleable iron, and the scrolls and jaws of steel.

Diameter	Price	Diameter	Price
3 inches	34s.	15 inches	134s.
4 ,,	42s.	18 ,,	159s.
6 ,,	67s.	21 ,,	200s.
9 ,,	88s.	24 ,,	250s.
12 ,,	109s		

Unless otherwise ordered, these chucks are always supplied with lathe jaws.

Add 10 per cent. to above list for chucks with four jaws. Add 20 per cent. to above list for chucks with two sets of jaws (lathe and drill).

BRITANNIA CO., COLCHESTER, England.

London Showrooms—100, Houndsditch. *All Letters to Colchester.*

WHITON'S
IMPROVED AMATEUR CHUCKS

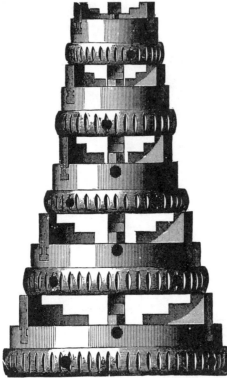

ARE very neat in design, and are intended for amateurs' use on foot and light power lathes, and for all classes of light work.

Although very light, they are strong and durable, the shell being made of malleable iron and the scroll and jaws of steel.

They are intended for attachment by means of a face plate.

They operate by hand or lever.

Diameter.	Weight about	With Lathe Jaws (as shewn in sketch)	With Lathe and Drill Jaws.
2 inches	$\frac{3}{4}$ pounds	19s.	24s.
$2\frac{1}{2}$,,	$1\frac{1}{4}$,,	21s.	26s.
3 ,,	$1\frac{3}{4}$,,	23s.	28s.
4 ,,	$3\frac{1}{2}$,,	27s.	34s.
5 ,,	5 ,,	32s.	38s.

Above Prices include Levers and Face Plate Screws.

When ordering chucks to be fitted, it is necessary to send the lathe mandrel or a chuck which exactly fits it. Charge for back plate and fitting is about 10s.

Any American Scroll Chuck to order at usual list price.

BRITANNIA CO., COLCHESTER, England.

London Showrooms—100, *Houndsditch.*   *All Letters to Colchester.*

WHITON'S NEW AMATEUR INDEPENDENT REVERSIBLE JAW CHUCKS.

AN entirely new line of Independent Jaw Chucks for all kinds of light work, provided with 3 or 4 *independent, reversible steel jaws*, each of which is operated by a separate screw. Every variety of round, square, irregular or eccentric work may be held in them to be operated upon by the tool. The Chucks will hold with great firmness, and will take pieces considerably larger than the diameter of the Chucks. All are provided with circular lines on the face by which to set the jaws true for holding round work. There are no projecting screw heads. The thread on the screws extends to the outside of the Chuck, so that the jaw has a longer traverse than in other Jaw Chucks. All are attached to the lathe by means of a face plate, screws for which accompany each Chuck. The Chuck may be very readily taken apart.

The sizes 6in. and above are only made with 4 Jaws

PRICES.

Diameter.		Weight.		3 Jaws.		4 Jaws.
2 inch	...	¾ pound	...	27/- each	...	34/- each
2½ ,,	...	1¼ ,,	...	32/- ,,	...	38/-
3 ,,	...	2 ,,	...	36/- ,,	...	42/-
4 ,,	...	4 ,,	...	42/- ,,	...	50/- ,,
5 ,,	...	5¼ ,,	...	50/- ,,	...	59/- ,,

		Price.				Price.
6 inches diam.	...	75/- each		15 inches diam.	...	146/- each
7½ ,, ,,	...	84/- ,,		18 ,, ,,	...	184/- ,,
9 ,, ,,	...	96/- ,,		21 ,, ,,	...	230/- ,,
12 ,, ,,	...	125/- ,,		24 ,, ,,	...	271/. ,,

BRITANNIA CO., COLCHESTER, England.

London Showrooms—100, *Houndsditch.*   *All Letters to Colchester.*

Over 10,000 of these Vices in use.

INSTANTANEOUS GRIP PARALLEL VICES.

THE FIRST COST SAVED IN TWELVE MONTHS.

ALTHOUGH one of the most noticeable features of the present day is the extent to which labour-saving appliances have been successfully introduced, yet it may safely be said that in no branch has less progress been made than in Vices, articles which are so commonly in use everywhere. The old screw vice is still to be found in every workshop, large or small, and were it possible to estimate the amount of time spent in a twelve month in the repeated screwing up and unscrewing, it would show a great amount of mis-directed energy and a startling amount of wasted time. Fig. 1 represents one of the Engineer's Vices with instantaneous grip. These Vices are invaluable in enabling a man to fasten **INSTANTLY** any size of work. By raising the handle to a vertical position, the Sliding or Loose Jaw is at liberty to be moved, and can be adjusted at once to any thickness of article within the scope of the Vice. The work is held in one hand. and the loose jaw is, with the other hand, pushed against the work, and **by half-a-turn of the handle instantly fastened, all screwing being entirely dispensed with**. **These Vices will stand any amount of hard usage. The Grip is certain** and cannot relax, and from the fewness of working parts, it is almost an impossibility for them to get out of order.

The Racks are made of a Special Steel, suitably hardened, and as they **merely engage without rubbing,** will last an indefinite length of time. The method of fixing the loose Steel Jaws is also a great improvement over that adopted in ordinary Parallel Vices. They are easily removable at any time, which makes the cost of re-cutting trifling, compared with that of Wrought Vices.

The Vices can be swivelled round to any position on the bench, and are therefore particularly adapted for many classes of work otherwise bad to get to a Vice. They can be easily removed from one bench to another by taking off the wing nut and the screws. They can always be kept clean without trouble, as five seconds suffice to take one to pieces. No workshop ought to be without them. The whole first cost is saved in twelve months in economy of time, and through requiring no repairs.

See Illustrations and Prices next page.

BRITANNIA CO., COLCHESTER, England.
London Showrooms—100, Houndsditch.   All Letters to Colchester.

INSTANTANEOUS GRIP ENGINEERS' VICES.

For description see page 120.

In various Sizes and Styles for Engineers, Machinists, Founders, Gun Makers, Blacksmiths, Sewing Machine Makers, Brass Finishers, Amateurs, Jewellers, Dentists, &c.

BENCH VICES.

No. 11.	3 inch Jaws, to open 3 inches	... ...	£1 7 6
12.	3¾ ,, ,, 4 ,,	... ...	1 12 0
13	5 ,, ,, 5 ,,	... ...	1 18 0
14.	6 ,, ,, 6½ ,,	... ...	2 5 0
15.	7 ,, ,, 8½ ,,	... ...	3 5 0

N.B.—These Vices, from 5 in. Jaws and upwards, are supplied with Fast Handle, as shewn in Fig. 1, except specially ordered with long Loose Handle, as shewn in Fig. 2. For ordinary work, and particularly where there is much changing in and out of the Vice, the Fast Handles are certainly preferable, the Loose Handle only being recommended for very heavy Work.

For General Work No. 14 and No. 15 Vices are particularly recommended.

PORTABLE VICES.

No. 16	6 inch Jaws, to open 6½ inches	... ...	£4 15 0
17	7 ,, ,, 8½ ,,	... ...	6 0 0

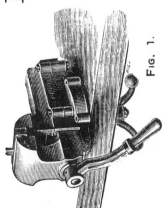

FIG. 1.

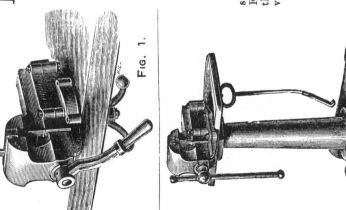

FIG. 2.

BRITANNIA CO., COLCHESTER, England.

London Showrooms—100, *Houndsditch.*   *All Letters to Colchester.*

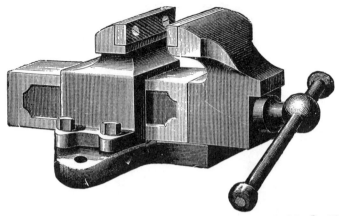

PARALLEL BENCH VICES,

With Steel Jaws, Made in Three Sizes.

	No. 1.	No. 2.	No. 3.
Measure across jaw	2¾ in.	3¼ in.	3¾ in.
Will open	3½ in.	4 in.	5 in.
Weight	11 lb.	18 lb.	29 lb.
Price	10/6	17/6	25/-

Castings and forgings for above Vice in the rough **4/- 6/9 10/-**
If planed and the screw turned and cut ... **7/6 12/- 18/-**

INSTANTANEOUS SELF-ADJUSTING AND SELF-ACTING

TUBE AND BOLT VICE.

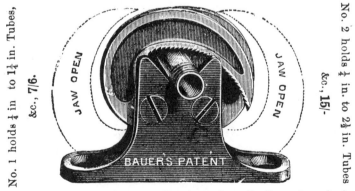

No. 1 holds ¼ in. to 1¼ in. Tubes, &c., **7/6.**

JAW OPEN

JAW OPEN

BAUER'S PATENT

No. 2 holds ½ in. to 2½ in. Tubes &c., **15/-**

THIS is the handiest and best, as it grips automatically and works in any position. It weighs only about one-fifth of the old-fashioned cast iron Tube Vices.

BRITANNIA CO., COLCHESTER, England.

London Showrooms—100, *Houndsditch.* *All Letters to Colchester.*

THE BRITANNIA COMPANY'S
ORNAMENTAL SLIDE REST,

As supplied with Lukin Lathe.

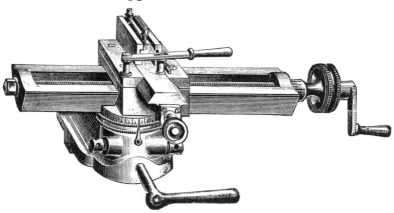

THE above illustration represents our Ornamental Slide Rest, constructed to suit a 5-in. Lathe, and embodying all the most material and useful improvements. It is arranged with a gun-metal cradle planed to fit the Lathe bed and slide along it to any part, and planed at top to receive an eccentric socket at right angles to the bed. The socket is 12 inches long, planed parallel at sides to slide along the gun-metal cradle, and adjust to any distance from axial line of centres. Within it is an eccentric shaft with eye and nut, a half turn of which rigidly secures it to the Lathe Bed. At its top rim it is turned and screwed, and fitted with a gun-metal ring with milled edge to turn by thumb and finger, to adjust the height of the cutter. The longitudinal slide is 12 inches long, made with a turned shank to fit into the socket of eccentric slide, and swivel to any angle, its circular bottom being graduated to 50° each side of centre. Along its upper face are graduations in 10ths of an inch, and it is fitted with a steel draw screw having 10 threads per inch, with cones at each end to take up wear, and with a split gun-metal nut to adjust to take up back lash. On the collar of the screw are 20 divisions to give an adjustment to 200ths of an inch, and it has a long milled edge knob for thumb and finger adjustment, and grooved for gut to enable it to be driven from overhead gear ; it also has a square at its end fitted with crank and handle. The top slide is made of gun-metal, fitted to longitudinal slide by loose adjusting strips, with a transverse slide carrying Tool Holder to suit $\frac{9}{16}$ inch tools, and actuated by a milled head thumb screw and garter slide, screwed to 20 per inch, graduated by an ingenious contrivance to 25 divisions, giving an adjustment of the tool to the greatest nicety. The garter slide is instantly detachable, enabling the slide and tool holders to be operated freely by lever.

A stop screw is fitted to the tool holder, and the face of the slide is graduated in 20ths of an inch.

The whole instrument is well devised, very complete, and accurately and carefully made.

Price   -   -   -   -   15 Guineas.

BRITANNIA CO., COLCHESTER, England.

London Showrooms—100, Houndsditch.   *All Letters to Colchester.*

Capstan or Turret Compound Slide Rests.

FOR BRASS FINISHERS AND ELECTRICIANS.

Send Template of Face and height of Centre.

Can be fitted to any Lathe. Great economisers of time.

THESE are designed for use on any ordinary plain Lathe, for brass finishers and others, where quantities of parts of uniform size and shape are to be produced, giving many of the advantages of the expensive turret lathes.

The evolving Head is constructed to hold five tools of any desired form for sliding, surfacing, pointing, parting, etc., enabling all such operations to be done at one setting of the work, and if the rest be used in conjunction with a headstock having a hollow spindle through which rods of brass or iron may be passed, studs, joints, pins, etc , with cheese or cup heads, or without heads, may be cheaply and quickly produced and cut off finished from the rod.

The "Capstan" or "Turret" Tool Holder is rotated by hand, held in desired position by lever and link motion (as seen in illustration), actuating a steel piston dropping into accurately fitting notches in a ring at the bottom of capstan, and the latter is then firmly locked in position by the handle at the top.

The Rests have compound sides having longitudinal and transverse traverse, and are prepared to bolt securely to any ordinary plain lathe, **or can be made to fit the saddle of a screw-cutting Lathe.**

Prices are as follows :

For Lathes having centres	3 in.	3½ in.	4 in.	4½ in.	5 in.	6 in.
Price	£6	£6 10	£7 10	£9	£10 10	£12 15

☞ The illustration is that of the 6 in. size.

LATHE CLAMPING DOGS, of various styles.

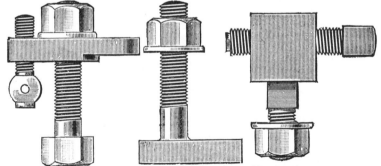

No. 1. No. 2. No. 3 pattern.

The above will be found very useful for securing the work to be bored or turned, to the f ce-plate on the Lathe.

Price, to suit 4-in. to 6-in. Centre Lathes : Pattern No. 1, 3/6 ; No. 2, 1/6 ; No. 3, 4/-

Other Sizes and Patterns made to order.

BRITANNIA CO., COLCHESTER, England.

London Showrooms—100, Houndsditch. *All Letters to Colchester.*

Britannia Co.'s Improved Compound Slide Rest.

To suit 2½ in. centre Lathe	-	£2 0 0
,, 3 in. ,,	-	2 10 0
,, 3½ in. ,,	-	3 0 0
,, 4 in. ,,	-	3 10 0
,, 4½ in. ,,	-	4 0 0
To suit 5 in. centre Lathe	-	£5 0 0
,, 6 in. ,,	-	6 0 0
,, 7 in. ,,	-	7 0 0
,, 8 in. ,,	-	8 0 0

Larger sizes to order at 20/- per inch.

These are made so that the Bottom Slide always remains at a right angle with the Lathe Bed, the Rest having a swivel arrangement, accurately graduated, for turning taper or conical work to any desired angle.

The bottom cover, extending nearly full length, excludes turnings and dirt from the screw and slide.

The materials are of the best. Screws are cast steel, gunmetal nuts, horn handles improved tool box, with hardened steel screws.

The workmanship is excellent. The slides, &c., are surfaced up, and the parts machine made.

Tool Holders with Plates or other Pattern to order.

PATENT DOUBLE DRIVING CARRIERS.

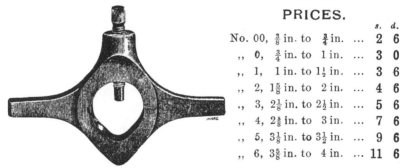

PRICES.

			s.	d.
No. 00,	⅜ in. to ¾ in.	...	2	6
,, 0,	¾ in. to 1 in.	...	3	0
,, 1,	1 in. to 1¼ in.	...	3	6
,, 2,	1⅝ in. to 2 in.	...	4	6
,, 3,	2⅛ in. to 2½ in.	...	5	6
,, 4,	2⅝ in. to 3 in.	...	7	6
,, 5,	3⅛ in. to 3½ in.	...	9	6
,, 6,	3⅝ in. to 4 in.	...	11	6

Equalize the strain, and are generally more useful than ordinary carriers.

"ONCE TRIED ALWAYS USED."

When the Lathe has not a Clement's driver, two studs in the face plate are required.

The smaller sizes can be sent per Parcel Post, at 3d. to 6d. extra.

BRITANNIA CO., COLCHESTER, England.

London Showrooms—100, *Houndsditch.* *All Letters to Colchester.*

BRITANNIA COMPANY'S
REGISTERED SCREW-CUTTING GUIDE

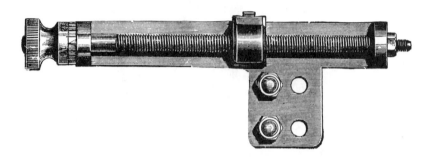

THE above appliance can be used on any Lathe. By its use the workman can regulate the depth of cut to the greatest nicety, and the use of the chalk mark, or any such expedient is unnecessary.

It can be used for inside or outside screw cutting, or other work requiring uniformity. It saves time from insufficiency of cut. It prevents the breaking of tools, or the work being torn out from the centres. It is a reliable stop for ornamental drilling and fluting.

While the Lathe is cutting this can be adjusted for the following cut. It only requires to be bolted upon the saddle of a Screw-cutting Lathe, and a projecting stud or screw fixed in the middle engages the stop.

It can also be used on ordinary Lathes with slide rest—in this case it must be fixed to the bed.

This is a tool which has long been wanted by engineers, and will also be appreciated by amateurs.

PRICES.

For 3 in. to 4 in. Centre Lathes	...	18s.
5 in. and 6 in. ,,	...	20s.
8 in. to 10 in. ,,	...	22s.

'TANNIA CO., COLCHESTER, England.

Showrooms—100, Houndsditch.   *All Letters to Colchester.*

THE 'CLIMAX' TOOL-HOLDER

(PATENT).

FOR LATHES, SHAPING AND PLANING MACHINES, &c.

THE advantages and great saving the Tool-holder possesses over the forged tool are proved by its adoption by the leading firms of engineers both in this country and in America.

The "Climax" Tool-holder is designed to meet the demand for a useful all-round cutting-tool, which will cut straight or irregular work, and into corners, and face either right or left, without altering its position in the slide rest.

The important improvement in this Tool-holder over those already in use lies in the fact that **side rake** as well as top rake can be given to the cutter, which thus always presents the **correct cutting angle to the work**. The object of this side rake is not only to make the tool **more keen** without sacrificing its strength, but to **relieve the feed screw** or gearing of strain by giving the tool a tendency to feed **along and into its cut**

The cutter is held perfectly rigid in any position by tightening a single nut.

This holder is invaluable for screw-cutting, as the cutter can be canted to suit the angle of any thread either V or square.

The "Climax" Tool-holder is made entirely of steel the bolt, etc., being case hardened, and is of the best workmanship and finish.

The cutting tools are of uniform section, made from the finest cast steel obtainable.

Cutters of Mushet's special self-hardening steel can be supplied for the larger sizes. This steel is strongly recommended, and machine tools should be worked at faster speeds, and with deeper cuts when using it.

Size of Shank	Section of Cutter	Suitable for use in Lathes to	Price of Tool-holder			Price of best Cast Steel Cutters Per dozen			Price of Mushet's Steel Cutters Per Dozen		
			£	s.	d.	£	s.	d.	£	s.	d.
$\frac{9}{16}$ in sq.	$\frac{5}{16}$ in. by $\frac{1}{8}$ in.	4 in. centres	0	13	6	0	4	6	—		
$\frac{5}{8}$ in. ,,	$\frac{3}{8}$ in. ,, $\frac{5}{32}$ in.	4½ in. ,,	0	14	0	0	5	0	—		
$\frac{11}{16}$ in. ,,	$\frac{1}{2}$ in. ,, $\frac{3}{16}$ in.	5 in. ,,	0	14	6	0	5	6	—		
$\frac{3}{4}$ in. ,,	$\frac{5}{8}$ in. ,, $\frac{1}{4}$ in.	6 in. .,	0	15	0	0	6	0	0	8	0
$\frac{7}{8}$ in. ,,	$\frac{5}{8}$ in. ,, $\frac{3}{8}$ in.	10 in. ,,	1	0	0	0	8	6	0	11	0
1 in. ,,	$\frac{7}{8}$ in. ,, $\frac{3}{8}$ in.	12 in. ,,	1	5	0	0	8	6	0	11	0
1¼ in. ,,	1 in. ,, $\frac{7}{16}$ in.	14 in. ,,	1	10	0	0	10	0	0	14	0
1½ in. ,,	1 in. ,, $\frac{7}{16}$ in.	16 in. ,,	1	15	0	0	10	0	0	14	0

Angle Gauges, **4/6** each.

Special Quotations for Larger Sizes.

BRITANNIA CO., COLCHESTER, England.

London Showrooms—100, *Houndsditch.*   *All Letters to Colchester.*

HAYDON TOOL HOLDER.

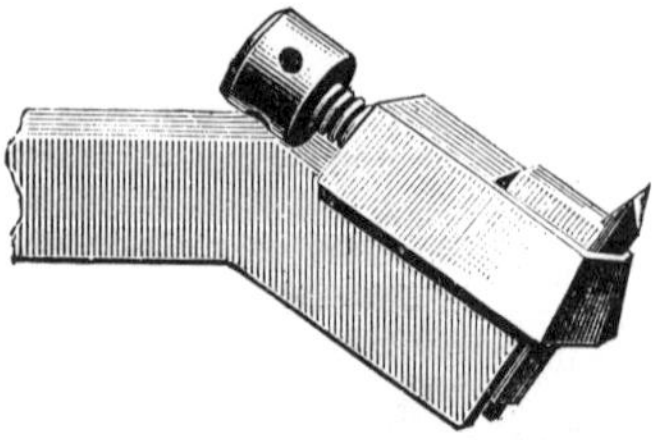

ADVANTAGES.

Users of these Holders save the cost and inconvenience of forging their tools.

The Cutters are easily sharpened to the correct angle.

By due attention to the instructions superior finish can be given to the work.

A stock of the small Cutters can be always kept sharpened, as they cost but little, and occupy a small space.

The steel of which the Cutters are made can be bought in 12 in. lengths at 6d. and cut off as required, or Cutters can be purchased at 6d. to 9d each.

Plain directions for sharpening Cutters to the EXACT ANGLE required for various metals, and how to use the tools to the best advantage, will be sent with each Bar. A diagram showing the various angles will prevent the possibility of errors in judgment.

SIZES AND PRICES.

			s.	d.				£	s.	d.
$\frac{3}{8}$in. holder for	3in. centre lathes,		9	6	$\frac{7}{8}$in. holder for	8in. centre lathes,			15	0
$\frac{7}{16}$ in. ,,	$3\frac{1}{2}$ in.	,,	10	0	1 in. ,,	10 in.	,,		17	6
$\frac{1}{2}$ in. ,,	4 in.	,,	10	6	$1\frac{1}{8}$ in. ,,	12 in.	,,	1	0	0
$\frac{5}{8}$ in. ,,	$4\frac{1}{2}$ & 5 in.	,,	11	0	$1\frac{1}{4}$ in. ,,	14 in.	,,	1	2	6
$\frac{3}{4}$ in. ,,	6 in.	,,	12	6						

PATENT TOOL HOLDER.

Invented by B. H. BENT, M.A., Demonstrator of Applied Mechanics, University of Cambridge.

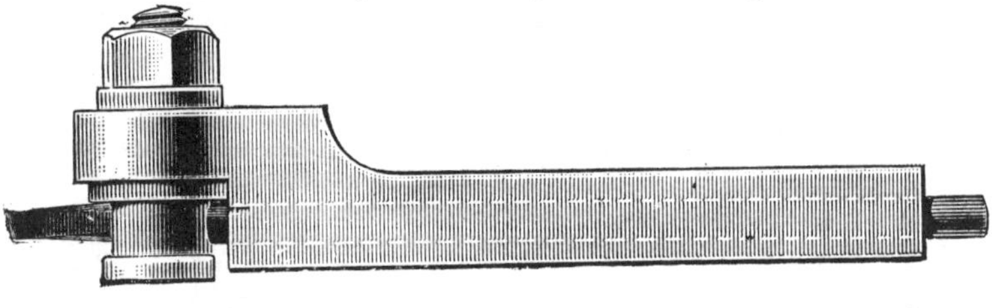

This is one of the best tool holders for boring and cutting internal threads. The cutters or tools can be made of round rod which is easy to obtain. They are held firmly, and in boring it is so easy to adjust depth of cut. Various sizes of steel can be used in the same holder.

It is an economical tool, no skilled smith being required to forge them. It can be used for ordinary turning and surfacing.

SIZES AND PRICES.

				s.	d.
$\frac{1}{2}$ in.	Holder, will suit Lathes	3 in. to 4 in. centre	.. ..	9	6
$\frac{5}{8}$ in.	,, ,,	$4\frac{1}{2}$ in. to 6 in.	.. ..	10	0
$\frac{3}{4}$ in.	,, ,,	$6\frac{1}{2}$ in. to 7 in.	.. ..	12	6
$\frac{7}{8}$ in.	,, ,,	$7\frac{1}{2}$ in. to 9 in.	.. ..	15	0
1 in.	,, ,,	10 in. to 12 in.	.. ..	17	6

Cutters for the Bents Holder, 6d. to 1/6 each.

BRITANNIA CO., COLCHESTER, England.

London Showrooms—100, *Houndsditch.* *All Letters to Colchester.*

GEAR CUTTER FOR LATHE.

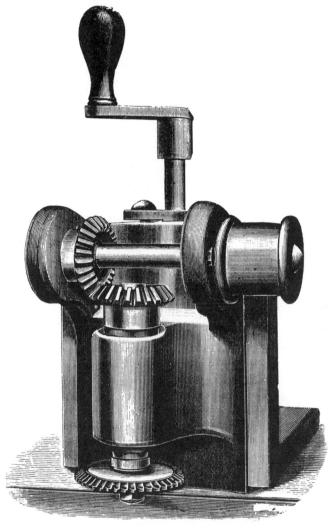

THE above illustration shows the new Gear Cutter; which can be fitted upon the slide rest of any lathe, and the cross and parallel slides are thus utilized to give the necessary traverse.

It is driven from an overhead pulley. The milling cutters are held on the spindle by the nut and washer. A Vertical slide gives the necessary vertical traverse.

This is a most useful adjunct to the lathe for fluting taps, milling key ways, spiral fluting, cutting bevel and worm wheels, &c. Wheels with any number of teeth can be accurately cut by means of a division plate. This has hitherto been an expensive appliance but the Makers have brought them within the reach of the amateur, who will, by its assistance, be able to accomplish many jobs hitherto quite beyond his reach. The price is £4 4s. 0d., adapted for lathes up to 6in. centres.

BRITANNIA CO., COLCHESTER, England.

London Showrooms—100, Houndsditch.   All Letters to Colchester.

E

PATENT
EXPANDING LATHE MANDREL.

Supplied to the Royal Arsenal and all the
principal Railway Works, &c.

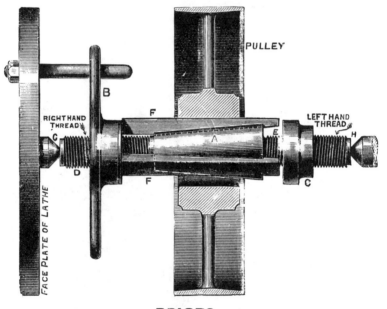

PRICES.

No.		£	s.	d.	Ex. Slides	No.		£	s.	d.	Ex. Slides
1 to take	$1\frac{1}{4}$ to $1\frac{5}{16}$	1	15	0	15/-	5 to take	3 to $3\frac{3}{8}$	3	15	0	15/-
2 ,,	$1\frac{5}{8}$ to $1\frac{7}{8}$	1	15	0	12/-	6 ,,	$3\frac{1}{2}$ to 4	4	5	0	16/-
3 ,,	2 to $2\frac{1}{4}$	2	5	0	12/-	7 .,	$4\frac{1}{8}$ to $4\frac{5}{8}$	5	0	0	17/-
4 ,,	$2\frac{3}{8}$ to $2\frac{5}{8}$	2	15	0	15/-	8 ,,	$4\frac{3}{4}$ to $5\frac{1}{2}$	5	10	0	18/-

**These Mandrels are Protected and Legal Proceedings
will be taken against any infringers.**

Gear Cutters, Stocks and Dies, Twist Drills. Portable Forges,
Anvils, Vices (for Iron or Wood), Mortising Machines, Band Saws.

Above are supplied, of reliable quality, at Moderate Prices.

BRITANNIA CO., COLCHESTER, England.

London Showrooms—100, Houndsditch.   All Letters to Colchester.

TWIST DRILLS.

Straight Shanks.

Diam. of Drills	Length of Drills	Price per Drill
$\frac{1}{16}$ in.	2 in.	4d.
$\frac{5}{64}$	$2\frac{3}{16}$	5d.
$\frac{3}{32}$	$2\frac{1}{8}$	5d.
$\frac{7}{64}$	$2\frac{9}{16}$	6d.
$\frac{1}{8}$	$2\frac{1}{4}$	6d.
$\frac{9}{64}$	$2\frac{15}{16}$	7d.
$\frac{5}{32}$	$3\frac{1}{8}$	7d.
$\frac{11}{64}$	$3\frac{5}{16}$	8d.
$\frac{3}{16}$	$3\frac{1}{2}$	8d.
$\frac{13}{64}$	$3\frac{3}{4}$	9d.
$\frac{7}{32}$	4	10d.
$\frac{15}{64}$	4	1/-
$\frac{1}{4}$	4	1/2
$\frac{17}{64}$	$4\frac{1}{4}$	1/3
$\frac{9}{32}$	$4\frac{1}{4}$	1/3
$\frac{19}{64}$	$4\frac{1}{2}$	1/4
$\frac{5}{16}$	$4\frac{1}{2}$	1/4
$\frac{21}{64}$	$4\frac{3}{4}$	1/6
$\frac{11}{32}$	$4\frac{3}{4}$	1/7
$\frac{23}{64}$	5	1/9
$\frac{3}{8}$	5	1/11
$\frac{25}{64}$	$5\frac{1}{4}$	2/-
$\frac{13}{32}$	$5\frac{1}{4}$	2/1
$\frac{27}{64}$	$5\frac{1}{2}$	2/2
$\frac{7}{16}$	$5\frac{1}{2}$	2/3
$\frac{29}{64}$	$5\frac{3}{4}$	2/4
$\frac{15}{32}$	$5\frac{3}{4}$	2/5
$\frac{31}{64}$	6	2/7
$\frac{1}{2}$	6	2/8
$\frac{17}{32}$	8	3/4
$\frac{9}{16}$	$8\frac{1}{4}$	3/9
$\frac{19}{32}$	$8\frac{1}{2}$	4/2
$\frac{5}{8}$	$8\frac{3}{4}$	4/8
$\frac{21}{32}$	9	5/1
$\frac{11}{16}$	$9\frac{1}{4}$	5/6
$\frac{23}{32}$	$9\frac{1}{2}$	5/11
$\frac{3}{4}$	$9\frac{3}{4}$	6/4
$\frac{25}{32}$	10	7/1
$\frac{13}{16}$	10	7/7
$\frac{27}{32}$	$10\frac{1}{2}$	8/1
$\frac{7}{8}$	$10\frac{1}{2}$	8/8
$\frac{29}{32}$	$10\frac{1}{2}$	9/3
$\frac{15}{16}$	$10\frac{3}{4}$	9/10
$\frac{31}{32}$	$10\frac{3}{4}$	10/5
1	11	11/-

Straight Shank Drills to Stubs' Letter Gauge.

Letter	Price per Drill	Price per Dozen
A	1/1	12/3
B	1/1	12/6
C	1/1	12/9
D	1/2	13/-
E	1/2	13/3
F	1/2	13/6
G	1/2	13/9
H	1/3	14/-
I	1/3	14/3
J	1/3	14/6
K	1/3	14/9
L	1/4	15/-
M	1/4	15/3
N	1/4	15/6
O	1/5	15/9
P	1/6	16/-
Q	1/7	17/-
R	1/8	18/6
S	1/9	20/-
T	1/10	21/-
U	1/11	22/-
V	2/-	22/9
W	2/1	23/6
X	2/2	24/3
Y	2/3	25/-
Z	2/4	25/6

Stubs' Steel Wire Gauge Straight Shanks.

Nos of Wire the Drills are made from	Entire Length of Drills	Price per Drill	Price per Dozen
1 to 5	4 in.	9d.	8/7
6 to 10	$3\frac{3}{4}$	8d.	7/10
11 to 15	$3\frac{1}{2}$	7d.	7/-
16 to 20	$3\frac{1}{4}$	7d.	6/4
21 to 25	3	6d.	5/5
26 to 30	$2\frac{3}{4}$	6d.	5/5
31 to 35	$2\frac{1}{2}$	5d.	4/6
36 to 40	$2\frac{1}{4}$	5d.	4/6
41 to 45	$2\frac{1}{16}$	4d.	3/8
46 to 50	$1\frac{7}{8}$	4d.	3/8
51 to 65	$1\frac{3}{16}$	3d.	2/9

Turned Drills with Taper Shanks, Tapping Sizes.

Diameter of Taps	Length of Drills	Price per Drill
$\frac{1}{4}$ in.	$6\frac{1}{8}$ in.	2/-
$\frac{5}{16}$	$6\frac{1}{4}$	2/1
$\frac{3}{8}$	$6\frac{1}{2}$	2/3
$\frac{7}{16}$	$6\frac{3}{4}$	2/5
$\frac{1}{2}$	$7\frac{1}{4}$	2/10
$\frac{9}{16}$	$7\frac{3}{4}$	3/4
$\frac{5}{8}$	$8\frac{1}{4}$	4/-
$\frac{3}{4}$	9	5/2
$\frac{7}{8}$	10	7/1
1	$10\frac{1}{4}$	8/8
$1\frac{1}{8}$	$10\frac{3}{4}$	10/5
$1\frac{1}{4}$	$11\frac{1}{4}$	12/9
$1\frac{3}{8}$	12	14/9
$1\frac{1}{2}$	$14\frac{1}{4}$	18/-
$1\frac{5}{8}$	$14\frac{3}{4}$	21/6
$1\frac{3}{4}$	$15\frac{1}{4}$	31/6
$1\frac{7}{8}$	$15\frac{1}{2}$	32/6
2	16	35/6

Bit Stock Drills.

Size	Price p. Doz	Price p. Drill
$\frac{1}{16}$	5/9	7d.
$\frac{3}{32}$	6/4	8d.
$\frac{1}{8}$	7/8	9d.
$\frac{5}{32}$	9/-	10d.
$\frac{3}{16}$	10/6	1/-
$\frac{7}{32}$	12/6	1/2
$\frac{1}{4}$	17/-	1/6
$\frac{9}{32}$	19/3	1/8
$\frac{5}{16}$	21/6	1/10
$\frac{11}{32}$	23/9	2/-
$\frac{3}{8}$	26/-	2/3
$\frac{13}{32}$	28/6	2/6
$\frac{7}{16}$	31/6	2/9
$\frac{15}{32}$	35/-	3/-
$\frac{1}{2}$	39/-	3/4

☞ Millimetre Drills, with Straight Shanks, of the same length and prices as the Taper Shanks, are kept in Stock from 6 to 25 m/m.

BRITANNIA CO., COLCHESTER, England.

London Showrooms—100, *Houndsditch.* *All Letters to Colchester.*

TWIST DRILLS

Turned, with Taper Shanks.

Diam. of Drills	Length of Drills	Price per Drill	No. and Price of Sockets for Drill	Milli-metres	PRICE
1/4 in.	6 1/8 in.	2/-	1	6	2/-
9/32	6 1/4	2/1	1	7	2/1
5/16	6 3/8	2/2	1	8	2/2
11/32	6 1/2	2/3	1	9	2/4
3/8	6 3/4	2/5	1	10	2/7
13/32	7	2/7	1	11	2/10
7/16	7 1/4	2/10	1	12	3/2
15/32	7 1/2	3/1	1	13	3/6
1/2	7 3/4	3/4	1	14	3/11
17/32	8	3/8	1	15	4/4
9/16	8 1/4	4/-	1	16	4/10
19/32	8 1/2	4/4	1	17	5/4
5/8	8 3/4	4/9	2	18	5/11
21/32	9	5/2	2	19	6/6
11/16	9 1/4	5/7	2	20	7/1
23/32	9 1/2	6/1	2	21	7/9
3/4	9 3/4	6/7	2	22	8/5
25/32	10	7/1	2	23	9/2
13/16	10	7/7	2	24	9/11
27/32	10 1/4	8/1	2	25	10/8
7/8	10 1/2	8/8	2	26	11/5
29/32	10 1/2	9/3	2	27	12/2
15/16	10 3/4	9/10	3	28	12/11
31/32	10 3/4	10/5	3	29	13/9
1	11	11/-	3	30	14/7
1 1/32	11	11/7	3	31	15/5
1 1/16	11 1/4	12 2	3	32	16/3
1 3/32	11 1/4	12/9	3	33	18/-
1 1/8	11 3/4	13/4	3	34	18/6
1 5/32	11 3/4	14/-	3	35	19/-
1 3/16	12	14/9	3	36	20/-
1 7/32	12	15/6	3	37	21/9
1 1/4	12 1/2	16/4	3	38	24/-
1 5/16	14 1/4	18/-	4	39	31/-
1 3/8	14 1/2	19/-	4	40	32/6
1 7/16	14 3/4	21/6	4	41	33/6
1 1/2	15	24/-	4	42	34/6
1 9/16	15 1/4	31/6	4	43	35/8
1 5/8	15 1/2	32/6	4	44	36/8
1 11/16	15 3/4	33/8	4	45	37/9
1 3/4	16	35/6	4	46	38/9
1 13/16	16 1/4	38/-	4	47	40/-
1 7/8	16 1/2	40/-	4	48	41/3
1 15/16	16 1/2	41/8	4	49	42 3
2	16 1/2	43/-	4	50	43/-
2 1/8	16 1/2	47/-	5	...	...
2 1/4	17 1/2	52/-	5	...	...
2 3/8	17 1/2	58/-	5	...	...
2 1/2	19	65/-	5	...	...
2 5/8	19	73/-	5	...	...
2 3/4	20 1/2	80/-	5	...	...
2 7/8	20 1/2	85/-	5	...	...
3	22	90/-	5	...	...

No. 1 Socket, 5/- — No. 2 Socket, 6/6 — No. 3 Socket, 8/6 — No. 4 Socket, 14/3 — No. 5 Socket, 40/-

No. 1 Socket, 5/- — No. 2 Socket, 6/6 — No. 3 Socket, 8/6 — No. 4 Socket, 14/3

SETS OF DRILLS, Nos. 1 to 5 MOUNTED ON STANDS.

	£		
1—Sets of Straight Shank Drills, 1/16 to 1/2 advancing by 32nds ...	£1	0	8
2—Ditto, by 64th ...	2	1	4
3—Sets of Wire Drills, Nos. 60 to 3/8 (65 Drills) ...	1	16	3
4—Sets of Wire Drills. Nos. 1 to 60 ...	1	8	6
5—Half Sets of Wire Drills. Nos. 1 to 60, alternate numbers	1	14	6
Jewellers' Sets, in case (36 Drills), Nos. 30 to 65 ...	0	18	3
Sets of Drills for Bit Stocks, 1/16, 3/32, 1/8, 5/32, 3/16, 7/32, 1/4, 6/16, 3/8.	0	10	6

☞ We would call attention to the Set of Sockets, Nos. 1, 2, 3, 4, and 5, in column 4 of Turned Drills. By use of these Sockets all further fitting of Drills to Machine is saved.

Bit-Stock Drills for use in Bit-Braces will be found especially useful to Carriage Builders and for general repairing, because holes may be drilled without removing the work. They can be used for either Wood or Metal.

BRITANNIA CO., COLCHESTER, England.

London Showrooms—100, *Houndsditch.*   *All Letters to Colchester.*

THE "ECLIPSE" ADJUSTABLE KEY

For taking off Oil Cups from all kinds of Wheels.

BY ROYAL LETTERS PATENT.

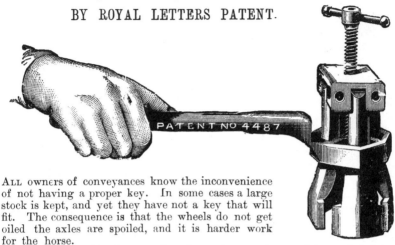

ALL owners of conveyances know the inconvenience of not having a proper key. In some cases a large stock is kept, and yet they have not a key that will fit. The consequence is that the wheels do not get oiled the axles are spoiled, and it is harder work for the horse.

These keys will take any size of cap, from $1\frac{3}{4}$ in. to $3\frac{1}{2}$ in., and, being a perfect fit. cannot destroy the corners.

The working parts are made of cast steel, and will last a lifetime.

Any special size made to order. One will be sent to any address on receipt of P.O.O. for **12/6**.

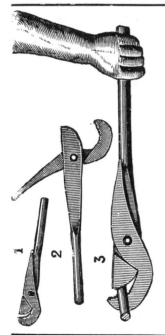

PIPE TONGS,

Which for utility, usefulness, and firmness of grip are unsurpassed.

In three sizes: No. 1 is 8 in. long, and will take from $\frac{1}{8}$-in. to $\frac{1}{2}$-in. pipe; No. 2 is 14 in. long and takes from $\frac{1}{2}$-in. to 1-in. coupling; No. 3 is 23 in. long, and takes from 1-in. to 2-in. coupling.

Acts as Pipe Tongs or Screw Key.

For screwing in studs or nuts with corners off, they are invaluable.

Price, £1 15s. the Set, net.

BRITANNIA CO., COLCHESTER, England.

London Showrooms—100, *Houndsditch.*   *All Letters to Colchester.*

STRONG NEW CAST-IRON PULLEYS

SUITABLE FOR GENERAL ENGINEERING PURPOSES.

Turned Flat or Rounding on Face.   Flat Faces always sent unless ordered otherwise.
Keyways cut or Set Screw fitted.

Diam.	Max. Bore	WIDTH ON FACE.								
		4 in.	5 in.	6 in.	7 in.	8 in.	9 in.	10 in.	11 in.	12 in.
ins.	ins.	s. d.	s. d.	s. d.	s. d.	s. d.	s. d.	s. d.	s. d.	s. d.
4	3	4 0	4 6	5 0						
5	3	4 6	5 0	5 6						
6	3	4 9	5 3	6 0						
7	3	5 3	5 9	6 6	8 6					
8	3	5 6	6 3	7 0	9 6	11 0				
9	3	6 0	6 9	7 6	10 0	11 6	13 0			
10	3	6 6	7 3	8 0	11 0	12 6	14 0	15 6		
11	3	7 0	7 9	8 6	11 6	13 0	14 6	16 0	18 0	
12	3	7 6	8 3	9 0	12 6	14 0	15 6	17 0	19 0	21 0
13	3	7 9	8 6	9 3	13 0	14 6	16 6	18 0	20 0	22 0
14	3	8 0	8 9	9 6	13 6	15 0	17 0	19 0	21 6	23 0
15	3	8 6	9 3	10 0	14 0	15 6	17 6	19 6	22 0	24 6
16	3	9 0	9 9	10 6	14 6	16 0	18 0	20 0	22 6	25 0
17	3	9 6	10 6	11 6	15 6	17 0	19 0	21 0	23 6	26 0
18	3	10 6	11 3	12 0	16 6	18 0	20 0	22 6	25 0	27 6
19	3	11 6	12 3	13 0	17 6	19 6	21 6	24 0	26 6	29 0
20	3	12 0	12 9	13 6	18 6	20 6	22 6	25 0	27 6	30 0
21	3	13 0	13 6	14 0	19 6	21 6	23 6	26 0	28 6	31 0
22	3	13 6	14 3	15 9	21 6	23 6	25 6	28 0	30 6	33 0
23	3	14 0	15 0	16 0	22 6	24 6	27 0	29 6	32 0	34 6
24	3	15 0	16 0	17 0	23 6	26 0	28 6	31 0	33 6	36 0
25	3	16 6	18 0	19 0	25 6	28 0	30 6	33 0	36 0	39 0
26	3	18 0	20 0	21 0	26 6	29 0	32 0	34 6	37 6	41 0
27	3	20 0	22 0	23 0	27 6	30 0	33 0	36 0	39 0	42 6
28	3	22 0	24 0	25 0	28 6	31 0	34 0	37 0	40 0	44 0
29	3	24 0	25 0	27 6	29 6	32 0	35 0	38 0	42 0	46 0
30	3	25 0	26 0	28 6	30 6	33 0	36 0	40 0	44 0	48 0
32	3	27 0	29 0	31 0	33 0	35 0	38 0	42 0	46 0	50 0
33	3	28 0	30 0	32 0	34 6	37 0	40 0	44 0	48 0	52 6
34	3	29 0	31 0	33 0	35 6	38 0	41 0	45 6	50 0	55 0
36	3	31 0	33 0	35 0	37 6	40 0	43 0	47 6	52 6	57 6
38	3	35 0	35 0	37 6	40 0	43 0	46 0	50 0	55 0	60 0
39	4	36 0	36 0	38 6	41 0	44 0	48 0	52 6	57 6	62 6
40	4	37 6	37 6	40 0	43 0	46 0	50 0	55 0	60 0	65 0
42	4	38 0	41 0	44 0	48 0	51 0	55 0	60 0	65 0	70 0
44	4	44 0	44 0	47 6	51 0	56 0	60 0	65 0	70 0	75 0
45	4	46 0	46 0	48 0	53 0	58 0	62 0	67 6	72 6	77 6
46	4	47 0	47 0	50 0	55 0	60 0	65 0	70 0	75 0	80 0
48	4	47 6	50 0	55 0	60 0	65 0	70 0	75 0	80 0	85 0
50	4	...	...	...	63 0	69 0	75 0	80 0	85 0	90 0
52	4	...	...	...	67 0	72 6	77 6	85 0	90 0	95 0
54	4	...	...	...	70 0	75 0	80 0	87 6	95 0	100 0
56	4	...	...	...	75 0	80 0	85 0	92 6	100 0	105 0
58	4	...	...	...	80 0	85 0	90 0	97 6	105 0	110 0
60	4	...	...	...	85 0	90 0	97 6	102 6	110 0	117 6

BRITANNIA CO., COLCHESTER, England.

London Showrooms—100, Houndsditch.   All Letters to Colchester.

WROUGHT-IRON SHAFTING.

It is of the greatest importance that shafting should be true and well turned, and buyers will do well to study the quality rather than the saving of a few shillings in the first cost.

We guarantee all our shafting true to Whitworth's gauge, turned in the lathe and polished.

We can turn shafting in lengths up to 24 feet, but as the Railway Company will not carry such long lengths, unless there are two tons, we advise shorter lengths being chosen.

Diameter .. inches	1	1¼	1½	1¾	2	2¼	2½	2¾	3	3¼	3½	4
Weight per foot, lbs.	2.62	4 09	5.90	8.03	10.49	13 27	16.39	19.84	23.60	27.70	32.13	41.97
Price .. per foot	1/-	1/2	1/4	1/6	1/9	2/2	2/8	3/4	3/10	4/6	5/2	6/10

Intermediate sizes charged at proportionate prices.

Fractions of 6 inches are charged as 6 inches. Pieces over 20 feet long charged 10 per cent. extra.

STEEL SHAFTING.

We are also in a position to supply this of the first quality, true and well turned.

Diameter .. inches	1	1¼	1½	1¾	2	2¼	2½	2¾	3	3¼	3½	4	4½	5	5½	6
Weight per foot, lbs.	2 67	4·17	6.02	8.19	10.70	13.54	16.72	20.24	24·07	28.25	32.77	42.81	54	67	82	97
Price .. per foot	1/2	1/4	1/6	1/10	2/2	2/8	3/2	3/8	4/6	5/3	6/-	7/6	9/6	13/-	16/-	20/-

Intermediate sizes charged at proportionate prices.

Fractions of 6 inches charged as six inches.

It is important in fixing shafting to have a sufficient number of Bearings, and the following table will be useful for general guidance, but these distances will of course vary according to the nature of the work put upon the shafting.

Diam. of Shaft in.	1	1¼	1½	1¾	2	2¼	2½	2¾	3	3¼	3½	4
Distance of Bearings	5ft.	6ft.	7ft.	7ft. 6in	8ft.	8ft. 6in.	9ft.	9ft. 6in	10ft.	10ft. 6in.	11ft.	12ft.

"J" HANGERS

WITH BRASSES.

Length of Brasses, 1½ diameters plus ⅝ inch.

These are specially designed for carrying countershafts, and short lengths of shafting.

Distance of Centre from Beam in. ..	8	10	12	14	14	16	18	20
Bore of Brasses	1¼	1½	1¾	2	2½	2½	2¾	3
Price	7/3	9/6	13/6	18/-	26/-	27/-	29/-	36/-

BRITANNIA CO., COLCHESTER, England.

London Showrooms—100, *Houndsditch.* *All Letters to Colchester.*

PLUMMER BLOCKS.

THE large demand for these articles has induced us to put down special plant for their manufacture, by means of which we are enabled to offer Plummer Blocks of a superior quality, at prices that will compare favourably with any house in the trade.

Planed on Sole, Bored, Faced, and fitted with Top and Bottom Brasses.

LIGHT SERIES.

Length of Brasses equal to 1½ in. Diameters.

Size of Bore ... ins.	1	1¼	1½	1¾	2	2¼	2½	2¾	3	3¼	3½	4
Weight of Brasses Finished	oz. 7	oz. 10	oz. 15	lb. oz. 1 4	lb. oz. 1 11	lb. oz 2 4	lb. oz 3 2	lbs. 4	lb. oz 4 12	lb. oz. 6 4	lb. oz. 7 11	lb. oz. 11 7
Length of Sole ins.	6¼	7¼	8¼	9 5/16	10	10¾	11½	12⅜	13 1/16	13¾	14½	16
Width of Sole ,,	1 1/16	1⅜	1¾	2 1/16	2⅜	2 11/16	3	3 5/16	3⅝	3 15/16	4¼	4⅞
Centres of Bolt Holes ... ,,	5⅛	6	6¾	7⅝	8¼	8⅞	9⅜	10¼	10⅞	11½	12	13½
Height of Centre from Sole ... ,,	1¼	1⅜	1⅝	1⅞	2	2⅜	2 7/16	2 11/16	2⅞	3 3/16	3⅜	3⅞
Price ... ... each	3/-	3/6	4/6	5/6	7/-	9/-	11/6	14/6	17/6	21 -	26/-	36 -
If with Babbitt's metal bearing instead of gun metal	3/6	4/-	5/-	6/-	8/-	10/-	12/6	16/-	19/-	23/6	29/-	40/-

MEDIUM SERIES.

Length of Brasses 1½ Diameters plus ⅝ inch.

Size of Bore ins.	1	1¼	1½	1¾	2	2¼	2½	2¾	3	3¼	3½	4
Weight of Brasses Finished	oz. 11	oz. 14	lb. oz. 1 7	lb. oz 2 2	lb. oz. 2 14	lb. oz 3 9	lb. oz. 4 12	lb. oz. 5 12	lb. oz. 7 2	lb. oz. 8 8	lb. oz. 10 4	lb. oz. 15 8
Length of Sole ins.	7¼	7¾	8⅜	10	10¾	11½	12⅜	13⅛	13⅞	14⅝	15⅜	18⅜
Width of Sole ,,	1 7/16	1 11/16	2 1/16	2⅜	2 11/16	3	3 5/16	3⅝	3 15/16	4 3/16	4 7/16	4⅞
Centres of Bolt Holes ... ,,	5⅞	5⅞	6 7/16	8 3/16	8¾	9 7/16	10⅛	10 13/16	11⅝	12¼	13⅛	14 11/16
Height of Centre from Sole ... ,,	1 5/16	1 9/16	1¾	2	2¼	2⅜	2⅝	2 13/16	3⅛	3⅜	3½	3 15/16
Price ... ... each	3/6	4/6	5/6	7/-	9/-	11/6	14/6	17/6	22/6	28/-	37/-	48/-
If with Babbitt's metal bearing instead of gun metal	4/-	5/-	6/-	8/-	10/-	13/-	16/6	20/-	25/-	30/-	42/-	54/-

EXTRA HEAVY SERIES.

Length of Brasses equal to Two Diameters.

Size of Bore ... ... inches	1¾	2	2¼	2½	2¾	3	3¼	3½	4
Weight of Brasses Finished	lbs. 3	lb. oz. 4 4	lb. oz. 5 4	lb. oz. 6 8	lbs. 8	lb. oz 9 12	lbs. 12	lbs. 14	lb. oz. 20 12
Length of Sole ... ... inches	10¾	11¾	12 11/16	13½	14¼	15⅛	15⅞	16¾	18¼
Width of Sole ... ... ,,	2 7/16	2⅞	3⅜	3¾	4¼	4⅝	5 1/16	5⅝	6⅛
Centres of Bolt Holes ... ,,	8¼	9	9 13/16	10 9/16	11¼	11¾	12⅝	13¼	14⅝
Height of Centre from Sole ... ,,	2⅛	2 7/16	2⅝	2 13/16	3 1/32	3¼	3½	3¾	4 3/16
Price ... ... each	10/-	12/6	16/-	19/-	22/6	27/6	38/-	42/	57/-
If with Babbitt's metal bearing instead of gun metal	11/-	14/6	18/-	21/6	25/6	31/-	38/-	47/6	64/-

Intermediate sizes same price as next size larger.

☞ All our Plummer Blocks are Planed on Sole.

Any of the Plummer Blocks can be made with oil catchers cast on each side, if specially ordered.

SIZE	1in. to 1¾in.	2in. to 2¾in.	3in. to 4in.
Price (any series) extra, each	1/-	1/6	2/-

BRITANNIA CO., COLCHESTER, England.

London Showrooms—100, *Houndsditch.* *All Letters to Colchester.*

WALL BOXES.

THESE Wall Boxes are of new design with curved top and flange, giving them a very neat appearance when fixed. They are planed to receive Plummer Block, and prices include Bolts for same, but not the Plummer Block.

For 4½ in. wall, will take any Plummer Block up to 2 in. ...	£0 6 0
,, 4½ in. ,, ,, ,, ,, 3 in. ...	0 10 0
,, 9 in. ,, ,, ,, ,, 1½ in. ...	0 8 0
,, 9 in. ,, ,, ,, ,, 2¼ in. ...	0 12 0
,, 9 in. ,, ,, ,, ,, 2¾ in. ...	0 16 0
,, 9 in. ,, ,, ,, ,, 3½ in. ...	1 2 6
,, 9 in. ,, ,, ,, ,, 4 in. ...	1 7 6
,, 9 in. ,, ,, ,, ,, 5 in. ...	2 12 6

☞ All our fittings are Planed to receive Plummer Block.

Bracket Bearings, A Standards, Wall Brackets, Sling Hangers, Sill Plates, Wrought Iron Slings, &c., supplied.

FLANGED COUPLINGS.

ORDINARY PATTERN.

THE importance of having shafting coupled up securely and true cannot be over-estimated, and although many patent and novel couplings are before the public, there are none to beat the old-fashioned Flanged Coupling, securely keyed on to the shaft and faced down true after keying on.

These Couplings are bored, faced, turned all over, key-grooved, bolt-holes reamered, and fitted with turned bolts and nuts.

The price for keying on, &c., includes grooving the shafts, providing keys, keying on the couplings, and facing down afterwards.

Size of Bore ... ins.	1	1¼	1½	1¾	2	2¼	2½	2¾	3	3¼	3½	4
Diameter of Flange ,,	4¾	5¼	5⅝	6	6⅞	7⅜	7¾	8¼	9¼	9½	9⅞	12
Thickness of ea. Flange ,,	⅝	⅝	¾	$\frac{13}{16}$	⅞	1	$1\frac{1}{16}$	1⅛	$1\frac{3}{16}$	1¼	1⅜	1½
Length over all ... ,,	3⅝	4⅛	4½	5⅛	5¾	6¼	6¾	7⅛	7¾	8¼	8¾	9¾
Price ... per pair	**6/-**	**6/6**	**7/6**	**9/6**	**12/-**	**14/-**	**18/-**	**21/-**	**25/-**	**28/-**	**32/-**	**40/-**
Keying on and facing down ... ... ,,	4/-	4/6	5/-	6/-	6/8	7/6	8/-	9/-	10/-	12/-	13/-	15/-

Intermediate sizes same price as next size larger.

Flanged Couplings with recessed Bolts.

Size of Bore ... ins	1	1¼	1½	1¾	2	2¼	2½	2¾	3	3¼	3½	4
Diameter of Flange ,,	6¼	6½	6¾	7¼	8¼	8¾	9¼	9¾	10½	11	11½	12¼
Thickness of ea. Flange ,,	1⅛	1⅛	1⅛	1⅛	1⅜	1⅜	1⅜	1⅜	1⅝	1⅝	1⅝	1⅝
Length over all ... ,,	3⅝	4¼	4½	5⅛	5¾	6¼	6¾	7⅛	7¾	8¼	8¾	9¾
Price ... per pair	**8/6**	**9/6**	**10/-**	**13/-**	**16/-**	**20/-**	**23/-**	**27/6**	**32/-**	**37/6**	**42/-**	**50/-**
Keying on and facing down ... ... ,,	4/-	4/6	5/-	6/-	6/8	7/6	8/-	9/-	10/-	12/-	13/-	15/-

Intermediate sizes same price as next size larger.

EITHER of the preceding Couplings can be made with one face recessed, the other projecting and accurately turned to fit tightly; this is of most value when Coupling up two shafts of different diameters.

Price

Up to 2 inch diameter, **2/-** per pair extra. Up to 3 inch diameter **3/6** per pair extra. Up to 4 inch diameter, **5/-** per pair extra.

LATHE & FRET SAW, No. 1.

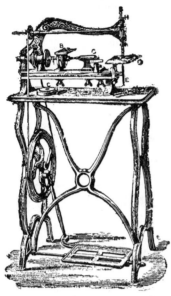

ADVANTAGES CLAIMED.

1.—It is a Lathe, Drill, Fret Saw, Circular Saw, Emery Grinder, and Polisher, in one compact tool, with heavy Fly Wheel.

2.—The Fret Saw works with a perpendicular stroke. and requires much less power than any other, while the quality of the work is superior. It will cut the most intricate designs in wood up to 1 inch thick.

3.—The table is adjustable, and drops to enable the Saw to enter another hole, without loss of time, and TILTS TO ANY ANGLE for inlaid work.

4.—It has an improved Clip, by which the Saw is instantly fixed, while the introduction of rollers behind the Saw prevents breakage. (The under tension is now fixed under the table instead of as shown).

5.—The adjustable Presser foot is introduced, and prevents the wood being jerked upwards.

6.—It has a horizontal Drill, for drilling holes for Fret work, and can be fitted with a vertical spindle with mitre gear wheels and 3 Drills for drilling metal, &c., price **12/6** extra.

7.—As a Lathe it is very durable, with planed bed, takes 8 in. by 4 in. between centres, conical Mandril, hardened centre, 3-in. Face Plate, Driver, 2 rests, square Thread in Barrel, same as a first-class Engineer's Lathe.

By means of an Emery and Buff Wheel fixed on Mandrel of Lathe. steel, stones, shells, &c., may be polished, and tools and knives sharpened.

These Tools are coming into favour with Ladies as well as Gentlemen, and are a most useful and never-ending source of amusement and profit.

Total Height—3 ft. 10 in., and will take 15 in. under the arm.

Weight—3 qrs. 20 lbs.

Price, with Horizontal Drill, 6 Saws, Oil Can, Spanner, and Turnscrew **£5 5 0**

Machine, without Stand, Fly Wheel, or Treadle ... **3 15 0**

Any of the following useful attachments can be had extra if desired, viz.:

	s.	d.
Circular Saw	4	0
Emery Wheel for Grinding Steel, Stones, Shells, &c. ...	4	0
Buff Wheels for polishing the same (fine or coarse) each	2	0
Mandrel, with Screw Collars for holding Saw or Wheels ...	6	0
Platform, with Guide for Circular Saw	10	6
Vertical Drill Spindle, with Mitre Gear Wheels to fit in place of Fret Saw Spindle with 3 Drills for Metal, &c.	12	6

Fret Saws, **4d.** per dozen, or **3/-** per gross

BRITANNIA CO., COLCHESTER, England.

London Showrooms—100. Houndsditch.   All Letters to Colchester.

NOTICE TO FRETWORKERS.

FRET SAW, No. 8.

With Improved Tension.

Not a Toy, but a useful Tool.

The presser foot prevents jerking of the work.

——-

Price, with horizontal and vertical Drill,

£3.

Cuts ½ in. easily.

Compare this before you purchase.

It is worth two of many others.

Will cut metals.

Has a durable Blower.

Weight 74 lbs.

Screw Collar for holding Emery Wheel, **2/6.** Polishing Brushes, **1/-** each. Emery Wheels, **2/-** each. Drills, **1/-** per dozen.

The Fret Saw as illustrated fills a want which has long been expressed. The advantages claimed for this over every other Saw are to the Practical Fret Cutter of considerable importance.

1.—True Vertical Stroke.

2.—Without any upper spring to offer resistance, the tension is **instantly put on or off by altering the thumb-nut** so that when fixing a new saw the tension is taken off by a turn of the nut. This gives *entire freedom of action,* however tight the tension.

3.—It will cut metal up to $\frac{1}{16}$ in. thick. Will cut ½ in. wood easily, and thicker at proportionate speed.

4.—It has a heavy two-speed fly-wheel, 14 in. diameter, weight 17 lbs., which ensures *steadiness of working* in either metal or wood.

5.—It will take in work 20 in. long under the arm.

6.—The table extends the *whole distance under the arm,* and gives *ample space* for the work.

7.—It is made *to tilt* for doing inlaid work. 8.—It has an *efficient* blower.

9.—It is *more substantial* than most Fret Saws.

BRITANNIA CO., COLCHESTER, England.

London Showrooms—100, *Houndsditch.* *All Letters to Colchester.*

FRET SAW, No. 3

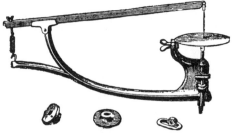

Price, 30s.

Can be made for any Lathe. It is secured by a bolt and nut under the
Lathe Bed. Fixed in one minute.

NOTE. — In ordering, it is necessary to give the exact height from bed to centre, an
accurate sketch or zinc template of size and form of Lathe bed, and to send the Lathe
mandrel to fit the catch plate to nose-screw; or if a correctly-fitted chuck is sent, it
will answer the latter purpose as well.

"WINDSOR" FRET SAW

Is constructed entirely of iron and steel, except
the arms, which are of tough wood for quietness
and lightness. The work table is 32 in. from the
floor, and is made to tilt for inlaying. The upper
arm throws back to enable the end of the saw to
be inserted for internal work.

The stand is nicely japanned. The driving
wheel is 12 in. in diameter, with a 5 in. balance
wheel. It will admit 18 in. under the arm.
The saw clamps are hung on pivots, and will
hold firmly the finest or coarsest saw. It is
fitted with an automatic blower and a drill
shaft. A drill, wrench, and six saws accompany
each machine.

The most surprising thing of all, however, is
its cheapness, for

The Price is only 17s. 6d.

If required to be sent by rail—box to pack, 2s.

TESTIMONIALS.

"I received the WINDSOR quite safely a few days ago. I put it together the same
night, and find that it works very well indeed, and shall recommend it to my
friends."

"I have to-day returned the case the WINDSOR came in. I have tried the Machine.
and like it very much."

"I received the Machine yesterday in proper order, and find that it works in a very
satisfactory manner"

BRITANNIA CO., COLCHESTER, England.

London Showrooms—100, *Houndsditch.* *All Letters to Colchester.*

BENCHES

FOR

CARPENTERS & CABINET MAKERS.

30 in. high from floor.   Extra height if required **1/-** per inch extra.

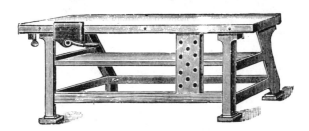

THE above represents a strong bench for wood workers.   The supports are of iron, and firmly held together by bolts and screws, thus avoiding the nuisance of a rickety bench.   It is fitted with a screw stop, shown on left, which is a great improvement on the old plan.

The tops are of sound well-seasoned wood firmly bolted together.

Shelf is provided for tools.

			£	s.	d.
No. 1 Price with Deal Top, 5 ft. by 18 inches	...	...	3	4	0
No 2 ,, Hard Wood Top	...	...	3	16	6
No. 3 ,, Deal Top, 6 ft. by 22 inches	...	...	3	8	6
No. 4 ,, Hard Wood Top	...	...	4	4	0
No. 5 ,, Deal Top, 7 ft. by 22 inches	...	...	3	14	6

These Benches are fitted with Patent Instantaneous Grip Vices.

Vices for these Benches are on Page 142.

☞ Improved Bench Knives or Back Stops for firmly securing work upon the bench extra **3/6** each.

Small Hardwood Amateur Work Benches, with tools ; 2 ft. 10 in. long, **22/-** 3 ft. 10 in , **36/-** ; 4 ft. 4 in., **52/-**

BRITANNIA CO., COLCHESTER, England.

*London Showrooms—*100, *Houndsditch.*   *All Letters to Colchester.*

INSTANTANEOUS GRIP JOINERS' VICES.

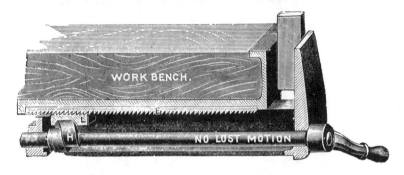

No. 0.—Width of jaw, 7½ in., opens 6 in.   ... Price, 12/6

No. 1.—Width of jaw, 9 in., opens 12 in.   ...   ,,   16/-

Fitted with Steel Backs.

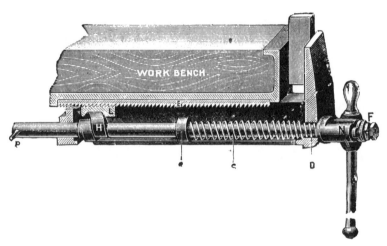

No. 2.—Size across jaws, 9 in., opens 12 in.   ... Price, 18/-

No. 3.—Size across jaws, 10½ in. opens 13 in. ..   ,.   21/-

Above have Steel Racks.

BRITANNIA CO., COLCHESTER, England.

London Showrooms—100, *Houndsditch.*   *All Letters to Colchester.*

PATENT

PLANE IRON, CHISEL & TOOL SHARPENING MACHINE.

Price, 8s. 6d. each.

THIS useful Machine is fast taking the place of the Oil Stone, being so simple in use, and giving the work a much better finish. A boy can sharpen a Plane Iron and ensure having a straight and true edge in less time than the most experienced workman could with a stone.

NOTE.—When grinding on the grindstone, which, as a rule, is UNTRUE, we advise that you do not let the cutting edge touch the stone, but leave about $\frac{1}{64}$th of an inch; then finish the tool on the above Sharpening Machine. By this means your tools will always have a straight edge ; and much time be saved.

Can be used on Bench as shown, but it is more convenient if fixed on a post or wall.

SIR, *Waddesdon, April 5th,* 1889.

The Plane Iron and Chisel Sharpening Machine you supplied me with some months since, must supply a longfelt want.

I have no hesitation in saying it is most economical with regard to saving time, and puts the edge of tools to much greater truth than the ordinary way. The consequence is better work. It only wants to be known to command a ready sale.

Yours truly, H. H. SHERWIN.

DEAR SIR, *Bicester Road, Aylesbury, March 6th,* 1889.

I have been using your Patent Sharpening Machine for Plane Irons and Chisels the last few weeks, and find it a great improvement on the oil stone, a good edge is easily obtained and in much less time, and I think when known will be extensively used.

Yours truly, W. ROADS.

DEAR SIR, *The Printing Works. Aylesbury.*
May 10th, 1889,
In reply to your application, we beg to state that we have now had your Tool Sharpening Machine in use for a long time, and cannot speak too highly of its merits; and on account of its truth, is much preferred to the ordinary oil stone.

Yours faithfully,
For HAZELL, WATSON & VINEY, Lim.,
H. JOWETT, *Manager.*

BRITANNIA CO., COLCHESTER, England.

London Showrooms—100, *Houndsditch.* *All Letters to Colchester.*

IMPROVED MITRE CUTTERS.

No. 1 ... ... **15/-**	No. 2 .. ... **30/-**
Cuts 2-in. Mouldings.	To cut 4-in. Mouldings.
Extra Cutter **3/-**	Will cut Architrave and Panel Mouldings up to 4 in. with great precision.
☞ **Cuts Mitres for Picture Frames without injury to Gilt Surface.**	Extra Cutter **6/-**

CORNER CRAMPS.

		Takes	Per Pair.
No. 1	... ...	$1\frac{3}{4}$ in. ...	... **2/-**
No. 2	... ...	$2\frac{3}{4}$ in. ...	... **3/-**
No. 3	... ...	4 in. ...	... **5/-**

WOOD-WORKING MACHINERY.
MORTISING MACHINES.
CIRCULAR SAWS, for Foot or Steam Power, &c.

BRITANNIA CO., COLCHESTER, England.

London Showrooms—100, Houndsditch. All Letters to Colchester.

THE 'BRITANNIA' MORTISE MACHINE.

We have put into this Machine all the additions & improvements that experience suggests.

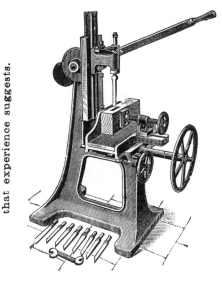

Many of our Mortise Machines are working various kinds of wood to the satisfaction of the users in all parts of the world.

In designing and constructing the above Machine, our great aim has been to make a MORTISE MACHINE at a low price, and which for simplicity, efficiency, and accuracy in all its working parts, cannot be surpassed.

It is suitable for working either hard or soft wood, thus making it a most acceptable Machine for all classes of Joiners, Builders, Cabinet Makers, &c., &c.

The Frame itself is made in one casting. By this means a strength and solidity is given to the Machine, which is not only very desirable, but very necessary where good work is required to be done.

The Wrought Iron Lever which is used for bringing the chisel down to its work, is so placed that when the workman is using the Machine he stands in an easy and convenient position for operating on, and seeing the work he is doing.

The Chisels are made from a high class steel, specially manufactured for mortising purposes. A class of steel which a great many years' experience has taught us is the best for mortise chisels.

Each Chisel is fitted with a pin, which fits in a slot hole in a taper socket in chisel box, this keeps it immovable and perfectly true in reversing, thus by a half-turn of chisel box handle, the chisel is reversed truly.

This Machine will mortise 6 in. deep, and take work on the moveable table 15 in. by 8 in. Weight of machine, 3 cwt. 3 qrs. ; with Boring Apparatus, 4 cwt.

Price of Machine, including 8 chisels, ¼in. to ¾in., one spanner, and one core driver (without Boring Apparatus) **£8**

Price of Machine (with Boring Apparatus, including three bits for iron, and three for wood) **£9**

Self-coring chisels, extra **10s.**

BRITANNIA CO., COLCHESTER, England.

London Showrooms—100, Houndsditch. All Letters to Colchester.

WALL BORING MACHINE.

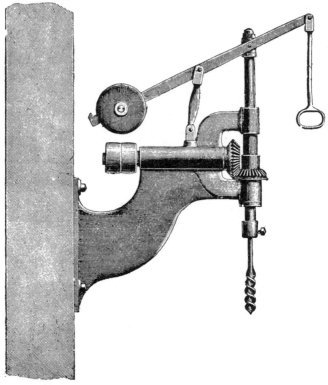

THE above machine has been specially designed to meet the demand for a cheap Boring Machine, for the use of builders, cabinet makers, &c., &c.

It is capable of boring holes in all kinds of hard or soft wood with efficiency and despatch. Where room is an object this machine will be found to be very convenient on account of the very small space it requires.

The boring spindle revolves in a strong cast iron frame, firmly bolted to a wall, and is counter-balanced by weight and lever.

It is driven by bevel tooth gear and fast and loose pulleys, and the spindle is raised or lowered to suit various depths of work required by means of wrought handle attached to weight lever, as shown in front of machine.

Size ... to bore holes up to	2 in. diameter and 8 in. deep.
Approximate Weight	2 cwts.
Average Power required	$\frac{1}{2}$-horse.
Size of Driving Pulleys	5 in. by $2\frac{1}{2}$ in.
Speed of Driving Pulleys	500 revolutions.
Price	£6 10s.

BRITANNIA CO., COLCHESTER, England.

London Showrooms—100, Houndsditch.   *All Letters to Colchester.*

HORIZONTAL COMBINED
SLOT MORTISING & BORING MACHINE.

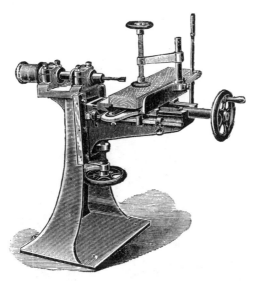

This illustration represents a machine that will be found very useful for making mortises, and for doing the boring required in joiners', builders', or cabinet makers' work.

It is self-contained, takes up little room, and may be fixed in any part of a workshop.

The mortises are formed by a revolving bit of specially improved shape, for boring or routing either hard or soft wood.

The wood to be bored or mortised is placed upon a planed table, carried by a strong bracket attached to frame of machine ; the bracket is fitted with hand-wheel and screw, by which it can be readily raised or lowered, to suit position of holes or slots to be made. The table is worked to and fro by lever in front of machine, and backward and forward by hand-wheel and screw.

Each machine is complete with stops or gauges, so as to regulate depth and length of slots to be worked.

SIZES	Approximate Weight	Average Power Required	If supplied without Countershaft		If supplied with Countershaft		Price of Machine as shown and described above	Price of Machine as a Boring Machine only
			Size of Driving Pulleys	Speed of Driving Pulleys	Size of Driving Pulleys on Countershaft	Speed of Driving Pulleys on Countershaft		
No. 1, to mortise slots 2 in. wide by 8 in. long	8 cwt.	$\frac{1}{2}$ horse	4 by 2 in.	4,000	6 by 3 in.	800	£25	£20
No. 2, to mortise slots 1¼ in. wide by 6 in. long	4½ ,,	½ ,,	3 by 2 in.	5,000	5 by 2½ in.	800	£15	£12

Countershaft for either machine, £4 extra.

BRITANNIA CO., COLCHESTER, England.

London Showrooms—100, *Houndsditch.* *All Letters to Colchester.*

BRITANNIA COMPANY'S
NEW BAND SAW
With Revolving and Tilting Table and Adjustable Fence.
(WHIBLEY'S PATENT.)

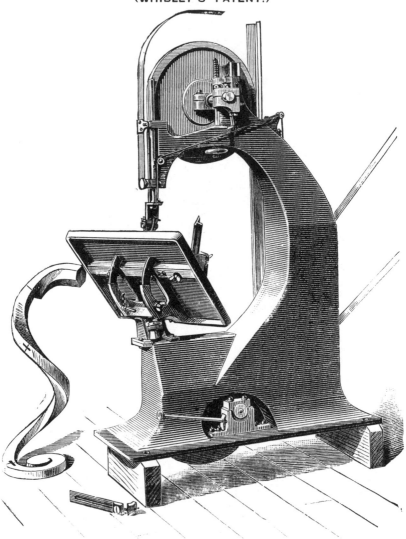

(For description see opposite page).

BRITANNIA CO., COLCHESTER, England.
London Showrooms—100, *Houndsditch.*   *All Letters to Colchester.*

BRITANNIA COMPANY'S

NEW BAND SAW

With Revolving and Tilting Table and Adjustable Fence.

(WHIBLEY'S PATENT).

(For illustration see opposite page).

THE most perfect machine of its kind yet introduced. The main body is a heavy hollow box casting, within which the driving pulleys and belt and striking gear are contained, leaving the outside of the machine clear for operator. The table tilts through an angle of 60 degrees, and can be freely revolved around the saw and secured in any position, and it is fitted with a most ingenious patented sliding fence. The saw pulleys are constructed of wood, numerous thin boards of mahogany glued and screwed together with grain in opposite direction, and with turned cast-iron hub and washer plate, avoiding arms. The saw guides are adjustable, and upper one counterbalanced.

The machine possesses many advantages over others, among which may be named the following :—

1. All ordinary work done on Band Saw Machines can be done by this machine, but with greater facility.
2. The table cants through a greater angle than any other.
3. The table can be revolved freely around the saw, and instantly secured in either one of four primary positions at right angles or at any intermediate angle.
4. The patent fence, combined with the revolving table, enables work to be done which cannot be done on any other machine, viz., all forms of oblique solids of equal or similar parallel sections ; twist cuts in work of double curvature. as rails of circle upon circle curvature, twisted wreaths of staircase handrails &c., can all be cut quickly. with ease and precision, which hitherto have all been done entirely by hand at the bench. involving much expenditure of time and highly skilled labour.
5. Square. angular, and oblique plane cuts of every description can be made accurately to gauge dimensions in every direction.

The saw pulleys are	...	... 30 in. diameter
Table	...	2 ft. 7 in. by 2 ft. 9 in
Total height of machine	...	... 8 ft. 9 in.
Floor space ...	...	5 ft. 6 in. by 2 ft. 3 in.
Approximate weight	...	... 1 ton 2 cwt
Price, complete	...	...

BRITANNIA CO., COLCHESTER, England.

London Showrooms—100, *Houndsditch.*   *All Letters to Colchester.*

THE IMPROVED
BAND SAW MACHINE.

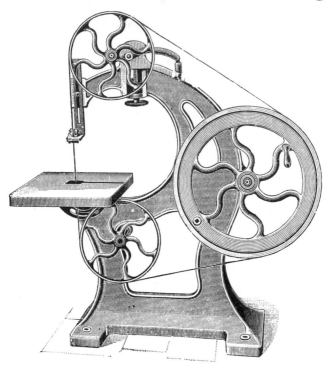

It is strongly built, the pillar being one solid casting; it is compact and complete in itself, occupies little room, and works by hand with greater ease than any other hand machine of its class. We introduce it to the trade with full confidence in its working, feeling certain it will not fail to give satisfaction.

It is fitted with tension motion to allow for expansion or contraction of saw whilst working. The table is made to cant for cutting work on the bevel. It will admit of work 11 in. deep.

When worked by steam power, speed of driving pulleys should be about 100 revolutions per minute.

The above represents a useful Band Saw for Hand or Steam Power.

No. 1 Size, with band saw pulleys each 16 in. diameter, and fly-wheel 28 in. diameter, with angle bracket for tenoning, one screw-key, and one $\frac{3}{8}$ in. saw, sharpened and set ready for use. Weight, 5 cwt. 2 qrs. ... ... **Price £10 10 0**

No. 2 Size, with band saw pulleys each 20 in. diameter, and fly-wheel 32 in. diameter, with angle bracket for tenoning, one screw-key, and one $\frac{3}{8}$ in. saw sharpened and set ready for use. Weight, 7 cwt. ... ... **Price 13 10 0**

A Boring Apparatus, with 1 in. auger, may be attached to either machine ... ... Price extra **2 0 0**

Either machine may be made so as to work by steam power, by placing a pair of pulleys behind fly-wheel, one pair 9 in. pulleys ... ... Price extra **0 12 6**

One pair 12 in. pulleys ... ... ,, **0 15 0**

Belt, fork, and striking gear for ditto ... ,, **0 12 0**

BRITANNIA CO., COLCHESTER, England.

London Showrooms—100, *Houndsditch.*   *All Letters to Colchester.*

PLAIN BAND SAW MACHINES

WE have re-arranged and thoroughly overhauled all our Band Saw Machines, and the above is an illustration of them as *now* made.

The main frame is a cored casting, in *one* piece, securing strength and preventing vibration when in operation.

The machines are fitted with wrought-iron pulleys of special construction, truly bored, turned and balanced, made light but strong, thus greatly reducing the strain on the saw, which often results from the starting or stopping of the machine when heavier pulleys are used ; they are faced with best India-rubber tyres, making an elastic bed for the saw. Top pulley is made to rise and fall and is fitted with canting arrangement to guide the saw to the centre, or any part of the face, to suit different widths of saws. Bottom pulley works in adjustable gun-metal bearings secured to the lower portion of main frame.

They are fitted with lever and weight tension arrangement, which gives sufficient elasticity to the saw to compensate for any variation in the length of the saw, brought about by the change of temperature or strain.

Saw guides, consisting of anti-friction rollers made of hardened steel, to receive the back thrust of the saw, with wooden pieces for the sides, are fitted immediately above and below the table ; the upper guide is adjustable vertically, so as to support the saw, and suit the different thicknesses of wood to be sawn.

The table is truly planed on the surface, and is fitted with canting arrangement by quadrant and wheel for working stuff on the bevel.

SIZES.	Approximate Weight.	Average Power required.	Diameter of Saw Pulleys.	Size of Driving Pulleys.	Speed of Driving Pulleys.	PRICE.
No. 1, to cut 20in deep	36 cwt.	2 horse	48in.	18 by 5in.	350	£60
No. 2, ,, 18in. ,,	29 ,,	1 ,,	42in.	15 by 4in.	400	46
No. 3, ,, 18in. ,,	21 ,,	1 ,,	36in.	14 by 4in.	450	40
No. 4, ,, 16in. ,,	15 ,,	½ ,,	30in.	12 by 3½in.	500	30
No. 5, ,, 13in. ,,	12 ,,	½ ,,	24in.	10 by 3in.	300	26

BRITANNIA CO., COLCHESTER, England.

London Showrooms—100, Houndsditch.   *All Letters to Colchester.*

IMPROVED
FRET SAW MACHINE.

The engraving herewith represents our Fret Saw Machine, it is used for sawing carved and irregular work, and is especially useful for Cabinet Makers, Manufacturers of Pianofortes, or others who have fret work to do of any kind whatever, it will do the most delicate work, or it will saw timber up to 4 in. deep.

The Machine is self-contained, the frame being very strong, thus giving great rigidity to it.

It is fitted with very simple but effective straining Apparatus, consisting only of a lever, to one end of which the saw is attached in such a manner that it is readily fixed or released.

The tension motion is so arranged that it is equally the same at every part of the stroke.

The table has a planed surface, and is fitted with canting arrangement, so that work may be cut out to any required bevel.

Weight about	..	10 cwts.	Driving Pulleys	..	6 in. by 3 in.
Table	.. ..	30 in. square	Speed of Driving Pulleys	..	1000
Average Power ..	..	¼-horse	**Price**	.. ..	**£25.**

BRITANNIA CO., COLCHESTER, England.

London Showrooms—100, Houndsditch.   All Letters to Colchester.

HAND POWER COMBINED
Circular and Band Sawing Machine.

For the use of Joiners, Builders, Cabinet
Makers, Coach Builders, &c. It is also
very useful for Contractors, as it is
readily moved from place to place
where required.

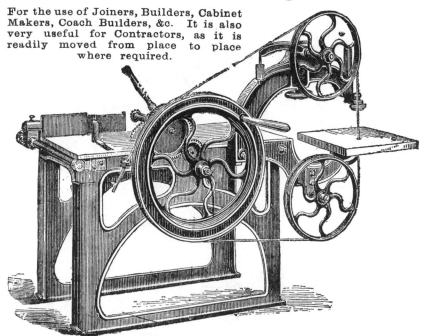

THE table for above Bench is 4 feet by 2 feet, substantially made of iron,
planed true on top. It is fitted with Rising and Falling Spindle, Self-acting
Feed Motion ; Parallel Fence, made to cant so as to cut bevels, and also to
turn over end of bench, to be out of the way of cross-cutting. It is also fitted
with Weight and Roller for keeping timber to Fence.

With this Bench one man can cut three inches deep at the rate of ten feet
in four minutes, or two inches deep at the rate of ten feet in two minutes,
thus effecting a saving of 150 per cent. over what can be done with the
Hand Saw.

Band Saw Apparatus is fitted with square table, made so as to cant over
for cutting to any bevel. With this may be cut any irregular, curved. or
ornamental design, with an ease not attained before by any Hand-power
Machine. The Band Saw is fitted with a new arrangement for securing
equal tension to saw at all times.

Approximate Weight, 8 cwt. 2 qrs. Band Saw Pulleys, 16 in diameter.

Price of above Machine, with one each 9 in. and 14 in. Circular and one
⅜ in. Band Saw, for Hand and Steam Power £24 0 0
Ditto if with Boring Apparatus and one Auger 26 0 0
Ditto if for Steam Power only and not for Hand 23 10 0
Ditto if for Hand Power only 22 0 0
Ditto without Band Saw attachment, including 2 Circular Saws, viz.,
9 in. and 14 in., 6 rollers and carriers for extending the Bench, and
2 extra change wheels for Feed Motion 12 10 0
Ditto if without Feed Motion, and without rollers and carriers for
extending the Bench 10 10 0

For an extra charge of 10s., this Bench can be prepared to work either by Steam
or Hand, as occasion requires.

BRITANNIA CO., COLCHESTER, England.

London Showrooms 100, *Houndsditch.* *All Letters to Colchester.*

CIRCULAR SAW BENCH.

For Wood or Metals ; with Rising Table ; to be driven by any ordinary foot power.

6¾ in. long by 10 in. wide at base ; table, 9¾ in. by 6 in. ; fast and loose pulleys, 1⅝ in. diameter by 1 in. wide ; height of bench, 4⅝ in. ; will take a 3¾ in. circular saw.

Price, £2 2s. 0d.

USEFUL SAW

LIGHT WOOD OR METAL WORK.

Size of Table,

19 in. by 19 in.

Size of Table,

19 in. by 19 in.

Price, £8.   Cheaper Pattern, £6 15s.

BRITANNIA CO., COLCHESTER, England.

London Showrooms —100, Houndsditch.   All Letters to Colchester.

SMALL FIXED SPINDLE BENCH.

THE engraving represents a small but very useful Circular Saw Bench for amateurs, or to place amongst the joiners or workmen of any kind of manufactory where wood has to be worked.

It is handy for cross-cutting odd lengths. or for ripping light work. With a circular saw 14 in. diameter it will cut 4 in. deep.

It occupies but a small space, takes little power to drive it, and the price is such as to place it within the reach of any one to whom such a machine would be serviceable.

Surface of table is 2 ft. 9 in. × 1 ft. 6 in., and admits a saw up to 14 in. diameter. Saw spindle is made of steel, and works in adjustable brass bearings. It is complete with fast and loose pulley, and strap-guider, as shown.

SIZE.	Approximate Weight, net.	Average Power Required	Driving Pulleys	Speed of Driving Pulleys.	PRICE.
Size of table, 2ft 9in × 1ft 6in, and prepared for taking a saw 14in diameter	4 cwt 2 qrs	½ horse	4 in × 2½ in	2,000 revs.	£7

BRITANNIA CO., COLCHESTER, England.

London Showrooms—100, *Houndsditch*.   *All Letters to Colchester.*

THE NEW PATENT SAW

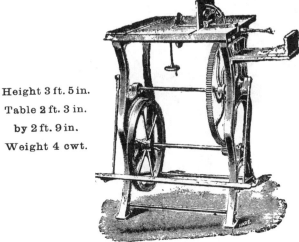

Height 3 ft. 5 in.

Table 2 ft. 3 in.

by 2 ft. 9 in.

Weight 4 cwt.

Height 3 ft. 5 in.

Table 2 ft. 3 in.

by 2 ft. 9 in.

Weight 4 cwt.

Including one each 8 in. Rip and Cross-Cut Saws, and one 6 in. Saw, with one pair of Bevel Washers for Grooving, **£15**.

Fret Arm to suspend from ceiling, for Fret Cutting, **£2 10s**.

Two Mitre and Cross-Cut Gauges, **17/6**.

If 12 in. Cross-Cut Saw instead of 8 in., **5/-** extra.

Adjustable Boring Table at side, including Chuck and 9 Bits, from $\frac{1}{4}$ in. to $1\frac{1}{2}$ in., **22/6**.

Mortising Attachment, **£3 10s**.

Centre-Bits fitted—$\frac{1}{4}$ in., **8d.** ; $\frac{3}{8}$ in., **8d.** ; $\frac{1}{2}$ in., **8d.** ; $\frac{5}{8}$ in., **8d.** ; $\frac{3}{4}$ in., **8d.** ; 1 in., **10d.** ; $1\frac{1}{8}$ in., **1/-** ; $1\frac{1}{4}$ in., **1/-** ; $1\frac{1}{2}$ in., **1/2**.

The Saw can be worked at 1500 Revolutions per Minute.

A Handle at left can be used as auxiliary to, or in lieu of Treadle—Price **7/6**. This Saw will cut 10 ft. of inch wood in a minute.

Especially adapted for Pattern Makers, Cabinet Makers, Joiners, Picture Frame Makers; for Vertical or Circular Sawing. Groove Cutting, Dowelling, Drilling, Dovetailing, Mortising, and Moulding up to $\frac{7}{8}$ in.

BRITANNIA CO., COLCHESTER, England.

London Showrooms—100, Houndsditch.   All Letters to Colchester.

PATENT DOVETAILING APPARATUS

As fixed on Patent Saw.

Price for Ordinary Size,

£2 2s. 0d.

See Special Circular.

Can be fitted to any saw
with rising spindle or table.

CAUTION.

The above appliance is patented.   Users or makers infringing will be proceeded against

BRITANNIA CO., COLCHESTER, England.

London Showroom—100, *Houndsditch.   All Letters to Colchester.*

NEW SAW BENCHES.

THIS Saw Bench is recommended as a very firm and substantial tool ; it is made with either stationary or rise and fall table, and the larger sizes can be fitted with drag motion if required. All the parts are planed together, the table is planed and polished, the spindle has three long necks, and is fitted up with lock nuts of improved design for taking up all side wear ; the fence is in every way adjustable, and will swing clear over end for cross cutting. Complete with belt guide and necessary screw keys.

To admit Saw diameter.	Table. in. in.	Will cut fully through.	Diam. and width of Pulley. in. in.	Revoltns. per minute.	Price Rising Top.	Price Stationary Top.
18 in.	40 by 20	7 in. deep	5 by 3	1400	£12 10	£10 0
26 in.	48 by 24	10 in. ,,	6 by 3½	1200	13 10	11 0
32 in.	58 by 27	12 in. ,,	7 by 3½	1000	17 10	15 10
34 in.	66 by 33	14 in. ,,	9 by 4	950	20 0	17 0
38 in.	72 by 36	16 in. ,,	10 by 5	850	23 0	18 10
42 in.	90 by 38	18 in. ,,	12 by 5	800	26 0	22 0

CIRCULAR SAWS (Cast Steel)—New.

4	4½	5	6	7	8	9	10	12	14	16 inch
3/2	3/6	4/3	5/-	5/8	6/8	7/9	9/-	11/3	14/-	16/9

18	20	22	24	26	28	30	32 inch
£1 1	£1 5 3	£1 9 6	£1 13 8	£2	£2 6 3	£2 13 3	£3 2

34	36	38	40	42	44	46	48 inch
£3 12 9	£4 4	£5 1 6	£5 12	£6 6	£7 10 6	£8 8	£9 9

50	52	54	56	58	60 inch
£13 6	£14 14	£16 16	£19 19	£21 14	£23 16

Perforated Saws 10 per cent. extra.

BRITANNIA CO., COLCHESTER, England.

London Showrooms—100, Houndsditch.   All Letters to Colchester.

SELF-ACTING SAW BENCHES.

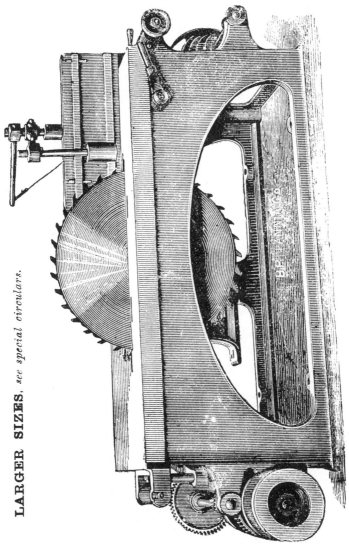

LARGER SIZES, *see special circulars.*

These Benches are useful for cutting planks or battens into boards or scantlings. The tops are planed true on the surface, and are fitted with strong parallel fence, to which is attached pressure lever and roller for keeping timber to fence whilst being sawn into boards, &c.

The main framing is cast all in one piece, and the surface and all facings are truly planed. The self-acting motion is driven from saw spindle, and is arranged so that the rate of feed may be varied from 15 to 60 feet per minute. The saw spindle is of steel, working in massive gun-metal bearings, 3 in number, one of which is bolted to side of bench, to carry off end of saw spindle. The benches are constructed in such a manner that spindle is readily taken out when required for cleaning purposes.

They are made in the following Sizes:

No. 1 Size, 8 ft. 9 in. long and 3 ft. 2 in. wide, to take in a Saw 48 in. diameter, to cut timber 21 in. deep; weight about 35 cwt.; power required, 4-horse; driving pulleys, 15 in. by 5 in.; speed, 850 .... £55

No. 2 Size, 6 ft. long and 3 ft. wide, to take in a Saw 42 in. diameter, to cut timber 18 in. deep; weight about 28 cwt.; power required, 3-horse; driving pulley, 12 in. by 4½ in.; speed, 950 .... £45.

No. 3 Size, 5 ft. 6 in. long and 2 ft. 9 in. wide, to take in a Saw 36 in. diameter, to cut 15 in. deep; weight about 23 cwt.; power required, 3-horse; driving pulleys, 10 in. by 4½ in.; speed, 1,100 .... £36

BRITANNIA CO., COLCHESTER, England.

London Showrooms—100, Houndsditch. All Letters to Colchester.

ROGERS' PATENT SAW SHARPENER.

Each Machine includes Three Wheels, Hart's Patent.

SEMI-AUTOMATIC.

Pitch, Angle, and Depth of Teeth can be regulated with ease.

Any boy can work them.

Will save their cost in a few months.

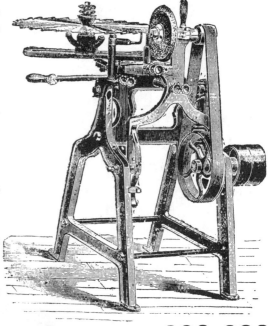

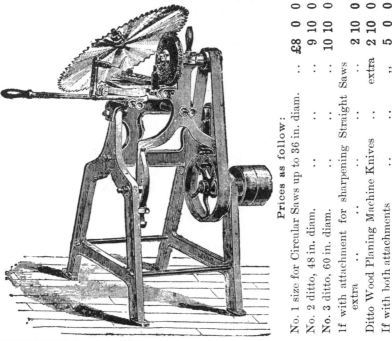

Prices as follow:

	£	s.	d.
No. 1 size for Circular Saws up to 36 in. diam.	£8	0	0
No. 2 ditto, 48 in. diam.	9	10	0
No. 3 ditto, 60 in. diam.	10	10	0
If with attachment for sharpening Straight Saws extra	2	10	0
Ditto Wood Planing Machine Knives extra	2	10	0
If with both attachments ,,	5	0	0

BRITANNIA CO., COLCHESTER, England.

London Showrooms—100, *Houndsditch.*   *All Letters to Colchester.*

IMPROVED
Small Hand-Planing & Jointing Machine

IN designing the above, careful attention has been given to produce a Hand Planer on the most modern principles, for making true surfaces and edges, stop chamfering, squaring, bevelling, &c., &c., and at the same time to place it in the market at an especially low price.

The Frame is of cast-iron, of strong section, and cast in one solid piece, top end of which is prepared with long slides on the bevel for receiving the tables, also the bearings for carrying cutter spindle.

The tables are extra long, each measuring three feet; this is an important feature in a machine used for surfacing and trueing up long stuff, and is indispensable in preparing wood for glued joints, &c., &c. They are fitted on the bevel slides, prepared on frame to receive them, and each is made to rise and fall independently for regulating the depth of cut.

The Fence for above is made with an entirely new and simple arrangement for bevelling, is readily set, and is very firm when screwed up.

The Cutter Block and Spindle are of steel, in one forging; they work in long and substantial phosphor bronze bearings, fitted with self-oiling lubricators.

The Pulley on the Spindle is 3½in. diameter and 3in. wide, and should make 4,000 to 5,000 revolutions per minute.

SIZES	Approximate Weight with Countershaft	Average Power required	Size of Driving Pulleys on Countershaft	Speed of Driving Pulleys on Countershaft	PRICE of Machine with Countershaft	PRICE of Machine without Countershaft
No. 1, to work stuff 12in. wide	9 cwt.	⅓ horse	6 by 3in.	800 revols.	£22	£18
No. 2, ,, 9in. ,,	8 cwt.	⅓ horse	6 by 3in.	800 ,,	19	15

BRITANNIA CO., COLCHESTER, England.

London Showrooms—100, *Houndsditch.* *All Letters to Colchester.*

F

PANEL PLANING & THICKNESSING MACHINE.

THIS machine has been designed with a view to meet the several requirements of builders, cabinet makers, joiners, pattern makers, etc.

Makers of lap boards, cigar boxes and cases will find it very useful, as it is specially adapted for their class of work. By a little alteration of pressure bar and chip guard, it can be made so as to work sash bars, window bars, and other kinds of moulded work. The framework is all one casting, made very strong to prevent any vibration or tremulous motion; the adze is made of steel, and planed out on two sides to form a back iron up to the knives, and revolves in long gun-metal bearings

The feed rollers are made of wrought iron, and the pressure is readily adapted with strong springs, for either light or heavy work. The table is made strong and planed perfectly true on the top, and is fitted with two friction rollers working in gun-metal steps. These rollers are adjustable, and can be set to stand slightly above the top of the table.

The feed motion can be thrown out of gear instantly, and varied for three rates of feed. The table is made to rise and fall to suit various thicknesses of timber, by means of hand wheel and screw fixed on side of machine.

Size.	To work stuff.	Take in stuff up to	Weight Cwts.	Power required.	Driving Pulleys.	Speed of ditto.	PRICE.
No. 4	15 in. wide	4 in thick	13	1 h.p.	6 in. by 3 in.	800	£26 0 0
No. 3	18 ,,	5 ,,	16	1½ ,,	7 in. ,, 3 in.	800	32 10 0
No. 2	24 ,,	5½ ,,	20	1½ ,,	8 in. ,, 3 in.	800	40 0 0
No. 1	30 ,,	6 ,,	30	2 ,,	8 in. ,, 4 in.	750	60 0 0

Any of the above-named Machines may be arranged so as to work moulds up to 5 in. wide at an extra cost of 15/-, and may be fitted with an apparatus for canting the table so as to plane work on the bevel, thus making an invaluable machine for the pattern room of an engineer's or machinist's works, at an extra cost of £3.

BRITANNIA CO., COLCHESTER, England.

London Showrooms—100, *Houndsditch.*   *All Letters to Colchester.*

The " A I " Combined Hand and Power Feed
PLANING & THICKNESSING MACHINE.

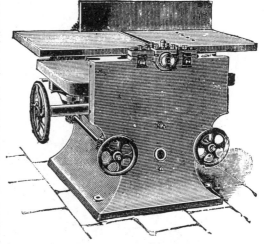

THE above engraving represents a Combination Planing Machine that unites all the functions of the two machines when separate; it is simple in construction, and it occupies little space, which in some cases is a very important consideration. It is specially adapted for the following work :—

Taking out of twist any kind of stuff, making glue joints surfacing straight or tap r work, bevelling. chamfering, or squaring up. It will plane with power feed under the cutter, panels or boards any thickness, from one eighth of an inch to the size the machine is specified to take in.

The machine is of very substantial construction, the main frame being cast all in one piece The table on which the stuff to be worked is placed for passing under the cutter. is fitted with special adjustable slides, having large wearing surfaces, and is raised or lowered by means of one screw ; this screw being fixed under centre of table, only requires one pair of bevel wheels and one hand-wheel, whilst in other machines, to attain the same purpose, two screws and three pairs of bevel wheels are necessary, thus the above machine is simplified and rendered less liable to get out of order.

The top tables, on which work is placed for passing over the cutter, are made in halves. each half having a separate rising and falling motion. each regulated by hand-wheel and screw. These tables can be readily drawn apart when it is required to change or sharpen the irons

A fence is fitted on the top table, which is arranged to cant to any required bevel.

All the feed rollers are made of wrought-iron, the front top roller being grooved so as to grip the work. and the necessary pressure is got by weights or springs. made adjustable to suit light or heavy work. The two bottom friction rollers are fitted in the table. These rollers can be adjusted as required for the various kinds of wood to be worked.

A flexible pressure bar is placed on each side of the cutter-block, which keeps the work dead on the table whilst undergoing the process of planing.

In designing this machine, care has been taken to place the gearing and driving pulleys at the back of the machine. thereby leaving the front, where the operator stands, quite clear and free from the danger of getting entangled in the same.

The cutter-block is of an improved form, made from a special quality of steel, and the necks in which it revolves are of phosphor bronze, extra long, and fitted with self-oiling lubricators.

The various adjustments are so arranged that the workman can make changes quickly, no part of the machine being in the way of any other part.

Each machine is provided with a gauge for indicating the thickness of stuff it will plane under the cutters.

SIZES.	Approximate Weight	Average Power required.	Size of Driving Pulleys on Countershaft	Speed of Driving Pulleys on Countershaft	PRICE
No. 1, to take work 24 in. wide & 6 in. thick	28 cwt. 2 qrs.	2 horse	8 in. by 4 in.	800 revols.	£62 10
No. 2, ,, 18 in. ,, 6 in. ,,	24 ., 0 ,,	1½ ,,	7 in. ,, 3 in.	800 ,,	52 10
No. 3, ,, 15 in. ,, 5 in. ,,	17 ,, 0 ,,	1½ ,,	6 in. ,, 3 in.	800 ,,	44 0

BRITANNIA CO., COLCHESTER, England.

London Showrooms—100. Houndsditch. All Letters to Colchester.

COMBINED
Planing, Thicknessing & Moulding Machine

This machine is an improvement on the Panel Planing and Thicknessing Machine, and is designed with a view to meet the demand for a machine that will occupy but a small space, and yet be as efficient in its working as a large machine.

It will surface and thickness up stuff from $\frac{1}{8}$ in. to 5 in. in thickness, and it will plane work on three sides at one operation up to 18 in. wide and 4 in. thick.

It will plane, joint, tongue, and groove, work skirtings, strike mouldings, work window and sash bars, and will be found a most valuable machine for joiners, carpenters, cabinet makers, pattern makers, &c.

The side adzes are of steel, and work in long gun-metal bearings. The cutter blocks are wrought iron, and fitted loose on spindles, so as to be removed when required.

The brackets for carrying the spindles are made very strong, and can be adjusted by means of hand wheel and screw on each side of machine, to suit the various widths of work to be done.

The feed rollers and gearing are of wrought iron, very powerful and effective. Three rates of feed to suit various thicknesses.

The machine is complete with countershaft, spanners, lubricators, &c.

Sizes.	To work stuff on three sides at one operation.	Approx. Weight.	Average Power required.	Size of Driving Pulley.	Speed of Driving Pulleys.	Prices.
No. 1	30 in. by 5 in.	35 cwt.	$2\frac{1}{2}$ horse	10 in. by 4 in.	750 revltns.	£90
No. 2	24 in. ,, 5 in.	28 ,,	$2\frac{1}{4}$,,	8 in. ,. 4 in.	800 ,,	60
No. 3	18 in. ,, 5 in.	22 ,,	2 ,,	8 in. ,, 4 in.	800 ,,	52
No. 4	15 in. ,. 4 in.	18 ..	$1\frac{1}{2}$ ..	7 in. ,. 3 in.	800 .,	40

BRITANNIA CO., COLCHESTER, England.

London Showrooms—100, Houndsditch.   All Letters to Colchester.

Self-Contained Circular Moulding Machine.

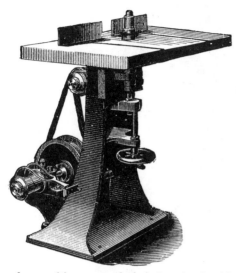

THE above is expressly designed to meet the want for a light and handy Moulding Machine for the many varieties of irregular and circular work required in a cabinet maker's, joiner's, or builder's works —it occupies but a small space, and will do work as clean, effective, and as quickly as the most expensive machine of its class.

The spindle is carried by a frame which is adjustable, vertically by screw and hand-wheel; the frame is planed and fitted to the column so that the pull of the belt comes *against* the body of the machine, thus lessening the possibility of vibration.

The driving to the spindle is communicated through a countershaft attached to the back of the column, this countershaft being fitted with a suitable driving pulley.

The spindle is so arranged that either square cutter blocks, washers with slots through, or solid steel cutters may be used on it, as may be most suitable for the work required to be done.

The table is made of iron, having an opening for projection of spindle, which is fitted with various sized washers to suit light or heavy work.

As shown above the machine is complete with guiding fence for doing straight work ; when required a fence can be supplied specially made for use when doing circular or irregular work.

At a small extra cost the spindle can be made to work reversible for convenience when working cross-grained stuff.

Machine is supplied complete with one square cutter block, 3 in. deep, one pair of washers with slots through for holding irons, the necessary making-up rings for opening in table, spanners, &c.

SIZE.	Average Power required.	Approximate Weight.	Diam. of Driving Pulleys.	Speed of Driving Pulleys.	PRICE.			Price of Machine with additional fence for circular & irregular work.			Price of Machine with reversing motion to spindle, and only straight fence			Price of Machine with reversing motion & straight & circular fences.		
					£	s.	d.	£	s.	d.	£	s.	d.	£	s.	d.
To work 3in. deep ...,	½-horse	5 cwt.	4 in.	1000	15	0	0	15	12	6	16	2	6	16	15	0

BRITANNIA CO., COLCHESTER, England.

London Showrooms—100, *Houndsditch.*　　*All Letters to Colchester.*

PATENT PLANING MACHINE.

THE machine – as represented above—will plane Venetian blind laths, reed laths, heald laths, lap boards, stuff for cigar boxes, or other light work.

It will also smooth floor boards skirting boards, stairs steps, drawer sides and fronts, and various other kinds of joiner work, after having passed through a machine having revolving cutters.

The work is done by a stationary knife fitted in a knife box, and fixed in cast-iron table.

Each machine is supplied with two knives and knife boxes, so that one may be sharpened whilst the other is in use.

The work to be planed is fed up to and past the knife by a roller of large diameter. made of India-rubber. and revolving at such a high rate of speed that it will plane the stuff as rapidly as the hand can place it on the table, with a finish that cannot be surpassed by any other process.

The table is made to rise and fall by hand-wheel and screw to suit various thicknesses of work required to be planed.

SIZES.	Length of Table.	Approx-imate Weight.	Average power required.	Size of Driving Pulleys.	Speed of Driving Pulleys.	PRICE.
To plane stuff 3in. wide	3ft. 2in.	4 cwt.	$\frac{1}{4}$-horse	18in. × 4in.	500 revs	£12 10
,, ,, 5in. ,.	4ft. 0in.	8 ,,	$\frac{1}{2}$,,	20in. × 4in.	300 ,,	26 0
,, ,. 7in. ,,	4ft. 4in.	9 ,,	1 .,	30in. × 5in.	250 ,,	30 0
,, ., 9in. ,,	4ft. 4in.	10 ,,	1 ,,	30in. × 5in.	250 ,,	45 0
., ,, 11in. ,,	—	16 ,,	$1\frac{1}{4}$,,	36in. × 6in.	250 ,,	70 0
,, ,, 12in. ,,	—	17 ,,	$1\frac{1}{4}$,,	36in. × 6in.	250 ,,	75 0

BRITANNIA CO., COLCHESTER, England.

London Showrooms—100. *Houndsditch.*   *All Letters to Colchester.*

IMPROVED SINGLE DEAL FRAME.

The machine illustrated is a compact, easily managed, and efficient Deal Frame, requiring very little foundation, and only such excavations as are required for removing the sawdust.

These Frames will saw one deal into several boards at one operation, and can be run with one or various saws as required.

The column is very firmly designed, and spreads at the base to insure sufficient strength against any strain it can possibly be put to.

The crankshaft is carried at the bottom of the column, and is fitted with fast and loose pulleys.

The Saw Frame is of wrought iron, thus combining great strength with lightness, and can be driven at a very high speed.

The fence can be readily adjusted to the thickness of boards required, without altering the position of first saw.

The timber is fed through the machines by means of fluted rollers, driven by eccentric, and gearing from the crankshaft, and weighted press rollers keep the deal in position while being sawn, thus ensuring a continuous and parallel passage of the deal.

Cast iron standards are supplied, if required, for carrying the deals as they enter or leave the frame.

Size	To take Deal	Horse Power required	PRICE			Extra for carrying standard		
1	14 in. × 6 in.	2½	£67	10	0	£4	15	0
2	18 in. × 6 in.	3	78	0	0	4	15	0
3	18 in. × 12 in.	4	89	0	0	4	15	0

Saws extra.

BRITANNIA CO., COLCHESTER, England.

London Showrooms—100, *Houndsditch.*　　*All Letters to Colchester.*

ARMENIAN GRINDSTONES

To work by hand, foot, or power, mounted on strong Cast Iron or Wood frames, well painted and varnished. These Stones are of the **Best Fine Grit**, and well adapted for all kinds of Edge Tools. All Stones are fitted with Turned Wrought Spindles and Plates screwed on, to ensure their keeping true, having no wood wedges to get loose, and are sent out with Treadle and loose Handle, complete for immediate use.

No. 1 Grindstone, 12 in. × 2 in.

For Bench, with Iron Troughs.
Hand Machines.

No. 000	...	6 in. × 2 in.	...	**7/6**
,, 00	...	8 in. × 2 in.	...	**10/-**
,, 0	...	10 in. × 2 in.	...	**12 6**
, 1	...	12 in. × 2 in.	...	**15/-**
,, 2	...	14 in. × 2 in.	...	**17/6**
,, 3	...	16 in. × 2 in.	...	**20/-**
,, 4	...	18 in. × 2½ in.	...	**22/6**

For Bench, with Pulleys for Power.

No. 5 ... 18 in. × 2½ in. ... **31/6** | No. 6 ... 18 in. × 3½ in. ... **34 6**

No. 10 Grindstone, 22 in. × 3 in.

Grindstones mounted with Wood Troughs and Stands.

No. 7	...	18 in. × 2½ in.	...	**£1 6 6**
,, 8	...	18 in. × 3 in.	...	**1 9 0**
,, 9	...	20 in. × 3½ in.	...	**1 14 0**
,, 10	...	22 in. × 3½ in.	...	**1 17 6**

With Anti-friction Rollers.

No. 11	...	24 in. × 4 in.	...	**£2 5 0**
,, 12	...	26 in. × 4 in.	...	**2 16 6**
,, 13	...	30 in. × 5 in.	...	**4 4 6**

Wrought Iron turned Spindles and Plates, with Bearings, Crank and Handle.

					s.	*d.*
To suit Grindstone,	2½ in. wide	...	...		9	6
,,	,,	3 in. ,,	...	...	13	0
,,	,,	4 in. ,,	...	...	15	0
,,	,,	5½ in. ,,	...	...	19	0

BRITANNIA CO., COLCHESTER, England.

London Showrooms—100, Houndsditch.   *All Letters to Colchester.*

ARMENIAN GRINDSTONES.

With Iron Troughs and Stands, for Hand and Treadle.

No. 14, 18 in. × 2½ in.

		£	s	d
No. **14.**—18 in. × 2½ in., plain bearings ...		£1	14	0
,, **15.**—18 in. × 3½ in., plain bearings ...		1	17	0
,, **16.**—18 in. × 2½ in., anti-friction bearings ...		1	18	6
,, **17.**—18 in. × 3½ in., anti-friction bearings ...		2	1	6
No. **18.**—21 in. × 3 in., plain bearings ...		2	4	6

Larger size Grindstones, for power only, with very heavy Cast Iron Troughs and Frames, Fast and Loose Pulleys.

No. 29, 42 in. × 6 in., £8 15 0

,, 30, 42 in. × 8 in., 10 0 0

,. 31, 48 in. × 8 in., 11 17 6

,, 32, 24 in. × 4½ in., with solid wrought iron frame, Government pattern 4 7 6

Wrought or Cast Iron Hoods and Galvanized Water Cans, with Taps, fitted to any of the above stones at an extra cost.

No. 29, Grindstone, 42 in. × 6 in.

BRITANNIA CO., COLCHESTER, England.

London Showrooms—100, *Houndsditch.* *All Letters to Colchester.*

ARMENIAN GRINDSTONES

WITH STRONG CAST-IRON TROUGHS & FRAMES.

	£ s. d.
No. 19.—21 in. by 4 in., with anti-friction rollers ...	£2 10 0
,, 20.—24 in. by 4 in., with bearings ...	2 15 0
,, 21.—24 in. by 4 in., with anti-friction rollers ...	2 17 6
,, 22.—24 in. by 5 in., extra strong frame and anti-friction rollers ...	3 9 0
,, 23.—26 in. by 4½ in., with anti-friction rollers ...	3 15 0
,, 24.—28 in. by 4½ in. ...	4 2 0
,, 25.—30 in. by 4½ in. ...	5 0 0
,, 26.—30 in. by 6 in. ...	5 5 0
,, 27.—36 in. by 5 in., with pulley for power ...	6 17 0
,, 28.—36 in. by 8 in., with pulley for power ...	7 17 6

Fast and loose pulleys fitted to any of the above, 18/- per pair extra.

No 21 Grindstone, 24 in. by 4 in.

BRITANNIA CO., COLCHESTER, England.

London Showrooms—100, *Houndsditch.*   *All Letters to Colchester.*

DOUBLE BLAST BELLOWS

No. 101.

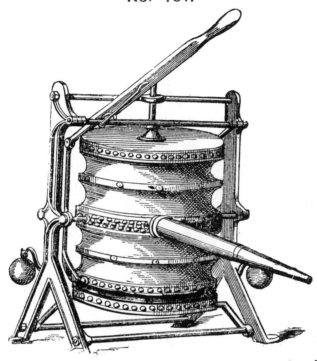

						£	s.	d.
Sizes —18 inches ...	...	...	...	...		5	15	0
20 ,, ...	...	...	...	...		6	12	0
22 ,, ...	...	...	...	...		7	14	0
24 ,, ...	...	...	...	...		8	16	6
26 ,, ...	...	...		...		9	18	0
28 ,, ...	...	...	...	...		11	10	0
30 ,, ...	...	...	...	...		13	8	0
32 ,, ...	...	...	...	...		15	0	0
34 ,, ...	...	. .	...	...		17	10	0
36 ,, ...	...	...	...	...		20	0	0

On account of the expense of carriage, the weights are not included in
Price, and are not sent with the Bellows.

BRITANNIA CO., COLCHESTER, England.

London Showrooms—100, *Houndsditch.*   *All Letters to Colchester.*

PATENT
CIRCULAR IRON-ENCASED RIVET FORGE.

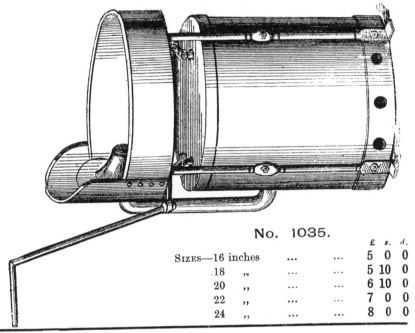

No. 1035.

				£	s.	d.
Sizes—16 inches	...	...		5	0	0
18 ,,	...	...		5	10	0
20 ,,	...	...		6	10	0
22 ,,	...	...		7	0	0
24 ,,	...	...		8	0	0

PATENT CIRCULAR FORGES.

No. 1037.

Sizes—16 in. £4 12.   18 in. £5.   20 in. £5 16
22 in. £6 15.   24 in. £7 18.

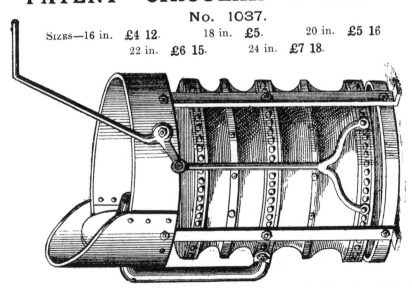

BRITANNIA CO., COLCHESTER, England.

London Showrooms—100, Houndsditch.   *All Letters to Colchester.*

IMPROVED NEW PATTERN
WROUGHT-IRON PORTABLE FORGES.

No. 1036.

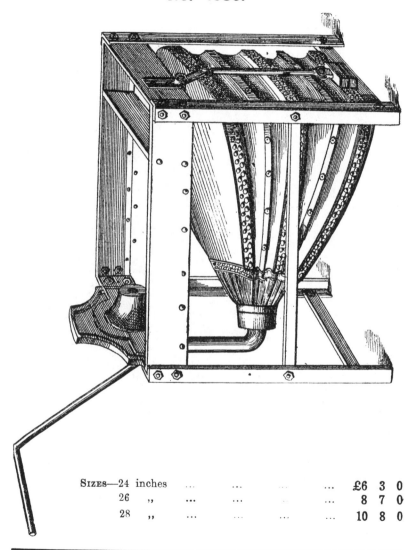

Sizes—24 inches	...	...	...	...	£6	3	0
26 ,,	...	...	...	...	8	7	0
28 ,,	...	...	...	...	10	8	0

BRITANNIA CO., COLCHESTER, England.

London Showrooms—100, *Houndsditch.* *All Letters to Colchester.*

IMPROVED HAND-POWER SCREWING MACHINES,
FOR IRON GAS TUBES OR BOLTS.

MADE with either solid or adjustable dies as preferred. Machines with adjustable dies screwing at once over. It is strongly recommended to have extra Speed Wheels (as fitted to Cutting off Machine as per drawing below) for increasing the speed when screwing smaller sizes. See prices page 175.

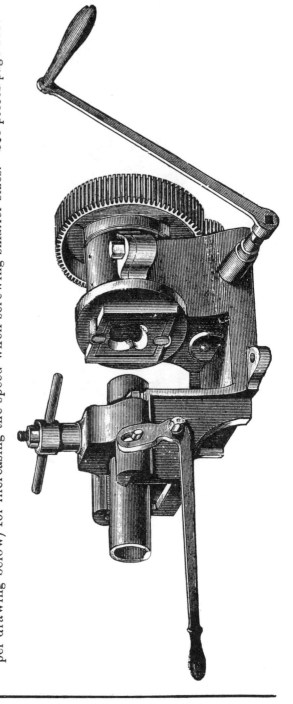

BRITANNIA CO., COLCHESTER, England.

London Showrooms—100, Houndsditch.　　*All Letters to Colchester.*

IMPROVED HAND-POWER SCREWING MACHINES

(For Illustration see page 174.)

No.			Size for Screwing		Sets of adjustable dies	£	s.	d.		£	s.	d.
No. 1a	Size for	Screwing	¼ ⅜ ½ ¾ 1 inch Iron Gas Tubes	with	3 sets of adjustable dies	9	0	0	ditto solid dies	8	0	0
,,	,,	,,	½ ⅝ ¾ ⅞ 1 inch Bolts	,,	5 ,, ,,	10	8	0	,,	8	0	0
No. 2a	,,	,,	1 1¼ 1½ 1¾ 2 inch Iron Gas Tubes	,,	1 ,, ,,	13	0	0	,,	13	0	0
,,	,,	,,	¼ ⅜ ½ ¾ 1 1¼ 1½ 1¾ 2 inch Gas Tubes	,,	3 ,, ,,	15	0	0	,,	14	11	0
,,	,,	,,	1 1⅛ 1¼ 1⅜ 1½ inch Bolts	,,	3 ,, ,,	15	0	0	,,	12	10	
,,	,,	,,	½ ⅝ ¾ ⅞ 1 1⅛ 1¼ 1⅜ 1½ inch Bolts	,,	7 ,, ,,	19	0	0	,,	14	1	0
No. 2c	,,	,,	1½ 1¾ 2 2¼ 2½ 3 inch Iron Gas Tubes	,,	1 ,, ,,	20	10	0	,,	20	10	0
,,	,,	,,	1 1¼ 1½ 1¾ 2 2¼ 2½ 3 inch Iron Gas Tubes	,,	2 ,, ,,	21	18	0	,,	22	0	0
No. 3a	,,	,,	2 2¼ 2½ 3 3½ 4 inch Iron Gas Tubes	,,	1 ,, ,,	28	0	0	,,	26	10	0

Extra Adjustable Dies,
Nos. 1a 2a 2c 3a size Machines,
16/- 20/- 28/- 33/- per set.

Extra if fitted with extra Speed Wheels,
Nos. 1a 2a 2c 3a size Machines,
20/- 25/- 32/- 40/- per pair.

Extra Solid Dies, Nos. 1a 2a 2c 3a size Machines.

½	⅝	¾	⅞	1	1⅛	1¼	1⅜	1½ in. Bolts.
7/-	7/-	7/-	10/-	10/-	20/-	20/-	20/-	20/-

¼	⅜	½	⅝	¾	1	1¼	1½	1¾	2	2¼	2½	2¾	3	3¼	3½	4 in. Iron Gas Tubes
7/-	7/-	7/-	10/-	10/-	10/-	20/-	20/-	20/-	20/-	30/-	30/-	30/-	45/-	45/-	45/	each.

Cutting-off apparatus for Tubes for Nos. 1a 2a 2c 3a size Machines.
16/- 28/- 30/- 33/- each.

	Nos. 1a	2a	2c	3a
Extra if fitted with 3 speed Cone or fast and loose Pulley to work by power	35/-	40/-	48/-	54/-
Extra if mounted on cast-iron Stand	40/-	50/-	70/-	85/-
Extra for Overhead Driving Gear	85/-	110/[illegible]	145/-	160/-

BRITANNIA CO., COLCHESTER, England.
London Showrooms—100, Houndsditch. All Letters to Colchester.

WHITWORTH'S PATENT GUIDE STOCKS & DIES.

No. 32.
(WHITWORTH'S STANDARD THREAD)

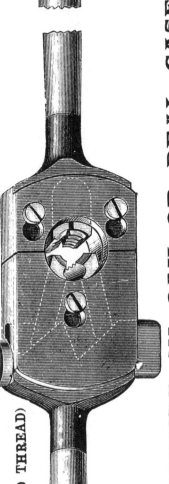

IF FITTED IN OAK OR DEAL CASES.

	RANGE OF SIZES.		With Taper and Plug Tap to each size, and Tap Wrenches.		With Taper 2nd and Plug Tap to each size, and Tap Wrenches.		With Taper 2nd, Plug and Master Tap to each size, and Tap Wrenches.	
			Deal Case.	Oak Case.	Deal Case.	Oak Case.	Deal Case.	Oak Case.
			£ s. d.	£ s. d.	£ s. d.	£ s. d.	£ s. d.	£ s. d.
No. 1 set to screw		fitted into 1 case	11 3 0	11 13 0	12 12 0	13 2 0	14 0 0	14 15 0
,, 2 ,,		1 ,,	11 10 0	12 0 0	13 0 0	13 10 0	14 17 0	15 7 0
,, 3 ,,		1 ,,	12 18 0	13 8 0	14 13 0	15 3 0	16 15 0	17 5 0
,, 4 ,,		1 ,,	16 3 0	17 0 0	18 9 0	19 6 0	21 4 0	22 1 0
,, 5 ,,		1 ,,	16 12 0	17 9 0	18 19 0	19 16 0	21 17 0	22 14 0
,, 6 ,,		1 ,,	19 5 0	20 2 0	21 18 0	22 15 0	25 0 0	25 19 0
,, 7 ,,		1 ,,	23 6 0	24 4 0	26 18 0	27 16 0	31 1 0	31 19 0
,, 8 ,,		1 ,,	23 12 0	24 10 0	27 6 0	28 4 0	31 13 0	32 11 0
,, 9 ,,		1 ,,	25 1 0	25 19 0	29 0 0	29 18 0	33 12 0	34 10 0
,, 10 ,,		2 cases	36 2 0	37 15 0	41 15 0	43 8 0	48 12 0	50 5 0
,, 11 ,,		2 ,,	44 7 0	46 0 0	51 17 0	53 10 0	60 14 0	62 7 0
,, 12 ,,		2 ,,	45 15 0	47 8 0	53 11 0	55 4 0	62 13 0	64 6 0

OTHER RANGES OF SIZES MADE TO ORDER.

BRITANNIA CO., Colchester, England.
London Showrooms—100, Houndsditch.   All Letters to Colchester.

WHITWORTH'S PATENT GUIDE STOCKS AND DIES.

(WHITWORTH'S STANDARD THREAD.)

No. 32.

For illustration see page 176.

TO SCREW.	With Taper and Plug Tap to each size.	With Taper 2nd, and Plug Tap to each size.	With Taper 2nd, Plug and Master Tap to each size.	TO SCREW.	With Taper and Plug Tap to each size.	With Taper 2nd, and Plug Tap to each size.	With Taper 2nd, Plug and Master Tap to each size.
	£ s. d.	£ s. d.	£ s. d.		£ s. d.	£ s. d.	£ s. d.

(WHITWORTH'S STANDARD THREAD.)

Detailed numeric table with columns for *TO SCREW* sizes (in fractional inches) and corresponding prices in pounds, shillings, and pence for the three tap configurations.

BRITANNIA CO., COLCHESTER, England.

London Showrooms—100 Houndsditch.   *All Letters to Colchester.*

DIRECT ACTION GUIDE STOCKS AND DIES.

No. 71.
(WHITWORTH'S STANDARD THREAD)

IF FITTED IN OAK OR DEAL CASES.

No.		RANGE OF SIZES.	With Taper and Plug Tap to each size, and Tap Wrenches.		With Taper 2nd and Plug Tap to each size, and Tap Wrenches.		With Taper 2nd, Plug and Master Tap to each size, & Tap Wrenches.	
			Deal Case	Oak Case	Deal Case	Oak Case	Deal Case	Oak Case
			£ s. d.	£ s. d.	£ s. d.	£ s. d.	£ s. d.	£ s. d.
No. 1	set to screw — fitted into 1 case		8 8 0	8 17 0	9 18 0	10 7 0	11 7 0	11 16 0
,, 2	1 ,,		8 12 0	9 1 0	10 5 0	10 14 0	11 16 0	12 5 0
,, 3	1 ,,		10 3 0	10 12 0	11 19 0	12 8 0	13 16 0	14 5 0
,, 4	1 ,,		12 1 0	12 16 0	14 5 0	15 0 0	16 12 0	17 7 0
,, 5	1 ,,		12 3 0	12 18 0	14 12 0	15 7 0	17 2 0	17 17 0
,, 6	1 ,,		14 3 0	14 16 0	16 14 0	17 0 0	19 9 0	20 4 0
,, 7	1 ,,		18 5 0	19 5 0	21 15 0	22 11 0	25 9 0	26 4 0
,, 8	1 ,,		18 9 0	19 5 0	22 1 0	22 17 0	25 17 0	26 13 0
,, 9	1 ,,		20 0 0	20 16 0	23 17 0	24 13 0	27 18 0	28 14 0
,, 10	2 cases		28 16 0	30 5 0	34 14 0	36 3 0	40 11 0	42 0 0
,, 11	2 ,,		35 8 0	36 17 0	42 18 0	44 7 0	50 11 0	52 0 0
,, 12	2 ,,		37 0 0	38 0 0	44 14 0	46 3 0	52 11 0	54 0 0

OTHER RANGES OF SIZES MADE TO ORDER.

BRITANNIA CO., COLCHESTER, England.

London Showrooms—100, Houndsditch. All Letters to Colchester.

DIRECT ACTION GUIDE STOCKS & DIES.

No. 71.

(WHITWORTH'S STANDARD THREAD.)

(For Illustration see page 178.)

TO SCREW	With Taper and Plug Tap to each size. £ s. d.	With Taper 2nd, and Plug Tap to each size. £ s. d.	With Taper 2nd, Plug and Master Tap to each size. £ s. d.
...	1 9 0	1 14 0	1 19 0
...	1 17 0	2 4 6	2 11 0
...	2 13 0	2 14 0	3 2 0
...	2 6 0	3 3 0	3 14 0
...	2 8 0	2 18 0	3 7 0
...	1 18 6	2 7 6	2 15 0
...	2 0 0	2 10 0	2 18 0
...	2 7 0	2 17 0	3 7 0
...	2 8 0	2 19 0	3 10 0
...	2 14 6	3 16 0	3 4 0
...	2 16 0	2 14 6	3 19 0
...	3 3 0	3 7 0	3 4 0
...	3 4 0	3 9 0	4 2 0
...	2 14 0	3 13 0	4 6 0
...	2 16 0	3 18 0	4 12 0
...	3 4 0	3 11 0	5 8 0
...	3 14 0	4 7 0	3 19 0
...	3 7 6	4 2 6	4 17 0
...	3 12 0	4 9 0	5 7 0
...	3 19 0	4 16 0	5 14 0

TO SCREW	With Taper and Plug Tap to each size. £ s. d.	With Taper 2nd, and Plug Tap to each size. £ s. d.	With Taper 2nd, Plug and Master Tap to each size. £ s. d.
...	3 3 0	3 18 0	4 13 0
...	3 17 0	4 16 0	5 14 0
...	4 2 0	5 2 6	6 4 0
...	3 16 6	4 10 0	6 11 0
...	3 18 6	4 13 6	5 9 0
...	4 12 0	4 16 6	5 14 0
...	4 10 6	5 11 0	6 10 0
...	4 16 0	5 12 6	6 15 0
...	4 5 0	5 19 0	7 4 0
...	5 4 0	6 9 6	7 15 0
...	6 10 0	6 10 0	6 16 0
...	4 13 0	5 9 0	8 19 0
...	4 16 0	5 11 0	6 12 0
...	5 10 0	5 14 0	6 16 0
...	5 8 0	6 7 0	7 4 0
...	7 3 0	6 17 0	7 14 0
...		8 3 0	8 7 0
...		8 18 0	9 18 0
...			10 12 0

TO SCREW	With Taper and Plug Tap to each size. £ s. d.	With Taper 2nd, and Plug Tap to each size. £ s. d.	With Taper 2nd, Plug and Master Tap to each size. £ s. d.
...	5 17 0	7 5 6	8 13 0
...	6 4 0	7 12 6	9 4 0
...	7 6 0	9 2 0	10 18 0
...	7 12 0	9 8 0	11 8 0
...	8 18 0	11 1 0	13 8 0
...	8 10 0	10 7 0	12 4 0
...	8 18 0	11 19 0	12 19 0
...	9 18 0	11 3 0	14 2 0
...	10 13 0	13 3 0	15 16 0
...	11 17 0	14 17 0	17 19 0
...	9 18 0	12 0 0	14 9 0
...	10 10 0	13 0 0	15 8 0
...	11 0 0	13 18 0	16 14 0
...	12 0 0	15 0 0	17 18 0
...	14 10 0	16 10 0	19 10 0
...	14 10 0	18 10 0	22 13 0
...	18 0 0	19 5 0	23 12 0
...	16 10 0	24 8 0	29 3 0
...	21 8 0	21 10 0	25 16 0
...		28 2 0	34 5 0

BRITANNIA CO., COLCHESTER, England.

London Showrooms—100, Houndsditch. All Letters to Colchester.

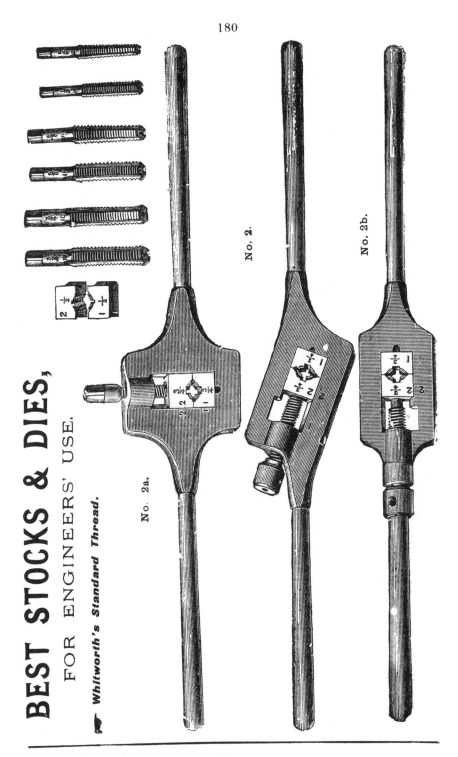

BEST STOCKS & DIES,

FOR ENGINEERS' USE.

Whitworth's Standard Thread.

No. 2a.

No. 2.

No. 2b.

BEST STOCKS & DIES for ENGINEERS' USE.

(WHITWORTH'S STANDARD THREAD.)

TO SCREW.	With Taper and Plug Tap to each size. £ s. d.	With Taper 2nd. and Plug Tap to each size. £ s. d.	With Taper 2nd. Plug and Master Tap to each size. £ s. d.	TO SCREW.	With Taper and Plug Tap to each size. £ s. d.	With Taper 2nd. and Plug Tap to each size. £ s. d.	With Taper 2nd. and Master Tap to each size. £ s. d.	TO SCREW.	With Taper and Plug Tap to each size. £ s. d.	With Taper 2nd. and Plug Tap to each size. £ s. d.	With Taper 2nd. Plug and Master Tap to each size. £ s. d.
	1 0 0	1 4 0	1 9 0		2 7 0	3 0 0	3 15 0		4 8 0	5 11 0	6 19 0
	1 5 0	1 10 0	1 17 0		2 16 0	3 11 0	4 10 0		4 14 0	6 1 0	7 13 0
	1 10 0	1 17 0	2 5 0		3 7 0	3 19 0	5 1 0		5 6 0	6 16 0	8 12 0
	1 15 0	2 3 0	2 14 0		3 7 0	3 4 0	5 4 0		5 13 0	7 6 0	9 6 0
	1 17 0	2 5 0	2 15 0		2 16 0	3 9 0	4 6 0		6 12 0	8 11 0	10 18 0
	1 9 0	1 15 0	2 3 0		2 16 0	3 11 0	4 9 0		6 10 0	8 4 0	10 1 0
	1 10 0	1 17 0	2 5 0		3 7 0	4 3 0	5 2 0		6 19 0	8 18 0	11 1 0
	1 17 0	2 5 0	2 15 0		3 12 0	4 5 0	5 8 0		7 16 0	9 16 0	12 0 0
	1 18 0	2 7 0	2 18 0		3 17 0	4 13 0	5 18 0		8 3 0	10 12 0	13 5 0
	2 0 0	2 16 0	3 0 0		3 16 0	4 18 0	6 3 0		9 0 0	12 3 0	15 5 0
	2 12 6	2 1 0	2 11 0		4 8 0	4 2 0	5 3 0		8 10 0	9 19 0	12 2 0
	2 19 0	2 9 0	3 3 0		3 4 0	4 3 0	6 5 0		9 3 0	10 16 0	13 6 0
	2 0 0	2 10 0	3 9 0		3 6 0	4 6 0	7 4 0		10 4 0	11 15 0	14 12 0
	2 3 0	2 14 0	3 14 0		3 17 0	4 18 0	5 3 0		10 10 0	12 18 0	15 17 0
	2 8 0	2 19 0	4 7 0		3 19 0	5 14 0	5 10 0		11 10 0	13 15 0	17 6 0
	2 16 0	3 10 0	3 16 0		4 12 0	5 4 0	6 7 0		10 0 0	15 2 0	19 6 0
	2 0 0	2 10 0	4 6 0		3 6 0	5 2 0	6 14 0		13 15 0	18 5 0	16 10 0
	2 8 0	3 0 0	4 9 0		4 9 0	6 9 0	7 18 0		12 0 0	16 3 0	23 0 0
	2 13 0	3 8 0			5 0 0		8 4 0		16 5 0	22 4 0	20 10 0
	2 16 0	3 11 0									28 10 0

STOCKS AND DIES FITTED IN OAK OR DEAL CASE TO ORDER.

BRITANNIA CO., COLCHESTER, England.

London Showrooms—100, Houndsditch.   All Letters to Colchester.

SOLID DIE STOCK.

MADE TO SCREW UP TO 3 in. AT ONCE GOING OVER.

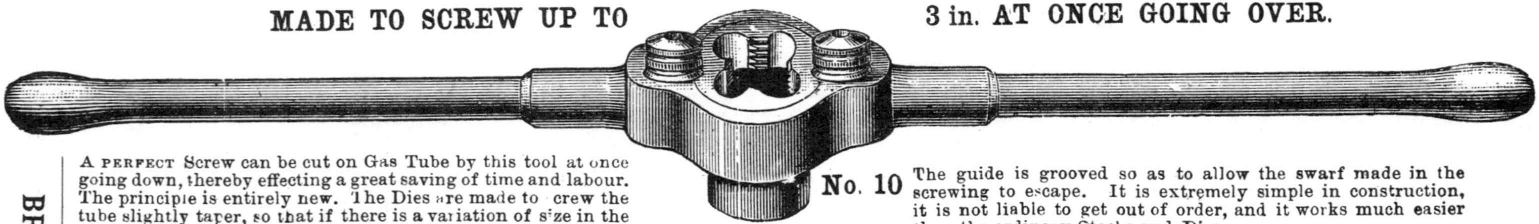

No. 10

A PERFECT Screw can be cut on Gas Tube by this tool at once going down, thereby effecting a great saving of time and labour. The principle is entirely new. The Dies are made to screw the tube slightly taper, so that if there is a variation of size in the gas fittings, tubes screwed by this tool will fit equally well.

The guide is grooved so as to allow the swarf made in the screwing to escape. It is extremely simple in construction, it is not liable to get out of order, and it works much easier than the ordinary Stocks and Dies.

Size of Stock.	TO SCREW	With Taper and Plug Tap to each size £	s.	d.	Without Tap £	s.	d.
A	¼ ⅜	1	2	0	0	15	6
	⅛ ¼ ⅜	1	10	0	1	1	0
B	½ inch only ...	1	4	0	0	19	6
	⅜ ½	1	11	0	1	3	0
	¼ ⅜ ½	1	18	0	1	7	0
	⅛ ¼ ⅜ ½ ...	2	6	6	1	13	0
C	¾ inch only ...	1	14	0	1	8	0
	½ ¾	2	2	0	1	11	6
	⅜ ½ ¾	2	12	0	1	18	0
	½ ⅝ ¾	2	14	0	1	18	0
	¼ ⅜ ½ ¾ ...	3	4	0	2	7	0
	⅜ ½ ⅝ ¾ ...	3	7	0	2	7	0
	¼ ⅜ ½ ⅝ ¾ ..	3	19	0	2	16	0
D	1 inch only ...	2	1	0	1	12	6
	¾ 1	2	12	0	1	8	0
	½ ¾ 1	3	3	0	2	4	6
	⅜ ½ ¾ 1 ...	3	17	0	2	14	6
	½ ⅝ ¾ 1 ...	3	18	6	2	14	6
	¼ ⅜ ½ ¾ 1 ...	4	10	6	3	5	0
	¼ ⅜ ½ ⅝ ¾ 1 ...	5	6	0	3	15	6
E	1¼ inch only ..	2	16	0	2	4	6
	1 1¼	3	10	0	2	10	6
	¾ 1 1¼	4	10	0	3	4	6
	½ ¾ 1 1¼ ...	5	8	0	3	18	0
	⅜ ½ ¾ 1 1¼ ...	6	5	0	4	11	6
	½ ⅝ ¾ 1 1¼ ...	6	7	0	4	11	6
F	1½ inch only ...	3	12	0	2	18	0
	1¼ 1½	4	16	0	3	10	6
	1 1¼ 1½ ...	6	0	0	4	7	0
	¾ 1 1¼ 1½ ...	7	4	0	5	5	0
	½ ¾ 1 1¼ 1½ ...	8	7	0	6	3	0
G	1¾ inch only ...	4	14	0	3	12	0
	1½ 1¾	6	4	0	4	9	0
	1¼ 1½ 1¾ ...	7	14	0	5	8	0
	1 1¼ 1½ 1¾ ...	9	4	0	6	10	0
	2 inch only ...	5	0	0	3	12	0
	1½ 2	6	10	0	4	9	0
	1¼ 1½ 2 ...	8	0	0	5	8	0
	1½ 1¾ 2 ..	8	17	0	5	13	0
	1 1¼ 1½ 2 ...	9	10	0	6	10	0
	1¼ 1½ 1¾ 2 ...	10	5	0	6	12	0
	1 1¼ 1½ 1¾ 2 ...	11	16	0	7	15	0
H	2¼ inch only ...	6	5	0	4	5	0
	2 2¼	9	1	0	5	14	0
	1½ 2 2¼ ...	11	5	0	7	3	0
	1¾ 2 2¼ ...	11	12	0	7	3	0
	1¼ 1½ 2 2¼ ...	13	5	0	8	12	0
	1½ 1¾ 2 2¼ ...	13	16	0	8	13	0
J	2½ inch only ...	8	5	0	5	14	0
	2¼ 2½	11	17	0	7	6	0
	1½ 2 2½ ...	13	12	0	8	18	0
	2 2¼ 2½ ...	14	7	0	8	19	0
	1½ 2 2¼ 2½ ...	17	4	0	10	11	0
K	3 inch only ...	12	16	0	9	3	0
	2½ 3	17	7	0	11	3	0
	2 2½ 3 ...	20	15	0	13	3	0
	2¼ 2½ 3 ...	21	7	0	13	3	0
	2½ 2¾ 3 ...	23	0	0	13	12	0
	2 2¼ 2½ 3 ...	24	15	0	15	3	0
	2¼ 2½ 2¾ 3 ...	27	0	0	15	12	0

PRICE OF EXTRA DIES & GUIDES FOR ABOVE STOCKS	A	B	C	D	E	F	G	H	J	K
Size of Stocks	A	B	C	D	E	F	G	H	J	K
Extra Dies	3/6	4/9	6/6	7/6	10/-	13/6	17/-	21/-	24/-	30/-
Extra Guides	1/6	1/9	2/6	3/-	3/6	4/6	6/-	7/6	8/6	10/-

BRITANNIA CO., COLCHESTER, England.

London Showrooms—100, Houndsditch. All Letters to Colchester.

STOCKS & DIES FOR BRASS & COPPER TUBE.

With Taper and Plug Tap to each size.

No. 16.

TO SCREW.	PER SET	TO SCREW.	PER SET	TO SCREW.	PER SET
$\frac{1}{4}$ iron and $\frac{3}{8}$, $\frac{1}{2}$ brass	25/6	$\frac{1}{4}$, $\frac{3}{8}$, $\frac{1}{2}$, $\frac{5}{8}$ brass tube	29/-	$\frac{5}{8}$, $\frac{3}{4}$, $\frac{7}{8}$ brass tube ...	44/-
$\frac{1}{4}$, $\frac{3}{8}$, $\frac{1}{2}$ brass ...	25/6	$\frac{3}{8}$, $\frac{1}{2}$, $\frac{5}{8}$, $\frac{3}{4}$	33/-	$\frac{3}{4}$, $\frac{7}{8}$, 1	50/-
$\frac{3}{8}$, $\frac{1}{2}$, $\frac{5}{8}$	25/6	$\frac{1}{4}$, $\frac{3}{8}$, $\frac{1}{2}$, $\frac{5}{8}$, $\frac{3}{4}$ ...	37/-	$\frac{5}{8}$, $\frac{3}{4}$, $\frac{7}{8}$, 1	60/-

No. 57.

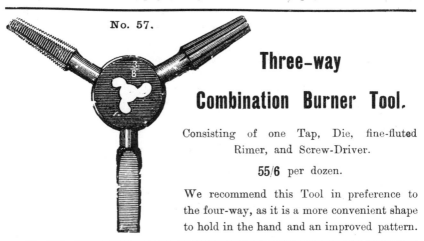

Three-way
Combination Burner Tool.

Consisting of one Tap, Die, fine-fluted Rimer, and Screw-Driver.

55/6 per dozen.

We recommend this Tool in preference to the four-way, as it is a more convenient shape to hold in the hand and an improved pattern.

TUBE CUTTER.

For Cutting Cast Iron Main Pipes.

No. 27.

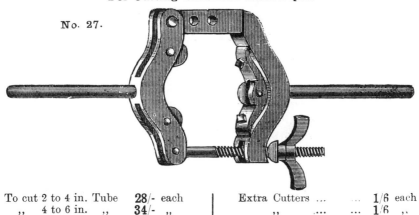

To cut 2 to 4 in. Tube	28/- each	Extra Cutters ...	... 1/6 each
,, 4 to 6 in. ,,	34/- ,,	,, ...	... 1/6 ,,
,, 5 to 8 in. ,,	40/- ,,	,, ...	... 1/6 ,,

BRITANNIA CO., COLCHESTER, England.

London Showrooms—100, Houndsditch.   *All Letters to Colchester.*

No. 5.				No. 5a.				
IMPROVED				**FLUTED**				
## Rimer Tap,				## Rimer,				
FOR GAS MAINS.				**FOR GAS MAINS.**				
Sizes $\frac{1}{2}''$	$\frac{5}{8}''$	$\frac{3}{4}''$	1	Sizes $\frac{1}{4}''$	$\frac{3}{8}''$	$\frac{1}{2}''$	$\frac{5}{8}''$	$\frac{3}{4}''$
Each 4/3	5/-	5/9	7/6	Each 1/5	1/9	2/3	2/6	2/9
Sizes $1\frac{1}{4}''$	$1\frac{1}{2}''$	$1\frac{3}{4}''$	2''	Sizes 1''	$1\frac{1}{4}''$	$1\frac{1}{2}''$	$1\frac{3}{4}''$	2'
Each 10/6	13/6	20/-	24/-	Each 4/-	5/3	6/9	10/	12/9

No. 33.

Brass

Gas Taps,

TAPER OR PLUG.

PRICE PER DOZ.

$\frac{1}{4}''$	$\frac{3}{8}''$	$\frac{1}{2}''$	$\frac{5}{8}''$
8/6	10/-	11/6	12/6

$\frac{3}{4}''$	$\frac{7}{8}''$	1''
17/-	25/-	34/-

Burner Taps.

No. 7a. With Rimer & Turnscrew combined, **25/** per doz.

No. 56. **8/6** doz.

No. 7. With Handle, **17/-** doz.

Single Wheel Tube Cutter.

No. 23.

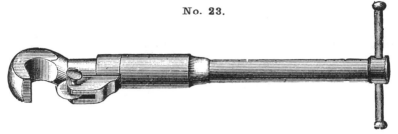

To Cut $\frac{1}{4}$ to 1 inch Tube, **12/9** each.   Extra Cutters, **1/-** each.
,, $1\frac{1}{4}$ to 2 ,,   ,,   **18/-** ,,   ,,   **1/6** ,,
,, $2\frac{1}{4}$ to $3\frac{1}{2}$,,   ,,   **29/-** ,,   ,,   **1/6** ,,

BRITANNIA CO., COLCHESTER, England.

London Showrooms—100, Houndsditch.   All Letters to Colchester.

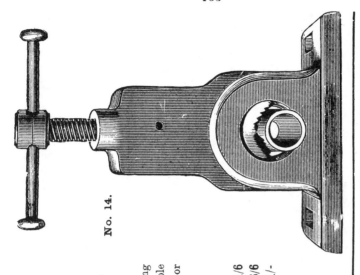

No. 14.

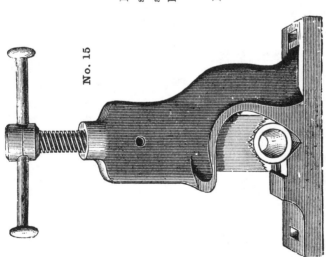

No. 15

IMPROVED
TUBE VICES.

For holding Tube while being screwed or cut off. It is portable and can be fastened to a post or handcart by two bolts.

No. 1, to take 1¼ to ½ in. ... 21/6
" 2, " 2 to ¾ in. ... 26/6
" 3, " 3 to 1¼ in. ... 41/-

BRITANNIA WORKS, COLCHESTER, ENGLAND.

☞ ALL LETTERS TO BRITANNIA WORKS, COLCHESTER.

BRITANNIA CO., COLCHESTER, England.

London Showrooms—100, Houndsditch.   *All Letters to Colchester.*

HYDRAULIC LIFTING JACKS.

Tested to Tons.	Height when down	Run out.	Weight lbs.	PRICE.						
	Inches.			Lifting.			Lifting and Traversing.			
				£	s.	d.	£	s.	d.	
3	19	6	34	3	0	0	5	5	0	
4	23	10	57	3	15	0	5	15	0	
6	24	10	68	4	0	0	6	5	0	
8	26	11	76	4	10	0	7	0	0	
10	27	12	86	5	0	0	7	10	0	
12	27	12	96	5	10	0	8	0	0	
15	28	12	104	6	0	0	9	0	0	
20	28	12	132	6	10	0	10	0	0	
30	29	12	174	7	10	0	13	10	0	
40	29	11	206	9	0	0	15	10	0	
50	29	11	264	10	10	0	20	0	0	
60	29	10	364	12	10	0	22	10	0	

ALLIX'S PATENT
ROLLER TUBE EXPANDER.

As supplied to Her Majesty's Government,
The Japanese Government, &c.   The Principal Boiler Makers.
Shipping and Railway Companies.

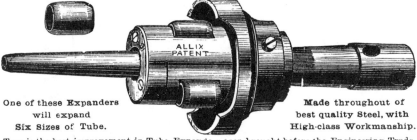

One of these Expanders
will expand
Six Sizes of Tube.

Made throughout of
best quality Steel, with
High-class Workmanship.

This is the best improvement in Tube Expanders ever brought before the Engineering Trade, one of these Expanders being equal to from 3 to 7 of the ordinary make, according to size. The advantage of a tool covering so many sizes is obvious.   They are made of steel throughout, the rollers being of the finest cast steel, solid, and specially tempered.   We have numerous Testimonials as to its economy and efficiency.   Each Expander is supplied with an extra set of rollers and 2 mandrels.

Letter.	Outside Diameter of Tube.	PRICE.			Letter.	Outside Diameter of Tube.	PRICE.		
	Expanding from	£	s.	d.		Expanding from	£	s	d.
A	$\frac{5}{8}$ to $\frac{7}{8}$ in.	2	0	0	J	$2\frac{1}{2}$ to $3\frac{1}{8}$ in.	3	12	6
B	$\frac{3}{4}$,, 1 ,,	2	5	0	K	$2\frac{3}{4}$,, $3\frac{1}{2}$,,	3	17	6
C	$\frac{7}{8}$,, $1\frac{1}{8}$,,	2	7	6	L	3 ,, $3\frac{3}{4}$,,	4	2	6
D	1 ,, $1\frac{1}{4}$,,	2	10	0	M	$3\frac{1}{4}$,, 4 ,,	4	12	6
E	$1\frac{1}{4}$,, $1\frac{5}{8}$,,	2	10	0	N	$3\frac{1}{2}$,, $4\frac{1}{2}$,,	5	5	0
F	$1\frac{3}{8}$,, $1\frac{3}{4}$,,	2	12	6	O	$3\frac{3}{4}$,, 5 ,,	5	17	6
G	$1\frac{5}{8}$,, 2 ,,	2	15	0	P	4 ,, $5\frac{1}{4}$,,	6	10	0
H	2 ,, $2\frac{1}{2}$,,	3	0	0	Q	$4\frac{1}{2}$,, 6 ,,	7	5	0
I	$2\frac{1}{4}$,, $2\frac{7}{8}$,,	3	7	6	R	5 ,, $6\frac{1}{2}$,,	9	0	0

Delivered Free on Rail in London.
To denote the Size when ordering it is sufficient to give the Capital Letter as above.

BRITANNIA CO., COLCHESTER, England.
London Showrooms—100, Houndsditch.   All Letters to Colchester.

IMPROVED HOISTING CRABS.

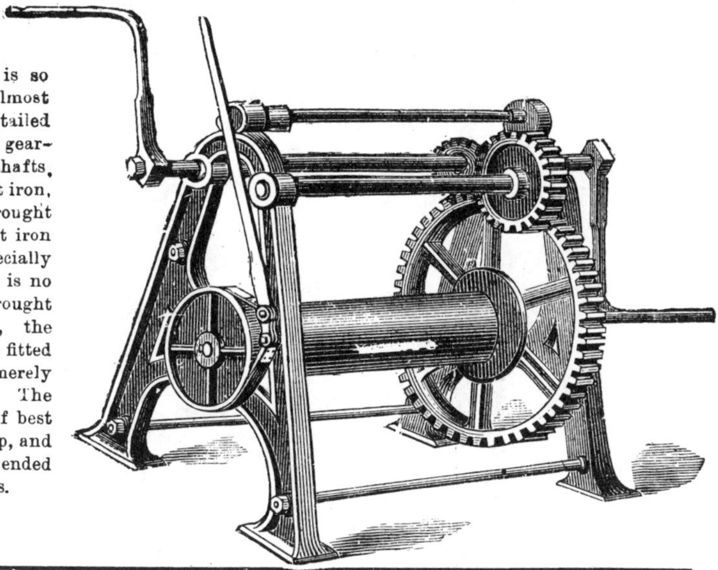

THE general construction is so well known that it is almost unnecessary to give any detailed description. The barrel and gearing are of cast iron; all shafts, also handles, are of wrought iron, and the sides, of cast or wrought iron, as required. Wrought iron sides are preferable, especially for export orders, as there is no risk of breakage When wrought iron sides are supplied, the bearings for the shafts are fitted into the plates, and not merely riveted on to the plates. The Crabs are strongly made, of best materials and workmanship, and can be confidently recommended as really serviceable articles.

POWER.		DIMENSIONS.			PRICE						
Will Lift.		Barrel.			Cast-Iron Sides.			Extras.			
With 2 & 3 Sheave Blocks	Direct from Barrel	Diam.	Length Between Flanges.	"B.B." Tested Chain.	With Brake. Price Each.	Improved Screw Brake.	Without Brake. Price Each.	Wrought-Iron Sides.	Brass Bushing.	"B.B." Tested Chain.	2 and 3 Sheave Blocks.
Tons.	Cwts	Inches.								per Foot.	
SINGLE PURCHASE.											
2	8	4	12	1/4	£4 3	£4 10	£3 8	£1 13	17/-	-/7	£2 10
3	12	4	14	5/16	4 10	4 18	3 14	1 13	17/-	-/9	3 10
4	16	4½	16	3/8	5 5	5 14	4 7	1 16	19/-	-/11	5 5
5	20	5	18	7/16	6 0	6 15	5 3	1 17	19/-	1/2	8 0
6¼	25	5¼	20	7/16	7 15	8 10	6 12	2 0	21/-	1/2	8 0
7½	30	5¾	20	½	9 5	10 5	8 0	2 4	21/-	1/5	13 15
9	36	6	22	9/16	11 5	12 6	9 0	2 10	24/-	1/8	16 10
DOUBLE PURCHASE.											
4	16	4½	16	3/8	£6 0	£6 12	£5 4	£2 4	23/-	-/11	£5 5
5	20	5	18	7/16	6 18	7 13	6 0	2 4	23/-	1/2	8 0
6¼	25	5¼	20	7/16	8 16	9 10	7 10	2 7	26/-	1/2	8 0
8	32	5¾	20	½	9 17	10 15	8 11	2 10	27/-	1/5	13 15
9	36	6	22	9/16	10 6	11 5	9 0	2 12	27/-	1/8	16 10
10	40	6	22	9/16	11 0	12 0	9 15	2 15	30/-	1/8	16 10
11¼	45	6	22	5/8	12 0	13 0	10 15	2 17	32/-	2/-	19 10
12½	50	6½	24	5/8	12 15	13 15	11 8	3 0	35/-	2/-	19 10
13¾	55	7	25	11/16	14 5	15 8	12 18	3 5	40/-	2/5	23 10
15	60	7⅜	27	¾	15 15	16 18	14 2	3 11	45/-	2/11	28 0
17½	70	7⅜	27	¾	19 16	21 0	17 15	4 0	50/-	2/11	30 0
20	80	8	28	13/16	27 0	28 10	24 0	4 10	51/-	3/3	38 0

EXTRAS.

WARPING DRUMS; FAST and LOOSE PULLEYS, for working by power; ANGLE IRON FRAMING to Wrought-iron Sides. BARRELS can be had Concave, with Ribs for "Fleeting" the Rope or Octagon; or length can be made to suit special requirements. CRAB MOUNTED ON TROLLEY, for Contractors' purposes. WESTON'S SAFETY BRAKE.

BRITANNIA CO., COLCHESTER, England.

London Showrooms—100, *Houndsditch.* *All Letters to Colchester.*

GREEN'S PATENT FOOT PRESSES

Great Speed, Economy, and Accuracy.
Both Hands of the Operator at liberty. Great Saving of Labour
Special Designs to suit all Trades.

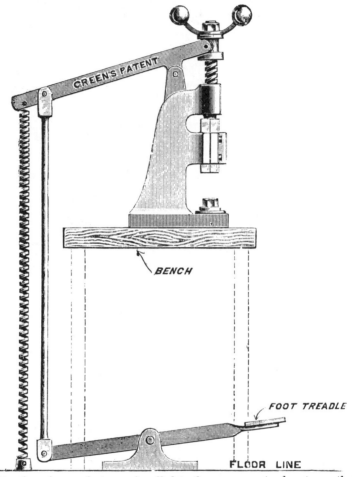

THE attention of manufacturers is called to the very great advantages these Presses have over the ordinary kind. They are arranged to be worked by the **Foot** instead of by **Hand**—thus enabling the operator to have **both** hands at liberty to manipulate the work; thereby saving a great amount of time and making it **easy** to perform **rapid** operations with these Presses that are not possible with any others.

The improved arrangement of the Levers in combination with the screw and weighted "Fly," very greatly increases the power and efficiency of the Press, making it quite easy to work.

They are made and finished in first-class style; the screw and all the working parts being case-hardened.

PRICE from £6 10s.

BRITANNIA CO., COLCHESTER, England.

London Showrooms—100, *Houndsditch.* *All Letters to Colchester.*

THE "BRITANNIA"
LETTER COPYING PRESSES.

No. 2.

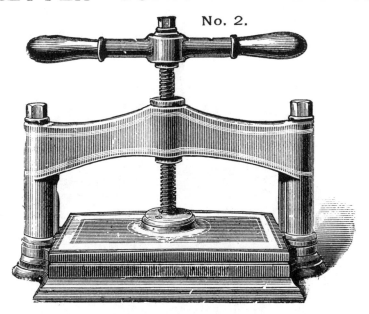

FOOLSCAP. 15 in. by 10 in.

	£	s.	d.
Extra Strong, Machine Planed, Gunmetal Washer and Nuts, Japanned Fillet	2	12	6
Extra Ornamented and Finished	3	0	0
Gun-metal Handles	0	8	0

STANDS FOR THESE PRESSES.

	£	s.	d.
Birch, Polished, with 1 Drawer	1	3	0
Do. 2 Drawers	1	5	0
2 Flaps, extra	0	10	0
Mahogany, Polished, 1 Drawer	1	9	0
Do. 2 Drawers	1	13	6
2 Flaps, extra	0	12	6

BRITANNIA CO., COLCHESTER, England.

London Showrooms—100. Houndsditch.   *All Letters to Colchester.*

THE "BRITANNIA"
LETTER COPYING PRESSES.

No. 1.

LARGE QUARTO 12 in. by 10 in.

	£	s.	d.
Japanned Black Marble with Iron Washer ...	1	1	0
Japanned Black Marble with Brass Washer and Nut and Surfaces Machine Planed ...	1	5	0
Japanned Ornamentally and of very superior finish	1	10	0
Brass Ball Handles, extra	0	6	0

STANDS FOR THESE PRESSES.

	£	s.	d.
Birch, Polished, with 1 Drawer	0	19	0
Do. do. with 2 Drawers	1	1	0
Do. do. with 2 Drawers and 2 Flaps ...	1	8	6
Mahogany, Polished, with 1 Drawer	1	4	6
Do. do. with 2 Drawers	1	9	0
Do. do. with 2 Drawers and 2 Flaps	1	17	6

BRITANNIA CO., COLCHESTER, England.

London Showrooms—100, Houndsditch. All Letters to Colchester.

NOTICE.

AGENTS are being appointed for the Sale of our

ENGINEERS & WOODWORKERS'

TOOLS.

Also for the "Facile" Patent

PETROLEUM

OIL ENGINES.

BRITANNIA COMPANY,

COLCHESTER, ENGLAND.

London Showrooms — 100, Houndsditch. All Letters to Colchester.

BRITANNIA CO.

DESIGNERS AND MAKERS

Of over 300 varieties of LATHES, SHAPERS, DRILLING & MILLING MACHINES and other WOOD and IRON WORKING MACHINERY.

SPECIAL TOOLS

MADE TO ORDER.

BRITANNIA WORKS,

COLCHESTER.